Criminal Justice in Guernsey
1680–1929

Criminal Justice in Guernsey
1680–1929

Rose-Marie Crossan

MÒR MEDIA LIMITED

First published 2021
Mòr Media Limited, Benderloch, Argyll, Scotland
www.mormedia.co.uk

ISBN 978-1-9196371-2-9 (paperback)

A catalogue record for this book is available from the British Library.

Contents

Illustrations

Maps

Plates

Figures

For Jonny

Acknowledgements

I would like first and foremost to express my gratitude to the staff of Guernsey's Greffe, Priaulx Library, Island Archives and Museum Service for their assistance in the course of my research and in tracking down illustrations. I am also most grateful to Helen Crossan for her help in preparing my text for publication. More indirectly, I would like to acknowledge a long-standing debt to historians of Guernsey Darryl Ogier, Richard Hocart and Gregory Stevens Cox, whose work has provided a firm foundation for my own research. Finally, I offer my affectionate thanks to my husband Jonathan, to whom this book is dedicated and without whose support it would not have been written.

Rose-Marie Crossan, MA (Oxon), PhD
Guernsey, July 2021

Abbreviations

Billet	*Billet d'Etat*[1]
GG	Greffe, Guernsey[2]
IA	Island Archives, Guernsey
O in C	Order in Council[3]
Ord	Ordinance of the Royal Court
PL	Priaulx Library, Guernsey
NA	National Archives, Kew
TSG	*Transactions of La Société Guernesiaise*

[1] *Billets d'Etat*, which contain the agenda and supporting material for States meetings, will be referred to by the date of the meeting for which the *Billet* was compiled, and will be found in the bound volumes held at the Priaulx Library.

[2] Records held by the Greffe, Island Archives and other record offices will be referred to by their date, followed, where relevant, by the institution's reference code. A detailed description of each record will be found in the Bibliography.

[3] Orders in Council and Ordinances issued prior to 1950 will be referred to by their name and/or date, and, unless otherwise stated, will be found in the published volumes held at the Priaulx Library or in the registers of *Ordonnances* and *Ordres du Conseil* at the Greffe. Post-1950 legislation will be found online at www.guernseylegalresources.gg.

Notes on the text

1.   Most of Guernsey's official records prior to the mid-twentieth century are in French. Where I have felt it necessary, I have provided translations silently and without reproduction of the original. Any French words and phrases left untranslated (except the titles of certain local officials and institutions) are italicised.

2.   Guernsey's parishes have both French and English names. For consistency, I use the English version throughout, and render those prefixed 'St' with a terminal 's' unpreceded by an apostrophe (to reflect general usage, where the final 's' has become accreted to the names, as in the British towns of St Albans, St Helens, St Andrews etc.).[1]

3.   Before the nineteenth century, Guernsey's currency was the French *livre tournois* (divided into *sols* and *deniers*). Local exchange rates were variable, but the standard eighteenth-century London rate was 14 *livres tournois* to £1 sterling. Where an equivalent is required for the purposes of this book, I have used a conversion table in an eighteenth-century Guernsey almanac.[2] After France replaced the *livre tournois* with the *franc* in the early nineteenth century, the *livre tournois* was superseded in most local contexts by the Guernsey pound (although some judicial fines continued to be denominated in *tournois* well into the twentieth century). Because one Guernsey shilling was deemed equivalent to one *franc*, the Guernsey pound was worth 19s 2½d sterling until 1921, when it was fixed at parity with sterling. All sums in pounds, shillings and pence relating to local affairs from the early nineteenth century onwards are in Guernsey values.

4.   Many Guernsey surnames are preceded by particles (*De* Sausmarez, *Le* Marchant, *De La* Rue, etc.). According to historian and linguist Marie De Garis, 'the property-owning classes always used capital letters for the prefixes [but] the artisan classes used the more humble small letters.'[3] In this study, capitals are used for all particles, irrespective of class.

5.   Dates before 1752 are Old Style but adjusted to a year beginning 1 January.

6.   The names of all individuals convicted of crimes after 1900 are withheld or changed, as are the names of their victims.

[1] The parish of *St Pierre du Bois* is known in English both as St Peter in the Wood and St Peters. I have used the latter form.
[2] *Anon., Almanach Journalier à l'Usage de l'Ile de Guernesey* (Guernsey, 1797).
[3] M. De Garis, *Dictiounnaire Angllais–Guernesiais* (Chichester, 1982), p. 114.

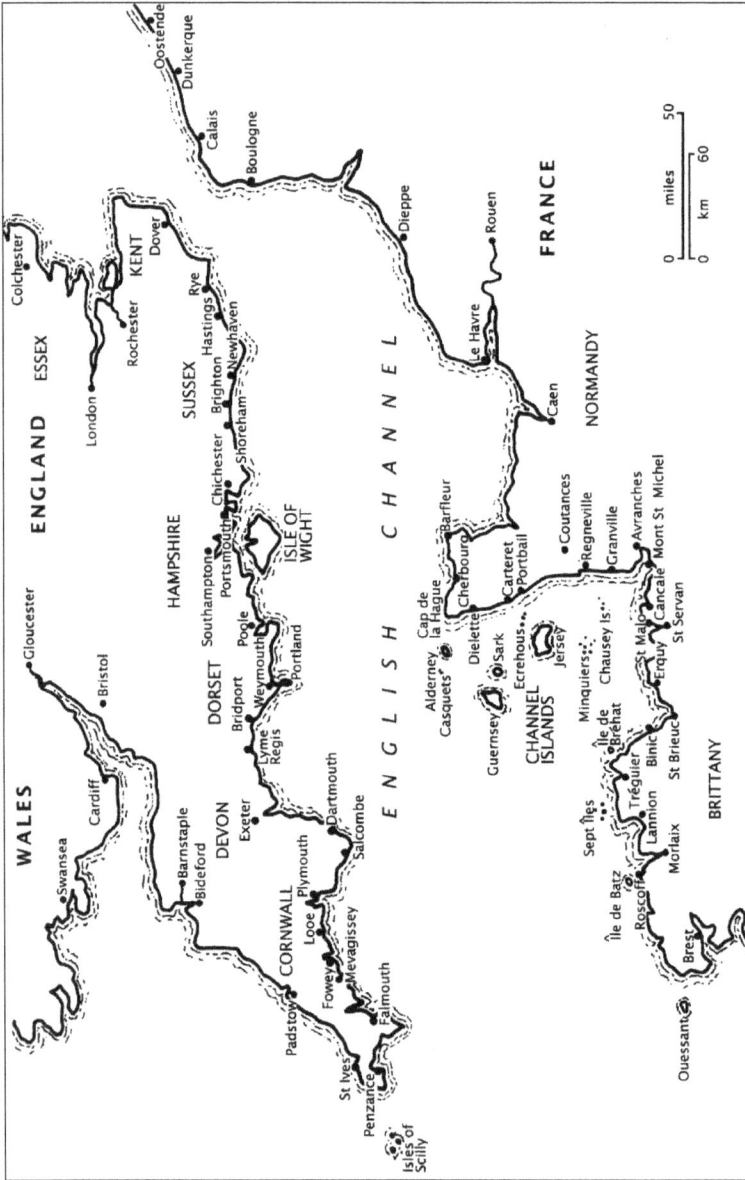

Map 1. Channel Islands and adjacent French and English coasts

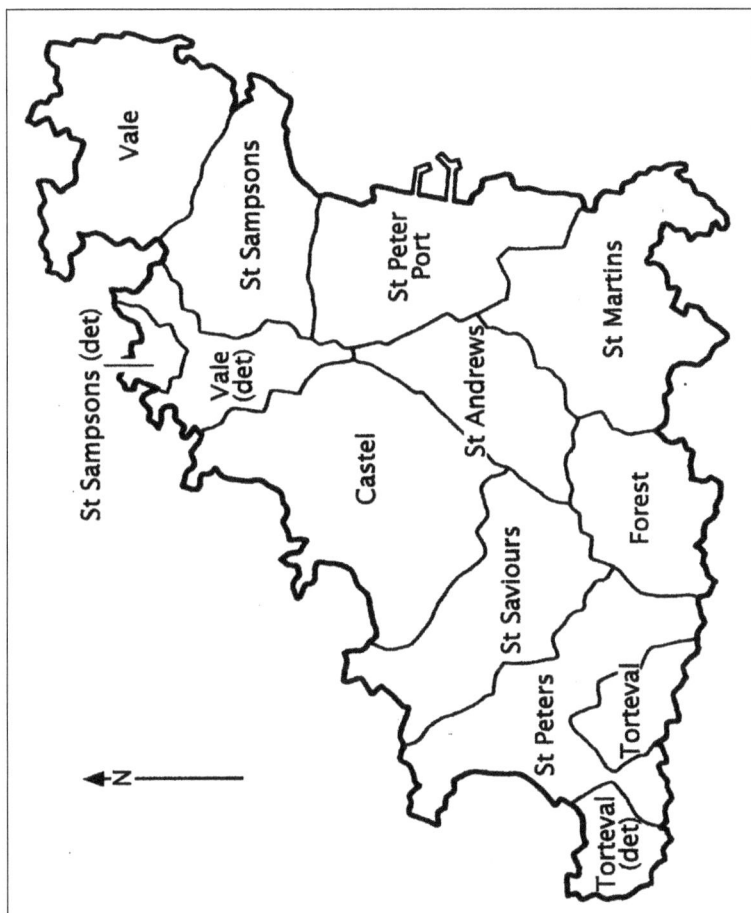

Map 2. Parishes of Guernsey

Introduction

This introduction is divided into two parts. The first will establish the general rationale for this study, outline the approach adopted, and detail the sources used. The second will set the scene for future chapters by tracing the origins not only of Guernsey's system of law but also its system of government, whose functioning between the 1680s and 1920s will be described as background to the main theme.

Part 1: General

Crime was one of the first subjects to be explored after social history was opened up as a field of academic enquiry in the 1960s and 1970s. It was studied alongside such topics as welfare, the family, childhood and gender, as European and American historians sought to construct a new 'history from below' from hitherto neglected sources. Although by no means lacking in materials for such studies, Guernsey's historians came late to the field, and it was not until the 1990s that the first modern works of insular social history appeared.[1] In the three decades since that time, many aspects of this field have been explored, but, to date, there have been no full-length works on crime.[2] This is surprising, given that criminal history lends itself well to studies of discrete areas over defined time periods. With an area of just 24½ square

---

[1] D.M. Ogier, *Reformation and Society in Guernsey* (Woodbridge, 1996); G. Stevens Cox, *St Peter Port, 1680–1830: The History of an International Entrepôt* (Woodbridge, 1999). Both began life as PhD theses.

[2] Although Dr Darryl Ogier included an analysis of Royal Court crime records in his study of the Reformation period (Ogier, *Reformation and Society*, pp. 114–57), and later published two important essays on criminal subjects: 'New-born child murder in Reformation Guernsey', in G. Dawes (ed.), *Commise 1204: Studies in the History and Law of Continental and Insular Normandy* (Guernsey, 2005), and 'Glimpses of the obscure: the witch trials of the Channel Islands', in A. McShane & G. Walker (eds), *The Extraordinary and the Everyday in Early Modern England* (Basingstoke, 2010).

miles, only one criminal court, only one series of criminal court registers, and no external appeals, Guernsey forms the ideal subject.

Legal history (as distinct from criminal history) focuses on the origin and development of laws and legal systems, and has long been a respectable academic discipline. Again, Guernsey (and the Channel Islands in general) are good candidates for a study of legal history. This is chiefly because they retained their own law after transferring their political allegiance from Normandy to England. Theirs was thus a very different experience from that of other non-English parts of the British Isles, such as Ireland and Wales, where English law was imposed after the English assumed ascendancy. It was different, too, from that of the Isle of Man, where the overlordship of English noblemen encouraged the early engrafting of English law. Indeed, Guernsey had more similarities with Scotland, which retained its own legal system after becoming a part of the United Kingdom in 1707. Scotland's retention of its legal system has been recognised as fundamental to that country's preservation of a strong separate identity. As one Scottish legal historian has said, 'the law draws physical boundaries in geographical space, shaping and giving identity to that space'.[3] A legal history of Guernsey can help determine the extent to which this was also true here.

Since Guernsey's legal history is not readily separable from its social history, this study will address both aspects in tandem. It will also encompass the whole Bailiwick of Guernsey, which includes the smaller islands of Alderney, Sark, Herm and Jethou. While the last two were part of Guernsey for judicial purposes, Sark and Alderney both had their own courts, which operated under the same law as Guernsey but had a limited criminal jurisdiction, beyond which offenders were sent to Guernsey to be tried.[4] Such crimes as were committed in these islands and tried by Guernsey's Court will form part of our study.

This book spans the 250 years between 1680 and 1929. It is divided into three sections which each comprise a period of continuity followed by a period of transition. The first section stretches from the beginning of the

---

[3] L. Farmer, *Criminal Law, Tradition and Legal Order: Crime and the Genius of Scots Law, 1747 to the Present* (Cambridge, 1997), p. 2.

[4] The criminal jurisdiction of the Sark court was limited throughout our period to petty offences liable to up to three days' imprisonment or a small fine. Until 1848, the Alderney court had no criminal jurisdiction whatever. After this date, it had the power to try minor offences attracting prison sentences of up to one month and fines of up to £5.

study to the mid-1760s; the second from the mid-1760s to the mid-1840s; and the third from the mid-1840s to the end of our period. Each of the sections is sub-divided into chapters exploring changes in the composition of the judiciary and criminal justice infrastructure; changes in the law and its application; and changes in the number and nature of crimes and criminals which came before the Court. Throughout the process, an effort is made to relate local changes to contemporaneous developments in Britain, Jersey and France.

The principal source on which this study draws are the records of Guernsey's Royal Court. The earliest surviving Court registers date from 1526 and are kept at Guernsey's Greffe.[5] Of chief importance are the crime registers, known as *Livres en Crime*, which begin in 1563. Volumes 6 to 60 of these contain an unbroken record of all cases of a criminal nature spanning the period covered by this book. Also important are the Greffe's registers of Ordinances and Orders in Council, which furnish an account of legislative developments, and Royal Court Letter Books, which shed light on influences prompting legislative change.

Away from the Greffe, local newspapers, which survive from 1791 at Guernsey's Priaulx Library, are invaluable for filling in (the sometimes large) gaps left by the crime registers. Police and prison records held by the Island Archives also provide useful information, as do the National Archives' records of correspondence between insular and British authorities, which provide insights into metropolitan attitudes to Guernsey's criminal justice system, and enable us to assess the role of external pressure in effecting changes to that system.

---

[5] The medieval records of the Royal Court, almost certainly in roll form, have not survived. It has been surmised that at some time, probably early in the sixteenth century, the Court changed from rolls to bound registers, after which the earlier rolls were lost or destroyed (J.H. Le Patourel *et al* (eds), *List of Records in the Greffe, Guernsey, Volume 1* (London, 1969), p. 13).

Part 2: Law and government

Origins, pre-1300

The Channel Islands are closer to France than to England. Guernsey lies just 27 miles off Normandy's Cotentin peninsula, Alderney is a mere 10 miles from the French coast. Until the thirteenth century, the Islands shared a common history with north-west France. They are thought to have become part of the Roman Empire at the same time as Gaul, and, like adjacent parts of what later became Normandy, to have been inhabited after the Romans' departure by a Gallo-Roman population under the Frankish monarchy. From the early 800s, this part of the French kingdom was destabilised by the arrival of the Vikings who began by raiding coastal areas and in due course established permanent settlements. Between 911 and 933, the French monarchy reached an accommodation with the Vikings, by means of which the Duchy of Normandy was formed, and overlordship over it was ceded to the invaders in return for homage to the French king. The Channel Islands are believed to have been incorporated into the territory of the new Duchy along with the Cotentin peninsula some time after 933.[6] Duke William's conquest of England in 1066 brought no change to his relationship with the French king, from whom he and his successors continued to hold Normandy in return for homage. Neither did it bring any change to the Channel Islands, which simply continued as part of the Duchy.

The major transformation came after 1204, when King John of England fell into a dispute with the French king which led to the forcible re-incorporation of the Duchy into the French royal domain. After a short military campaign in the early summer of 1204, mainland Normandy submitted to King Philippe II. With the Duchy in French hands, it became imperative for the English Crown to hold on to the Islands.[7] Located at the western entrance to the Channel, they controlled the main shipping route

---

[6] Professor John Le Patourel has asserted that that from 867 until the early 900s, the Channel Islands, along with the Cotentin, had briefly been part of the kingdom of Brittany (J.H. Le Patourel, 'Guernsey, Jersey and their environment in the Middle Ages', *TSG*, 19 (1975), p. 439).

[7] This paragraph is based on J.A. Everard & J.C. Holt, *Jersey 1204: The Forging of an Island Community* (London, 2004), pp. 79–126.

between England and the monarchy's remaining territories in south-west France. They also served as advanced posts from which the activities of the French might be observed, and defensive bulwarks against the future invasion of England by France. The Norman tenants-in-chief of insular fiefs were confronted with the choice of either transferring their allegiance to the English Crown or forfeiting their lands. Since most of these were nobles who also held estates in mainland France, many opted to abandon their local holdings in order to retain their core domains. This left many of the Islands' former sub-tenants holding their lands directly of the Crown. Having effectively become tenants-in-chief themselves, these islanders assumed a status they would never otherwise have enjoyed – and which predisposed them to support the new regime.

After a few decades of instability, the Channel Islands' status *vis-à-vis* their larger neighbours was largely settled in the 1250s. There were two watersheds. Firstly, in 1254, Henry III formally granted the Islands to his son, the future Edward I, 'in such manner that the said lands … may never be separated from the Crown [and] should remain to the Kings of England in their entirety for ever'.[8] This set the pattern for Guernsey's future relationship with the monarchy. Although it meant that whoever henceforth was king of England was by that fact also lawful sovereign of the Channel Islands, the relationship was a personal one. The Islands were never politically subsumed into the realm of England, nor, later into the United Kingdom. The second important event of the 1250s was the signing of the Treaty of Paris in 1259. This treaty witnessed Henry III's abandonment of the title of Duke of Normandy, while at the same time confirming the monarch's right to the Islands.[9]

As sovereign of the Islands, the English king ruled them directly, with the advice of his Privy Council. His representative in the Islands was a royal official known as the Warden (or alternatively Keeper or *Custos*) who was responsible for all of the Channel Islands and the conduct of all aspects of government. These Wardens were often absent and delegated day-to-day tasks to resident subordinates drawn from the new insular elites. The Warden's local agents were sometimes referred to as his *ballivi* or bailiffs, a generic term for officials in medieval times.

---

[8] J. Loveridge, *The Constitution and Law of Guernsey* (1975; Guernsey, 1997 edn), p. 1.
[9] D.M. Ogier, *The Government and Law of Guernsey* (2005; Guernsey, 2012 edn), p. 206.

One function which came to be performed by *ballivi* was the administration of justice. This was above all a practical arrangement, since the native *ballivi* would have known the relevant local laws and procedures, while the Warden (could he have spared the time to be present) would not.[10] In this, the *ballivi* were assisted by twelve *jurati*, officers who are thought to have originated under King John.[11] By the beginning of the fourteenth century, the local *ballivi* and *jurati* in Jersey and Guernsey (whom we may now call the Bailiff and Jurats) appear to have been functioning as a court in much the same way they were destined to function for the next several centuries – the Bailiff presiding over cases, and the Jurats determining them.[12] Administering justice in the king's name, these insular courts were entitled to the designation 'Royal'.

As the principal standing bodies in their respective islands, the Royal Courts of Guernsey and Jersey also took over from the Warden responsibility for much of the Islands' routine civil administration. At first the Royal Courts simply held the Warden's authority in commission. At some point in the fourteenth century, however, their assumption of direct responsibility for these duties was tacitly accepted. As John Le Patourel later remarked, the fact that Islanders had a law of their own was 'the *fons et origo*' of their development towards self-government.[13]

---

[10] Everard & Holt, *Jersey 1204*, p. 155.

[11] A document known as the 'Constitutions of King John' instituted twelve *coronatores jurati*, sworn Crown officers who were to keep the rights pertaining to the Crown. The originals of the 'Constitutions' do not survive, but a document dated 1248 is held at the National Archives which Judith Everard and James Holt suggest may reflect the terms of a document which could have been issued by John between 1204 and 1216. Everard and Holt speculate that these *coronatores jurati* were modelled on the coroners first instituted in England in 1194, whose original duty it was to investigate breaches of the peace and infringements of the Crown's rights (Everard & Holt, *Jersey 1204*, pp. 157–9). Other scholars posit that they might be based on the *jurati* serving free towns created by John in his other French territories (J. Havet, *Les Cours Royales des Iles Normandes* (Paris, 1878), p. 54; J.H. Le Patourel, *The Medieval Administration of the Channel Islands, 1199–1399* (London, 1937), pp. 115–16).

[12] Note that the officers referred to in English as 'Jurats' were usually called *magistrats* or *jurés* in the records of the insular courts, which were kept in French throughout our period.

[13] Le Patourel, *Medieval Administration*, p. 109.

Law, pre-1300

Everard and Holt have identified as crucial to the continuation of Norman law in the Islands a mandate issued to the Warden in 1218 by the Regents of the infant King Henry III ordering that he should 'cause to be observed in these same Islands the assizes which were there in the times of our predecessors.'[14] The 'assizes' referred to were those conducted by the itinerant Norman justices who had been visiting the Islands for at least the previous century on circuit from mainland Normandy.[15] The purpose of these assizes was to try serious crimes such as homicide, rape and arson which were known in Normandy as *les plaids ducaux* or *les plaids de l'épée* and in England as the pleas of the Crown. Everard and Holt assert that the significance of this mandate lay in the fact 'that the king undertook not to introduce new laws or innovations in the exercise of royal jurisdiction, substantive or procedural'. In the view of Everard and Holt, conditions in the early thirteenth century made this undesirable as well as impractical. Replacing Norman customary law with an unfamiliar system risked exacerbating an already volatile situation, and was in any case unnecessary since the Plantagenets believed that Normandy would soon be restored to their rule and the Islands would resume their status as part of the Duchy.[16] They further note that, although this measure may originally have been intended as temporary, 'with time it became enshrined and immutable'.[17] Following this development, assizes dealing with serious crimes appear to have been held in the Islands every three years, while less serious offences – known as *les plaids vicomtaux* – were despatched on an ongoing basis.[18] Professor Le Patourel has observed that the term *plaids vicomtaux* continued to be used in the Islands well into the post-Norman period to distinguish the ordinary sessions of the courts from the assizes.[19]

By the end of the thirteenth century, the responsibility of local courts for all aspects of insular justice seems to have become well established.

---

[14] Everard & Holt, *Jersey 1204*, p. 91. King John had died in 1216.
[15] Le Patourel, *Medieval Administration*, p. 42.
[16] Everard & Holt, *Jersey 1204*, p. 156.
[17] *Ibid.*, p. 164.
[18] Le Patourel, *Medieval Administration*, p. 42.
[19] *Ibid.*, p. 44.

Nevertheless, the events of a thirty-year period at the beginning of the fourteenth century called it sharply into question, and for a while it hung in the balance. This episode is worth briefly recounting here if only because it led to the re-confirmation of the *status quo ante*. Between 1299 and 1331, six royally commissioned judicial eyres (on the model of the English General Eyre) were sent to the Islands to take the pleas of the Crown, from which men connected with the administration in the Islands were gradually excluded.[20] Although every commission contained an instruction that the proceedings should be in accordance with 'the laws and customs of the Islands', Islanders became concerned that their liberties and privileges were being swept away, and the eyre of 1331 culminated in rioting in Guernsey. By this time, however, the General Eyre was in full decline in England, and this proved to be the last such eyre ever held in the Channel Islands.[21] It was followed in 1341 with the Islands' first royal charter, which explicitly confirmed the Channel Islanders in all their 'privileges, liberties, immunities, exemptions, and customs'.[22] Nineteen further charters were issued by successive sovereigns.

Government, post-1300

The fourteenth and fifteenth centuries saw the gradual separation of the Channel Islands into two distinct Bailiwicks. The Bailiwick of Guernsey comprised Alderney, Sark, and the smaller islands; that of Jersey only its own 46 square miles, plus some outlying reefs. By the early 1300s, each Bailiwick had its own seal; from 1465, each Bailiwick (usually) had its own charter; and

---

[20] The General Eyre was a short-lived experiment of the thirteenth and fourteenth centuries. Instituted by Edward I, it was 'an impressive demonstration of royal power' whereby royally commissioned justices travelled around the country investigating all the judicial and administrative business transacted in an area since the last Eyre, and inquiring by 'what warrant' persons claimed rights and privileges (T.F.T. Plucknett, *A Concise History of the Common Law* (1929; Boston, 1956 edn), p. 103).

[21] The episode of the eyres is recounted in detail in Le Patourel, *Medieval Administration*, pp. 54–66.

[22] The immediate motivation for this charter seems to have been Edward III's need to secure the Islands' loyalty in the context of his intervention in a war over succession to the Duchy of Brittany (T. Thornton, *The Charters of Guernsey* (Bognor Regis, 2004), pp. 2–4).

from 1485 each Bailiwick had its own Warden.[23] All these changes had a cumulative effect, and by the sixteenth century at the latest, the Bailiwicks can be said to have become completely sundered. Their political, legal and administrative structures thenceforth evolved in different ways.

Although judicial autonomy was understood to be among Guernsey's privileges, the precise content and nature of these privileges was not spelt out in the relatively brief royal charter of 1341. Subsequently, they became better defined, and in this respect, a document of 1441 is important. This document, known as the *Précepte d'Assise*, purported to set out in detail the privileges, immunities, customs and usages of Guernsey endorsed by the visiting English justices of 1331, and also contained other material from the intervening period.[24] One of the chief privileges the document set out was the right of the insular court to try all matters arising in the island. One of the chief immunities was the freedom of islanders from process of English courts in matters arising locally. Other insular privileges and immunities which were eventually formally recognised (some in the *Précepte* and others in royal charters) included exemption from military service outside the Islands, freedom of trade with England, and freedom from English taxation.

Throughout the period dealt with by this book, the Crown retained its representative in the Bailiwick. By the opening of our study in 1680, he was no longer known as the Warden but the Governor. From the early eighteenth century onwards, the Governorship was usually bestowed upon a high-ranking army officer at the end of his career.[25] The substantial emoluments attached to the post (an entitlement to local Crown revenues) were a form of reward for long service.[26]

---

[23] Le Patourel, *Medieval Administration*, p. 52; Thornton, *Charters*, pp. 32, 46.

[24] For an accessible text, see H. De Sausmarez, 'Guernsey's Précepte d'Assise of 1441: translation and notes', *Jersey & Guernsey Law Review* (June 2008). The *Précepte d'Assise* was accepted by the English Privy Council as an authoritative statement of local law and practice in 1583.

[25] R. Hocart, *Guernsey in the Reign of Charles II* (Guernsey, 2020), p. 178.

[26] The Crown revenues, which amounted to c.£1,250 in 1680, comprised corn and money rents due on private properties; tithes of grain; *champart* of grain, and *poulage*, both in Crown fiefs; the profits of Crown lands, including the islands of Herm and Jethou; *treizième* (a duty on sales of realty); duties upon certain items of merchandise imported and exported; anchorage dues on vessels in the roadstead; and forfeited goods (Hocart, *Charles II*, p. 37). For *champart* see Chapter 3, n. 7; for *poulage*, see Chapter 2, n. 77.

After Lord Hatton (Governor between 1670 and 1706), no Governor resided locally nor performed his duties in person. These duties were instead delegated to resident Lieutenant Governors, whom Governors paid from their own purse. In our period, the responsibilities of Lieutenant Governors were chiefly military. They were in overall command of both the British garrison and local militia. In addition, they acted as conduits for communication between British and insular authorities and had specific duties relating to foreigners and security. On a political level, their powers were circumscribed. The Lieutenant Governor's consent was required for a States meeting, which he had a right to address.[27] However, he had no vote in the assembly, no veto, and no executive power. In 1835, the position of Governor was abolished, and Lieutenant Governors became salaried British government appointees.

By the opening of our period, Guernsey's ten parishes were playing an important role in the island's day-to-day running. Dr Darryl Ogier has dated the establishment of the parishes to the early eleventh century, though little is known of parochial structures at this time.[28] In our period, the parishes exercised civil as well as ecclesiastical functions. As well as organising and financing the upkeep of parish churches and churchyards, they also bore responsibility, at various times, for parochial roads and sea walls, parochial policing, parochial poor relief and parochial schools. Each parish possessed a body elected by the adult male ratepayers which was known as the Douzaine.[29] Among other things, this body was responsible for assessing and levying parochial taxation and apportioning parochial expenditure. At the apex of parish structure were the two Constables, also elected by the adult male ratepayers.[30] As well as bearing responsibility for public order, the

---

[27] The nature and role of the States will be described below.

[28] D.M. Ogier, 'The origins of Guernsey's parishes and the ownership and maintenance of their ancient church buildings', *The Jersey Law Review*, 9 (2005), p. 326.

[29] Douzeniers were twelve in number in all parishes aside from the Vale, which had sixteen, and St Peter Port, which had twenty (between 1844 and 1948, St Peter Port also had an additional forty-eight 'cantonal' Douzeniers, serving on four subsidiary Douzaines). Although service was nominally for life, Douzeniers were allowed, by convention, to retire at sixty.

[30] They were usually elected annually, but some parishes tended to re-elect their Constables from year to year; in 1778 the Royal Court ordered that no-one should serve as Constable for more than three years without calling an election (R. Hocart, *An Island Assembly: The Development of the States of Guernsey, 1700–1949* (Guernsey, 1988), p. 3).

Constables acted as parish treasurers and executive officers of their Douzaines, and, until 1844, one Constable from each parish sat and voted in the States. Owing to their exercise of these functions, Guernsey's parish Constables were of considerably higher status than their nominal counterparts in England. They were elected from among the leading families of their parish, and a proportion of them went on to become Jurats of the Royal Court.

For much of our period, the Royal Court functioned as Guernsey's principal legislative, as well as judicial and administrative body. The origin of its legislative powers is obscure, but it was certainly exercising them by the time of the earliest Court registers, which, from the 1520s, record the promulgation of Ordinances at thrice-yearly sessions called *Chefs Plaids*, or Chief Pleas.[31] These Ordinances concerned such matters as maintenance of roads and streams, regulation of markets, weights and measures, hunting, taverns, and much else. Sometimes they could also be declaratory of existing law and custom. What the Royal Court could not do by means of Ordinances was to alter the customary law, make new substantive law, or create new taxes, since it was generally understood that such measures could only be instituted by Order of the King in Council.

The highest tier of local government was the States. According to Professor Le Patourel, this body was a simple 'afforcement of the court' which arose in the fifteenth or sixteenth century to deal with business felt to require a wider measure of consultation and consent than could be achieved by the Royal Court alone.[32] By definition, such business was exceptional, and, at the beginning of our period, the States met as little as once a year. The matters with which they dealt were, typically, the control of food supplies in times of want, the maintenance of St Peter Port harbour, the purchase of arms and equipment for the militia, and the quartering of garrison soldiers. At this time, the States were composed of thirty-two members: all the Jurats of the Royal Court, ten parish Constables, eight parish Rectors,[33] the Procureur (a Crown-appointed Law Officer, of whom more later), and the Bailiff, who as

---

[31] Chief Pleas was (and remains) the fullest form of the Royal Court, attended by the Bailiff, Jurats, Law Officers, tenants who owed suit of Court, the Advocates (from 1619), and one Constable from each parish (from 1801). As well as making Ordinances, Chief Pleas also fixed the monetary equivalent of rents due in kind.

[32] Le Patourel, *Medieval Administration*, pp. 117–18.

[33] The ten parishes had just eight Rectors between them because, until 1859 and 1867 respectively, St Sampsons/the Vale, and Torteval/the Forest each formed one living.

well as presiding over the judicial and legislative sessions of the Royal Court, also presided over the States.[34]

Aside from its deliberative role, the States also had an elective role. In this capacity, as the States of Election, the body comprised all the members of the deliberative States, together with both Constables and the entire Douzaines of each parish. Its functions were to elect the Jurats of the Royal Court and another Court officer known as the Prévôt, and, from 1844, also to approve applications for the levying of island-wide general taxes.[35]

When it came to legislating, the States themselves had no Ordinance-making powers, and their decisions could only be given force by Ordinances of the Royal Court. As mentioned earlier, Ordinances could not be used to introduce major new laws or new forms of taxation. Until the late eighteenth century, this caused no major problems, since Ordinances sufficed to meet most States' purposes. However, the early 1800s saw an upsurge in States activity which was initially caused by the need to build new infrastructure, and for which, ultimately, new forms of taxation were required. In response to these novel demands, the States evolved a new way of legislating peculiar to themselves.

Details of the new legislative system took time to mature, but in its fully fledged form, the system operated as follows: proposals for new laws were tabled for debate in the States, and a vote was taken after an exchange of views.[36] If the proposals were approved in general terms, they were passed to the Law Officers for drafting in the form of what became known as a *projet de loi*. The *projet* was then passed back to the States for further debate, which

---

[34] The constitution of the States underwent three reforms over our period: the first, in 1844, replaced the Constables with fifteen Douzaine delegates; another in 1899 introduced nine Deputies elected on an island-wide ratepayer franchise; and a third in 1920 doubled the number of Deputies and gave the vote to all men over twenty and women over thirty.

[35] Hocart, *Island Assembly*, p. 3.

[36] Until 1844, proposals could only be tabled by the Bailiff (although they might emanate, via him, from other sources). The 1844 States Reform Law allowed a majority of any one of the three estates (Jurats, Rectors and Douzaine delegates) or any ten members to request the Bailiff to submit a proposal to the States, after which he was required to convene them for that purpose within a reasonable time. In 1864, an article was added to the 1844 Law permitting any two members to submit a written proposition to the Bailiff, who had to submit it to the States within two months, and if the States voted to entertain it, it was then submitted to them at a subsequent meeting for a decision (Hocart, *Island Assembly*, pp. 28, 44, 60).

might oblige the Law Officers to introduce modifications. After final approval by the States, the *projet* was forwarded to the Privy Council along with a petition praying for its ratification. When the Council gave their sanction (sometimes not without negotiation), these *projets de loi* were returned in the form of Orders in Council which were then registered as insular laws by the Royal Court. An early instance of this mode of legislating came in the form of an Order in Council of 18 May 1803 which sanctioned a States' *projet* to build a new prison. Other instances in the first half of the nineteenth century were a new inheritance law and a law on marriage and civil registration which were sanctioned by Orders in Council of 1840.[37] During the second half of the nineteenth century, the frequency with which the States passed such laws increased as social and economic conditions became more complex and public expectations changed. This brought about a gradual diminution of the Royal Court's legislative activities and a corresponding increase in those of the States.[38]

As regarded finances, the island was largely independent. The British government limited its spending strictly to the military sphere. It paid the expenses of the garrison, partly funded the militia, and contributed towards the construction and upkeep of some (though not all) insular fortifications. Domestic needs were met exclusively from domestic resources. Parochial expenses were funded from rates raised on the value of all the real and personal property of parishioners whose assets exceeded a certain threshold. The Royal Court had no fixed source of funding, but raised revenue by means of lotteries between the late eighteenth and early nineteenth centuries, and also briefly enjoyed an income from harbour dues in the early twentieth century. For capital projects, the States relied on island-wide general taxes. These were levied on all insular ratepayers on a similar basis to parochial rates, but were unpopular with islanders and used on fewer than thirty occasions during our period.[39] For day-to-day outgoings, the States were initially limited to harbour dues and import duties, supplemented by a tax on innkeepers from 1780. In 1813, however, they were compelled to boost their revenues with a new income stream when they took over maintenance of sea

---

[37] O in Cs, 13.7.1840, 3.10.1840.
[38] The process culminated in the wholesale transfer of the Royal Court's Ordinance-making powers to the States in 1948.
[39] Hocart, *Island Assembly*, pp. 9, 10, 92.

defences from the parishes. This took the form of the *impôt*, a duty on locally sold spirits. An Order in Council of 1814 authorised the States to levy this duty for five years to provide funding for sea defences. However, as States spending for other purposes mounted, the States were obliged to apply for permission to renew the *impôt* in 1819, and on successive occasions throughout the nineteenth century.[40] On each occasion, the objects on which the proceeds of the *impôt* were to be spent were subject to British government agreement, and, to an extent, this restricted the States in the projects they were able to contemplate. It was not until the introduction of insular income tax in 1919 that the States were finally freed from such financial tutelage.

Until 1688, the Channel Islands were subject to the personal rule of the monarch, who, in concert with his Privy Council, could intervene in local affairs as he saw fit. This ceased with the accession of William III and the limitation of the monarchy's powers. Thereafter, the royal prerogative was to some extent assumed by government ministers and departments, although exercised through the Privy Council. Following the creation of the Home Office in 1782, this department assumed oversight of Channel Island affairs, with the Privy Council retaining an intermediary role.[41] Aside from its supervision of finances and law-making, the British government by and large respected the Islands' autonomy. Nevertheless, perhaps encouraged by their growing involvement in Island affairs, some eighteenth- and nineteenth-century governments asserted their ability, in certain circumstances, to extend Acts of Parliament to the Islands. This was problematic, since the Islands had never been part of England or the United Kingdom, and were hence not represented at Westminster. When, on a number of occasions, British governments sought to impose Acts on the Islands against their will, insular authorities resisted with vehemence. The position never explicitly resolved, but by the late nineteenth century, the constitutional convention had become established that – given the Islands' lack of representation – legislation should not be extended to them without serious cause, and, even then, not without their prior consultation and consent. The definition of

---

[40] *Ibid.*, pp. 25–6.
[41] Ogier, *Government and Law*, p. 225.

matters on which Westminster could legislate for the Islands then developed pragmatically.[42]

Law, post-1300

The law which English monarchs had allowed Channel Islanders to retain in the early thirteenth century was Norman customary law (*la Coutume normande*), to which had been added certain usages which had evolved in the Islands. Customary law can be said to consist of a body of laws and legal practices which have grown up gradually within a specific region and are applicable to that region only. Throughout the *ancien régime*, most of northern and western France operated at least partly under regional *Coutumes*. Indeed, this part of the country was known as *le pays de droit coutumier* to distinguish it from southern France, *le pays de droit écrit*, which by the thirteenth century had largely adopted written Roman law. France as a whole had about 700 distinct regional *Coutumes*.[43]

Norman customary law was based on a substrate of Frankish law. This had governed north-western France for centuries before the Normans' arrival, and Norman customs and usages had grown organically out of it. The *Coutume normande* is thought to have crystallised into a distinctive body of law in its own right in the period between 1049 and 1079.[44] French regional *Coutumes* began to be committed to writing in the twelfth century. The Norman *Coutume* was one of the first. The earliest Norman custumal, known as *Le Très Ancien Coutumier*, was composed of two parts, the first dating from

---

[42] Among subjects addressed by such legislation in the late nineteenth and early twentieth centuries were merchant shipping, copyright, posts and telegraphs (Hocart, *Island Assembly*, p. 86).

[43] B. Lenman & G. Parker, 'The state, the community and the criminal law in early modern Europe', in V.A.C. Gatrell, B. Lenman & G. Parker, *Crime and the Law: The Social History of Crime in Western Europe since 1500* (London, 1980), p. 32.

[44] S. Poirey, 'L'esprit of Norman customary law', in P. Bailhache (ed.), *A Celebration of Autonomy, 1204–2004: 800 Years of Channel Islands' Law* (Jersey, 2005), pp. 17, 20, 69.

the 1190s, and the second from 1218-23.[45] It was originally written in Latin, but a French translation appeared in the late 1230s. A further custumal thought to have been compiled between 1234 and 1258 emerged towards the end of the century in a Latin version referred to as the *Summa de Legibus*. A French translation of the *Summa*, later known as *Le Grand Coutumier de Normandie*, followed between 1270 and 1302.

Between them, *Le Très Ancien Coutumier* and *Le Grand Coutumier* contained about 600 customary laws, and like most French *Coutumes*, they focused primarily on the transmission of property. One scholar has likened *Le Grand Coutumier* to 'a flow chart of how land, cash, offices, and mobile goods might pass across generations, genders, and degrees of kinship'.[46] Only around one-tenth of *Le Grand Coutumier* dealt with what we would now think of as crime. The most accessible edition of this work currently available is Judith Everard's *Le Grand Coutumier de Normandie*, published in 2009.[47] This is the version which will be referred to here. Most of the matter relating to crime is found in Part II, Section 1 of the book, about two-thirds of which concerns such subjects as homicide, robbery, assault and defamation.[48]

There is evidence that *Le Grand Coutumier* was known of in the Channel Islands as early as 1309.[49] By the opening of the period dealt with in this study, it had been joined – in Guernsey's case, at least – by two other seminal texts, by which it was to some extent superseded. The first of these texts was Guillaume Terrien's 1574 commentary on Norman law.[50] Terrien's book was one of a long series of digests of Norman law and customs written by and for

---

[45] The remainder of this paragraph is based on J.A. Everard, 'L'ancienne [sic] Coutumier de Normandie: the laws and customs by which the duchy is ruled', in G. Dawes (ed.), *Paris 1259: Studies in the History and Law of Continental and Insular Normandy* (Guernsey, 2016), pp. 203, 205-8, 210–11, 213–15.

[46] Z.A. Schneider, *The King's Bench: Bailiwick Magistrates and Local Governance in Normandy, 1670-1740* (Woodbridge, 2008), p. 8.

[47] J.A. Everard (tr), *Le Grand Coutumier de Normandie: The Laws and Customs by which the Duchy of Normandy is Ruled* (Jersey, 2009). Everard's text is a translation of the *Summa de Legibus* as published in W.L. De Gruchy, *L'Ancienne Coutume de Normandie* (Jersey, 1881), which De Gruchy copied from G. Le Rouillé, *Le Grant Coustumier du Pays & Duché de Normendie* (Paris, 1534).

[48] Everard (tr.), *Grand Coutumier*, pp. 280-375.

[49] Everard, 'L'ancienne [sic] Coutumier de Normandie', p. 207.

[50] G. Terrien, *Commentaires du Droict Civil tant Public que Privé Observé au Pays & Duché de Normandie* (Rouen, 1574). My references are to the edition published in Paris in 1578.

lawyers.[51] His work took on a particular significance for Guernsey in 1581, when Crown officials requested Guernsey's authorities to set out the island's laws and customs in writing. Instead of basing themselves on *Le Grand Coutumier*, the compilers referred in preference to Terrien's work, which, having been published just a few years earlier, was the most up-to-date digest of Norman law.[52] The method they adopted consisted in going through Terrien's *Commentaires* section by section, specifying what accorded with, or varied from, local law and usage. The resulting statement was then ratified by an Order in Council of 27 October 1583 and assumed authoritative status. At first only available in manuscript, the statement was published as *L'Approbation des Lois* in 1715 and again in 1822.[53] This was Guernsey's second seminal legal text.

In its printed form, *L'Approbation des Lois* comprised a mere twenty-seven pages. The compilers adopted a broad-brush approach, often limiting themselves to a bald statement – 'yes, we use chapter such and such' or 'no, we do not use chapter such and such' – without going into detail as to precisely which parts of sometimes lengthy chapters were used, nor, usually, in the case of a negative, specifying what was done instead. As a code of laws, it was utterly deficient and attracted criticism from the first. One of its most scathing critics was the clergyman Thomas Le Marchant (1612–84), who wrote a detailed critique of *L'Approbation* a few decades after it was compiled.[54] It was Le Marchant's opinion that the Jurats who compiled *L'Approbation* had deliberately left gaps in it in order to allow themselves maximum flexibility and hence maximum power. He alleged that the Jurats' aim had been 'to exalt the authority of the Court of this Island, and to give

---

[51] Terrien was himself a lawyer who had served a number of important judicial offices, including that of president of the principal royal court of Dieppe.

[52] This was the second time Guernsey's authorities had attempted such a task; an account of local laws compiled in 1579, directly based on *Le Grand Coutumier*, had been rejected by the Privy Council, possibly because it was felt to be too archaic. For more on this episode, see Ogier, *Government and Law*, pp. 160–7.

[53] The 1822 edition is the one which will be referred to here: T. Tramailler (ed.), *Approbation des Lois, Coutumes, et Usages de l'Ile de Guernesey* (1715; Guernsey, 1822 edn).

[54] T. Le Marchant, *Remarques et Animadversions sur l'Approbation des Lois et Coustumier de Normandie usitées ès Jurisdictions de Guernezé*, 2 vols (Guernsey, 1826). Although published in 1826, Le Marchant's *Remarques* were written in the second half of the seventeenth century.

the Court powers as sublime, unlimited and arbitrary as possible.'[55] In writing his critique, Le Marchant adopted the same linear approach as the Jurats and worked his way through Terrien's *Commentaires* section by section. Unlike the Jurats, however, he did so with a fine-tooth comb, and – filling 711 pages – in rather more detail than *L'Approbation*. Le Marchant's book thus goes some way to filling in the gaps left by the earlier work, and it was treated by some later jurists as an authority.[56]

It should be noted at this point that Terrien's *Commentaires* differed substantially from *Le Grand Coutumier*. Though based on the *Coutume*, the book also incorporated all the major additions made to Norman law and procedure up to the 1570s. The title page of the *Commentaires* listed a whole host of disparate sources, including the fourteenth-century *Charte aux Normands*; the mid-fifteenth-century *Style de Procéder*; the 1515 *Style de Parlement*; decrees and decisions of the Norman *Echiquier* and *Parlement*; and French royal Ordinances – material from all of which was interspersed with Terrien's own detailed annotations.

Terrien's work was thus a far cry from the original *Coutume normande*, but, through the medium of *L'Approbation des Lois*, whole sections of it had become Guernsey law. In a submission to the nineteenth-century Royal Commission on Guernsey's criminal law, a leading local Advocate stated 'we look upon Terrien as being enacted. Terrien is held to be written law, so far as it is sanctioned by the Approbation des Loix'. Another Advocate declared 'our law, as far as it is recognized, is Terrien, approved by Queen Elizabeth, in the Approbation des Loix'.[57] In the investigation of Guernsey's criminal law and practice which follows, it will be my aim to determine to what extent such statements were true, and – if only partially true – to identify other forces which may have contributed to shaping the justice system between 1680 and 1929.

---

[55] *Ibid.*, 2, p. 314.
[56] See, for instance, Advocate Peter Jeremie in *Second Report of the Commissioners Appointed to Inquire into the State of the Criminal Law in the Channel Islands: Guernsey* (London, 1848), p. 106.
[57] *Ibid.*, pp. 92, 106. *Loix* is an archaic plural of *loi* used in the original document of 1583.

I
1680–1764: Gallic Style

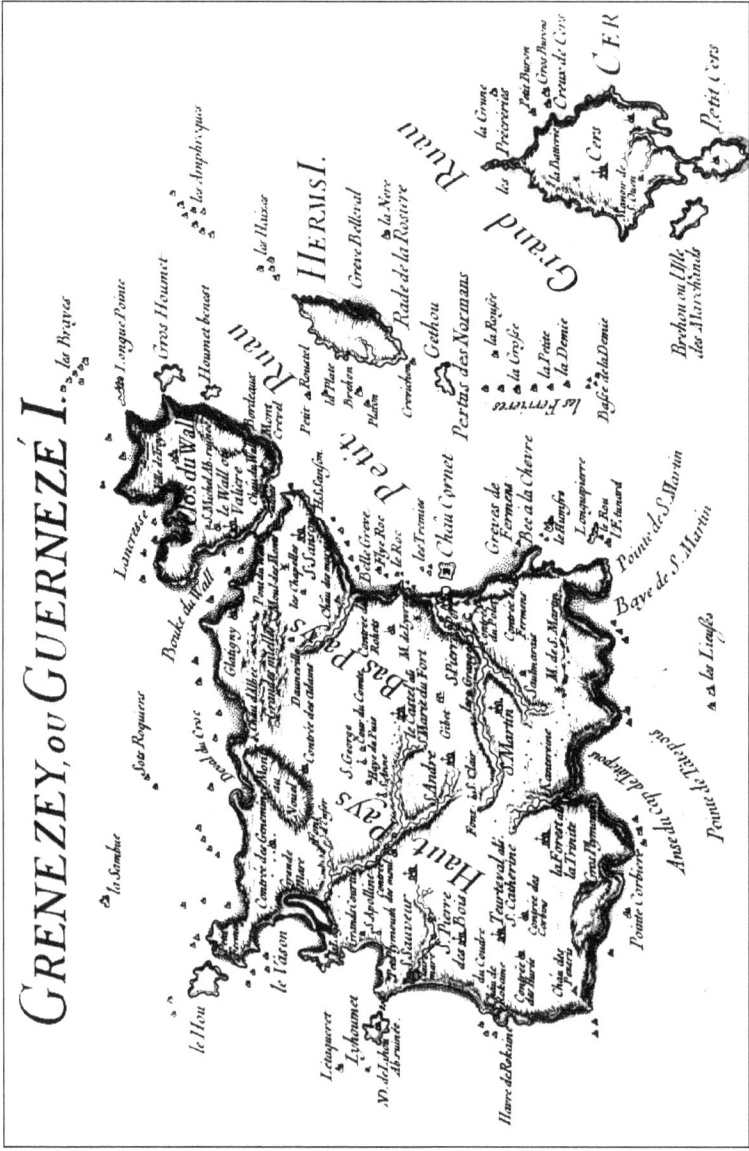

Map 3. Guernsey, 1689
Courtesy of the Priaulx Library, Guernsey

1

1680–1764: Background

In the period with which this chapter is concerned, Guernsey was an island physically in two parts. The northern tip was separated from the rest by a tidal channel whose bed of sand and mud was largely uncovered at low tide and could be crossed by means of stepping stones at intervals along its length. At its eastern end was a more substantial bridge which gave access to the detached portion at all times save when the tide was at its height. The channel was known as the Braye du Valle, and the land which it separated from the rest of the island was known as the Clos du Valle. It formed part of the Vale parish.

There are no hard statistics on Guernsey's population in the seventeenth century. Calculations made by Gregory Stevens Cox suggest an insular total of around 10,000 in 1680, with St Peter Port accommodating about a third of the population.[1] Situated mid-way down the east coast, St Peter Port possessed a good natural harbour and a sheltered roadstead in which ships en route from Britain to Biscay could ride out rough weather. By the late thirteenth century, hundreds of vessels were stopping by annually on voyages between northern and southern Europe.[2] By the early fourteenth century, when Guernsey's main market was moved to St Peter Port, what had been a small harbourside settlement became recognisably a town.[3]

---

[1] Using a multiplier of between 4 and 7 on an island total of 1,902 militiamen of which 521 were in St Peter Port, Dr Stevens Cox calculated that Guernsey's population in 1680 was between 7,608 and 13,314, and St Peter Port's between 2,084 and 3,647; taking the medians of the two figures in each case gives an insular population of 10,461 and a St Peter Port population of 2,865 (G. Stevens Cox, *St Peter Port, 1680–1830: The History of an International Entrepôt* (Woodbridge, 1999), p. 65).

[2] W. Stevenson, 'The Middle Ages, 1000–1500', in A.G. Jamieson (ed.), *A People of the Sea: The Maritime History of the Channel Islands* (London, 1986), pp. 42–3.

[3] Stevens Cox, *St Peter Port*, pp. 12, 50. The town accounted for only a small part of the total area of St Peter Port, but accommodated the largest proportion of that parish's population. It never developed any municipal institutions of its own, and was always run as part of the parish. Although the port of St Sampsons acquired a semi-urban fringe during the nineteenth century, St Peter Port remained Guernsey's only town throughout our period.

Plate 1. View of St Peter Port, 1680
By kind permission of the Royal Court

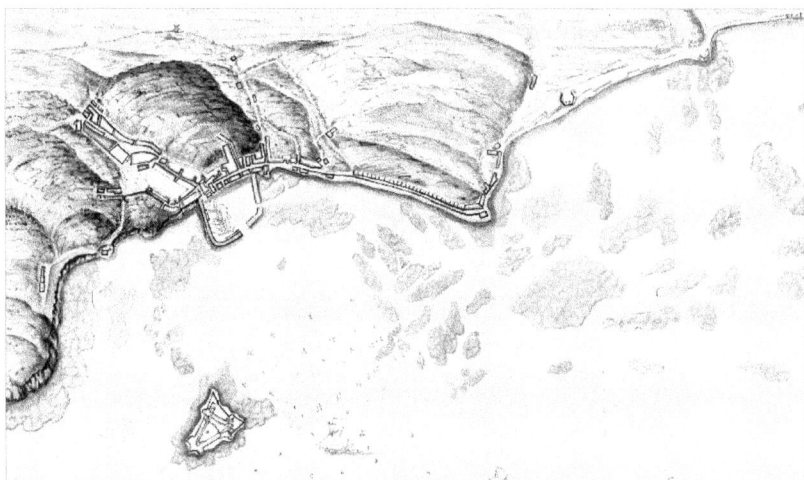

Plate 2. Plan of St Peter Port, 1680
By kind permission of the Royal Court
(note that the harbour is represented as having a north pier,
which was not in fact built until 1730)

As well as providing facilities for visiting vessels, St Peter Port was also the base of local shipowners and traders. In medieval times, Guernsey's trade consisted of little more than the export of small amounts of local produce, the import of essential commodities from France and England, and occasional voyages further south for wine.[4] The situation changed somewhat after 1481, when a Papal Bull made the Channel Islands 'neutral' in wartime by permitting them to continue trading with France during hostilities with England.[5] This gave a fillip to St Peter Port's traders, so that by the 1580s, local merchants had established themselves as significant middlemen in the Anglo-French wine trade. By this time, too, Guernsey-owned vessels had begun to take a tentative part in the infant Newfoundland trade.[6] For a great many years, however, Guernsey's trade, commensurate with its small population, remained relatively small-scale. Charles Trumbull, who visited Guernsey in 1677, observed that islanders owned only nine trading vessels, two of which went to Newfoundland, and seven to Bordeaux, St Malo, Holland and England.[7]

In the following decade, a political change occurred which was to have important repercussions for local trade. In 1689, at the beginning of England's Nine Years War against France, an Order in Council confirmed that a prohibition on the import of goods from France should also be observed in the Channel Islands.[8] Although it abolished their privilege of neutrality, the prohibition was accepted by Islanders, some of whom might have seen it as an opportunity to engage in privateering.[9] The Nine Years' War lasted until 1697, during which period a number of Guernsey shipowners did indeed fit out privateers. Having met with some success, they continued to do so in ensuing Anglo-French wars, gradually increasing the

---

[4] Stevenson, 'The Middle Ages', pp. 19–43.

[5] For a detailed account of the Bull, see D.M. Ogier, *Reformation and Society in Guernsey* (Woodbridge, 1996), pp. 37–8.

[6] J.C. Appleby, 'Neutrality, trade and privateering, 1500–1689', in Jamieson (ed.), *People of the Sea*, p. 59.

[7] R. Hocart (ed.), 'The Journal of Charles Trumbull', *TSG*, 21 (1984), p. 572.

[8] J.S. Bromley, 'A new vocation: privateering in the wars of 1689–97 and 1702–13', in Jamieson (ed.), *People of the Sea*, p. 109.

[9] 'Privateering' was the practice whereby civilian-owned vessels were permitted to participate in maritime warfare under a commission of war known as a letter of marque. This empowered them to attack enemy vessels and take them as prizes, with the proceeds shared between sponsors, shipowners, captains and crew.

size of their fleet.[10] Privateering in itself did not provide a secure foundation for a stable economy, since participants often experienced dramatic losses as well as spectacular gains. However, it did encourage the establishment of St Peter Port as an entrepôt, and, in due course, it led to an expansion of trade.

St Peter Port became an entrepôt almost by default as prize cargoes of wines, spirits, tobacco, tea and textiles were brought back to Guernsey by the privateers and stored in the town. Between 1719 and 1747, some twenty to thirty new warehouses were built to accommodate these goods.[11] Since most of the prize goods were luxury items subject to high duties in England, the interest of English smugglers was eventually aroused. These began to visit St Peter Port in their luggers and cutters to buy up supplies – so much so that, by the 1730s, Guernsey had become one of the main suppliers of contraband to smugglers on the south coast of England.[12] This in turn stimulated local entrepreneurs to set up manufactories for processing raw tobacco; operations for decanting wine and spirits into small barrels; and coopers' workshops for making the barrels.

As the demand from smugglers for dutiable goods remained as strong in peacetime as in war, local shipowners further responded by fitting out regular trading ships to fetch these goods from their places of origin. As a result, local shipowners and traders had by the mid-eighteenth century become full participants in the Atlantic trade, bringing in wine, brandy and textiles from France; rum from the West Indies; and tobacco from Maryland and Virginia.[13] In tandem with these developments, the entrepôt's clientele expanded as its growing reputation allowed it to develop a respectable role as depository and bulk-breaker for dutiable commodities destined for legal entry into Britain before the introduction of the bonding system.

Economically, this was by and large the point St Peter Port had reached by the end of the period dealt with in this chapter. However, the town was far from its apogee as entrepôt. As Ferdinand Tupper later observed, it was not until the reign of George III (1760–1820) that it entered its period of

---

[10] After the Nine Years War, there were three further major Anglo-French conflicts in the period ending 1764: the War of the Spanish Succession (1701–13), the War of the Austrian Succession (1740–8), and the Seven Years War (1756–63).

[11] Stevens Cox, *St Peter Port*, p. 21.

[12] A.G. Jamieson, 'The Channel Islands and smuggling, 1680-1850', in Jamieson (ed.), *People of the Sea*, p. 204.

[13] G. Stevens Cox, *The Guernsey Merchants and their World* (Guernsey, 2009), p. 7.

greatest prosperity and importance.[14] The narrative will be resumed in Chapter 4.

Socially, however, even these early economic changes had repercussions, not least the unprecedented influxes of sailors to crew the privateers. A document from the 1730s asserted that, during the War of the Spanish Succession (1710–13), Guernsey's thirty or forty privateers had 'employed not less than 1700 men, whereof about the one half belonged to the Island, and the remainder were English and Irish with some Dutch and other foreigners.'[15] This phenomenon was largely new to St Peter Port and had implications for the preservation of law and order.

At the same time, the recurrent wars also brought in large numbers of soldiers. St Peter Port had housed an English garrison since the thirteenth century. Based in Castle Cornet on an islet half a mile from the town, the garrison was originally raised by the Warden or Governor and paid from Crown revenues. From the beginning of our period, responsibility for the garrison was transferred to the Board of Ordnance, and the 'Governor's Guard' was replaced by troops from regular regiments.[16] In peacetime, the garrison had a complement of about sixty soldiers: Charles Trumbull found it manned by two companies of thirty men each in 1677.[17] In wartime, numbers were considerably higher. In the War of the Austrian Succession (1740–8), the garrison comprised some 200 men.[18] In the Seven Years War (1756–63), the number was at least 800.[19] At these times, the Castle could not provide sufficient accommodation, and islanders were required to find quarters for soldiers onshore. An Order in Council of 1691 gave the civil authorities the right to decide where and how these soldiers would be quartered. As many as possible were billeted in St Peter Port's public houses,

---

[14] F.B. Tupper, *The History of Guernsey and its Bailiwick* (Guernsey, 1854), p. 363.

[15] Memorial by Peter Carey, undated but probably 1739, PL, Watkins MSS, vol. 3.

[16] T.W.M. De Guérin, 'The English garrison of Guernsey from early times', *Transactions of the Guernsey Society of Natural Science and Local Research*, 5 (1905), pp. 67, 78.

[17] Hocart (ed.), 'Journal of Charles Trumbull', p. 573.

[18] Royal Court to Governor, November 1755, GG, Royal Court General Letter Book (first series), vol. 1.

[19] Secretary of State for War to Lieutenant Governor, 12.6.1756 and 13.6.1756, GG, Royal Court General Letter Book (first series), vol. 1. These letters announce the despatch to Guernsey of nine companies of Invalids (five of 50 men each, and the other four of 112 each) to reinforce the garrison, which then consisted of two companies of Invalids.

and the rest were distributed among the parishes.[20] Of a contingent of 397 men which arrived in August 1761, St Peter Port was allocated 147, and the other nine parishes between fifty and fifteen each, proportionate to their size.[21]

The other major influxes in the late seventeenth and early eighteenth centuries arose for religious reasons. This period saw three waves of Huguenot immigration. The first took place between 1685 and 1690 and was prompted by the revocation of the Edict of Nantes; the second took place between 1699 and 1700 and followed the end of the Nine Years War; the third trickled in slowly between 1717 and 1727. Some of the religious refugees stayed only briefly, but others put down more permanent roots. Gregory Stevens Cox has suggested that, by the end of the third wave, between eighty and one hundred Huguenot families had settled in St Peter Port.[22]

Aside from these Huguenots, St Peter Port saw relatively few strangers settle permanently in the first half of the eighteenth century. Leading merchants and shipowners were chiefly drawn from the long-standing native elite, who now mostly lived in town.[23] Natives also preponderated lower down the scale. Most artisans seem to have been local, save a few specialist craftsmen (shipwrights, coopers, etc.) brought in to supply skill shortages. Most shopkeepers and victuallers were local too, apart from a small handful attracted by growth in the service sector.[24] Much of the loading and unloading, portering, wine-decanting and tobacco-processing also appears to have been performed by local labour at this time, some native to St Peter Port, some newly arrived from the country parishes. A local census of 1728 shows that St Peter Port's population had risen from around 3,000 in 1680

[20] R. Hocart, *An Island Assembly: The Development of the States of Guernsey, 1700–1949* (Guernsey, 1988), pp. 5–6.

[21] Ord, 15.8.1761.

[22] Stevens Cox, *St Peter Port*, pp. 86–8.

[23] In 1677, Charles Trumbull commented 'what gentry they have in a manner live in the Town or near it' (Hocart (ed.), 'Journal of Charles Trumbull', p. 568).

[24] Stevens Cox, *St Peter Port*, pp. 83–5.

to a total of about 6,000.[25] By early-eighteenth-century standards, this made St Peter Port a fairly sizeable town.[26]

Plate 3. St Peter Port from Castle Cornet, 1739
© The British Library Board, K.Top.55.63.a

St Peter Port's lowest social stratum lived a precarious existence, always vulnerable to the economic downturns caused by weather, trade cycles and European politics. In 1722, a petition to the Privy Council complained that 'half the town's poor' were out of work.[27] The urban poor also suffered badly in the periods of food shortage and high grain prices which regularly afflicted much of northern Europe in the seventeenth and eighteenth centuries. Special measures were repeatedly initiated by the island's authorities to import and distribute emergency grain supplies.[28] In 1743, a workhouse

[25] The census was carried out by parochial authorities in order to assess grain requirements in a year of dearth. It counted only settled inhabitants, so sojourning soldiers, sailors and other non-natives would not have been included. The census gave a figure for St Peter Port of 4,350, but if we add a notional 1,500 for temporary residents, this brings the total to around 6,000. This figure may be an underestimate. In 1758, the Privy Council was informed that the island accommodated more than 3,000 sojourning strangers, most of whom would have resided in town (Lieutenant Governor to Privy Council, 28 Jan 1758, GG, Royal Court General Letter Book (first series), vol. 1). For 1728 census figures, see Stevens Cox, *St Peter Port*, p. 164.

[26] At a similar period, some English county towns, such as Lincoln and Warwick, only had populations of about 4,500 (C.W. Chalklin, *The Provincial Towns of Georgian England* (London, 1974), p. 18).

[27] 19.7.1722, PL, Watkins MSS, vol. 2.

[28] See, for instance, Acts of the States dated 10.6.1697, 15.7.1725, 19.4.1729, 7.11.1751, 10.8.1752, 23.6.1756, 10.3.1757, 21.2.1758 in G.E. Lee (ed.), *Actes des Etats de l'Ile de Guernesey, 1651–1780* (Guernsey, 1907).

known as the Town Hospital was established in St Peter Port in a bid to bring the parish's burgeoning relief expenditure under control.[29]

Physically, the fabric of the town remained medieval throughout the period dealt with by this chapter. In extent, it was limited to a strip running along the seashore, with a few spurs to the south and west. The town's narrow thoroughfares were lined with four- or five-storey granite houses, gable-ends fronting the street, many of them garnished with projecting jetties on their upper floors, some of which almost touched each other across the interjacent alleyways. In 1677, Charles Trumbull described the interiors of these houses, with their massive exposed beams and ancient cavernous fireplaces, as 'not built for ornament'.[30] In 1749, the Jurat (and later Bailiff) Samuel Bonamy declared of the town: 'its situation is very unpleasant, being built at the bottom of a hill close to the sea shore, and so confined for want of room, that the streets are narrow and irregular; there may be between three and four hundred houses in it.'[31]

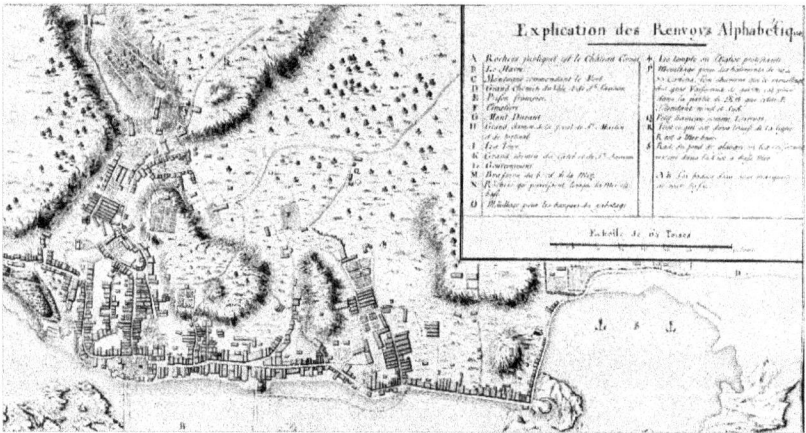

Plate 4. Plan of St Peter Port, 1759
Island Archives Service, Guernsey

[29] R.-M. Crossan, *Poverty and Welfare in Guernsey, 1560–2015* (Woodbridge, 2015), pp. 115–19.
[30] Hocart (ed.), 'Journal of Charles Trumbull', p. 571.
[31] S. Bonamy, *A Short Account of the Island of Guernsey A.D. MDCCXLIX*, British Library, Add MS 6253.

By the beginning of our period, some at least of St Peter Port's streets were paved with stone. Royal Court records show that paviours were brought over from England for this purpose as early as 1625.[32] This must have helped reduce dust and mud, but the town was far from clean. Each of the main streets had an open gutter into which householders were obliged by law to sweep their waste so that it could flow into the sea. However, this obligation was ill-observed, and much of the waste was simply tipped out of windows and left where it landed.[33] In 1728, a scavenger or street-cleaner was engaged by the parish to deal with the worst of the filth.[34] Prior to the installation of sewers in the early nineteenth century, the harbour served as the general repository for the town's ordure, with adjacent beaches also used for this purpose.

In the period between the 1680s and 1760s, carriages were unknown in St Peter Port. Even the better-off walked from one part of town to the other. When going into the countryside, they also went on foot, or else travelled on horseback. Paths leading out of town were mere muddy tracks across fields. Heavy goods moved about the town streets either on sledges drawn by oxen and horses, or slung on poles between the shoulders of two porters.[35]

Until the late eighteenth century, St Peter Port lacked a purpose-built marketplace, and foodstuffs displayed for sale cluttered the pavements on either side of the High Street – fish on mats towards the northern end; vegetables, eggs and butter lower down. At the bottom of the High Street, almost on the threshold of the Town Church, were the butchers' shambles where meat was cut up and sold in the open air.[36] As far as liquid sustenance was concerned, St Peter Port was well supplied. In 1764, it hosted eighty public houses and seventeen spirit-purveyors.[37]

As we have seen, the town's *raison d'être* was its harbour. In the seventeenth century, that harbour consisted of a single pier built in the 1580s which could shelter about thirty small vessels. In 1684, the States decided to enclose the harbour by building a second pier to the north. The work was started but money soon ran out. In the early 1720s St Peter Port's leading

[32] Ord, 3.10.1625.

[33] 'Notes on St Peter Port by Edgar MacCulloch', PL, Edith Carey Scrapbook no. 1.

[34] 19.1.1728, IA, AQ 0988/01.

[35] *The Guernsey and Jersey Magazine*, 3 (1837), pp. 233–5.

[36] Stevens Cox, *St Peter Port*, p. 51.

[37] 25.9.1764, IA, AQ 0988/01.

merchants raised a voluntary subscription, and by 1730 the northern pier was complete. The harbour did not however have a landward quay until after 1774.[38] In 1749, Samuel Bonamy described the harbour thus:

> it is built in the form of an half moon, with two moles or peers extending like two bended arms into the sea. The top of these peers is smooth, and paved with Swanidge stone, and there are posts for the ships to fasten their cables. These serve as a walk for the inhabitants, there being walls on each side. This harbour is capable of containing near an hundred vessels.[39]

As regarded the country parishes, the dearth-related census of 1728 showed a total population of 5,896.[40] While the figure for St Peter Port fell short of its actual population, the figure for the country parishes was almost certainly accurate, for the reason that most sojourning strangers were town-based. There was little to attract them to rural areas, since the economy of the nine country parishes (and the portion of St Peter Port which lay outside the town) was solidly based on agriculture. By the beginning of our period, most of Guernsey's productive land had been divided into small fields bounded by banks of earth and stone. Richard Hocart has written that the original open fields were gradually enclosed from the fifteenth century, with landowners consolidating their strips by purchase and exchange to form parcels suited to enclosure.[41]

The interior of the island was intersected by a multitude of tracks and paths giving access to the fields, but these were generally so narrow that they could only accommodate a single cart. They were also largely unmetalled, and although landowners were theoretically obliged to maintain thoroughfares bordering their property, many were so neglected that they were impassable in winter. This impeded travel between parishes to the extent that different parts of the island developed distinct sub-dialects.[42] Settlement in the countryside was dispersed, consisting largely of farmhouses and cottages situated amid the fields. Although there was some clustering of habitation around parish churches, there were no villages.

---

[38] Hocart, *Island Assembly*, p. 5; Stevens Cox, *St Peter Port*, p. 22.

[39] Bonamy, *Short Account*, p. 5.

[40] Stevens Cox, *St Peter Port*, p. 164.

[41] R. Hocart, *The Country People of Guernsey and their Agriculture, 1640–1840* (Guernsey, 2016), p. 73.

[42] *The Guernsey and Jersey Magazine*, 3 (1837), pp. 233–5.

Most of Guernsey's rural families owned the land on which they lived. At the opening of our period, the feudal structures which had succeeded the early-thirteenth-century departure of Norman seigneurs were still largely in place. The island remained divided into fiefs, 70 per cent of which belonged to the Crown and the rest to small private seigneurs.[43] Feudal dues remained payable on land within the fiefs, but owners were free to sell their properties and pass them on to their heirs. In the thirteenth century, most men recorded as holding land from the Crown were very small farmers indeed, since the majority held just one *bouvée*, which was equivalent to about five English acres.[44] In the 400 years between the thirteenth and seventeenth centuries, some families had enlarged their holdings by judicious marriages and astute management, and others had seen their holdings shrink as land was subdivided through inheritance.[45] However, in an island of less than 25 square miles, the average holding necessarily remained small. No figures exist for Guernsey farm sizes before the 1851 census. In default of better, however, the 1851 figures will serve as a guide to the position in earlier times. In 1851, 821 Bailiwick farmers gave details of their holdings, of which between 725 and 750 were located in Guernsey.[46] There were just three farms of over 50 acres in the whole Bailiwick.[47] Over 90 per cent of farms were under 25 acres in size, with 38 per cent 9 acres or less. Most of the families who lived on these holdings would have worked their land themselves, and only hired additional labour to help out at peak times. As an Englishman once observed,

---

[43] Hocart, *Country People*, p. 23.

[44] J.H. Le Patourel, *The Medieval Administration of the Channel Islands, 1199–1399* (London, 1937), pp. 76–7.

[45] Guernsey had a system of modified partible inheritance whereby the eldest son was entitled to the principal dwelling and a fixed area around it, while other siblings had a share of the remaining land.

[46] 1851 census report, Parliamentary Papers 1852–3, LXXXVIII (available at www.histpop.org). We cannot be sure of the precise number of Guernsey farms, because the census report did not disaggregate them from those elsewhere in the Bailiwick.

[47] In 1812, Thomas Quayle had noted the existence of 'eight or nine' farms of over 50 acres, so some had clearly been broken into smaller units between that date and 1851 (T. Quayle, *General View of the Agriculture and Present State of the Islands on the Coast of Normandy subject to the Crown of Great Britain* (London, 1815), p. 249).

Guernsey's country people were 'a hard-working and a hard-faring race of husbandmen'.[48]

The primary aim of a Guernsey holding was to sustain the family that lived on it. However, restraining their own consumption, families would have reserved their best produce for market in order to earn much needed cash. The larger the holding, the larger the marketable surplus, and the more secure the family. Although Guernsey's land was fertile and its climate benign, the 38 per cent of families owning fewer than 9 acres could probably not have lived by farming alone.[49] Here the holding would have functioned as an adjunct to another occupation, providing food for the household and/or cash-earning crops, while their owners worked primarily as fishermen, stonemasons, carpenters, and so on. Knitting, a by-employment in which all household members could engage, also provided support to the rural economy. In the 1650s, it was claimed that more than 6,000 islanders in both country and town eked out a living by knitting stockings on a piece-work basis.[50] This trade was organised by St Peter Port merchants using raw wool imported under licence from England. Finished goods were at first exported mostly to France, but switched to England in the late seventeenth century. The export of locally knitted stockings played an important part in Guernsey's economy until at least the 1780s.[51]

From a nadir around the beginning of our period, rural fortunes seem to have been on an improving trend over the years covered by this chapter. In 1680, the countryside had yet to recover from the crisis which had beset it around the time of the English Civil War. During the War, which began in 1642, islanders took the side of Parliament, while Castle Cornet was held for the king by the Governor, who blockaded St Peter Port harbour with the Castle guns and only surrendered in 1651. The nine years of blockade disrupted trade and led to widespread distress. Land under tillage diminished as the conflict made demands on cultivators' time, and they were further discouraged from production by the dues and tithes still levied on their harvests. Levels of indebtedness increased, and a number of countrymen lost

---

[48] J. Jacob, *Annals of some of the British Norman Isles constituting the Bailiwick of Guernsey* (Paris, 1830), p. 162.

[49] Richard Hocart has estimated that a landholding of at least 8 to 14 acres would have been necessary for a family to live entirely off the land (Hocart, *Country People*, p. 216).

[50] Hocart, *Country People*, p. 60.

[51] *Ibid.*, pp. 63–4, 66–8.

their land through insolvency.[52] After 1689, however, the developing entrepôt and periodic influxes of soldiers and sailors increased demand for locally produced food and gradually improved the situation in the countryside. By the 1750s, the country parishes were in a distinctly better position than they had been sixty years earlier. As Richard Hocart has observed, many rural houses were built or improved, and rural schools founded or extended in this period.[53]

Nevertheless, benefits from increased sales of comestibles were unevenly distributed, and it was the farmers able to produce in volume who garnered the bulk of the profits. For the rest of the country population, the picture was mixed. Evidence suggests that rural inequalities may even have increased. Certainly, rural in-migration to St Peter Port was gathering pace over this period.[54] Growing numbers of young country men were moving to town to work as labourers or seamen, and young women to work as domestics. Emergency grain supplies in times of dearth continued to be needed in rural areas, and the country parishes founded a workhouse of their own – the Country Hospital – in 1751.[55]

The last few paragraphs have dwelt on differences between town and country. However, islanders from all parts had many characteristics and experiences in common. The rest of the chapter will focus on these. To begin with, all local males between sixteen and sixty shared an obligation to serve in the insular militia.[56] For the first three decades of our period, each parish had an infantry company (save St Peter Port, which had four), commanded by a parish captain assisted by a lieutenant and ensign.[57] These officers were commissioned by the Governor, who was in overall command of the militia. During the early eighteenth century, the militia was reorganised into regiments. In 1711, the First (or Town) Regiment was created, composed of men from St Peter Port and St Sampsons. With it came a command structure

[52] *Ibid.*, pp. 147–50. See also 'Historical notices of the Channel Islands, no. 13', *The Guernsey and Jersey Magazine*, 4 (1837), pp. 296–7.

[53] Hocart, *Country People*, pp. 153–7.

[54] Stevens Cox, *St Peter Port*, p. 66.

[55] Crossan, *Poverty and Welfare*, pp. 27–8, 58.

[56] Guernsey had had a militia since at least the mid-fourteenth century (E. Parks, *The Royal Guernsey Militia: A Short History and List of Officers* (Guernsey, 1992), p. 5).

[57] J. Warburton, *A Treatise on the History, Laws and Customs of the Island of Guernsey* (Guernsey, 1822), pp. 61–2.

of colonels and subordinate officers. The Second (or North) Regiment followed in 1717, for men from the Castel and Vale parishes, and the Third (or South) Regiment in 1743, for men from St Martins, St Andrews, the Forest, St Saviours, St Peters and Torteval.[58] By 1750, some 1,800 men were serving in these regiments under three colonels, twenty captains, three majors, fifteen lieutenants and sixteen ensigns.[59] In the period here, Guernsey's militia was subject to the jurisdiction of the Royal Court rather than the British army. Periodically, the Court passed Ordinances to regulate conditions of service, and breaches of regulations were tried in the criminal division of the Court.

Islanders also shared a common religion, which was Protestant and Anglican. As Samuel Bonamy stated in 1749, 'at present the church of England is the only communion among us, there being not one dissenter to my knowledge, either protestant or papist.'[60] This situation had, however, only prevailed for about seventy years. The Protestant Reformation had originally come to Guernsey from Normandy, brought by refugee clergymen whose Protestantism was of a Calvinist character (the norm in sixteenth-century France). Thus, when the Reformation had run its course and Guernsey had completed its transition from Catholicism to Protestantism, the regime which established itself had been Calvinist and Presbyterian.[61] Presbyterianism was to endure as Guernsey's 'established' religion for approximately a century (hence the island's support for the parliamentary cause during the English Civil War). Ultimately, it was brought to an end by the restoration of the English monarchy in 1660. The king appointed an Anglican Dean to Guernsey in 1662 with an order to introduce the Anglican liturgy to the island.[62] Subsequent measures to engraft Anglicanism upon the population stimulated a certain amount of resistance among islanders and clergy, notably on the part of Thomas Le Marchant (Presbyterian minister and author of *Remarques et Animadversions*), who was imprisoned for a time for his refusal to conform.[63] While these measures were ultimately successful,

[58] Parks, *Guernsey Militia*, p. 9.

[59] V. Coysh, *Royal Guernsey: A History of the Royal Guernsey Militia* (Guernsey, 1977), p. 9.

[60] Bonamy, *Short Account*, p. 14.

[61] For an account of the process, which culminated in the 1560s, see Ogier, *Reformation and Society*, pp. 62–83.

[62] R. Hocart, *Guernsey in the Reign of Charles II* (Guernsey, 2020), pp. 58, 59, 67–8.

[63] *Ibid.*, pp. 77–9, 96, 113, 165–6.

and Presbyterianism had more or less died out by the end of the seventeenth century,[64] a latent Calvinism seems nevertheless to have underlain the surface for many decades, assisted by the fact that most of Guernsey's parochial rectors continued to come from France.[65] Even in the early nineteenth century, parish churches still lacked baptismal fonts, clergymen still shunned the surplice, and no Anglican bishop visited Guernsey, nor performed a confirmation service, until 1818.[66]

Guernsey's latent Calvinism only served to fuel a strong anti-Catholicism. The accession of the Catholic King James II in 1685 was not enthusiastically received in the island, particularly when Captain Charles Macarty and Colonel John Legge, both apparently Roman Catholics, were appointed Lieutenant Governors, and Catholic troops were quartered at Castle Cornet.[67] Thomas Dicey recounts that, as soon as news reached Guernsey of the landing of William of Orange in Devon in 1688, Jurats arranged for the Protestant soldiers of the garrison to take Castle Cornet from the Catholics and place the Lieutenant Governor under detention.[68]

Language was another trait all islanders had in common. In their homes, fields, workshops and counting-houses, all natives spoke a variant of Norman French which had established itself locally after the island became part of Normandy in the tenth century. It differed in many ways from 'standard' French, which was based on the Parisian dialect. If called upon to distinguish their local tongue from standard French, Guernseymen might have called it *guernésiais*, or adopting a standard French term, *patois*.[69]

Guernsey's *patois* had no written form, as was the case with most French regional *patois*. During the twelfth and thirteenth centuries, Parisian French had gradually established itself as the standard form for written texts

---

[64] *Ibid.*, p. 174.

[65] Jonathan Duncan informs us that in 1768, of Guernsey's eight rectors, one was Swiss, six French, and one of recent French extraction (J. Duncan, *The History of Guernsey* (London, 1841), p. 570). Guernsey's parochial livings were of such low value as to be unattractive to local men until benefices were augmented in the early nineteenth century.

[66] W. Berry, *The History of the Island of Guernsey* (London, 1815), p. 262; Duncan, *History of Guernsey*, p. 351.

[67] Hocart, *Charles II*, p. 162.

[68] T. Dicey, *An Historical Account of Guernsey* (London, 1751), pp. 155–7.

[69] The word *patois* (archaically rendered *patrois*) is derived from the low Latin *patriensis*, meaning 'of the fatherland'.

throughout northern France. By the time the surviving series of Royal Court registers began in the 1520s, it was also used in local Court records. This paralleled the adoption of standard French in legal and administrative documents in mainland Normandy.[70] In the sixteenth century, standard French also became the language of insular religion when the francophone clerics who introduced Calvinism substituted French for Latin in local churches. Over time, the use of standard French was extended to all the formal contexts of civic life – government, the judiciary, education and religion – while *guernésiais* remained ubiquitous in private communication and domestic life.[71] In the late seventeenth and eighteenth centuries, all social classes probably had some knowledge of both. Although the common people spoke only *guernésiais*, they heard French in church, and they were taught to read and write in French in their parish schools. Islanders higher up the social scale used *guernésiais* with servants, tradesmen and the lower orders generally. Those who lived in the countryside also spoke *guernésiais* among themselves. The urban mercantile elite used standard French for record-keeping and correspondence, and may also have spoken it with their peers.

The final characteristic which all seventeenth- and eighteenth-century islanders had in common was their marked sense of social hierarchy. This was perhaps exaggerated by the fact that stratification was compressed compared with larger nations with wider wealth gaps. Status was indicated by title. Scions of the wealthiest and most respected families were designated Monsieur ('Mr'). Better-off farmers, shopkeepers and business owners were designated Sieur ('Sr'), and the large residue of journeymen artisans, smallholders, unskilled labourers and domestic servants were denied any title at all.

Different social strata pursued different life courses, and although they constantly interacted in daily life, closer forms of contact, such as marriage, were taboo, even between families farming 10 as opposed to 5 acres. In this period, a person's rank was particularly important in determining the extent to which he could participate in public life. In the countryside, parochial

---

[70] In Normandy, as in the rest of France, French was made the official language of the law courts by the Ordinance of Villers-Cotterêts in 1539 (Z.A. Schneider, *The King's Bench: Bailiwick Magistrates and Local Governance in Normandy, 1670–1740* (Woodbridge, 2008), p. 186).

[71] The technical term for this division of roles between two languages, or variants of a language, which was fairly common in Europe at this period, is diglossia.

offices were handed down through dynasties composed of leading farmers. In St Peter Port, they were monopolised by the mercantile elite. Only people at the highest social level, many of whom could trace their pedigrees back to the thirteenth century, could expect to be elected Jurats. These people attached great importance to their status. As Richard Hocart has observed, they counted themselves as 'nobles' in the French sense of the word, wearing swords on formal occasions, having themselves painted in wigs and lace, and acquiring coats of arms. Above all, they expected to be obeyed and deferred to by their inferiors.[72]

Within the confines of Guernsey's small community, a mutual consciousness of rank was all-pervasive. This consciousness was fully reflected in the registers of the Royal Court, whose use or omission of titles pinpointed the social position of everyone the Court dealt with. Against this background, the next chapter will begin by looking more closely at the nature and composition of the Court between 1680 and 1764. The second half of the chapter will then focus in detail on the intricacies of seventeenth- and eighteenth-century criminal procedure.

---

[72] Hocart, *Country People*, pp. 208–9, 215.

2

1680–1764: Courts, Personnel and Procedure

Courts

By the end of the thirteenth century, it had become an established principle in France, England and other parts of Europe, that judicial power was exercised by delegation from the Crown.[1] In keeping with this idea, criminal justice was the exclusive prerogative of Guernsey's Royal Court throughout the period dealt with by this book. We should however briefly note the existence of a number of other courts in Guernsey at the beginning of our period. There were a handful of seigneurial courts and one ecclesiastical court. The seigneurial courts performed functions for landholders on their fiefs, such as passing contracts and overseeing the division of estates among heirs.[2] None, however, had any criminal jurisdiction. As for the ecclesiastical court, having been abrogated during the Presbyterian era, it had only been operating in its revived form for eighteen years at the beginning of our period. The jurisdiction of the court was not regulated by any Canons (since none were ever promulgated for Guernsey), so that the extent of its powers was largely a matter of convention between the church and the Royal Court. In 1677, Charles Trumbull had described 'all the authority' of the ecclesiastical court as 'in a manner devoured by the other'.[3] The ecclesiastical court's functions

---

[1] T.F.T. Plucknett, *A Concise History of the Common Law* (1929; Boston, 1956 edn), p. 81; J.-M. Carbasse, *Histoire du Droit Pénal et de la Justice Criminelle* (2000; Paris, 2014 edn), p. 432.

[2] The Royal Court nevertheless maintained a concurrent jurisdiction over these functions, and, over the years covered by this study, it gradually came to monopolise responsibility for them (D.M. Ogier, *The Government and Law of Guernsey* (2005; Guernsey, 2012 edn), pp. 108–9).

[3] R. Hocart (ed.), 'The Journal of Charles Trumbull', *TSG*, 21 (1984), p. 579.

were strictly church-related, comprising such matters as the granting of marriage licences, the hearing of abjurations by Roman Catholics, the disciplining of clergy, the sequestration of vacant benefices, and so on.[4]

As noted above, this left the Royal Court with sole cognizance of all criminal causes arising in Guernsey. There was, moreover, no appeal from the decisions of the Royal Court in its criminal capacity. Although the Court was supervised by the Privy Council, which exercised a prerogative appellate jurisdiction, the Council had itself specifically disallowed appeals 'in any cause criminal or of correction' in a comprehensive Order in Council of 9 October 1580 which set out the rules for appeals.[5] This was confirmed by a further Order in Council of 22 February 1638.[6] The sole restriction on the Court's criminal powers was that, in accordance with ancient practice (partly derived from the *Coutume*), the punishment – though not the cognizance – of three distinct matters was reserved to the Crown. These were treason, coining, and assaulting the Bailiff or Jurats in the exercise of their office.[7]

As befitted a forum for the exercise of royal justice, Guernsey's courthouse belonged to the Crown, which also paid all the other costs of Guernsey's justice system.[8] The courthouse, known locally as *la Cohue*, was located in a medieval building in a town street aptly named 'La Plaiderie'. The building also functioned as a repository for dues paid in kind by landholders on Crown fiefs. The wheat and other commodities of which these dues consisted were stored in one part of the building, while the Royal Court met in a room set aside for the purpose of justice, accessed by public and Court members alike through a single door. Below the room was a cellar where prisoners were confined during breaks in their trial. In 1664, the Governor, Lord Hatton, sen.,

---

[4] D.M. Ogier, *The Government and Law of Guernsey* (2005; Guernsey, 2012 edn), p. 23. On the model of English ecclesiastical courts until 1857, the court also granted probate in respect of personal estates.

[5] In England and Wales, there was also no right of appeal in criminal matters (save by writ of error, and even then only in misdemeanours) until the Court of Criminal Appeal was created in 1907 (Plucknett, *History of the Common Law*, p. 213).

[6] *Second Report of the Commissioners Appointed to Inquire into the State of the Criminal Law in the Channel Islands: Guernsey* (London, 1848), p. 42.

[7] H. De Sausmarez, 'Guernsey's Précepte d'Assise of 1441: translation and notes', *Jersey & Guernsey Law Review* (June 2008). See also J.A. Everard (tr), *Le Grand Coutumier de Normandie* (Jersey, 2009), p. 232.

[8] Crown revenues were collected by official Receivers, who paid the costs of justice before passing the residue to the Governor.

had observed that both the inside and outside of this building were more reminiscent of a barn than a court of justice.[9] It was no better in our period. In 1700, the Court arranged for the interior of *la Cohue* to be assessed by two master carpenters who reported back that parts of it were on the verge of collapse.[10] Little was done, and despite sporadic attempts to improve the situation during the course of the eighteenth century, Guernsey's courthouse remained dusty and ramshackle throughout.

Plate 5. Old courthouse, La Plaiderie
(photographed in 1929)
© The Priaulx Library, Guernsey

This being so, the Court sometimes found it more convenient to meet at the Bailiff's house.[11] Indeed, the Bailiff's house was a particularly convenient venue for meetings when the Court was sitting in its 'ordinary' capacity, since this iteration of the Court required the attendance of only two Jurats and the Bailiff or Lieutenant Bailiff (although there was no upper limit on the number

[9] E.F. Carey, 'La Plaiderie', *TSG*, 10 (1929), p. 401.
[10] Entries for 3 and 21 December 1700, PL, Watkins MSS, vol. 2.
[11] T. Le Marchant, *Remarques et Animadversions sur l'Approbation des Lois et Coustumier de Normandie usitées ès Jurisdictions de Guernezé*, 2 vols (Guernsey, 1826), 2, pp. 2, 83.

of Jurats who could attend if they wished). The usual business of the Ordinary Court (also known as *la Cour de Meubles*) was to adjudicate on civil actions concerning personal property. Importantly for our purposes, however, it also had a criminal role. This was to try petty offences summarily, and to conduct the preliminary investigation of more serious crimes in order to decide whether there was a case for proceeding. The other form in which the Royal Court sat was the Full Court (also known as *la Cour d'Héritage*). Sittings of the Full Court required the attendance of at least seven Jurats together with the Bailiff or Lieutenant Bailiff.[12] The chief business of the Full Court was to deal with civil actions concerning real property. However, it also tried serious criminal offences on indictment, in which case it was known as *la Cour Criminelle*.

At the beginning of our period, the Ordinary Court sat on Mondays and the Full Court on Wednesdays and Saturdays.[13] The Court operated a system of terms. Since at least the sixteenth century, the judicial year had been divided into three terms and three *quartiers*. Each term lasted six weeks and began about a fortnight after each session of Chief Pleas.[14] The three *quartiers* took in not only the terms but the vacations which followed them. An Ordinance of 1608 laid down that the twelve Jurats should be divided into groups of four, each group to serve the Ordinary Court on a rota basis for one *quartier* annually (Christmas to Easter, Easter to Michaelmas, Michaelmas to Christmas).[15] This resulted in the Ordinary Court acquiring the alternative name of *la Cour du Quartier*. The Full Court normally only sat in term, but it could try serious crimes out of term on the petition of a prisoner already in custody who would otherwise have had to wait several months for the start of the next term.

---

[12] Although, by convention, if fewer than seven Jurats were present in Guernsey, then the full number of those actually in the island sufficed (*Second Report*, p. 108).

[13] J. Warburton, *A Treatise on the History, Laws and Customs of the Island of Guernsey* (Guernsey, 1822), p. 78. Note that this *Treatise*, though published under the name of Warburton in 1822, has since been identified as the work of Christopher, First Viscount Hatton, Governor of Guernsey between 1670 and 1706 (D.M. Ogier, 'The authorship of Warburton's treatise', *TSG*, 22 (1990), pp. 871–7).

[14] Chief Pleas were held on the first Monday after 29 September, the first Monday after 15 January, and the second Monday after Easter Sunday. For more on Chief Pleas, see Introduction.

[15] Ord, 3.10.1608. For a detailed account of the system, see J. Havet, *Les Cours Royales des Iles Normandes* (Paris, 1878), pp. 133–4.

During the period covered by this study, the series of Court registers known as *Livres en Crime* recorded all cases of a criminal nature, irrespective of whether they were heard in the Ordinary Court or the Full Court. They also recorded a good deal else. Since Jurats were in effect making law when they delivered judgment, the distinction between a judgment and an Ordinance was sometimes hard to draw, thus the early crime registers recorded material in the nature of Ordinances.[16] Other extraneous matter included the swearing in of hangmen and Vingteniers,[17] orders for the maintenance of strangers,[18] and orders for the confinement of the insane.[19] The registers also recorded all inquests and some, though by no means all, witness depositions.[20]

As regarded criminal proceedings, the crime registers were far from recording only final verdicts. Every separate procedural stage of a trial was also recorded in the books. In the period between 1680 and 1764, an average of 43 per cent of recorded sittings of the Royal Court in its criminal capacity were purely procedural.

At this point, we should also note what was *not* recorded in the crime registers. There were two significant omissions, both of which concerned the Ordinary Court. The first was in relation to preliminary investigations. When, in such cases, the Court decided that there was insufficient evidence to warrant a trial, no record of the proceeding was entered in the book.[21] The second was in relation to summary trials, of which no record was kept when

---

[16] On 3 May 1684, for example, the Court ordered that anyone depositing ordure in front of houses belonging to two named town parishioners would be liable to a fine of 3 *livres tournois* (GG, *Crime*, vol. 6).

[17] A Vingtenier was a lowly parochial officer who collected taxes in his vingtaine (originally a district containing twenty households) and called the militiamen of the district to duty.

[18] That, for instance, issued to Jeanne Pallot in respect of Englishwoman Elizabeth Rix on 11 February 1721 (GG, *Crime*, vol. 9).

[19] That, for instance, issued to Nicolas Gallienne in respect of his father Pierre Gallienne on 19 September 1724 (GG, *Crime*, vol. 10).

[20] The depositions of witnesses in particularly important cases are to be found at the back of registers 6 to 13, after which the recording of depositions in crime registers ceased. Although depositions were thereafter preserved elsewhere among the Court's records, most were lost during a 'decluttering' exercise after World War II (J.H. Lenfestey (ed.), *List of Records in the Greffe, Guernsey, Volume 3* (Guernsey, 1983), p. 5).

[21] *Second Report*, pp. 10, 164.

they did not produce a conviction.[22] This makes it impossible to for us know the total number of cases brought to Court and defeats any attempt to assess acquittal rates at summary level.[23]

Personnel

All the major offices in Guernsey's Court system were occupied by members of local elite families. Although the status of most such families was originally based on landholding, their properties were small and tended to become smaller by virtue of Guernsey's system of modified partible inheritance. Thus they vigorously took up opportunities to bolster their incomes, whether by engaging in trade, privateering, or judicial office-holding. Judicial offices were a source not only of income, but of private power and influence to their holders, and, as Richard Hocart has observed, they fought hard to preserve them.[24]

The highest office in the Royal Court was that of Bailiff, who also presided in the States and was regarded as Guernsey's civic head. By an Order in Council of 27 May 1674, his appointment had been reserved exclusively to the Crown. The Bailiff was paid an annual retainer from Crown revenues which had stood at 30 *livres tournois* (about £2 2s) since the fourteenth century. He also enjoyed certain Court fees. Laurent Carey, writing in the mid-eighteenth century, enumerated the following: one shilling for pronouncing a judgment; 4d for enrolling a cause; 2d for signing a minute; 8d for sealing an official letter; 3s 6d for issuing strangers with permits to sell their goods in the streets; 3s 6d for authorising the arrest of a stranger in a civil matter.[25] Over time, the list of chargeable items grew longer and the fees higher.

---

[22] *Ibid.*, p. 57.

[23] Crime registers only began to record dismissals and discharges at summary level in 1925. This coincided with the arrival of an English stipendiary magistrate and was probably at his direction.

[24] R. Hocart, *Guernsey in the Reign of Charles II* (Guernsey, 2020), p. 179.

[25] L. Carey, *Essai sur les Institutions, Lois et Coutumes de l'Île de Guernesey* (Guernsey, 1889), p. 33–4. Laurent Carey lived between 1723 and 1769, and served as a Jurat for the last four years of his life. His essay was published posthumously.

The Bailiff was entitled to appoint a Lieutenant Bailiff from among the Jurats to carry out his duties in his absence. Because the arrangement was a private one, the Lieutenant Bailiff received nothing from Crown revenues, but enjoyed 'all the appurtenances and profits that belong to the Bailiff in his absence'.[26] If a Bailiff died in office, the arrangement with his Lieutenant lapsed, and the Jurats elected from among themselves a *Juge Délégué* who would perform the role of Bailiff until another was appointed by the Crown. *Juges Délégués* were paid *pro rata* from Crown revenues for their service, and they also received the fees due to the Bailiff.

Five men served the office of Bailiff in the period covered by this chapter: Sir Edmund Andros, Jean De Sausmarez, brothers Josué and Eléazar Le Marchant, and Samuel Bonamy.[27] These men were all members of top-tier families, and all had forebears who were Jurats. The Le Marchant family in particular had long dominated the Royal Court, boasting five previous Bailiffs and a dozen Jurats.

The first three Bailiffs of our period were frequently absent from Guernsey, so their Court duties were performed by Lieutenant Bailiffs (or, in the case of Jean De Sausmarez, who did not appoint a Lieutenant, a *Juge Délégué*). When Josué Le Marchant died in 1751, it was established that Bailiffs must reside locally and should not leave the island without the permission of the King in Council.[28]

Although the Bailiff presided over sittings of the Court, he was not a judge in the modern sense of the word (no Bailiff appointed during the eighteenth century had any professional background in the law). His role was more that of a master of ceremonies, co-ordinating proceedings and ensuring the observance of forms. When a decision was required on a technical matter such as the admissibility of evidence or the correct procedure to be followed, the Bailiff was obliged to ask the opinion of the Jurats and to follow the majority view. Similarly, his task at the end of a trial was to pronounce, rather than render, judgment. Judgment was rendered by the Jurats, who (until as late as 1964) were judges of law as well as fact. Each Jurat had a vote as to verdict and sentence, and the majority view prevailed.

[26] Hocart (ed.), 'Journal of Charles Trumbull', p. 582.
[27] See Appendix 1.
[28] Carey, *Essai sur les Institutions*, p. 32.

Until the beginning of the seventeenth century, Jurats had been elected by islanders at large, but a Royal Commission of 1607 restricted voting to an electoral college, and in due course this became known as the States of Election.[29] In the period dealt with by this chapter, Jurats' elections were held in the courtroom at La Plaiderie, and voting was *viva voce*. Each member of the States of Election had one vote, and the election was decided by simple majority. Throughout our period, the power and prestige of a Jurat were such that these elections attracted considerable public interest. An Order in Council of 1673 prohibited Jurats from obtaining votes by bribes, feasting, drinking, promises, threats, or other corrupt means.[30]

Jurats' elections were not open to all comers. Social status, and to some degree wealth, were prerequisites: the fifteenth-century *Précepte d'Assise* had stated that Guernsey's Jurats should be 'douze Hommes dez plus notablez et discres sages loyaulx et Riches en la dicte ysle'.[31] Roman Catholics were ineligible, as the post-Reformation Jurats' oath required them to renounce the Papacy.[32] Brewers and publicans were also supposedly ineligible, as the 1607 Royal Commission had introduced a ban on candidates from such backgrounds (however, two Jurats who served in the current period – Isaac Carey (1673–85) and his nephew Pierre Carey (1719–44) – are both known to have been brewers).[33]

Once elected, Jurats were obliged to serve for life, and their duties could absorb considerable time. It was not necessary to obtain a man's consent to put his name forward for election, and a number found themselves elected against their will. Their options for evading service were limited. A Jurat-elect who refused to take the oath could be imprisoned (as was Laurent Carey in 1764),[34] and the only effective mode of self-extrication was to leave the island. Time-served Jurats whose ability to work was impaired by illness or old age were permitted to petition the Privy Council for their discharge. However,

---

[29] R. Hocart, *An Island Assembly: The Development of the States of Guernsey, 1700–1949* (Guernsey, 1988), p. xi.

[30] O in C, 21.11.1673. See also R. Hocart, 'Elections to the Royal Court of Guernsey, 1821–1844', *TSG*, 19 (1979), pp. 494–514.

[31] 'Twelve of the most distinguished and discreet men, wise, loyal and rich, from the said island' (H. De Sausmarez, 'Guernsey's Précepte d'Assise of 1441: translation and notes', *Jersey & Guernsey Law Review* (June 2008).

[32] Only in 1950 was a law passed re-establishing the eligibility of Catholics to become Jurats.

[33] Hocart, 'Elections to the Royal Court', p. 496.

[34] Hocart, *Island Assembly*, p. 14.

the petitioning process could prove expensive, and until the nineteenth century, individual Jurats were obliged to fund it from their own resources. Many thus simply stopped attending Court when their health deteriorated without seeking a formal discharge.[35]

Thomas Dicey tells us that, up to the end of the sixteenth century, Jurats gave their services *gratis*.[36] From the early seventeenth century, however, they were entitled to a range of fees similar to those enjoyed by the Bailiff, as also dues from what were called the *Poids du Roi* (where certain commodities were officially weighed out).[37] In addition to this, along with other Court members, they were treated to a dinner at Crown expense following every session of Chief Pleas, and on each occasion the Court passed a sentence involving forfeiture of property.[38] Such perquisites did not, however, amount to much in monetary terms. Even in the mid-nineteenth century, most Jurats did not make more than £15 a year from Court-related activities.[39]

During the period dealt with here, some fifty-three Jurats occupied a seat on the bench.[40] Between them, they shared just eighteen surnames, most of which had featured in the list of Jurats for centuries. No fewer than nine bore the name Andros, and eight bore the name Le Marchant. There were in addition six Careys, six De Beauvoirs, and four Bonamys. Four of these Jurats (three Le Marchants and a Bonamy) went on to become Bailiff.[41]

The minister and writer Thomas Le Marchant, who died in 1684, described the Jurats as 'brothers, cousins, sons-in-law, fathers-in-law, and other close relatives by blood and by marriage'.[42] The bench was a tight-knit

---

[35] In 1759, for example, the ailing Jean De Havilland stopped attending Court after thirty years' service but remained a Jurat until his death in 1770 (R. Hocart, *Peter de Havilland: Bailiff of Guernsey: A History of his Life, 1747–1821* (Guernsey, 1997), p. 3).

[36] T. Dicey, *An Historical Account of Guernsey* (London, 1751), p. 81.

[37] Carey, *Essai sur les Institutions*, p. 36.

[38] D.M. Ogier, 'Chief Pleas dinners', *Guernsey Law Journal*, 28 (2000), pp. 79–82. All capital sentences and sentences of more than seven years' banishment automatically entailed forfeiture of the guilty party's property.

[39] Anon., 'The Channel Islands', *The Eclectic Review*, 17 (1845), p. 545.

[40] For a list of Jurats who served between 1680 and 1929, see PL, LOF920 LIS. This list was compiled by local historian Edith Carey in the 1930s. Miss Carey compiled similar lists of all Court officers.

[41] From the 1750s, most Bailiffs were appointed from the ranks of sitting Jurats, which had not previously been the case.

[42] Le Marchant, *Remarques et Animadversions*, 1, p. 21.

oligarchy, with one generation of the same group of elite families succeeding another. Laurens Fiott replaced his father on the bench in 1742; Jean Andros replaced his in 1747; Richard De Beauvoir replaced his in 1764, and so on. Nephews could also replace uncles, as Josué Le Marchant, who was elected to fill the seat vacated by his uncle Eléazar Le Marchant in 1716. By convention, fathers and sons were not supposed to occupy seats at the same time,[43] but brothers occasionally sat together, as did the aforementioned Josué and his brother (confusingly, another Eléazar).

Most of these Jurats were involved in trade and lived in St Peter Port, where they could be close to the harbour, warehouses, counting-houses and other merchants. There were, however, always one or two country Jurats on the bench. Not only were Jurats supposedly representative of the whole community, but, as Richard Hocart points out, in an urban-dominated Court, a rural Jurat or two could come in useful for their knowledge of country ways.[44] Just under a quarter of those elected between 1680 and 1764 appear to have been country-based.

The average term served by Jurats between 1680 and 1764 was twenty-four years, with two serving over fifty years and only five serving fewer than ten years. The average age at election of Jurats gaining seats in this period was thirty-five, with six only in their twenties when elected.[45] The staggered nature of elections, with most Jurats only replaced when they died, meant that there was usually a balance between the experienced and inexperienced. More often than not, just under half of the Jurats on the bench at any one time had served for more than twenty years, with the other half for lesser periods ranging from nineteen years to just one or two years. This would have provided junior members with an opportunity to learn the ropes in the presence of a significant cohort of well-seasoned seniors – which was just as well, given that none of these men had any formal education in the law.

Aside from the Bailiff and Jurats, other vital members of the Royal Court were HM Procureur and HM Comptroller, collectively known as the Law Officers or Crown Officers. The duties of Procureur and Comptroller overlapped, but we shall look in detail at the Procureur first. This officer, one of whose chief functions was to act as a public prosecutor, seems to have been

---

[43] *Second Report*, p. 238.
[44] Hocart, 'Elections to the Royal Court', p. 496.
[45] Of the forty Jurats elected between 1680 and 1764, I have been able to find ages for thirty. I base my statements on these.

based on a French judicial officer of the same name. In France, *les Procureurs du Roi* first appeared as royal officers in 1302 when they were given the role of superintending the prosecution of offences involving fines and forfeitures, which were major sources of royal revenue.[46] The notion that it fell to the state to conduct criminal prosecutions became entrenched in France during the course of the fourteenth century, and similar systems were eventually instituted in many European countries, including Scotland, where Procurators Fiscal served as public prosecutors from the late 1500s.[47]

Payments to a 'king's advocate' featured regularly in local Wardens' accounts from the mid-1300s, although the title 'Procureur' was not used in official documents before the 1441 *Précepte d'Assise*.[48] Their function as public prosecutors may only have developed gradually, in emulation of their French namesakes. Philippe Le Geyt, writing in reference to Jersey, which had a similar system, thought that the role had 'established itself gradually on the model of our [French] neighbours'.[49] Whatever the case, HM Procureur was by our period apparently acting as prosecutor in all criminal actions heard before the Royal Court. Thomas Le Marchant wrote in the mid-seventeenth century: 'the king's Procureur … is a party in all criminal causes'; 'Warburton' observed towards the end of the century: 'the procureur and contrôleur are to be joined in the prosecution of … cause[s] from first to last'.[50]

[46] A. Esmein (tr, J. Simpson), *A History of Continental Criminal Procedure with Special Reference to France* (Boston, 1913), pp. 114–16.

[47] L. Farmer, *Criminal Law, Tradition and Legal Order: Crime and the Genius of Scots Law, 1747 to the Present* (Cambridge, 1997), pp. 43, 82, 85. Note, however, that this was not the case in England and Wales, where, for most of the period covered by this study, the task of prosecution lay with the victim rather than the state.

[48] J.H. Le Patourel, *The Medieval Administration of the Channel Islands, 1199–1399* (London, 1937), p. 94; Ogier, *Government and Law*, p. 124.

[49] P. Le Geyt, *Les Manuscrits de Philippe Le Geyt, Ecuyer, Lieutenant-Bailli de l'Ile de Jersey, sur la Constitution, les Lois et les Usages de cette Ile*, 4 vols (Jersey, 1846–7), 1, p. 19. Philippe Le Geyt lived between 1635 and 1716. His manuscripts, published posthumously, were written in the second half of the seventeenth century.

[50] Le Marchant, *Remarques et Animadversions*, 2, p. 225; Warburton, *Treatise*, p. 123. I use the word 'apparently' here, because the fact that the Procureur (and/or Comptroller) invariably played a part in criminal prosecutions is not always clear in late seventeenth- and early-eighteenth-century crime registers. On this matter, see opening paragraphs of Chapter 3.

Like that of the Bailiff, the appointment of the Law Officers was reserved to the Crown. Also like the Bailiff, both Procureur and Comptroller were paid a small annual retainer from Crown revenues (10 *livres tournois* or about 14s 4d), and derived the rest of their emoluments from fees. The oath of HM Procureur bound the incumbent to observe the ancient usages of the island, to maintain the rights of His Majesty, and to prosecute and defend the king's causes. This meant that, aside from acting as prosecutor in criminal cases, he was expected to attend all Court sittings in order to provide guidance and advice to the Court.[51] He was also obliged to provide legal advice to the Governor, Lieutenant Governor and Receiver of Crown revenues, and to represent the Crown in actions concerning Crown domains or revenues, as well as drafting conveyances and leases in respect of Crown land. For each individual piece of work, the Procureur charged the Crown a separate fee.[52]

One important function associated with HM Procureur's role as Court advisor was the drafting of Ordinances, which he shared with his colleague the Comptroller. The Law Officers' opinion on the merits of any proposed measure had to be heard before the Jurats voted to approve or reject it, and it fell to the Law Officers to draft the measure in its final form. The Procureur performed a similar advisory role for the States, in which he had a vote as well as a seat. He also enjoyed voting rights in the States of Election.

The Comptroller's post appears to have been created in the second half of the fifteenth century.[53] In criminal cases, the Comptroller usually prosecuted jointly with the Procureur, appearing beside him in Court. Whilst paid the same retainer and performing similar duties, the Comptroller was understood to be the Procureur's junior and took a smaller share of the work. Nevertheless, he was not formally under the Procureur's authority and could dissent from the latter's opinions when addressing the Court. Only in relation to the States did the Comptroller enjoy clearly inferior powers to the

---

[51] This was a duty shared with the Comptroller.

[52] Law Officers to Privy Council, 6.4.1835, 'Law Officers' salaries', 'Privy Council', vol. 2, Royal Court Library, IA. Aside from Crown work, HM Procureur also had other fee-earning functions within the Court. The most lucrative of these was the processing of applications for Court-licensed activities, which, in time, came to include innkeeping, butchery, theatrical performances, the installation of kilns and distilleries, and much else. He also had a monopoly over the drafting of causes for the appointment of *tuteurs* (guardians of minors) and *curateurs* (guardians of adults without legal capacity).

[53] Ogier, *Government and Law*, p. 125. The French name for this officer was *le Contrôle du Roi*.

Procureur, since he was not accorded a seat or vote in the States of Deliberation until 1899, nor admitted to membership of the States of Election until 1901. From 1738, both Procureur and Comptroller were permitted by Order in Council to appoint deputies to perform their duties during illness or absence.[54] Neither of these posts occupied their incumbents full-time. Indeed, they formed just one part of their income-earning portfolio. Both Law Officers practised privately as Advocates. Some held other official posts, and many also participated in business and commerce.

Procureurs came from broadly the same social background as Jurats and Bailiffs, with some Comptrollers from a slightly lower rung. In the years covered by this chapter, four men served as Procureur and six as Comptroller.[55] There was no necessary progression from one post to the other. Only the first two of the six Comptrollers ultimately became Procureurs: Josué Tramalier (or Tramailler), who served as Procureur between 1667 and 1701, and Elizée Roland, 1701–8. None of the three Comptrollers appointed after 1701 progressed to the rank of Procureur, although they all served terms of more than twenty years.

After the death of HM Procureur Elizée Roland in 1708, two Procureurs, neither of whom had previously served as Comptroller, between them dominated the first half of the eighteenth century: William Le Marchant, who was appointed at the age of 27 in 1708 and served for 36 years, and Jean De Sausmarez, who was appointed at the age of 38 in 1744 and served for 30 years. Both Le Marchant and De Sausmarez also held the post of Receiver of Crown revenues during part of their tenure as Procureurs.[56] Neither Le Marchant or De Sausmarez (nor indeed any late seventeenth- or early eighteenth-century Procureur) subsequently became Bailiff.

The Greffier, or Court clerk, was next in the Court hierarchy. The existence of such an officer is attested from the early fourteenth century, but there is no evidence that he was known by the title of Greffier until the sixteenth century.[57] Like the Bailiff and Law Officers, the Greffier was

---

[54] O in C, 10.11.1738.

[55] Appendix 2.

[56] To modern minds, this suggests a conflict of interest, since the fines and forfeitures exacted from parties they successfully prosecuted as Procureurs would enter their coffers as Receivers – not to mention the fact that Procureurs who also served as Receivers were effectively billing themselves for their services to the Crown.

[57] Ogier, *Government and Law*, p. 129.

appointed by the Crown. In Warburton's *Treatise* his duties are described as follows:

> to draw up and to enter into the books of registers, all acts, orders, judgments and sentences of the court, and to keep all the records thereunto belonging … to inregister all bargains and sales of lands or rents, and to deliver copies under his signature, when required, of all such matters of record, as are to be found in the registers.[58]

The Greffier received an annual retainer of 10 *livres tournois* from Crown revenues but, like most Court officers, derived most of his income from fees, which he charged for all his Court activities aside from judicial recording. Again, this was just one part of the portfolio of resources from which incumbents made a living, and they paid clerks and copyists to do most of the day-to-day work. Six men served the post of Greffier during the period covered by this chapter. The majority were members of elite families.

The office of Prévôt was also generally occupied by members of Guernsey's top tier.[59] Based on an ancient Norman office, the existence of a Prévôt is attested from the earliest days of the Court.[60] The Prévôt, who, like the Jurats, was elected by the States of Election, was the executive officer of the Royal Court and had to attend all Court sittings in person or by deputy. According to Warburton's *Treatise*, his office was

> to bring all criminals before [the court] to be tried, and to take care to see the sentence of the court executed upon them. He executes all arrests upon persons and goods, and gives seizure and possession, as he shall be ordered by the court … He has custody of the weights and measures, and is to seal and guage [sic] such as are used by any person in the island.[61]

Like the Greffier, the Prévôt was paid an annual retainer of 10 *livres tournois* and charged separate fees for his various Court activities (as also for kindred private work such as debt-collecting). Again, he paid deputies to perform most of the routine tasks. Four men held the office of Prévôt during the period 1680–1764. Two bore the surname Andros, one was a Le Marchant

---

[58] Warburton, *Treatise*, pp. 54–5.
[59] In later centuries, the name of this officer was anglicised to Sheriff.
[60] Le Patourel, *Medieval Administration*, pp. 93–4; Ogier, *Government and Law*, p. 131.
[61] Warburton, *Treatise*, pp. 55–6.

and the other a Gosselin. One of these Prévôts, Jean Andros (1670–86), also appears to have served simultaneously as Receiver.

A similar post, though less remunerative, was that of Sergeant.[62] This too was based on an old Norman office, and incumbents were anciently known as *Bedeaux*.[63] The Sergeant's duties included delivering summonses and other procedural documents, summoning the officers of the Court when required, assisting the Prévôt to escort prisoners, serving as court usher, and taking care of the courtroom.[64] The Sergeant was directly appointed by the Governor, received a small salary from Crown revenues and was also entitled to certain fees. Twelve men served as Sergeant between 1680 and 1764. By and large, they were not from the top tier of Guernsey society, since the post was less profitable, less prestigious, and required the incumbent to perform most of the work. Interestingly, some of the Sergeants in this period appear to have been Huguenots – literate people who had fled to the island without property and were obliged to make a living by their own wit. Jean-Jacques Condamine, born in Nîmes in 1711, was Sergeant between 1744 and 1764. Jean Bord and Jean Roche, who served in the 1680s and 1730s respectively, might also have been Huguenots, although their origins have not been researched.

The Sergeant's duties were to some degree shared by thirteen unpaid officers known as *Bordiers*. These were the owners of thirteen properties known as *bordages*. They were obliged by their conditions of tenure to act as ushers in sessions of the Full Court, to escort prisoners under the direction of the Prévôt, and to deliver summonses and procedural documents within their own *bordages*.[65]

The Royal Court appointed a number of Advocates with exclusive rights of audience at the Bar. These were the modern incarnation of *les conteurs*, mentioned in *Le Grand Coutumier*, by whom accused persons in Norman courts could opt to be defended.[66] In Guernsey, there is evidence of a body of professional pleaders by at least 1323.[67] In the period dealt with here, the number of Advocates was not formally limited, but it was unusual for more

[62] Also spelt 'Sergent' or 'Serjeant'.

[63] Le Patourel, *Medieval Administration*, p. 94.

[64] Havet, *Cours Royales*, p. 101.

[65] R. Hocart, *The Country People of Guernsey and their Agriculture, 1640–1840* (Guernsey, 2016), p. 34; Le Patourel, *Medieval Administration*, p. 84.

[66] Everard (tr), *Grand Coutumier*, pp. 270, 338.

[67] Havet, *Cours Royales*, p. 95.

than four or five to be active at any one time. When one Advocate retired or died, another would be sworn in to replace him.[68]

As well as acting as counsel, Guernsey Advocates also performed work which in England might be done by attorneys rather than barristers: drawing up wills, deeds and contracts; settling estates; recovering debts, and so on. This they shared with a number of *hommes d'affaires* or *agents de loi* who did not have rights of audience at the Bar. In the period covered by this chapter, no formal qualifications were required of *agents de loi*, and nor, indeed, were they required of Advocates.

It seems likely that most Advocates of this period learned their craft chiefly by apprenticeship. Some (perhaps the majority) may also have spent time in Normandy, but they would probably have done so informally – attending the courts to observe French lawyers in action, frequenting the libraries to read textbooks and commentaries, and perhaps occasionally sitting in on lectures at Caen.[69] Formal study here would have been of limited use. Until 1680, Caen University (as all French universities) taught only Roman law and Canon law. Thereafter, French law was introduced to the curriculum, but Norman law – based on the *Coutume* – was not formally taught at Caen until 1908.[70]

Sixteen men were sworn in as Advocates of the Royal Court between 1680 and 1764.[71] Something under half of them were from Guernsey's traditional elite. Most of the others were from local families further down the scale, but, interestingly, there were two Advocates of Huguenot descent: Jean Hubert (admitted in 1714) and Pierre Coutart (admitted in 1718). The former was

---

[68] Warburton, *Treatise*, p. 57.

[69] Caen University (the regional university of Normandy) hosted one of the largest law faculties outside Paris, with an average of over 200 new matriculations a year between 1680 and 1785 (R.L. Kagan, 'Law students and legal careers in eighteenth-century France', *Past & Present*, 68 (1975), p. 72). An attempt was made to find the names of Guernsey Advocates in the 87 matriculation registers covering this period (Archives départementales du Calvados, D/708–794). However, matriculants' names being in their thousands, the attempt was abandoned.

[70] M.H. Nézard, 'Allocution, séance d'ouverture', in *Travaux de la Semaine d'Histoire du Droit Normand tenue à Guernesey du 8 au 13 Juin 1938* (Caen, 1939), p. 40. See also M.E. Bridrey, 'Les études de droit normand au collège des droits de l'ancienne université de Caen', in *Travaux de la Semaine d'Histoire du Droit Normand tenue à Guernesey du 26 au 30 Mai 1927* (Caen, 1928), pp. 85–219.

[71] Appendix 3. The swearing-in of Advocates was recorded in the volumes of *Jugements, Ordonnances et Ordres du Conseil* until 1772, and thereafter in the registers of *Ordonnances*.

descended from Gilles Hubert and his wife Marie Troussey, who had arrived in Guernsey from Normandy in the seventeenth century.[72] The latter was the son of Pierre Coutart and Anne Cougot, who had sought refuge in Guernsey around 1700.[73] Both of these Advocates produced sons who also became lawyers. As befitted their origins, the majority of Advocates in this period were designated 'Sieur' rather than the higher-status 'Monsieur'. Two of them became Sergeants. The Advocates and lesser Court officers formed something of a caste at this time, with extensive inter-marriage among the families involved.

It remains to mention a number of other officers who, though not technically members of the Royal Court, were sworn into office by the Court and played a significant part in the criminal justice system. The first was the Receiver (or Receiver General, as he was later known). This office can be traced back to the early fourteenth century.[74] The Receiver was appointed by the Governor and collected the Crown revenues on his behalf.[75] In 1682, the Crown revenues amounted to 18,820 *livres tournois* or about £1,268 sterling.[76] These revenues made up the Governor's remuneration, and, after Court officers' salaries, prison expenses, courthouse costs, and expenses associated with punishments (floggings, executions, etc.) had been paid, the Governor kept the balance. Receivers were usually paid with a share of what they had collected. The last Receiver under this system (which changed after the death of the last Governor in 1835) took as his payment the product of the *poulage* and the interest on any cash balances in hand.[77] The post of Receiver could be fairly lucrative, and again formed part of a portfolio of activities engaged in by the twelve men who held it between 1680 and 1764. Most of these men were members of Guernsey's elite, who delegated the physical job of collection to paid agents and employees, while they pursued interests of their own.

---

[72] Hubert family file, PL.

[73] Coutart family file, PL.

[74] Ogier, *Government and Law*, p. 211.

[75] The Governor was free to appoint as many Receivers as he liked, and during the mid-eighteenth century, there were often two in office simultaneously.

[76] Warburton, *Treatise*, p. 113.

[77] 'Channel Islands Finance' (HM Treasury, 1909), Royal Court Library, IA. The *poulage* was an annual due on dwelling-houses which had originally been paid in fowls and eggs.

At the opposite end of the scale but also sworn in by the Court was the official hangman, who carried out not only executions but corporal punishments such as floggings, brandings and amputations. In the thirteenth century, the job of executioner formed part of the services of one of the *Bordiers*, but by our period it was a salaried post whose incumbent rejoiced in the formal title of *Exécuteur des Hautes Oeuvres*.[78] His appointment lay with the Governor, though usually delegated to the Receiver, who paid him from the Crown revenues. Philippe Le Geyt reported in the late seventeenth century that Guernsey's hangman received a retainer equivalent to about £15 sterling per year, together with a separate fee for every punishment he carried out.[79]

Five hangmen were sworn in during the period covered by this chapter.[80] Like executioners everywhere, they were reviled. As Vic Gatrell has observed, 'upon the executioner was lodged as upon a scapegoat the evil that justice had to do.'[81] It was not a job that anyone in this period volunteered to perform, least of all native islanders, who might be required to inflict unspeakable punishments upon neighbours and acquaintances. As elsewhere in Europe, the role therefore generally went to a non-native, usually a criminal himself, reprieved or let off lightly on condition he agreed to serve as hangman. Only one of the hangmen appointed in the current period was a local man: Etienne Robert of St Andrews, appointed in 1697. Of the others, three were French and one was English. Their swearings-in, recorded in the crime registers, always incorporated a statement that the man concerned had taken the job of his own volition, as well as an admonition to the public not to taunt or insult the incumbent. This echoed the repeated royal *arrêts* issued in contemporary France to shield executioners from rough handling by the mob.[82]

Another unglamorous post essential to the functioning of the criminal justice system was that of the gaoler (or *Portier*, as he was known in Guernsey). However, before describing this role, we shall first say a few words

---

[78] Havet, *Cours Royales*, p. 106.

[79] Le Geyt, *Manuscrits*, 4, p. 207.

[80] Appendix 4.

[81] V.A.C. Gatrell, *The Hanging Tree: Execution and the English People, 1770–1868* (Oxford, 1994), pp. 99–100.

[82] Z.A. Schneider, *The King's Bench: Bailiwick Magistrates and Local Governance in Normandy, 1670–1740* (Woodbridge, 2008), pp. 203–4.

about the prison. In the Middle Ages, several Guernsey fiefs had kept lock-ups to hold offenders prior to trial or punishment, in addition to which a few were also held at St Peter Port's fourteenth-century Tour de Beauregard.[83] By Tudor times, Castle Cornet had become the island's general prison. As noted above, the Castle, which was also garrison headquarters, was on an islet about half a mile off St Peter Port. In bad weather, prisoners might have to wait some time before a boat was sent out to collect them, so there was a half-way house in the form of the pier guardhouse, built in 1619, where they could be held while awaiting transport. A document from 1749 tells us that the prison in Castle Cornet consisted of three rooms:

> one room for the Porter's lodgings, and one under the same for persons arrested for Debts, neither of them above ten feet broad and not fourteen in length. The third room (called La Basse Fosse) is a cave under ground ... designed for Criminal convicts, and other Delinquents.[84]

The document concerned was a Royal Court petition requesting the release of £1,000 from Crown revenues for the construction of a new prison on dry land. Not only was the Castle prison difficult of access, it was also far from escape-proof, and the fact that the Castle was controlled by the British military engendered continual disputes with the civil authorities. This petition went unheeded, as indeed had an earlier petition from the States in 1718.[85]

---

[83] D.M. Ogier, 'Notes on Guernsey's Georgian prison and its antecedents' (unpub. typescript, 1999), IA, AM 001–13.

[84] Royal Court to Privy Council, 14.10.1749, GG, Royal Court General Letter Book (first series), vol. 1.

[85] Act of 15.10.1718, G.E. Lee (ed.), *Actes des Etats de l'Ile de Guernesey, 1651–1780* (Guernsey, 1907).

Plate 6. Prison tower, Castle Cornet
Courtesy of Guernsey Museums & Galleries (States of Guernsey)

Plate 7. Plan of prison tower, 1739
Courtesy of Guernsey Museums & Galleries (States of Guernsey)

The gaoler was appointed by the Governor and paid a small retainer from Crown revenues. He also received a customary duty on wine, salt and earthen pots unloaded in the island. Like others involved in Guernsey's justice system, however, his main income came from fees. At the beginning of our period, the gaoler charged a fee equivalent to about 2d sterling every time a prisoner was admitted, every time a prisoner was discharged, and every time a prisoner was produced before Court, as also a 2d subsistence fee per prisoner per day.[86] Prisoners were supposed to pay these fees themselves, but if any prisoner were destitute of means, his fees would be paid from Crown revenues. Out of his receipts, the gaoler fed and watered the prisoners, minimising what he spent to maximise his own profit. He also sold wine, spirits, bedding and other commodities to prisoners, again taking a profit for himself. This was the standard way in which prisons were run all over Europe at this period.

Eleven men served as gaolers during the years covered by this chapter, most of them local. The post was not prestigious but nevertheless represented a useful adjunct to the income of someone from the middling ranks. Gaolers regarded it only as a part-time activity, exercising some other occupation in tandem. The post was sometimes handed down from father to son, as in the case of Pierre Gosselin and his son Jean, who served the office concurrently between 1723 and 1736. It was also sometimes passed between brothers, as in the case of Nicolas and William Henry, who successively held the post for 34 years from 1753.

The last office we shall mention here is that of parish Constable, who was also sworn in by the Royal Court. The earliest extant record mentioning Constables by name – as *les connestables des parroesses* – dates from 1481.[87] As stated in the Introduction, Guernsey's Constables represented their parishes in the States and acted as parochial treasurers as well as exercising public order functions. In performing these functions, their powers were extensive. Operating autonomously, they could consign delinquents to the stocks and drunkards to the town lock-up. They could also arrest whom they wished without a warrant, and search premises without a warrant.

For the first fifty-five years of our period, the two elected Constables of each parish sufficed to keep order in their parishes without the assistance of

[86] Warburton, *Treatise*, pp. 60–1.
[87] Ogier, *Government and Law*, p. 4.

auxiliaries.[88] In 1736, however, St Peter Port's Douzaine decided that a supplementary force was needed in town on account of the increasing population. In the autumn of that year, the Court passed an Ordinance authorising the Douzaine to appoint whatever number of assistant constables it saw fit, to be sworn in for one year at a time.[89] The Ordinance added that it might be advisable for all insular parishes to follow suit. The nine country parishes did not take this advice, but St Peter Port soon established a force of four assistant constables, chosen annually by the Douzaine from the ranks of retailers and artisans, to serve under the direction of the parish Constables without remuneration and without a choice in the matter. Many shopkeepers and tradesmen dreaded the call, not least because the duties placed considerable demands on their time and exposed them to maltreatment. Some fought their appointment in Court, but, by and large, the Court backed the Douzaine and obliged the men to serve their term.[90] It was with these assistant constables, rather than the principal Constables, that a comparison may be drawn with English parish constables.

Procedure

As noted in the Introduction, Guernsey's criminal law and procedure were by our period based not on the Norman *Coutume* but on a document known as *L'Approbation des Lois*. This document specified which parts of Guillaume Terrien's 1574 *Commentaires du Droict Civil Observé au Pays & Duché de Normandie* accorded with, or varied from, local law and usage, and had assumed authoritative status after its ratification by the Privy Council in 1583.[91]

---

[88] Note that in Jersey, although parishes had only a single Constable, their policing work was shared with a team of parochial Centeniers, Vingteniers and Constables' Officers (R.G. Le Herissier, *The Development of the Government of Jersey, 1771–1972* (Jersey, 1973), p. 101).

[89] Ord, 4. 10.1736.

[90] See, for instance, the case of Sr Pierre Rabey, whose request for exemption was rejected by the Court on 18 February 1738 (PL, Watkins MSS, vol. 3).

[91] T. Tramailler (ed.), *Approbation des Lois, Coutumes, et Usages de l'Ile de Guernesey* (1715; Guernsey, 1822 edn); G. Terrien, *Commentaires du Droict Civil tant Public que Privé Observé au Pays & Duché de Normandie* (1574; Paris, 1578 edn).

Criminal matters occupied only a small proportion of Terrien's *Commentaires*. The work filled 728 pages, which were divided into sixteen books. Only one of these, Book XII, specifically concerned crime, though sundry matters of a quasi-criminal nature were treated in other Books. Book XII, entitled 'Des Crimes et des Procez Criminels', dealt with both substantive and procedural law (though essentially from a procedural point of view). It was sub-divided into forty-six separate chapters, of which *L'Approbation* endorsed thirty-five. For the most part, *L'Approbation*'s endorsements were qualified, suggesting differences (sometimes specified, sometimes not) between Guernsey's practice and that followed in Normandy. What is striking is that virtually the only chapters endorsed *without* reservation were those purely concerned with procedure.[92]

By the time Terrien was writing, Norman criminal procedure was based entirely on French royal legislation.[93] Normandy had been reintegrated into the French royal domain for almost 400 years, and royal justice had long since assumed control and supervision of all courts in the kingdom. In order to understand the procedure specified in Terrien, we must thus briefly summarise its development under the French monarchy.

An Ordinance of Louis IX issued in 1258 is widely regarded as the foundation of modern French criminal procedure. This Ordinance introduced the 'romano-canonical' system, which derived from the Roman law of treason and was first used in French Canon law courts.[94] The romano-canonical system involved the secret examination by judges of individual witnesses under oath. This procedure, defined as 'inquisitorial', was intended to replace proof by ordeal, duel or compurgation, which had been outlawed by the Vatican in Canon law trials in 1215.[95] In ensuing years, inquisitorial

---

[92] Chapters 1–4, 7, 27–32, 36–40 (Terrien, *Commentaires*, pp. 461–5, 468, 496–511, 520–31). See also Tramailler (ed.), *Approbation*, pp. 22–6.

[93] Terrien, *Commentaires*, p. 509.

[94] W.F. McDonald, *Criminal Prosecution and the Rationalization of Criminal Justice* (Washington, 1991), pp. 41–2; J.H. Langbein, *Prosecuting Crime in the Renaissance: England, Germany, France* (Cambridge, Massachusetts, 1974), p. 213.

[95] Proof by ordeal, duel or compurgation had been widely used in France since the time of the Franks (compurgation was a procedure whereby an accused person could formally exculpate himself by swearing his innocence on the Gospels, supported by three oath-helpers). *Le Grand Coutumier* had specified that serious crimes such as homicide or robbery could be dealt with by judicial duel or trial by battle, and lesser assaults might be handled by compurgation (Everard (tr), *Grand Coutumier*, pp. 36–46, 284–92).

procedure was adopted in many European countries. However, it was never adopted in England, which, while in due course also eschewing ordeals and duels, retained a vision of the criminal trial as essentially a contest between accuser and accused.

French criminal procedure continued to develop over the two centuries after 1258. In 1498, something of a watershed was reached when Louis XII's *Ordonnance de Blois* systematically codified developments in French criminal procedure to date, and enshrined the distinction between two methods of proceeding which came to be known as *la procédure extraordinaire* and *la procédure au petit criminel.*[96] In 1539, François I's *Ordonnance de Villers-Cotterêts* further elaborated on the distinction between *la procédure extraordinaire* and *au petit criminel* and definitively fixed the rules of both. In 1670, the Villers-Cotterêts Ordinance was superseded by Louis XIV's *Ordonnance Criminelle de Saint-Germain-en-Laye*, which refined and systematised the methods of proceeding already sanctioned by the previous Ordinances. This Ordinance was to govern criminal procedure in French courts until the Revolution of 1789.

At the opening of our period in the 1680s, Guernsey's criminal procedure was fairly closely based on the French royal Ordinances, and it replicated the essential distinction between *la procédure extraordinaire* and *la procédure au petit criminel*. Guernsey's version of *la procédure extraordinaire* was described in Warburton's *Treatise*.[97] This procedure, which was also known locally as *la procédure au grand criminel*, was used for the most serious crimes – those liable to the death penalty or to banishment for more than seven years.[98] It began with the Ordinary Court sitting *in camera* to hear preliminary evidence from witnesses in order to decide whether there were grounds for proceeding against a suspect.[99] Questioning was led by the Law Officers, the accused was

---

[96] Carbasse, *Histoire du Droit Pénal*, pp. 215–17.

[97] Warburton, *Treatise*, pp. 123–4. It was also described, largely unchanged, in *Second Report*, pp. xxii–xxv, which on p. 127 gives a fully worked example from the crime register dating from 1638. The French version of *la procédure extraordinaire* is detailed in Carbasse, *Histoire du Droit Pénal*, pp. 218–22.

[98] Since banishment for seven years or more entailed forfeiture of the criminal's property (as did capital punishment), it was conceived of as 'civil death'.

[99] In cases where there had been a grave crime but no evident perpetrator, the Ordinary Court could, as an initial step, order a general inquiry (*grande enquête*) in which it was open to any person with evidence to present themselves for examination on oath. This procedure was, however, rare.

not present, and witness statements were not recorded. If the Court decided there was indeed a case to answer, an *acte d'accusation* was drawn up and recorded in the crime register.[100] The Court also ruled as to whether the accused was to be remanded in custody, or released on bail to appear in Court at a later date.

The next stage of the procedure also took place before the Ordinary Court, again sitting *in camera*. This session was devoted to the accused's *interrogatoire*. Alone, unacquainted with the evidence against him, and without the assistance of counsel, he (or she) was questioned by the Court, again led by the Law Officers, on the testimony they had heard from preliminary witnesses. This time, the accused's responses were formally recorded. At this stage, the Court could still decide to dismiss the case and discharge the accused, but, if they decided to proceed with the case, the accused was asked to enter a plea and choose an Advocate.[101] If the accused pleaded not guilty, the Law Officers were directed to prove the charge and could instruct the Constables to set about gathering further evidence.

The third stage, again before the Ordinary Court, consisted of the formal examination of prosecution witnesses.[102] These were examined individually on oath, *in camera*, and in the absence of the accused, his counsel and other witnesses. The Greffier or his deputy recorded their depositions in writing.

The fourth stage was known as the *recolement*. Its purpose was to finalise the testimony of prosecution witnesses. The witnesses were summoned to a further private sitting of the Ordinary Court. Their original depositions were read out to them. They were then required, on oath, either to confirm all they had previously said, or to make alterations as they saw fit. This was followed, sometimes on the same day, by the fifth stage, the *confrontation*. The prosecution witnesses were again summoned before the Ordinary Court *in camera*, but, on this occasion, the accused was present, assisted by his or her

---

[100] *Actes d'accusation* usually consisted of a short recital of the accused's alleged actions. Notwithstanding that such *actes* were not the exact equivalent of English indictments, the term 'indictment' will be used here as shorthand for *actes d'accusation*.

[101] All persons accused of serious crimes had the right to be defended by an Advocate of the Royal Court. The chosen Advocate was compelled to act, but could charge the accused fees. In the event of conviction, the goods of the offender were liable for the costs of both prosecution and defence.

[102] The number of witnesses in criminal trials was limited to twelve for the prosecution and twelve for the defence.

Advocate. He or she was given an opportunity to recuse the witnesses.[103] Those remaining were then re-sworn, their depositions were re-read to them, and they were cross-examined by the accused's Advocate. After this, witnesses for the defence could be called to give evidence, but only if such evidence was deemed relevant by the Court. They were first examined by the accused's Advocate, and then by the Law Officers. Again, all questions and answers were recorded in writing.

Once these five distinct stages had been completed, the sixth and final stage was little more than a formality. This was the public trial before the Full Court. The trial began with the reading out of the *acte d'accusation* and *interrogatoire*, following which Jurats could be recused.[104] Then the depositions of both prosecution and defence witnesses were read out. After this, the accused's Advocate put the case for the defence. This was followed by speeches from the Law Officers, at the end of which they submitted their *conclusions*, which included their view as to the extent of the accused's culpability and suggestions for a sentence. The Bailiff then summed up, and each of the Jurats, in order of seniority, stated their own opinions as to both verdict and sentence. When they had finished, a vote was taken, again encompassing both verdict and sentence, and a simple majority sufficed to determine the case (with a casting vote to the Bailiff if Jurats were tied). Once a determination had been reached, it fell to the Bailiff to conclude the proceedings by informing the accused of the Court's decision (which he was obliged to hear on bended knee).

Perhaps owing to the extensive preliminary groundwork, acquittals in trials *au grand criminel* were rare. However, when it did happen that an accused person was acquitted, the formula used was one that might have been heard in any French court. The Law Officers were instructed 'to be silent' – '*les dits Officiers du Roi à silence envers* [the accused] *en la cause qu'ils ont contre lui*'.[105]

---

[103] In our period, the following witnesses could be recused: the father, mother, son, husband, wife, cousin, special friend or known enemy of the accused; anyone who was deaf, blind, undergoing a similar trial, reputed to have committed serious crimes, or who had defended or advised the accused. This was partly based on Roman practice, transmitted via France (Carey, *Essai sur les Institutions*, pp. 225–6).

[104] Generally only if they were a party to the cause, or for reasons of kinship (Warburton, *Treatise*, p. 10).

[105] For France, see A. Bruneau, *Observations et Maximes sur les Matières Criminelles* (Paris, 1715), p. 269.

For moderately serious crimes – typically those liable to whipping, a substantial fine, or banishment for up to six years, – the Royal Court evolved its own idiosyncratic variant of this procedure, which became known as *la procédure au criminel ordinaire*. This variant, while retaining the preliminary investigation and *interrogatoire*, dispensed with the further stages of deposition-taking, *recolement* and *confrontation*. Instead, the case went straight from *interrogatoire* to trial before the Full Court. This trial was open to the public, and followed much the same sequence as the final public session of trials *au grand criminel*, save that evidence was given and witnesses were examined orally on the day, and no depositions were recorded in writing.[106]

We should note at this juncture that Guernsey's adoption of French procedure had led to significant divergences with Jersey, which had no equivalent of *L'Approbation* and retained many features of medieval Norman procedure. A case in point was that of *l'enquête du pays*. This was a customary procedure to which a person accused of a serious crime could opt to submit in the hope of proving his innocence. Described in *Le Grand Coutumier*, it involved taking the opinions of a panel of twenty-four men from the district where a crime had allegedly been committed, and convicting only on the recommendation of at least twenty.[107] In Jersey, a version of *l'enquête du pays* survived until 1864 in the form of the twenty-four-man *grande enquête* used in certain criminal trials.[108] *Enquêtes du pays* were undoubtedly known in Guernsey in medieval times,[109] but there had already been a significant departure from them by at least the mid-sixteenth century. Thomas Le Marchant said that the Royal Court had 'invented a new form of *enquête*' for the witch trials which took place between 1563 and 1650, in which numbers of witnesses vastly exceeded twenty-four, and convictions might be secured on the evidence of just two or three of them.[110] Le Marchant's contention as to large numbers of witnesses was corroborated by evidence collected by

---

[106] *Second Report*, p. xxv.

[107] Everard (tr), *Grand Coutumier*, pp. 292–300.

[108] *First Report of the Commissioners Appointed to Inquire into the State of the Criminal Law in the Channel Islands: Jersey* (London, 1847), pp. xxx, xxxv–xxxvi. *La Loi (1864) réglant la Procédure Criminelle* transformed the twenty-four-man panel into a regular jury, with the result that juries are still used in Jersey today, while they are not used in Guernsey.

[109] For an example, see p. 26 of John Le Patourel's manuscript translation of the Guernsey Assize Roll of 1299 (PL).

[110] Le Marchant, *Remarques et Animadversions*, 2, pp. 66, 219–20.

Darryl Ogier in his recent study of witch trials.[111] Dr Ogier however also found large numbers of witnesses in *enquêtes* held before witch trials began and in *enquêtes* into other crimes such as infanticide.[112] It seems likely, therefore, that the witchcraft episode only accelerated the demise of an institution which was already in terminal decline. At all events, Terrien stated in chapter 31, Book XII of his 1574 *Commentaires* that *l'enquête du pays* was no longer in use in Normandy, and *L'Approbation* accepted this chapter without demur.[113] The Court instituted no *enquêtes du pays* in the period dealt with by this study.

Another ancient component of criminal procedure which survived in Jersey but not in Normandy or Guernsey were the *harèles* or parochial juries of presentment which had been used in both insular and mainland Normandy in medieval times.[114] These were panels of six or twelve men from the parish in which an offence had been committed who conducted the preliminary investigation and drafted the indictment on which the accused was, if necessary, brought before royal justice. Without these parochial juries, according to Judith Everard and James Holt, 'royal justice could not have functioned, and there would have been a breakdown in law and order'.[115] In Jersey, *harèles* survived in the form of *l'endîtement* (a panel composed of thirteen members of the parochial police in the parish where a crime was alleged to have been committed) until they were abolished by the *Loi (1864) réglant la Procédure Criminelle*.[116] In Guernsey, *harèles* – at least as juries of presentment – seem to have disappeared by the mid-sixteenth century. Darryl Ogier notes that, in Guernsey, allegations of witchcraft in the period

[111] D.M. Ogier, 'Glimpses of the obscure: the witch trials of the Channel Islands', in A. McShane & G. Walker (eds), *The Extraordinary and the Everyday in Early Modern England* (Basingstoke, 2010), p. 180.

[112] D.M. Ogier, 'New-born child murder in Reformation Guernsey', in G. Dawes (ed.), *Commise 1204: Studies in the History and Law of Continental and Insular Normandy* (Guernsey, 2005), pp. 133–4, 140.

[113] Terrien, *Commentaires*, pp. 508–9; Tramailler (ed.), *Approbation*, p. 25.

[114] Havet, *Cours Royales*, pp. 116–18; Le Patourel, *Medieval Administration*, pp. 96, 99.

[115] J.A. Everard & J.C. Holt, *Jersey 1204: The Forging of an Island Community* (London, 2004), pp. 173–5.

[116] J. Kelleher, *The Triumph of the Country: The Rural Community in Nineteenth-Century Jersey* (1994; Jersey, 2017 edn), p. 289.

1563–1650 were brought directly to the Law Officers, while in Jersey they were referred to these Officers only after a parochial *endîtement*.[117]

Although there are no records of *harèles* in our period, there is nevertheless evidence to suggest that this institution enjoyed something of an afterlife in Guernsey in the form of the twelve-man panels sworn in for the purpose of inquests. The practice of holding inquests, known locally as *levées de corps*, originated in the *Coutume*, which specified that people who had been killed could not be buried until seen by justice.[118] During the period covered by this chapter, Guernsey inquests were usually held on the spot where a body had been found, and twelve *hommes dignes de foi* from the neighbourhood were sworn in to give evidence as to whether or not there was a criminal case to answer.[119] This practice (which was later to change) was perhaps the last, somewhat withered, manifestation of the *harèle*.

A further difference between the islands resulting from Guernsey's adoption of French procedure was that judicial torture was at some point introduced to Guernsey, while it remained unknown in Jersey. There was no provision for torture in the Norman *Coutume*, but it had been adopted in France following the introduction of the romano-canonical system, and could be inflicted as part of *la procédure extraordinaire* if the accused refused to respond to questions in his *interrogatoire*.[120] Terrien went into some detail on torture in his *Commentaires*, and, again, *L'Approbation* unreservedly endorsed the chapters in which he dealt with this topic.[121]

Torture was certainly used in sixteenth-century Guernsey, where Darryl Ogier has found evidence of it, *inter alia*, in witch trials.[122] According to 'Warburton', however, the practice was dropped from the judicial repertoire when the witch trials came to an end around 1650.[123] In this, Guernsey was also following French practice, where, from a similar point in time, judicial

---

[117] Ogier, 'Glimpses of the obscure', pp. 178–9.

[118] Everard (tr), *Grand Coutumier*, pp. 274–8.

[119] Warburton, *Treatise*, p. 128. This was the reason why inquests were recorded in the crime registers. Though few *levées de corps* resulted in criminal prosecutions, the evolution of the Guernsey inquest is an interesting subject in itself and will be examined in Appendix 9.

[120] McDonald, *Criminal Prosecution*, pp. 42–3; Carbasse, *Histoire du Droit Pénal*, p. 206.

[121] Terrien, *Commentaires*, pp. 383–6, 526–8; Tramailler (ed.), *Approbation*, pp. 21, 25.

[122] Ogier, 'Glimpses of the obscure', p. 181.

[123] Warburton, *Treatise*, p. 126. See also Le Marchant, *Remarques et Animadversions*, 2, p. 250.

torture was 'virtually unused' in the provinces.[124] Thus, although torture might have remained theoretically permissible in Guernsey, it did not survive as an ongoing practice in the period dealt with here, and no records have been found of its use.

As noted earlier, French royal Ordinances made an important distinction between *la procédure extraordinaire* and *la procédure au petit criminel*. We shall now turn our attention to the latter, which saw particularly heavy local use in the period dealt with here.[125] This was the procedure adopted for less serious offences involving personal injury: physical and verbal assaults, threats, and defamation. Based on Roman practice, it had been used in southern France since the thirteenth century, and had spread from there to the rest of the country. Actions *au petit criminel*, which were closely related to civil actions, had a twofold aim. The first and arguably most important was to secure compensation for the injured party. The second was to punish the perpetrator in the name of the king. Prosecution was thus in the joint name of the *partie civile* and the king's Procureur. However, the *partie civile* initiated the prosecution and bore the risks.[126]

In Guernsey in the period covered by this chapter, such semi-civil actions were usually referred to either as *causes en petit criminel* or, reflecting the joint nature of prosecutions, *causes en adjonction*.[127] These actions were heard before the Full Court, with HM Procureur acting as joint prosecutor with the plaintiff, and HM Comptroller acting for the defence.[128] In its Guernsey incarnation, the procedure was highly formalistic, and each of its stages was recorded in the crime registers. An initial sitting of the Court gave permission for the action to proceed and formally granted the plaintiff *l'adjonction* of the Procureur. There then followed further procedural sittings in which each side called (and was given the opportunity to recuse) witnesses. Once these preliminaries were over, the actual trial would follow a *viva voce* procedure similar to a civil hearing. The prosecution spoke first, then the defence, then

[124] Schneider, *King's Bench*, p. 195.

[125] *La procédure au petit criminel* was described by Terrien in a chapter endorsed without comment by *L'Approbation* (Terrien, *Commentaires*, pp. 506–7; Tramailler (ed.), *Approbation*, p. 25).

[126] Carbasse, *Histoire du Droit Pénal*, pp. 211–12, 215–16.

[127] They were also sometimes known as *causes mixtes*.

[128] Residents of Sark could pursue such actions in their own court (where they appear to have been treated as a purely civil matter), but the Alderney court lacked this power and residents were obliged to pursue *causes en adjonction* in Guernsey (*Second Report*, pp. 197, 200).

witnesses on both sides were heard, then the two counsel spoke again in the same order, with the last word (in contrast with trials *au grand criminel*) always going to the defence.[129] The Jurats collectively determined both verdict and penalty, which, if the defendant was found guilty, usually took the form of damages to be paid to the plaintiff, together with a small fine to the Crown, and costs.[130] If the plaintiff was non-suited (*mis à la folle adjonction*), he would be charged with the costs of the proceedings, in addition to which he could also be fined if the Court judged that he had made a malicious allegation. If both parties were deemed to be at fault, they could both be sentenced to pay a fine to the Crown as well as to share costs.

Another semi-civil action dealt with in this fashion was the action of *nouvelle dessaisine*. This action also existed in both Normandy and England. It was described in *Le Grand Coutumier* and Terrien's *Commentaires*.[131] In England, where it was known as 'novel disseisin', its purpose was to recover lands of which a plaintiff had been wrongfully dispossessed.[132] In Guernsey, its scope was considerably broader, though it still concerned real property.[133] As was the case in semi-civil actions for assault or defamation, the Procureur adjoined himself to the plaintiff, and the Comptroller acted for the defendant. The action went through multiple procedural stages, and the final trial followed civil forms. If the Court found against the defendant, he was sentenced to restitution, costs, and any damages, as well as to pay a small fine to the Crown. If the plaintiff was non-suited, he was sentenced to pay a fine to the Crown and costs.

Cases relating to the use of *clameur de haro* were the third form of semi-civil action heard by the Full Court. The *clameur* was an age-old institution. Like the English hue and cry, its original purpose was to summon aid to a victim when a crime was being committed, and it was described in these terms in the thirteenth-century *Grand Coutumier*.[134] In ensuing centuries, use of the *clameur* in both Normandy and Guernsey departed radically from its

---

[129] The process, virtually unchanged since the seventeenth century, is described in *Second Report*, pp. xxv, pp. 187–90.

[130] In defamation cases, the guilty party was usually also ordered to make a public retraction, which he did at the bar of the Court immediately after sentencing.

[131] Everard (tr), *Grand Coutumier*, pp. 382–94; Terrien, *Commentaires*, pp. 259–62.

[132] Plucknett, *History of the Common Law*, pp. 358–60, 412.

[133] The scope of the action will be fully described in Chapter 3.

[134] Everard (tr), *Grand Coutumier*, pp. 238–45.

original purpose and became restricted to stopping wrongful interference with a person's possession of immovable property. It was described in these terms in Terrien, in a chapter endorsed by *L'Approbation*.[135] In our period, by performing the *clameur*, an islander could impose an immediate injunction upon the alleged perpetrator of such interference.[136] The injunction would lapse after a year and a day without a further Court order, during which time the person who had raised the *clameur* could bring an action against the alleged wrongdoer in support of his *clameur*, or the person impeded by the *clameur* could bring an action against the person who had raised it to have the *clameur* set aside. These actions were dealt with in much the same way as *causes en adjonction* and actions of *nouvelle dessaisine*, with the Procureur adjoining himself to the plaintiff, and the Comptroller acting for the defendant. Whichever of the parties was found to be in the wrong was sentenced not only to pay a fine to the Crown and costs, but also to twenty-four hours' imprisonment, which was termed in the registers of the period *un regard de château*.[137]

Prosecutions of Ordinance breaches were the fourth and final form of semi-civil action. These too were heard before the Full Court, and the reporter of the breach, known as *le délateur*, would be joined with the Procureur in the prosecution, while the Comptroller enjoyed monopoly rights to the defence.[138] If convicted, the accused would be fined and charged with the costs of the prosecution, but if he was acquitted, the *délateur* would be liable for both Court costs and Law Officers' fees. Prosecutions under Ordinances could be cumbersome. They were often contested, requiring the calling of witnesses over several sittings and usually taking months between launch and determination. Prosecutions under the Acts of Parliament which applied to Guernsey (though few in our period) were conducted in the same way as prosecutions under Ordinances.

---

[135] Terrien, *Commentaires*, pp. 272–3; *Approbation*, p. 17.

[136] The person seeking an injunction had to recite the words '*Haro! Haro! A l'aide mon Prince. On me fait tort*', followed by the Lord's Prayer, kneeling and before two witnesses. He had then formally to apprise the Bailiff or Lieutenant Bailiff (or, if they were unavailable, two Jurats) that he had raised *la clameur*, following which, and within twenty-four hours of the original proceeding, he had to register his *clameur* at the Greffe.

[137] Warburton, *Treatise*, pp. 100–1. This was because persons undergoing twenty-four-hour detention in *clameur* cases were lodged in the pier guardhouse (which had a view of the Castle) rather than the Castle itself.

[138] *Second Report*, p. 52.

The only other type of criminal action it remains to mention are summary prosecutions. These were undertaken in respect of trivial offences. In summary trials, the proceedings (entirely oral) took place in a single public session of the Ordinary Court, with the Law Officers conducting the prosecution.[139] Use of counsel was permitted but not mandatory as in trials *au grand criminel.*

The extent to which all these different actions were used varied considerably. In the first part of the next chapter, we will examine the incidence and distribution of each type of action and the reasons which motivated their use. Following this, we will look in detail at the offenders with whom the Court dealt, the nature of their offending, and the ways in which their offences were punished.

[139] But see opening of Chapter 3.

3

1680–1764: Crime

The period between 1680 and 1764 was spanned by nine *Livres en Crime*.[1] This chapter is based on a reading of each, during which notes were taken, a tally was kept of the number of cases determined, and all register entries during five evenly spaced quinquennia were recorded in detail. These quinquennia cover the years 1680–4, 1700–4, 1720–4, 1740–4 and 1760–4.

We should observe at the outset that, for the first fifty years of our period, the format of the crime registers was anything but consistent. The way in which particulars were recorded can only be described as haphazard, and details which were inserted in some entries might be omitted in others. In a number of cases, information was lacking as to who was conducting the prosecution, and the terse wording fails to rule out the possibility that one party might simply have been actioning another. It is true that Thomas Le Marchant and 'Warburton' asserted that the Law Officers were a party to every criminal cause.[2] However, it is not completely inconceivable that, despite their assertions, prosecution by these Officers was – at least in early years – reserved only for more serious cases.[3] Having raised this possibility, my own surmise – in the light of later and better-kept registers – is that the wording in these entries merely reflected the fact that the victim initiated the prosecution, it being then taken for granted that the Law Officers carried the case forward in Court. There is, however, no way to be certain of this. Only from the late 1730s did the format of the crime registers become more

---

[1] Volumes 6 (1660–1704) to 14 (1758–72).

[2] T. Le Marchant, *Remarques et Animadversions sur l'Approbation des Lois et Coustumier de Normandie usitées ès Jurisdictions de Guernezé*, 2 vols (Guernsey, 1826), 2, p. 225; J. Warburton, *A Treatise on the History, Laws and Customs of the Island of Guernsey* (Guernsey, 1822), p. 123.

[3] Leaving it to victims in other cases, as in England, to prepare the trial themselves, assemble witnesses and lay out the evidence in court. For English procedure, see J.M. Beattie, *Crime and the Courts in England, 1660–1800* (Oxford, 1986), p. 35.

standardised. The improvement in recording seems broadly to have coincided with a change of Greffier, when Josué Gosselin replaced Thomas Dobrée in 1737.

Between the 1680s and 1760s, an average of just thirty-seven criminal cases were determined annually. There were random upward and downward fluctuations, but these were produced by relatively insignificant changes in prosecution levels, such as in the 1720s, when the average rose to fifty-nine cases a year owing to an unusually zealous enforcement of Ordinances. There was, however, no definite trend, and, with an average of twenty-six cases per year, the 1760s were not very different from the 1680s, which had an average of twenty-nine per year.

The ratio of purely procedural sittings to those which resulted in a verdict was fairly high throughout the period, with a tendency to rise as time went on. In the quinquennium 1680–4, about one-third of sittings were purely procedural; this rose to nearly one-half in 1760–4. The number of Jurats present at each sitting was also high. Over our five sample quinquennia in aggregate, more than two-thirds of criminal sittings were attended by at least seven Jurats.

Some 82 per cent of sittings over the five quinquennia took place on a Saturday, which was the appointed day for sittings of the Full Court. The small number of sittings which took place on other days were concentrated in the first half of the week. There were also a few emergency sittings on a Sunday – nine in total across the five quinquennia.[4] Sittings took place throughout the year, but most were held in term-time, with peaks in February/March, May/June and November/December, shortly after the opening of each term. January and August were the quietest months of the year, with just a handful of sittings in each.

In an average of 86 per cent of criminal cases across our quinquennia, the accused was male. Ages were not recorded in crime registers. Neither, save in the most serious cases, was the accused's place of origin. That said, some 71 per cent of those standing trial in the sample quinquennia bore identifiably Guernsey surnames, with a further 12 per cent bearing French names, and 12 per cent bearing names from Great Britain and Ireland.[5]

---

[4] Such as on Sunday 9 February 1724, when the Court was summoned to attend an inquest on Jean Russeq, found dead in the harbour (GG, *Crime*, vol. 9).

[5] Married or widowed females were invariably prosecuted under their maiden names, although their husbands' names were also given.

Figure 1 divides all criminal cases determined over our sample quinquennia into four major categories: Ordinance infractions; other semi-civil actions; trivial offences prosecuted summarily; and serious crimes prosecuted on indictment.

Figure 1. Distribution of criminal cases over 5 quinquennia, 1680–1764

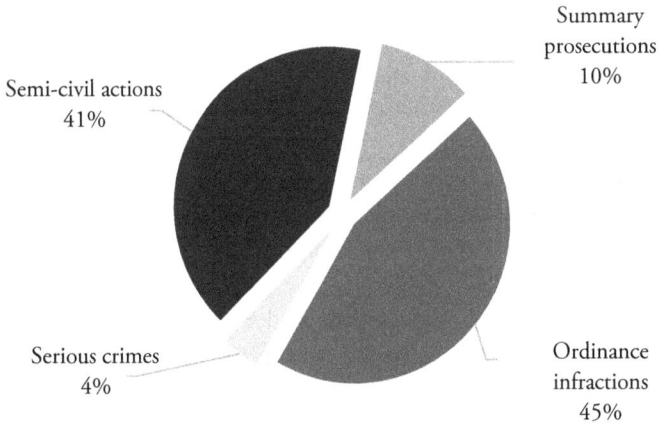

Serious crimes comprised by far the smallest proportion of offences dealt with by the Court – an average of only 4 per cent of all criminal cases across the five quinquennia. The actual number of such crimes was minimal: about one per year over the period 1680–4, rising to just under two per year in the period 1760–4. Perhaps more surprisingly, summary prosecutions comprised the next lowest proportion. At just 10 per cent of cases, this translated into five or so summary prosecutions each year, with numbers fairly stable across the whole period. At the other end of the scale, Ordinance infractions formed the largest proportion of the Court's criminal business: 45 per cent of cases across the five quinquennia. This translated into sixteen or so prosecutions per year. The second largest proportion, at 41 per cent of cases, consisted of the major semi-civil actions (*nouvelle dessaisine* and *causes en adjonction* for personal injury). There were about fourteen such actions annually.

Ordinance infractions

Ordinances passed by the Royal Court in the period between 1680 and 1764 regulated a wide variety of matters: the sale, import and export of food and drink; the maintenance and salubrity of town streets; militia matters; the gathering of seaweed, stones or sand from the shore; hunting; fishing; and 'disciplinary' matters such as sabbath observance.

Breaches of Ordinances could only be punished by fines, which were specified in individual Ordinances. A portion of these fines went to the Crown revenues (often referred to in Guernsey as *le Fisc*), another portion to the *délateur* or informant, and, in offences with a 'moral' component (such as selling under weight), a further portion might go to parochial poor funds. Individual Ordinances specified which portions of the fines were due to whom. Owing to the obligation on a *délateur* to bear the costs of failed Ordinance-related prosecutions, such prosecutions were usually initiated by parochial Constables or assistant constables, which transferred financial risks to the parish.

Something over half of prosecutions under Ordinances over our sample quinquennia were of breaches which took place in town. Urban breaches fell into three main categories: liquor-licensing offences (at 24 per cent of all prosecutions, the largest single category); breaches of sanitary and traffic regulations (15 per cent of prosecutions); and breaches of Ordinances restricting the export and sale of foodstuffs in times of dearth (10 per cent).

Rural breaches were more diverse. About 10 per cent were hunting-related.[6] A further 5 per cent concerned the evasion of tithe or *champart*;[7]

---

[6] Compared with English game laws, Guernsey's hunting Ordinances were anodyne. They concerned only rabbits, hares, game birds and pigeons, since the island contained no large mammals. Ordinances of this period sought to restrict the hunting of such animals to a group of 'qualified' persons, typically Court members, clergy and large landowners. Fines for their infraction ranged from 20 to 30 *livres tournois* (about £1 9s to £2 3s). For more on this subject, see R. Hocart, *The Country People of Guernsey and their Agriculture, 1640–1840* (Guernsey, 2016), pp. 211–12.

[7] Tithe and *champart* were levied on corn, flax, peas, beans and vetch. The tithe was the eleventh sheaf, *champart* the twelfth. Tithe was originally an ecclesiastical due, but passed to the Crown in the fifteenth century. *Champart* was a seigneurial due owed to the fief. By an Ordinance of 1625, a cultivator was required to give the Seigneur or farmer of tithe or *champart* 24 hours' notice of his intention to remove harvested crops from his land, and most of those prosecuted under this Ordinance had attempted surreptitiously to remove sheaves before the official arrived (Hocart, *Country People*, pp. 28–33).

5 per cent concerned the collection of seaweed at prohibited times; and the rest were chiefly for failing to maintain *douits* (drainage ditches), diverting streams away from watermills, and allowing livestock to graze in public thoroughfares.

A further class of breaches concerned both urban and rural parishioners. These related to militia Ordinances and what we have termed 'disciplinary' Ordinances. Militiamen were typically prosecuted for failing to attend exercises, musters, parades or watch-duty. Between 1680 and 1764, just 3 per cent of Ordinance-related prosecutions fell under this rubric, most of them following the passage of a new militia Ordinance at the beginning of the Seven Years War.[8] However (as we will see in later chapters), numbers of prosecutions rose exponentially as other major wars followed from 1778 onwards. 'Disciplinary' Ordinances sought to regulate the morals and social activities of the populace, and had been common under the Presbyterian regime when, as well as sabbath observance, they covered such matters as drunkenness, fornication, and unseemly singing and dancing.[9] By our period, attitudes had relaxed, and although a few such Ordinances were issued in the late seventeenth and early eighteenth centuries,[10] enforcement was lax. There were fewer than two prosecutions per year under 'disciplinary' Ordinances across our sample, most of them targeting business activities pursued on a Sunday.

Acts of Parliament

The Westminster statutes which were extended to Guernsey between 1680 and 1764 consisted chiefly of Quarantine Acts (ordering that ships from ports afflicted with contagious diseases should be held offshore) and Acts governing trade and navigation. Any prosecutions initiated under these statutes were

---

[8] Ord, 19.1.1756.

[9] D.M. Ogier, *Reformation and Society* (Woodbridge, 1996), pp. 114–15.

[10] These Ordinances included one of 1703 prohibiting barbers from shaving their customers on a Sunday (Ord, 4.10.1703), and one of 1720 banning the communal night-time get-togethers known as *veilles* and *parteries de gâche* (Ord, 8.1.1720). *Veilles* were a form of 'working-bee', where people saved on heating and lighting by working together to the accompaniment of songs and story-telling. The term *parterie de gâche* literally meant cake-sharing and denoted a kind of party.

conducted according to the same procedure as for Ordinances (and, as such, have been included in our statistics on Ordinances). There were, however, few such prosecutions, in particular under the Quarantine Acts. Prosecutions under the Acts of trade and navigation were only slightly more common, as these Acts were far from enthusiastically enforced in Guernsey, which lacked a permanent British customs post in this period.[11] The few who were made the subject of such a prosecution could thus count themselves exceptionally unfortunate. In the spring of 1739, Mr Daniel Carey was fined for importing bohea tea from St Malo contrary to the provisions of two named statutes.[12] Later that year, Alderney resident Mr Thomas Le Cocq was successfully prosecuted under the same Acts for importing tea from St Malo to Alderney.[13] Such prosecutions continued sporadically throughout our period.

Semi-civil actions

We shall henceforth reserve the term 'semi-civil' exclusively to actions of *nouvelle dessaisine* and *causes en adjonction* for personal injury. At 41 per cent of cases in our sample quinquennia, these formed the second largest component of the Royal Court's criminal business. Personal injury actions comprised the majority of these *causes mixtes*, outnumbering actions of *nouvelle dessaisine* by four to one. The number of actions relating to *clameur de haro* was very small, so we will omit them from further discussion.[14]

---

[11] G. Stevens Cox, *St Peter Port, 1680–1830: The History of an International Entrepôt* (Woodbridge, 1999), p. 19; Hocart, *Country People*, p. 15.

[12] 7.4.1739, GG, *Crime*, vol. 12. These were, respectively, the Act for the Further Preventing of His Majesty's Subjects from Trading to the East Indies, and the Act for the Encouraging and Increasing of Shipping and Navigation.

[13] 19.5.1739, GG, *Crime*, vol. 12.

[14] Between 1727 and 1814, just eighteen *clameurs* were registered at the Greffe (K.M.S. Kirkegaard, 'Clameur de haro – the Norman connection' (unpub. Master's thesis, Copenhagen Business School, 2008), p. 21).

Nouvelle dessaisine

Originally intended as an action for recovering possession of lands, the action of *nouvelle dessaisine* was by 1680 used in Guernsey for recovering possession of many things which were only tangentially related to land. Principally used in a rural setting, it had almost become an action for theft – specifically rural forms of theft, where a person's greatest wealth lay in his farm buildings and appurtenances, and his fields, orchards and gardens. Thus, in 1683, Henry Allez actioned Jean Le Pettevin for having dismantled the mounting block outside his farmhouse and removed the stones for his own use; in 1708, Nicolas Brehaut actioned Pierre Brehaut for taking away a manure heap he was keeping at the foot of his outside staircase; in 1709, Josias De Putron actioned James Le Lievre for having cut and removed a quantity of furze from his furzebrake; and in 1711, Anne Fallaize actioned Pierre Marquand for taking a quantity of clover which was growing in her field.[15]

In an urban context, the action of *nouvelle dessaisine* was much rarer, although it could still sometimes be used. In 1710, for example, Mr Mathieu De Sausmarez was actioned by Sr Jean Bernard for taking away the grill covering the drain between their two houses. In 1735, Daniel Guerin was actioned for his wife's appropriation of someone else's church pew.[16]

The main motive behind these actions was to re-establish a right to the possession of the property and secure its restitution. Nevertheless, the guilty party was also obliged to pay a fine to *le Fisc* in recognition that his wrongdoing was against the public interest. Reflecting the predominance of private interests over public, however, this fine was normally no more than a token 18 *sols tournois* (about 1s 3d).

In some ways, the action of *nouvelle dessaisine*, as locally evolved, marked a transitional stage between the ancient notion that the taking of one person's property by another was essentially a private matter, and the modern idea that all thefts required public prosecution. Actions of *nouvelle dessaisine* declined as personal possessions and opportunities for theft proliferated with the development of a consumer society. From three or four actions per year between the 1680s and 1720s, they fell to fewer than one per year between

---

[15] 1.10.1683, GG, *Crime*, vol. 6; 8.5.1708, 4.6.1709, 17.6.1710, 9.6.1711, GG, *Crime*, vol. 7.
[16] 20.2.1710, GG, *Crime*, vol. 7; 11.1.1735, GG, *Crime*, vol. 11.

the 1740s and 1760s. In due course (though not in this period), the action died out and was superseded by straightforward prosecutions for theft.

Causes en adjonction

About a dozen *causes en adjonction* for personal injury were determined each year across our sample quinquennia, and, unlike *nouvelle dessaisine*, there was no fall-off in numbers as time went on. 'Injuries' giving rise to *causes en adjonction* covered a broad spectrum. They might be physical or they might be moral. Physical injuries ranged all the way from bruised fingers to broken limbs. Moral injuries ranged from blows to a person's dignity from a public insult or threat, to blows to his honour from the deliberate besmirching of his reputation. Many *causes* involved an element of all of these, with physical violence featuring as a component in 37 per cent.

At the most serious end of the scale were the injuries sustained in brutal attacks such as that by Michel Robert on Thomas Bonamy in 1704. Setting upon Bonamy as he walked along a road in St Andrews, Robert struck Bonamy several blows on the head and face without any apparent provocation, breaking the bridge of his nose and drawing blood.[17] For this he was ordered to pay Bonamy damages of 35 *livres tournois* (£2 10s) and a fine of 5 *livres tournois* (7s 6d) to *le Fisc*.[18] In 1740, Samuel Jamouneau was adjudged to a similar penalty when Sarah Le Ray won a cause against him for punching her repeatedly in the breasts and face, causing widespread bruising to her head and torso.[19]

At the lowest end of the scale stood public name-calling. *Guernésiais* insults seem to have covered a fairly narrow range. Men might be called *bougre* (bugger), *pourchiau* (swine); *crouin* (dirty beast), *gueux* (beggar) or *fripon* (rogue). Women were called *putain* (whore), *chienne* (bitch), *truie* (sow) – as also *sorcière* (witch) and *laronnesse* (thief). To the modern eye, these insults can seem trivial, but the preservation of personal dignity was vital in a face-to-face society, where public humiliation could entail loss of social credit. Hence the action of Castel Constables Sr James Moullin and Sr Nicolas Cohu

---

[17] Whenever blood was drawn, this was mentioned in the Court record as an aggravating factor – possibly in recognition that an open wound, if infected, could in some cases lead to death.

[18] 17.6.1704, GG, *Crime*, vol. 6.

[19] 3.5.1740, GG, *Crime*, vol. 12.

against Jean Breton and his wife in 1761 for calling them *deux bougres de pourchiaux* in front of several persons and saying that they ought to be thrown out of office – *le tout contre l'honneur, crédit et réputation des dits plaintifs*, as the stock formula ran. The Bretons were sentenced to pay the Constables 10 *livres tournois* (14s 4d) each and 18 *sols* (1s 3d) to *le Fisc*.[20]

Between these two ends of the scale came the various types of calumny or defamation. Both spoken defamation (slander) and written defamation (libel) could be dealt with as *causes en adjonction*, although Guernsey's lack of a printing press at this time meant that most calumnies were delivered orally. Originally, the Royal Court had based its punishment of defamation on chapter 29, Book XII of Terrien, which had been endorsed by *L'Approbation*.[21] Terrien had in turn based his chapter directly on *Le Grand Coutumier*, which had made a distinction between simply besmirching someone's reputation, and falsely accusing someone of a crime which might incur capital or corporal punishment. *Le Coutumier* termed these two types of defamation *laidenges simples* and *laidenges criminelles*.[22] In the latter, more serious, case, *Le Coutumier* prescribed a special penalty: a heavy fine, plus the performance of a self-abasing ritual whereby the perpetrator, dressed only in his undershirt and without shoes, knelt before the court with a candle in one hand and the tip of his own nose in the other, and made a public declaration that he had lied.[23] In the mid-1600s, however, Thomas Le Marchant wrote in his *Remarques et Animadversions* that the Court had abrogated this practice, and now dealt with both forms of defamation 'without any distinction whatever'.[24]

This lack of distinction persisted throughout the period covered by this chapter, and all those found guilty of defamation were punished merely by

---

[20] 31.10.1761, GG, *Crime*, vol. 14.

[21] G. Terrien, *Commentaires du Droict Civil tant Public que Privé Observé au Pays & Duché de Normandie* (1574; Rouen, 1654 edn), pp. 498–500; T. Tramailler (ed.), *Approbation des Lois, Coutumes, et Usages de l'Ile de Guernesey* (1715; Guernsey, 1822 edn), p. 24.

[22] J.A. Everard (tr), *Le Grand Coutumier de Normandie* (Jersey, 2009), pp. 350–4. *Laidenge* (or *lédenge*) was an archaic synonym for defamation not often used by the Guernsey Court, although a similar word – *laidure* – was used to signify an insult in *guernésiais*. It is thought to be derived from the Latin verb *laedere* meaning to hurt or injure.

[23] The nose-holding apology on bended knee (apparently derived from Scandinavia) was also part of the punishment for slander in the custom of the English borough of Preston (T.F. Plucknett, *A Concise History of the Common Law* (1929; Boston, 1956 edn), p. 483).

[24] Le Marchant, *Remarques et Animadversions*, 2, pp. 200, 205.

fining (modulated according to the gravity of the case) and a simple retraction and apology at the bar of the Court. Thus, when Sr William Rivoire won his case against Sr Nicolas Tourtel in 1742 for having falsely claimed that he had seen Rivoire sexually assault a girl in St Martins, Tourtel was simply sentenced to retraction and to pay 50 *livres tournois* (£3 11s 6d) to Rivoire and 10 *livres tournois* to *le Fisc* (14s 4d).[25]

The single instance of the nose-holding ritual for defamation that has been found in crime registers came during the period covered by Part II (below). It occurred in 1770, when John Craw was made to perform the nose-holding ceremony for defaming Sr John Howe, accompanying his gestures with the declaration 'I lied in what I wrote and alleged about the said Howe, because he did not commit the crime of which I accused him, and my words were untruthful'.[26] Craw, who seems to have been a particularly troublesome character, had been sentenced to a summary whipping during the course of Howe's action for his repeated insolence to the Court.[27]

One important point to note with regard to late-seventeenth- and early-eighteenth-century *causes* for defamation is that they could be in respect of deceased as well as living persons. The preservation of family honour was hugely important to Guernseymen of this period, and it was accepted that actions could be launched to restore it 'beyond the grave'. Thus in 1704, Thomas Olivier launched a *cause en adjonction* on behalf of his wife against James Tardif for an unspecified slander on Mrs Olivier's deceased father. The Court found in the Oliviers' favour, and Tardif was sentenced to pay 18 *livres tournois* (£1 5s 10d) to the plaintiffs and 18 *sols* to *le Fisc* (1s 3d). As usual in such cases, he was also ordered to retract his remarks and restore the deceased parent's good name at the bar of the Court.[28]

Before leaving this subject, we will briefly mention another semi-civil action which enjoyed a short-lived upsurge in our period. This was the action for *trèves*, which was related to *causes en adjonction*. The action for *trèves*, also heard by the Full Court and recorded in crime registers, was detailed in both *Le Grand Coutumier* and Terrien, and endorsed by *L'Approbation*.[29]

[25] 21.11.1742, GG, *Crime*, vol. 12.

[26] 16.6.1770, GG, *Crime*, vol. 14.

[27] 19.5.1770, GG, *Crime*, vol. 14.

[28] 11.11.1704, GG, *Crime*, vol. 6.

[29] Everard (tr), *Grand Coutumier*, pp. 306, 314; Terrien, *Commentaires*, pp. 500–1; Tramailler (ed.), *Approbation*, p. 24.

A procedure common to many French *coutumes*, where it was also known as *asseurement*,[30] it was functionally analogous to an English binding over order.[31] Persons who felt their physical safety or their property to be threatened by a specific individual or individuals could apply to the Court jointly with the Law Officers to compel these parties to appear before the Court and swear that they would not molest the applicants, their families or their goods. Interestingly, suits for *trêves* were largely absent from the crime registers in the first thirty years of this study, and seem only to have been rediscovered in the 1720s, from which point they became fairly numerous. They could on occasion fulfil quite important functions, as in 1752 when Mr William Carey was made to swear not to molest his separated wife after threatening to break into her house and 'smash everything to pieces'.[32] However, just as they had been rediscovered in the 1720s, suits for *trêves* appear to have relapsed into oblivion later in the eighteenth century.

Serious crime

Over the five quinquennia examined for this chapter, crimes tried on indictment amounted to just 4 per cent of all offences tried before the Royal Court. Of these, just over half involved theft, usually with some aggravating element; about a fifth involved serious interpersonal violence; and the remainder consisted of miscellaneous offences such as counterfeiting, sedition, perjury, and so forth. Notwithstanding that serious crime comprised such a small proportion of the Court's business, it is worth discussing in detail because it is in this category that important stages in the development of the law are most evident. We shall look first at the category of serious interpersonal violence, which comprised homicide, grievous wounding, and rape.

---

[30] N. Gonthier, *Le Châtiment du Crime au Moyen Age, XIIe-XVIe Siècles* (Rennes, 1998), pp. 51–2.
[31] J.A. Sharpe, *Crime in Early Modern England, 1550-1750* (1984; London, 1999 edn), pp. 52–3.
[32] 21.10.1752, 9.12.1752, GG, *Crime*, vol. 13.

Interpersonal violence

Homicide

Homicide was a blanket term for the killing of one person by another, whether intentional or not. There were sixteen homicide trials in Guernsey between 1680 and 1764. In ten of these, the victim was an adult and, in the remaining six, an infant. In the ten trials involving adult victims, nine of the accused were male and one female. Only the woman and one of the men were hanged. In the six trials involving infant victims, all the accused were women. Three of these women were hanged. Thus although fewer women than men were charged with homicide, a greater proportion of them suffered the death penalty for it. As will be seen below, this was partly owing to the circumstances in which the homicide took place.

All but two of the men tried for homicide were soldiers, another was a sailor, and another a civilian. Only the civilian was a native of Guernsey. Most of the soldiers killed their victims in a fight, and because the deaths were deemed unintentional, all but one escaped capital punishment.[33] The opening of our period, however, saw a serious misunderstanding between Channel Island Courts and the Privy Council concerning wilful and involuntary homicide. A Jersey homicide case of 1689 had led the Council to believe that Channel Island courts observed no distinction between degrees of culpability in homicides and subjected all found guilty to the death penalty.[34] In England, homicide had effectively been divided into wilful murder and manslaughter in Tudor times.[35] The defining feature of manslaughter was that it was unpremeditated, occurring as a result of an accident, a quarrel, in the heat of passion, or as a result of sufficient provocation. In the period covered here, most prisoners convicted of

---

[33] It had been established by this time that soldiers accused of criminal offences against civilians should be tried by the Royal Court rather than a court martial (R. Hocart, *Guernsey in the Reign of Charles II* (Guernsey, 2020), p. 162). This had in the past been disputed.

[34] The case is recounted in P. Le Geyt, *Les Manuscrits de Philippe Le Geyt, Ecuyer, Lieutenant-Bailli de l'Ile de Jersey, sur la Constitution, les Lois et les Usages de cette Ile*, 4 vols (Jersey, 1846–7), 1, pp. 324–5.

[35] Plucknett, *History of the Common Law*, p. 446.

manslaughter in England and Wales were granted benefit of clergy, burnt in the hand, and discharged.[36]

In March 1689, on account of their misapprehension, the Privy Council issued an Order to Channel Island Courts instructing them to suspend judgment of persons who had apparently killed without premeditated malice until the Sovereign in Council had been informed of the case and given his orders as to how to proceed.[37] A second Order was issued in identical terms in 1697, and a third in 1698, this time stipulating that judgment could be rendered in such cases, but, if a person was found guilty, infliction of the death penalty was to be stayed until His Majesty's pleasure was known.[38]

All of these Orders were issued on false premises, for Channel Island courts had long recognised a distinction between different types of homicide similar (though not identical) to that recognised in England. In Guernsey's case, the handling of homicide was governed by chapter 42, Book XII of Terrien, which set out various French Ordinances on royal pardons available to those who had killed involuntarily or unpremeditatedly.[39] *L'Approbation* had endorsed the chapter, commenting only that, in Guernsey, 'letters of remission, pardon or reprieve' would be accepted from the English Sovereign (rather than the French king as stated in Terrien).[40]

When, therefore, in 1699, Guernsey's Court requested the Privy Council's guidance in what it called in explicit terms a 'manslaughter' case,

---

[36] Beattie, *Crime and the Courts*, pp. 80–1, 88. Benefit of clergy, which did not exist in Guernsey, had developed in fourteenth-century England as compensation for the removal of the clerical right to be tried by church courts alone. This enabled convicted ecclesiastics to avoid capital punishment through a literacy test, proved by reading what was called the 'neck verse' (the opening of psalm 51). Those who proved they were literate would then be released. In 1487, benefit was extended beyond the clergy to all men who could prove literacy, but it was restricted to a single use. Before release, offenders were branded on the brawn of the thumb, and if they were convicted again, they were executed.

[37] O in C, 13.3.1689. This Order in Council is not in the register of *Jugements, Ordonnances et Ordres du Conseil* at the Greffe, although it is referred to by date in an entry of 1697. Its full text can be found in Le Geyt, *Manuscrits*, 1, pp. 325–6.

[38] O in Cs, 25.3.1697, 23.6.1698.

[39] Terrien, *Commentaires*, pp. 532–6.

[40] Tramailler (ed.), *Approbation*, p. 26. Aside from this, 'Warburton' described an ancient customary practice whereby a person deemed to have killed someone accidentally or unintentionally could simply be 'brought to touch the dead body' then set at liberty (Warburton, *Treatise*, p. 128). This practice appears to have become obsolete by 1680.

Council members were surprised.[41] The case concerned a soldier named Daniel Jones who, the Court said, had recently been convicted of the 'manslaughter' of a fellow soldier. Having sentenced Jones to be branded on the hand and banished for seven years, the Court had suspended execution of the sentence in light of the Orders in Council.[42] Counsellors were mystified: if Guernsey law recognised no distinction between types of homicide, why did the Court use the term 'manslaughter'? If all homicides attracted the death penalty, why was the sentence not capital? The Privy Council were in due course enlightened by a communication from Bailiff Edmund Andros who apprised them of the actual state of affairs, explaining that the Royal Court did not invariably inflict the death penalty for any and all sorts of homicide, but awarded lesser punishments according to the circumstances. This then prompted the Council to issue a further Order acknowledging that the original Orders had been made upon a misrepresentation, and restricting any future referrals to the Sovereign in Council to cases of capital punishment 'where the said Court shall think the Offender a fit object of His Majesty's Mercy, and no other'.[43] From this time onwards, Guernsey's law of homicide was to all practical purposes assimilated to that of England.

Between 1699 and 1764 only four further homicides involving adult victims came before the Court. In 1704, George Guille of the Castel was alleged to have murdered his uncle, but he escaped justice by fleeing the island;[44] in 1730, Françoise Litton was convicted of murdering her husband; in 1738, soldier Thomas Goff was convicted of murdering a fellow soldier;[45] and in 1753, Englishman John Kemp was accused of murdering a St Sampsons woman in her home. Of these, the Litton and Kemp cases are of particular interest, so we shall discuss them in detail.

[41] Royal Court to Privy Council, 13.11.1699, NA, PC 1/3190. The Court's letter was written in English.

[42] 12.9.1699, GG, *Crime*, vol. 6.

[43] O in C, 30.11.1699.

[44] 18.3.1704, 8.4.1704, GG, *Crime*, vol. 6.

[45] 28.3.1738, 13.5.1738, GG, *Crime*, vol. 11. Goff killed the soldier by stabbing him twice in the stomach in a guardroom fight. The Court deemed his actions intentional, and he was hanged without referral to the Privy Council.

On 14 October 1730, the Court ordered the detention of Françoise Litton (*née* Fontaine), a native of Normandy.[46] Her husband, Robert Litton, had recently died, and rumours were circulating that Françoise had poisoned him. The Court ordered an autopsy, and on 24 October, Mrs Litton was charged with deliberately killing her husband by putting arsenic or some other poison in his food. She denied the accusation but admitted that she had bought poison around the time her husband fell ill. She claimed that her purchase had been on behalf of her daughter-in-law who needed arsenic to kill rats.[47] This case presented the Court with major problems of proof. Under the 1670 *Ordonnance Criminelle de Saint-Germain-en-Laye*, which seems to have been used for guidance locally, four classic romano-canonical proofs were recognised as valid: confession; the testimony of two eye-witnesses; written documents; and conjectural proof.[48] None of these proofs were available in the Litton case. Two of Robert Litton's sons were willing to take the stand, but they were recused as witnesses on account of their relationship to the accused. Dr Darryl Ogier has remarked of the case that, a century earlier, Mrs Litton would have been tortured to secure a confession.[49] However, changes in public opinion denied the Court this option in 1730. In January 1731, the Royal Court decided to seek guidance from the Privy Council. The Council referred the matter to the English Attorney General, who replied – cautiously, and somewhat unhelpfully – four months later:

> It is hardly to be conceived that the Law of Normandy should be deficient in the Rules of Evidence for the proof of so heinous and detestable a crime, but if it were so, yet I apprehend that it would not be advisable for Your Majesty as Sovereign Legislator of Guernsey to make a new Law with a Retrospect to include the case

---

[46] The Litton case unfolds in entries dated 14.10.1730, 24.10.1730, 12.6.1731, 18.6.1731, GG, *Crime*, vol. 11. The case is also summarised in 'Judicial Proceedings', vol. XIII, pp. 183–94, Royal Court Library, IA and further details are contained in NA, SP 36/23/89.

[47] On 12 December 1730, the Royal Court passed an Ordinance enjoining shopkeepers to keep their supply of arsenic under lock and key, and only to sell it to persons known to them, or to persons accompanied by someone known to them.

[48] A. Esmein (tr, J. Simpson), *A History of Continental Criminal Procedure with Special Reference to France* (Boston, 1913), p. 256. Conjectural proof might be established where, for instance, two witnesses both saw a person leave a room with a bloody sword, then entered the room and found the still-warm body of someone killed with a sword.

[49] D.M. Ogier, *The Government and Law of Guernsey* (Guernsey, 2005; 2012 edn), p. 174.

now under consideration, which seems to be pointed at by one part of this representation.

The Attorney advised the Privy Council that the Court should be told

> to proceed to give their judgment thereupon, and that this application to Your Majesty (tho' preferred in a dutifull manner and with a good intention) is totally irregular, since Your Majesty cannot legally interpose in a cause there depending and not yet determined.[50]

Left thus to decide for themselves, the Court put aside their scruples as to romano-canonical niceties, found Mrs Litton guilty, and, on 12 June 1731, sentenced her to death. The King in Council was asked if he wished to exercise his prerogative of mercy, but no response was forthcoming. On 18 June 1731, the Court's sentence was confirmed, and a few days later Françoise Litton was hanged.

The case heralded a change in the Court's attitude to proof. Henceforward, the romano-canonical approach was increasingly eschewed in favour of the more flexible system used in England and Wales, where juries made convictions on the basis, not of rigid technical proofs, but on all admissible evidence, interpreted in the light of their own common sense. Darryl Ogier has seen this as a step towards the anglicisation of Guernsey's criminal justice system.[51] It certainly was, but it is also important to note that this was not inconsistent with contemporaneous developments in France, where courts were already convicting on partial proofs in non-capital cases, and where, by the mid-eighteenth century, the romano-canonical system remained in full effect only for the gravest crimes.[52]

The Kemp homicide case is also worth discussing, though for rather different reasons. John Kemp was a gunsmith, originally from Epping in Essex. He was arrested in March 1753 on suspicion of having murdered Mrs Judith Jehan (*née* Le Normand) at her home in St Sampsons, by striking her on the head with a hammer and cutting her throat.[53] Crime registers are silent

---

[50] P. Yorke to Privy Council, 30.4.1731, NA, SP 36/23/89. This was very different to the attitude displayed in the 'manslaughter' cases of the 1680s.

[51] Ogier, *Government and Law*, p. 174.

[52] The system of legal proofs was abolished altogether in 1791 (J.-M. Carbasse, *Histoire du Droit Pénal et de la Justice Criminelle* (2000; Paris, 2014 edn), pp. 255, 423, 438).

[53] The case spans the entries for 25.3.1753, 12.5.1753 and 19.5.1753, GG, *Crime*, vol. 13.

on a possible motive. Kemp pleaded not guilty, and chose Advocate Jean Hubert as his counsel. Possibly because evidence was proving hard to find, or perhaps due to the timing of the Easter vacation, there was a delay of several weeks in carrying the case through the Court. In the interim, John Kemp was kept in detention at Castle Cornet. In mid-May, Kemp unilaterally brought the case to an end by hanging himself in the prison with one of his garters. On the Saturday after Kemp's death, the Full Court ruled that his suicide was equivalent to a confession of guilt, and ordered that his body should the following Monday be dragged on a hurdle, with a noose around his neck, to a rocky outcrop on the east coast, there to be hanged in chains on a gibbet and left to decompose.[54] His property was to escheat to the Crown.

The Kemp case is of interest for two reasons. The first is that it was the only instance of gibbeting in the 250 years dealt with by this book. In previous centuries, gibbeting had not been uncommon; Thomas Le Marchant, writing in the mid-1600s, stated:

> aside from suffering the death penalty, corpses are sometimes deprived of burial in this island, and left to hang in chains until they fall into pieces … in order to serve as a terror and example to similar wrongdoers.[55]

In England, the gibbeting of hanged criminals continued sporadically until the 1830s,[56] but Kemp's was the last criminal corpse subjected to this practice in Guernsey.

A further point of interest elicited by the Kemp case is related to suicide. While John Kemp's gibbeting was more of a punishment for murder than for suicide, taking one's own life while in full possession of one's faculties was also regarded as a crime.[57] *L'Approbation* had unreservedly endorsed the chapter in Terrien which set out the punishment normally inflicted on persons found knowingly to have committed suicide: the victim's corpse was dragged through the streets to a burial place in unconsecrated ground, and all

---

[54] 19.5.1753, GG, *Crime*, vol. 13. The name of the rock was la Héronnière, near la Tonnelle in St Sampsons.

[55] Le Marchant, *Remarques et Animadversions*, 2, p. 173.

[56] V.A.C. Gatrell, *The Hanging Tree: Execution and the English People, 1770–1868* (Oxford, 1994), pp. 113, 268–9.

[57] This was also the case in much of Europe. For more detail, see S. Moore, 'The decriminalisation of suicide' (unpub. PhD thesis, London University, 2000), pp. 21–9.

his property was forfeited to the Crown.[58] In Guernsey, although this practice was uncommon (inquests finding mitigating factors such as temporary madness) it was still occasionally observed in seventeenth and eighteenth centuries.[59] Thus, after an inquest concluded that a soldier named William Shaw had knowingly taken his own life in May 1715, the Royal Court ordered the hangman to drag his body to the shore on a hurdle and bury it face down in the sand above the high water mark, his entire property to escheat to the Crown.[60]

Infanticide

In Guernsey, the killing of a newborn came under the general rubric of homicide, and 'infanticide' as such was never an offence in its own right. In a recent essay, Darryl Ogier has described an upsurge in prosecutions for this crime during the Presbyterian period, which he suggested might have been influenced by a French royal edict of February 1557 concerning concealment of pregnancy. This edict established the presumption that if a woman gave birth to a child later found dead without previously having revealed she was pregnant, she had probably killed it.[61] Infanticide was singled out for severe punishment by many European states at this period, and a similar statute against the offence was passed in England in 1624.[62] Historians have commented that, in this era of religious ferment and revival, such legislation was aimed as much against 'immoral' behaviour as against the killing of children.[63]

---

[58] Terrien, *Commentaires*, p. 481; Tramailler (ed.), *Approbation*, p. 23.
[59] Thomas Le Marchant went into detail on local lore and practice surrounding suicide in his *Remarques et Animadversions*, 2, pp. 176, 179.
[60] 26.5.1715, GG, *Crime*, vol. 7.
[61] D.M. Ogier, 'New-born child murder in Reformation Guernsey', in G. Dawes (ed.), *Commise 1204: Studies in the History and Law of Continental and Insular Normandy* (Guernsey, 2005), p. 139.
[62] The Act to Prevent the Destroying and Murdering of Bastard Children, which made premeditated infanticide a capital crime, and also established the same legal presumption as the French legislation, though with regard to unmarried mothers only.
[63] Beattie, *Crime and the Courts*, p. 113.

In the period from 1567 to the beginning of this study, ten women were executed in Guernsey for killing their infants. [64] This equated to roughly one per decade. In the period between 1680 and 1764, there was some abatement in severity. Although six women were brought before the Court for killing newborns, only three of them were found guilty of the full offence and hanged. The three women hanged for killing their babies were Marie Roze in 1685, Marie Sarre in 1688, and Catherine Des Landes in 1748. [65] Catherine Des Landes was the last woman in Guernsey to suffer the death penalty for killing her infant, although a man was hanged for killing his in the nineteenth century. [66] Catherine Des Landes was also the last woman to suffer the death penalty for any offence in Guernsey. The three other women accused of infanticide in the current period escaped hanging through a lack of direct evidence. They were found guilty only of concealing their pregnancies and given lighter punishments. [67] These were Rachel Moulin in 1727, Françoise Le Filliastre in 1756, and Judith Robin in 1758. [68]

All these women had characteristics in common, not least that they were young, unmarried, and living in someone else's household. Given these commonalities, we will look in detail at just one of the cases where the woman was hanged, and one where she was given a lesser sentence. To begin with the former: on 14 May 1694, the Court went to view the body of an infant found dead in la Grande Mare, a tract of water near the west coast. Witnesses at the scene declared that Marie Sarre had confessed to them that the infant was hers and that she had killed it. Marie was the unmarried daughter of Thomas Sarre, in whose house she lived. The Court ordered her immediate arrest and

---

[64] Dr Ogier found four such executions between 1567 and 1640 (Ogier, 'New-born child murder', pp. 142, 146–7). There were a further six between that date and 1679 (9.10.1650, 24.10.1656 (two women); 24.9.1658, GG, *Crime*, vol. 5; 18.3.1670, 8.4.1670, GG, *Crime*, vol. 6).

[65] 4.12.1685, 1.6.1694, GG, *Crime*, vol. 6; 7.5.1748, GG, *Crime*, vol. 13.

[66] The case of the man will be examined in Chapter 6.

[67] There was nothing in Terrien or local legislation making concealment a crime, and this verdict seems to have been based on the standard English practice where a birth had occurred in secret but no corpse, or no evidence of injury, was found.

[68] 27.4.1727, GG, *Crime*, vol. 10; 12.6.1756, 27.5.1758, GG, *Crime*, vol. 13. Two further cases of suspected infanticide were investigated in our period but came to nothing. Jane Brimble escaped from Guernsey before she could be brought to trial in 1763, and the case of Rachel Mollet was abandoned by the Court as unsubstantiated in 1764 (16.7.1763, 25.7.1763, 2.7.1764, GG, *Crime*, vol. 14).

detention in Castle Cornet. She was charged with having strangled the baby which she had conceived extra-maritally and to which she had given birth secretly and without help, hiding the body in her bed for two days, and finally disposing of it in la Grande Mare. A mere two weeks later, the Court found Marie guilty as charged and sentenced her to be hanged. The hanging was to be carried out immediately, without prior enquiry to the Privy Council as to mercy or reprieve.[69]

Plate 8. Hanging of Marie Sarre, 1694 [70]
By kind permission of HM Greffier

Françoise Le Filliastre, whose case occurred sixty years later, was fortunate enough to escape hanging. This was because the evidence against her was altogether more tenuous. Following reports in March 1756 that she had given birth to a baby which had never been seen, the Court ordered Françoise's arrest on suspicion of having killed it. The arrest of the putative father, Sr David Le Normand, with whom Françoise had been living, was also ordered.[71] Despite investigations, no trace of the infant was ever found. On 27 March, therefore, Françoise was charged not with having killed her baby, but with having concealed her pregnancy, having failed to prepare for the

---

[69] 14.5.1694, 1.6.1694, GG, *Crime*, vol. 6. Marie Roze and Catherine Des Landes were also hanged without prior reference to the Privy Council.
[70] 1.6.1694, GG, *Crime*, vol. 6. This drawing marks the register entry relating to Marie's execution. A number of such drawings (some contemporary, some clearly added at later dates) adorn the margins of crime registers until the mid-nineteenth century. They may have served as markers to locate particular crimes.
[71] It is possible, though not stated, that Françoise was Le Normand's servant.

baby's arrival and having failed to summon assistance in childbirth. David Le Normand was charged with removing the baby from the house and burying it in an unknown location. On 12 June 1756, both were found guilty as charged. Le Normand was fined 20 *livres tournois* (about £1 8s 8d), half of which was to go to the poor of St Sampsons. Françoise Le Filliastre was fined 100 *livres tournois* (£7 13s), and she was also ordered to perform what was termed *amende honorable* at the bar of the Court.[72] The use of this particular punishment with Françoise Le Filliastre created a precedent, for over the next eighty years, *amende honorable* was to become the standard punishment for concealment of pregnancy.

The verdict of concealment itself also became more common from this point, as presumptions of murder became less automatic and more women were given the benefit of the doubt. Attitudes in Guernsey were slowly changing. This mirrored parallel changes in both Britain and France, where a distinctly softer line towards women in such cases was also discernible from the mid-eighteenth century.[73]

Before leaving the subject of infanticide, a related case from 1758 represents what was perhaps the Royal Court's first punishment of abortion. On 2 May 1758, 24-year-old Judith Robin appeared before the Court accused of killing her illegitimate child. Judith declared that she had had a short-lived relationship with Michel De France the previous Christmas, after which she became pregnant. She however told the Court that her pregnancy had lasted only five months, for two of which she had lain ill in bed and consumed nothing but water. Continuing her narrative, she said that, at the

---

[72] 21.3.1756, 27.3.1756, 12.6.1756, GG, *Crime*, vol. 13. *Amende honorable* was a variant of the nose-holding ceremony mentioned above in connection with defamation. Those required to perform it were obliged to kneel barefoot at the bar of the Court dressed only in an undershirt, and crave forgiveness for their crime from God and from justice while holding a lighted candle. Originally an ecclesiastical punishment, it was widely used as a secular judicial punishment in *ancien régime* France. The 1670 *Ordonnance Criminelle de Saint-Germain-en-Laye* had set out the ritual in detail (Carbasse, *Histoire du Droit Pénal*, pp. 310–11). Darryl Ogier has reported the Court's use of *amende honorable* in the Calvinist period, but, in the century between the 1650s and 1750s, it was only used twice: in 1650, to punish the spreading of malicious rumours, and in 1716, to punish sedition (Ogier, *Reformation and Society*, p. 132; 6.11.1650, GG, *Crime*, vol. 5; 10.11.1716, GG, *Crime*, vol. 8).
[73] A.-M. Kilday, *A History of Infanticide in Britain, c.1600 to the Present* (Basingstoke, 2013), p. 7; N.W. Mogensen, 'Crimes and punishments in eighteenth-century France: the example of the pays d'Auge', *Social History*, 10 (1977), p. 351.

beginning of the sixth month, she had suffered a miscarriage while alone in her father's garden, and, showing the infant corpse to no one, had buried it on the spot. The Court ordered the infant's body to be exhumed and examined by doctors, as a result of which Judith was charged with having 'taken certain drugs or remedies aimed at the destruction of the child before birth'. She was found guilty of this charge and sentenced to three hours' exposure in the cage in the marketplace at St Peter Port.[74] As well as demonstrating the Court's flexibility in finding a 'crime' to fit the evidence, this also shows that 'remedies' against pregnancy were well known in eighteenth-century Guernsey, with the concomitant that many such cases may have been successfully 'cured' before ever reaching the stage of a trial.

Serious assault

At the beginning of our period, only two kinds of assault were routinely dealt with on indictment. The first were assaults perpetrated on civilians by soldiers and sailors. The second were assaults on the holders of public office in the performance of their duty. Thus, in June 1700, Corporal Charles Fitzpatrick was prosecuted on indictment for a vicious and unprovoked attack on Nicolas Le Pelley. Approaching Le Pelley from behind in the High Street, Fitzpatrick had struck him on the back of the head with his sword, slicing through his hat to the bone, and putting Le Pelley's life in danger for some weeks. This earned Corporal Fitzpatrick seven years' banishment, preceded by fifteen days on bread and water in *la basse fosse*.[75] The Court cracked down similarly hard on publican Robert Mack for throttling a Town Constable with his neckerchief in 1760. Mack was sentenced to 200 lashes of the cat o'nine tails, followed by six years' banishment.[76]

One type of serious interpersonal violence which was distinctly under-prosecuted in this period was domestic abuse. There was a widespread belief that a man had a right to chastise his wife, to which Guernsey fully subscribed. Terrien had restated a provision in *Le Grand Coutumier* allowing husbands to use 'reasonable' physical force against wives (as also children and

---

[74] 2.5.1758, 27.5.1758, GG, *Crime*, vol. 13. The punishment of caging will be described in detail later in this chapter.

[75] 1.6.1700, GG, *Crime*, vol. 6.

[76] 5.7.1760, GG, *Crime*, vol. 14.

servants) in a chapter endorsed by *L'Approbation*.[77] However, Guernsey's seventeenth- and eighteenth-century Courts seem to have regarded as 'reasonable' everything short of murder itself. In 1751, for example, William Warden was arrested for having beaten his wife so badly that her life was in peril. Two surgeons were sent to visit the woman and confirmed that she was in mortal danger as a result of heavy blows to her head, stomach, arms, and other parts of her body. In anticipation of her demise, Mrs Warden made a formal declaration that her husband was responsible for her injuries. When, however, the Court were informed a few days later that she was out of danger, William Warden was simply released, and no charges of any description were brought against him for the injuries he had clearly inflicted on his wife.[78] Indeed, not a single case of spousal violence was prosecuted in the entire period between 1680 and 1764. And even if attacks like William Warden's had been prosecuted, conviction would have been difficult, since, under Guernsey law, the testimony of wives against their husbands was not admissible in Court.[79]

Sexual crime

The eighty-five years covered here saw just three local trials for rape and one for attempted rape.[80] The Court's treatment of rape at this time was ostensibly governed by Terrien, who, in a chapter endorsed by *L'Approbation*, restated a provision in *Le Grand Coutumier* prescribing the death penalty for the forcible 'deflowering of a virgin', but cited a French legal decision of 1518 to the effect that men who raped females who had already 'abandoned themselves' might expect greater leniency.[81] The prime consideration here was not the harm done to the women themselves, but to the males who had property in them. Women who bestowed their favours freely did not generally belong to any

---

[77] Everard (tr), *Grand Coutumier*, pp. 346, 430–2; Terrien, *Commentaires*, pp. 16, 497; Tramailler (ed.), *Approbation*, p. 1.
[78] 17.6.1751, 22.6.1751, GG, *Crime*, vol. 14.
[79] *Second Report of the Commissioners Appointed to Inquire into the State of the Criminal Law in the Channel Islands: Guernsey* (London, 1848), pp. xxxi, 233.
[80] There were no trials for other forms of sexual assault.
[81] Everard (tr), *Grand Coutumier*, p. 282; Terrien, *Commentaires*, pp. 483–4; Tramailler (ed.), *Approbation*, p. 23.

man, so punishment for violating them need not be severe. The rape of unsullied daughters (or virtuous wives) deserved harsher retribution since this injured the interests of their fathers and husbands. All the assaults prosecuted in our period were reported by victims' male relatives rather than by victims themselves.

Although the punishment prescribed in Terrien was severe, standards of proof were also exacting. Not only did a woman have to prove actual penetration, she also had to demonstrate that it had been non-consensual, violent and resisted. This was made all the harder by the fact that Courts were all-male and tended to give the man in such cases the benefit of any doubt. This state of affairs at least partly accounts for the fact that there were no hangings of rapists in Guernsey between 1680 and 1764.

The first rape trial in our period was initiated on the report of a husband. In December 1699, Eléazar Blampied reported that his wife (whose Christian name was never mentioned) had been raped by soldier John Turner at the couple's home, which appears to have been a tavern or lodging house, with the assistance of two other soldiers. The words used in the register were straightforward – *violée* and *forcée*.[82] The rape had resulted in the miscarriage of the baby Mrs Blampied had been carrying. Turner was found guilty on 16 September the following year and sentenced to perpetual banishment (on pain of hanging if he returned), preceded by twelve lashes of the cat o'nine tails.[83] The two assisting soldiers were sentenced to the same punishment.[84]

The next case came to Court in the spring of 1712.[85] This concerned a six-year-old girl named Susanne Le Gallez, whom her father Jean Le Gallez alleged had been raped by soldier Robert Lewins. The charge was that Lewins had *cruellement violentée* the little girl *pour comettre Rapt sur son corps*. Susanne died a few days later from an infection caused by physical trauma. The child's death notwithstanding, the Court decided in July that there was insufficient proof to convict Lewins of rape. Nevertheless, because the testimony of

---

[82] 26.12.1699, GG, *Crime*, vol. 6.

[83] 16.9.1700, GG, *Crime*, vol. 6.

[84] 16.9.1700, GG, *Crime*, vol. 6. The Norman *Coutume*, as endorsed by Terrien and *L'Approbation*, prescribed that accomplices to a crime should be punished in the same fashion as those they abetted (Everard (tr), *Grand Coutumier*, p. 328; Terrien, *Commentaires*, p. 494; Tramailler (ed.), *Approbation*, p. 24).

[85] The relevant entries are 29.3.1712, 23.5.1712, 29.7.1712, GG, *Crime*, vol. 7.

several witnesses had aroused *de véhéments soupçons* in the mind of the Jurats, they sentenced the soldier to thirty-six lashes and perpetual banishment.[86]

The trial of sailor John Davis for the rape of Mrs Elizabeth Ollivier in 1758 had a similar outcome. Davis was accused of having intercepted Mrs Ollivier, who was pregnant, on the outskirts of town, pulling her into a field in order to commit *le crime de rapt sur sa personne*. Again, the lack of sufficient proof prevented a conviction, but again, *à raison des fortes et véhémentes présomptions et presque concluantes de lui*, Davis was banished for six years.[87]

The fourth and final case of our period took place in 1763. On this occasion, the charge was one of attempted rape. Lincolnshire man John Dawson had been in Guernsey for about two months and was lodging at a public house. In the spring of that year, the publican (a man by the name of Shaddock) reported that Dawson had attempted to rape his eleven-year-old daughter while she lay in bed beside her seven-year-old sister. Dawson confessed to having attempted sexual intercourse, although he sought to exculpate himself by claiming the child's consent and saying no violence was used. Dawson was treated remarkably leniently. On 9 July, he was sentenced to spend an hour in the pillory on market day, and thereafter to give security for his future good conduct or quit the island.[88]

There was not a single prosecution for sodomy during the entire period dealt with by this chapter. In England and Wales, sodomy was first criminalised by the 1533 Act for the Punishment of the Vice of Buggerie, which made both sodomy and bestiality liable to the death penalty. There was nothing on sodomy in Terrien, but neither was there anything on bestiality, and Guernsey's Court did occasionally prosecute offences of this nature. Darryl Ogier found three bestiality trials in the Presbyterian period, for which two men were hanged and one was banished.[89] Like myself in the later period, Dr Ogier did not find any trials for sodomy. There were two

---

[86] *Véhéments soupçons* (vehement suspicions) is a phrase which appears frequently in crime registers of this period. It was based on a French practice which had grown up in the fifteenth and sixteenth centuries to circumvent the romano-canonical law of proof, namely that, in the absence of full proof, an individual could be convicted with a lesser penalty if there were *de véhéments soupçons* of his guilt (Carbasse, *Histoire du Droit Pénal*, pp. 210–11). On this practice in relation to Guernsey, see also Warburton, *Treatise*, p. 127.

[87] 24.4.1758, GG, *Crime*, vol. 13; 27.5.1758, GG, *Crime*, vol. 14.

[88] 9.7.1763, GG, *Crime*, vol. 14.

[89] Ogier, *Reformation and Society,* p. 153.

more bestiality trials in the years covered here. Both perpetrators appear to have been soldiers. In 1680, John Hambleton was convicted on his own confession plus the testimony of one eye-witness, and sentenced to be whipped through the town and banished in perpetuity.[90] In 1707, Henry Batley was acquitted for lack of proof, but sentenced to eight days in *la basse fosse* for his 'foul and filthy language'.[91]

Property crime

Most of the property crime prosecuted on indictment between the 1680s and 1760s took the form of aggravated theft: typically, robbery with violence to persons or property; theft from a church; theft from a master or employer. Technically, however, there were no separate offences under the general heading of theft, which was entirely governed by custom.[92]

No case of aggravated theft was capitally punished in Guernsey during the years between 1680 and 1764 even though the death penalty had been used to punish theft in the past (and would be used again in the future). The standard punishment for a male who committed a serious theft in the early part of our period was whipping and ear-cropping, followed by banishment. Thus, in 1686, domestic servant Pierre Cadet was sentenced to thirty lashes, amputation of the right ear, and perpetual banishment for stealing a chest containing 50 *écus* (about £16 10s) from his master.[93] In the 1750s and 1760s, ear-cropping became rarer (though it continued sporadically till the end of the century), periods of banishment became shorter, and the corporal element of the punishment became more severe. In 1763, William Letocq of the Castel was sentenced to 100 lashes and three years' banishment for breaking into farm premises and stealing a quantity of barley.[94]

---

[90] 30.10.1680, GG, *Crime*, vol. 6.

[91] 21.6.1707, GG, *Crime*, vol. 7.

[92] Terrien's only contribution to the subject was the inclusion of a royal Ordinance making theft by ambush or forced entry punishable by breaking on the wheel, but *L'Approbation* neither accepted nor rejected this chapter, commenting only that hanging and burning were Guernsey's sole capital punishments (Terrien, *Commentaires*, pp. 477–8; Tramailler (ed.), *Approbation*, p. 23).

[93] 5.6.1686, GG, *Crime*, vol. 6.

[94] 23.10.1763, GG, *Crime*, vol. 14

In Guernsey as elsewhere, the vast majority of aggravated thefts were committed by males. Only one female was tried for theft on indictment in each of our sample quinquennia. The woman who suffered the harshest punishment for an aggravated theft in our period was Rebecca Le Pettevin. She was tried in 1699 for having stolen two pigs from Sr Jean Guille of the Rohais and two shrouds and a cloth from Castel Church. Her punishment was exemplary (chiefly because theft from a church was considered sacrilegious): seventy-two lashes (to be administered in two instalments) and perpetual banishment, on pain of hanging should she return.[95]

Miscellaneous serious offences

Counterfeiting

Counterfeiting (also known as coining) was one of the three crimes of which the punishment – though not the cognizance – was reserved to the Crown by the fifteenth-century *Précepte d'Assise*.[96] In the period dealt with here, it was punished capitally in both England and France, since offences against the monarch's coin were regarded as treason.[97] Guernsey, and the other Channel Islands, were however in an anomalous position as regarded counterfeiting because their circulating medium was not the coin of the realm with which they were politically associated. Jerseyman Philippe Le Geyt, writing in the late seventeenth century, observed that, in England, counterfeiters of foreign (as opposed to English) coin were not capitally punished, because they were guilty only of 'misprision' of treason, i.e., a serious offence falling short of full treason. Jersey, Le Geyt continued, was different: given that French coin had been the local circulatory medium 'since time immemorial', its falsification

---

[95] 11.3.1699, GG, *Crime*, vol. 6. Note that, following French practice (Carbasse, *Histoire du Droit Pénal*, p. 393), Guernsey's Court considered multiple offences collectively rather than singly at this period, each contributing to the severity of the penalty.

[96] H. De Sausmarez, 'Guernsey's Précepte d'Assise of 1441: translation and notes', *Jersey & Guernsey Law Review* (June 2008).

[97] Terrien addressed the matter in these terms in chapter 7 of Book XII, which was endorsed by *L'Approbation* (Terrien, *Commentaires*, p. 468; Tramailler (ed.), *Approbation*, p. 23).

was just as culpable as that of English coins in England and also deserved the death penalty.[98]

A similar attitude pertained in Guernsey. In the autumn of 1699, the Royal Court tried soldiers John Richards, William Cockley and John Campbell for making and uttering false French *demi-couronnes*.[99] The Court found all three men guilty, but, as instructed by *Le Précepte d'Assise*, stopped short of sentencing them. Instead they sent copies of trial documents to London so that the Sovereign in Council could determine the sentence. After due consideration, the Privy Council ordered the discharge of Campbell and Cockley, but the execution of John Richards.[100] The Court complied, and the unfortunate Richards was hanged the following January.[101] This was the only instance of capital punishment other than for homicide in the period 1680–1764. It is ironic that it was ordered by the English Privy Council in respect not only of the coin of a rival realm, but of an Englishman serving in the English army.

Sedition

In the reign of the Catholic King James II, a number of allegations of sedition were made to the Court by the island's military commander, Captain Edward Scott (who was probably a Catholic himself).[102] However, given Guernsey's very recent Presbyterianism, these allegations were received less than enthusiastically. In 1687, Jacques Hattenville was acquitted for lack of proof, and brothers Jean and George Blondel were banished for just one year.[103]

After the accession of the Protestant monarchs William and Mary in 1689, the Court tackled allegations of sedition with rather more energy. In 1707, at the height of the War of the Spanish Succession, they interpreted statements made by soldier Thomas White as potentially treacherous and referred his case to the Privy Council. Three witnesses had testified to having

---

[98] Le Geyt, *Manuscrits*, 3, pp. 462–3.

[99] 23.9.1699, GG, *Crime*, vol. 6.

[100] O in C, 21.12.1699.

[101] 15.1.1700, GG, *Crime*, vol. 6.

[102] Scott seems to have been standing in for the Lieutenant Governor, Colonel John Legge, during a period of absence.

[103] 3.12.1687, 7.12.1687, 12.12.1687, GG, *Crime*, vol. 6.

heard White inveigh against Queen Anne and the English army while drinking in Thomas Cowling's tavern in St Peter Port. Flourishing his rosary, White had apparently said 'God damn the Queen', expressed a desire to join the French army, and declared that he wished to join battle with English forces on Salisbury Plain. Having found White guilty, the Court were uncertain whether or not to pronounce sentence, since treason was one of the crimes they were debarred from sentencing by the *Précepte d'Assise*. They therefore sent the trial documents to the Privy Council and requested their guidance. Evidently, the Council did not regard the matter in quite so grave a light as the Jurats, since, a few months later, a letter was received informing them that White had been pardoned under the Royal Sign Manual and ordering his release.[104]

In 1716, in a case involving a Frenchman, the Royal Court showed no such hesitation. Having found French sailor Jean Pageot guilty of calling King George I a 'bastard' and uttering other 'scandalous and defamatory words against the sacred person of our Sovereign', they sentenced Pageot to perform *amende honorable* at the bar of the Court, followed by a spell in the cage until sunset, then eight days on bread and water in *la basse fosse*, the whole topped off with five years' banishment.[105]

Prosecutions for sedition continued sporadically between the 1720s and 1740s, but with progressively lighter punishments. One of the last cases of sedition prosecuted in our period occurred in 1755, when Irishman Andrew Macnamara was reported to the authorities for toasting the Pretender's health in Frecker's public house: 'Here is Charley Stewart's health and prosperity to the family of the Stewarts, wishing they may soon return to England'. In this instance, the Jurats merely sentenced Macnamara to ask George II's pardon on bended knee at the bar of the Court, and to pay the costs of his trial.[106]

---

[104] 25.10.1707, 3.10.1709, GG, *Crime*, vol. 7; Add Ch 76094, British Library.
[105] 27.10.1716, 10.11.1716, GG, *Crime*, vol. 8. The Court were interpreting the concept of sedition/*lèse-majesté* broadly, since Pageot, as a Frenchman, would have had no allegiance to the British monarch.
[106] 9.8.1755, GG, *Crime*, vol. 13.

Perjury

In chapter 19 of Book XII, Terrien reproduced an Ordinance of François I to the effect that persons convicted of falsification, perjury and subornation should incur the death penalty. *L'Approbation* endorsed the chapter with the note that, in Guernsey, 'falsifiers … perjurers and suborners are punished at the discretion of justice according to the gravity of the offence'.[107] Between 1680 and 1764, the Court dealt with only two forms of perjury, for neither of which offenders suffered the death penalty. The most common form was lying under oath during trials at the Royal Court. In minor cases, the penalty was a small fine, often complemented with the performance of *amende honorable*. In more serious cases, the punishment was harsher. In 1743, Sr Jean De Garis was sentenced to seven years' banishment as well as *amende honorable* for giving false testimony during a trial in which the accused might have incurred capital punishment.[108]

The second form of perjury dealt with by the Court comprised lying under oath to bodies and personages other than the Court itself. A particularly interesting case occurred in 1758, when Guernsey's Anglican Dean reported Englishman Francis Lipthorne for having falsely sworn that he was free to marry Mary Howard, when he was already married to another woman. The marriage appears to have gone ahead. Lipthorne was charged with perjury and ordered to be detained in Castle Cornet. However, he broke out of the Castle and escaped from the island before his trial could be completed.[109] The real interest in this case lies not in its being a prosecution for perjury but a prosecution for bigamy in the guise of perjury. It was in fact the Royal Court's first attempt at prosecuting bigamy criminally. Others were to follow later, by less indirect means.

---

[107] Terrien, *Commentaires*, p. 490; Tramailler (ed.), *Approbation*, p. 24. Subornation is defined as procuring another to swear falsely.
[108] 29.10.1743, GG, *Crime*, vol. 12. This trial, for highway robbery, was ultimately aborted, as the accused escaped from Guernsey mid-way through proceedings.
[109] 15.7.1758, 21.10.1758, GG, *Crime*, vol. 14.

Libel

As noted above, both spoken and written defamation were usually regarded as private matters and dealt with as *causes en adjonction*. There was, however, an important exception. In England, instances of libel (usually of a political nature) had begun to be prosecuted as crimes in the early 1600s.[110] Terrien had nothing to say on this subject, but the Royal Court, perhaps taking its lead from English practice, had by the eighteenth century arrogated to itself the right to prosecute certain libels as crimes. The libels in question invariably took the form of written slurs upon the Court itself, or upon individual Court members, in the exercise of their functions. Thus, in October 1740, the Court prosecuted Anthoine Salmon for publishing a letter containing defamatory statements against the Jurats and Law Officers, and, finding him guilty, sentenced him to one hour in the pillory followed by seven years' banishment. The Law Officers justified their prosecution of Salmon (who had been held at the Castle throughout the three-month summer recess) on the basis that the publication of such material 'tended to abase the authority which was reposed in the Court'.[111] This was the only type of libel which was publicly prosecuted at this period.

Prostitution

Rising numbers of soldiers and sailors in St Peter Port from the 1680s stimulated the demand for prostitution, and there appears to have been no shortage of women to supply it. At this period, prostitution does not seem to have been carried on in any organised way, but by freelancers operating from shared lodgings or public houses. Women who lived in this way were treated harshly by the Court. They were usually charged under the Court's general jurisdiction with fornication (*paillardize*) or living a life of debauchery and scandal (*une vie débauchée et scandaleuse*).[112] Often, these women were brought to Court in batches by the Town Constables, as Marie Havillant,

---

[110] Plucknett, *History of the Common Law*, pp. 488–96.
[111] 16.6.1740, 25.10.1740, GG, *Crime*, vol. 12.
[112] The Court had issued Ordinances proscribing fornication in the Calvinist era, but these were not used to punish prostitutes in our period.

Rachel Marchant, Christine Damy and Catherine Kanis, who were convicted together in the spring of 1683. The first two were sentenced to be whipped through the town; the last two were sentenced to seven years' banishment.[113]

Occasionally, publicans and others who hosted the prostitutes were also brought before the Court. In 1715, Thomas Clogs and his wife were convicted of keeping a 'scandalous and dissolute house'. Both were sentenced to eight days on bread and water in *la basse fosse*, to be followed immediately by seven years' banishment.[114]

Although prosecutions for keeping disorderly houses persisted, prosecutions for fornication by and large disappeared from crime registers after the early 1740s. In 1742, the parish of St Peter Port opened a workhouse, known as the Town Hospital. From this point onwards, detention in the workhouse became the parochial authorities' preferred method of managing prostitution.[115]

'Witchcraft' (as fraud on the credulous)

The last serious offence we shall examine here is that of witchcraft. Terrien made no comments on this subject – which was surprising, given that the whole of western Europe had been preoccupied with witch-hunting when he published his *Commentaires* in 1574.[116] Guernsey had itself been drawn into the witch craze. In the absence of any legislation, the Royal Court had held 116 witch trials between 1563 and 1650, of which an astonishing forty-six had resulted in execution and forty-one in banishment.[117]

---

[113] 10.3.1683, 17.3.1683, 31.3.1683, GG, *Crime*, vol. 6.

[114] 29.3.1715, GG, *Crime*, vol. 7.

[115] R.-M. Crossan, *Poverty and Welfare in Guernsey, 1560–2015* (Woodbridge, 2015), p. 197.

[116] The nearest thing to this subject Terrien contained was a piece of sixteenth-century legislation expelling gypsies from France and banning the publication of certain almanacs containing astrological forecasts; however, this chapter was rejected by *L'Approbation* (Terrien, *Commentaires*, pp. 476–7; Tramailler (ed.), *Approbation*, p. 23).

[117] M. McGuiness, 'The Guernsey witchcraft trials of 1617, the case of Collete Becquet', *Current Legal Issues*, 2 (1999), p. 624, cited in D.M. Ogier, 'Glimpses of the obscure: the witch trials of the Channel Islands', in A. McShane & G. Walker (eds), *The Extraordinary and the Everyday in Early Modern England* (Basingstoke, 2010), p. 188.

By the opening of our period, however, attitudes had begun to change. In France, an edict issued by Louis XIV in 1682 prohibited any further witch trials.[118] In England, the 1735 Witchcraft Act repealed all previous anti-witch legislation and made it illegal for anyone to claim that he or she had supernatural powers.[119] This statute marked the transition to modern judicial understandings of 'witchcraft', since its purpose was not to punish so-called 'witches' but to protect the credulous from fraudsters claiming occult powers.

Guernsey's population long remained a prey to self-proclaimed *sorciers* and *sorcières*, and notwithstanding the continued absence of any legislation, prosecutions of such people occurred sporadically throughout the period dealt with by this chapter. In 1724, for example, Anne Mouton was sentenced to seven years' banishment preceded by thirty lashes for purporting to foretell the future.[120] Six of Anne's lashes were to be administered outside the courthouse, twelve in front of the house where she lived, and twelve in front of the cage. Her sister Marie, convicted of the same crime, was sentenced to seven years' banishment, as also to accompany Anne through the streets, watching as she received her lashes.[121] Prosecutions such as these continued into the twentieth century, and will be addressed again in Parts II and III.

Summary prosecutions

In the period between 1680 and 1764, offences dealt with summarily by the Court formed a surprisingly small proportion of criminal cases. Analysis of our five sample quinquennia shows that they comprised about one-tenth of the Court's criminal business, amounting only to five or six cases per year. About a quarter of these prosecutions were for minor assaults, another quarter were for trivial thefts, and the remaining half were for miscellaneous offences such as misbehaviour in Court, failure to assist a Constable, public drunkenness and disorderly conduct (the last two accounting for only a small fraction of summary prosecutions). The usual punishment for an offence

---

[118] B. Garnot, *Crime et Justice aux XVIIe et XVIIIe Siècles* (Paris, 2000), p. 40.
[119] C. Emsley, *Crime and Society in England, 1750–1900* (1987; Harlow, 1996 edn), p. 5.
[120] The Jurats' harshness was increased by the fact, mentioned in the charge, that Anne also been living out of wedlock with a soldier.
[121] 25.4.1724, 30.5.1724, GG, *Crime*, vol. 10.

dealt with summarily in this period was a fine, although the Court might also impose short periods of detention in *la basse fosse*.

Minor assaults were regarded essentially as private matters, and the Court did not often trouble itself to prosecute them unless as *causes en adjonction*. From time to time, however, an incident might occur which the Court felt impelled to prosecute publicly as an example to others. One such case occurred in 1700, when, during Sunday service in the Town Church, an altercation between Marie Carey and Marthe Tramailler led to Marie violently expelling Marthe from a pew, only to be seized by her neckerchief and dragged out of the pew by Marthe's father, Sr William Tramailler. Marie Carey was fined 3 *lives tournois* (about 4s 4d) and William Tramailler 5 *livres tournois* (7s 2d), to be paid to the poor of the parish.[122]

In many ways, petty theft was also regarded by Guernsey's authorities as a private matter, and there was no effort proactively to detect and punish it. In such cases, the onus was almost entirely on the victim to bring his case to the Law Officers, and relatively few appear to have done so. Punishments for trivial thefts usually took the form of a fine, divided between the victim and *le Fisc*, together with an order to restore the stolen item.[123] When, for example, Thomas Le Filastre was summarily prosecuted for stealing cider from Abraham Le Lacheur in 1683, he was sentenced to return the cider, and to pay 3 *livres tournois* (4s 4d) to Le Lacheur and 18 *sols* (1s 9d) to the Crown.[124]

The small number of summary prosecutions for drunkenness and/or disorderly behaviour in our period almost all concerned soldiers and sailors. In 1742, a naval lieutenant was punished with an exemplary fine of 80 *livres tournois* (£5 14s 4d) for his and his crew's bad behaviour at Margueritte Touzel's public house.[125] In 1747, a number of foreign sailors were fined for creating a disturbance at a tavern belonging to James Dyer.[126]

---

[122] 15.6.1700, GG, *Crime*, vol. 6.
[123] Terrien noted that that it was possible in Normandy to institute a civil action for the return of a stolen item without first having the theft prosecuted criminally. *L'Approbation* endorsed the chapter concerned, but Thomas Le Marchant commented that a purely civil action in such cases was '*contre le style et pratique*' of Guernsey's Court (Terrien, *Commentaires*, p. 257; Tramailler (ed.), *Approbation*, p. 17; Le Marchant, *Remarques et Animadversions*, 1, p. 299).
[124] 3.11.1683, GG, *Crime*, vol. 6.
[125] 18.10. 1742, 19.10.1742, GG, *Crime*, vol. 12.
[126] 5.12.1747, GG, *Crime*, vol. 12.

In contrast to soldiers and sailors, drunken and disorderly locals scarcely figured in crime registers at all. These all seem to have been dealt with extra-judicially, with Constables using their peremptory powers to confine them in the parish stocks, or, in St Peter Port's case, in the lock-up next to the cage.[127] The last Ordinance relating to parochial stocks was issued in 1704. It instructed all parishes to renew their stocks and equip them with iron chains and padlocks, specifically so that Constables could use them to confine drunkards, the 'vicious' and the 'scandalous'.[128]

Punishments

Over the five quinquennia sampled for this chapter, the commonest mode of punishment was the fine. This reflected the predominance across the period of prosecutions under Ordinances, as also of semi-civil actions such as *causes en adjonction*, all of which could only be punished by fines. For purely criminal offences, a wider range of punishments was available: the death penalty, whipping and other corporal punishments, banishment, and imprisonment. In the following paragraphs, the mode and incidence of each of these will be examined in turn.[129]

Capital punishment

In the period dealt with here, hanging was Guernsey's sole mode of capital punishment. A total of six hangings took place in the island between 1680 and 1764, four of women and two of men (five were for murder and one for counterfeiting). In principle, all capital and corporal sentences were to be carried out on the day they were pronounced. In practice, hangings were

---

[127] This lock-up is mentioned in 10.5.1717, GG, *Crime*, vol. 8.

[128] Ord, 17.1.1704. The Ordinance specified that these stocks were to be paid for from church funds and situated in parish churchyards. It was objected to by the ecclesiastical court, which forbade churchwardens from paying for the stocks and banned them from church property (19.4.1704, 24.4.1704, 26.4.1704, IA, AQ 008/01). It is not known whether they were erected elsewhere.

[129] *Amende honorable* was also used as a punishment, but having been examined elsewhere, it will be omitted from consideration here.

deferred until the following Friday, so that a clergyman could prepare the prisoner for death.[130] Throughout the period dealt with here, executions took place on a piece of uncultivated Crown land in the parish of St Andrews.[131] The *Bordiers*, Sergeant, Prévôt, Greffier and Law Officers were obliged to accompany the condemned man on his journey from the gaol to the gallows, and to remain in attendance while the sentence was carried out.[132]

Public hangings everywhere attracted large crowds. They were intended to do so, in order to demonstrate that justice had been done and to serve as an object lesson to potential malfeasors. Philippe Le Geyt recounted that, in Jersey, schoolmasters closed their schools on execution days and brought their pupils to watch the execution.[133] Vic Gatrell has characterised eighteenth-century English hangings as 'plebeian festivals'.[134] A drawing from one of Guernsey's crime registers, reproduced below, gives an impression of the crowds expected at a hanging.

Plate 9. Crowds at an execution[135]
By kind permission of HM Greffier

---

[130] Warburton, *Treatise*, p. 126. On occasions when cases thought deserving of mercy were referred to the Privy Council, the interval could be much longer.

[131] The site was just off what is now Bailiff's Cross Road, near the crossroads with Rue du Monnaie and Rue des Truchots, on the Truchots side (F.C. Lukis, 'Reminiscences of Former Days in Connection with Guernsey', PL).

[132] Warburton, *Treatise*, pp. 127–8. This was also the case with corporal punishments.

[133] Le Geyt, *Manuscrits*, 3, p. 498.

[134] Gatrell, *Hanging Tree*, p. 590.

[135] 23.10.1802, GG, *Crime*, vol. 12.

The image depicts a simple post and yard, with no evidence of a platform or trap-door. In England, trap-doors were not routinely used until 1783, and each locality had its favoured method of ensuring a drop. In some parts of the country, the prisoner would be stood on a cart with the noose around his neck, and the cart would be driven away, leaving the person to swing. In other parts, the prisoner would ascend a ladder propped against the yard, and when the ladder was pulled away, he would similarly be left to swing.[136] In Jersey, the ladder method appears to have been preferred, and this was probably also the case in Guernsey.[137]

Corporal punishment

Guernsey had three main forms of corporal punishment during our period: exposure in the cage, exposure in the pillory, and whipping. On a small number of occasions, these punishments were complemented by ear-cropping or branding.

The cage was located in the island's marketplace, which in this period was at the southern end of the High Street, near the Town Church. Cages were also used in France and Britain. They could be of iron, wood, or simply of cane. It is known that a nineteenth-century Guernsey cage was made of wood, and it seems probable that the eighteenth-century one was also of this material. The cage was used for both men and women, particularly to punish offences with a 'moral' component. Exposure was invariably on market day (Saturday), when the prisoner would be kept in the cage for a set period of between one and four hours. Some prisoners were sentenced to more than one period of exposure, on successive market days.

The pillory was also located in the marketplace. Prior to the early 1760s, it was usually known as *le pilori* or *les collières* and appears to have consisted only of an upright pillar to which those undergoing punishment were attached by the neck.[138] In 1762, the Royal Court requested HM Receiver to pay for a new pillory as the old one had become too rotten to use.[139]

---

[136] Gatrell, *Hanging Tree*, pp. 51–3.
[137] Le Geyt, *Manuscrits*, 4, p. 208.
[138] *Pilori*, borrowed from Italian, meant simply a pole.
[139] 19.4.1762, GG, *Jugements, Ordonnances et Ordres du Conseil*, vol. 10.

Thereafter, this apparatus was generally referred to as *le carcan*, which was the usual French term for more sophisticated pillories with holes for hands and head. As with the cage, the pillory was used for offences with a 'moral' component, and exposure was for a set number of hours on market day. In both France and England, women as well as men were sentenced to the pillory. There is however no record in our period of any woman being sentenced to the pillory in Guernsey.

Whipping was also publicly administered, and used on women as well as men. The former were usually sentenced to fewer lashes than the latter, although the number increased for both sexes as the eighteenth century progressed.[140] Men would be stripped to the waist to undergo punishment; women, for the sake of decency, only had their shoulders exposed. No particular implement was specified, but drawings always depicted the cat o'nine tails. Some whippings were carried out entirely in the marketplace, but it was more common for prisoners to be paraded through the streets with their attendant phalanx of Court officials, and receive a set number of lashes at each of a number of prescribed stations. This would draw out the punishment, make it more of a spectacle, and maximise the number of people who saw it. Sometimes, the route might include the site at which the prisoner had committed his or her crime, but more often than not the spectacle followed a traditional itinerary. Exiting the courthouse door, the party stopped in the yard immediately in front of *la Cohue* for the administration of a few lashes; it then proceeded to the top of the High Street for a few more; from thence it moved on to the bottom of Fountain Street for the third instalment; and, finally, at *le lieu appelé le Parc* (the modern Park Street), the ordeal came to its climax: here the prisoner received his or her last and usually largest instalment of lashes, and was thereafter released to the care of friends who tended to his or her wounds. In 1738, this was the sequence followed by Elizabeth Havilland, who was sentenced to three lashes at each of the first three stations, followed by twelve at *le Parc* for having *mené une vie débauchée et scandaleuse*.[141]

---

[140] In earlier times, prisoners were often sentenced simply to be whipped until bloody (*à effusion de sang*), but from c.1700 a specific number of lashes was prescribed.

[141] 3.6.1738, GG, *Crime*, vol. 11.

Plate 10. Woman receiving a whipping, 1739 [142]
By kind permission of HM Greffier

Banishment

Banishment was a punishment long practised in Guernsey as well as other parts of Europe. It was essentially a means of ridding communities of undesirables in an era when long-term imprisonment was not an option. Terms of banishment in our period ranged from one year to perpetuity, with those sentenced to seven years and more suffering 'civil death' and forfeiting their property to the Crown. Prisoners had a choice of destination, with their passages paid for from Crown revenues. Frenchmen would presumably have chosen to return to France, and Englishmen to England. This would not have been an onerous prospect, especially for those whose property had not been confiscated. For native islanders, however, banishment was more daunting and dangerous. Once away from Guernsey, they were permanently severed from family, friends and acquaintances. If they chose England, they might find themselves in a place where they did not speak the language. If, on top of this, they had been stripped of their property, survival would be a problem – which might make further recourse to crime more likely. In this situation, banished persons might be tempted to return before the expiry of their term.

[142] 24.2.1739, GG, *Crime*, vol. 12.

The most severe sentences included a provision for such persons to be hanged if they came back, and none in our period did so. A few sentenced to lesser terms did however reappear, such as François Anderlot, who returned eight months into his banishment for theft in 1763. At this period, returning prematurely from banishment was not generally treated as a crime in itself, and prisoners were not usually given an extra punishment for doing so. Thus Anderlot was merely kept in custody until the master of the ship which brought him removed him again (on pain of losing a sum of money deposited with the Court).[143] In this case as in others, it was the ship's master who stood to suffer the greater penalty, though no banished persons were suffered to evade their sentence.

Imprisonment

In the period dealt with here, long-term imprisonment was not commonly used as a penal sanction anywhere in Europe. The idea of building large-scale prisons was not even contemplated before the end of the eighteenth century, and, in our period, such prisons as did exist were normally only used to detain individuals for debt, and to keep prisoners in custody during or pending a criminal trial. Nevertheless, many jurisdictions, particularly on the continent, did have *une basse fosse* ('black hole'), where criminals might be sent for a short, sharp shock. In Guernsey, sentences to *la basse fosse* were usually served on bread and water and did not normally exceed eight days. They were, however, comparatively rare.

What Guernsey did not have was a house of correction. Institutions of this kind, characterised by the compulsion on inmates to work for their keep, developed in various parts of Europe during the 1500s. The first such English institution was London's Bridewell, chartered in 1553 and originally intended for the destitute poor. In the late sixteenth century, Westminster began to pass statutes providing for the incarceration of petty offenders in these institutions, which subsequently became known as houses of correction. By 1630, a network of more than a hundred such houses covered the whole

---

[143] 5.6.1764, GG, *Crime*, vol. 14.

of England, and they played an important role in the penal system.[144] In Guernsey, Jurat Thomas De l'Isle made a bequest to the States in 1627 which he had intended to be used for the endowment of *une maison de correction*. For various reasons, however, the money was diverted to other purposes, and the house of correction was never built.[145] This omission does not appear to have caused problems in the era dealt with here, but it did have significant repercussions in later periods. These will be addressed in Part II.

Conclusion

Two general conclusions suggest themselves in respect of the Royal Court's handling of crime and punishment in the period from the 1680s to the 1760s. One concerns the intrinsic nature of Guernsey's criminal justice system. The other concerns the relationship between actual practice and the law as found in *L'Approbation*, Terrien's *Commentaires* (and, ultimately, *Le Grand Coutumier*).

Taking the former first, it is clear that Guernsey's criminal justice system in this period was more passive and responsive than it was proactive. Although the system recognised a duty to prosecute major crimes, this duty did not extend to tracking down and prosecuting all delinquent acts. Hence most of the Royal Court's criminal business was initiated by private parties and would never have come to judicial attention had not these parties taken it upon themselves to launch a formal action or make a complaint to the Law Officers. In many ways, the system functioned primarily as a dispute-resolution service, and only secondarily as a public enforcer of law and order. This was very much the pre-modern concept of legal order, and it was also the one envisaged in the medieval *Grand Coutumier*. The most obvious effect of this, as far as Guernsey between 1680 and 1764 was concerned, was the marked dearth of summary prosecutions.

Turning now to the relationship between the source texts of Guernsey law and actual practice. A twentieth-century student of the early-modern

---

[144] J. Innes, 'Prisons for the poor: English bridewells, 1555–1800', in F. Snyder & D. Hay (eds), *Labour, Law and Crime: An Historical Perspective* (London, 1987), pp. 42–122.
[145] Crossan, *Poverty and Welfare*, p. 51.

Channel Islands once commented of their Royal Courts that, although they were supposed to enforce the law 'as laid down in certain recognised text-books … in practice [the Courts] persisted in deciding cases according to what they thought right without regard to the letter of the code'.[146] This was less than fair. Guillaume Terrien's *Commentaires* (and *Le Grand Coutumier* before it) treated the subject of crime primarily from a procedural angle, so that there was no 'letter of the code', nor even a 'code' at all. At the very best – as far as substantive law was concerned – there were only guiding principles, so the relationship between textbooks and actual practice could scarcely be anything but a loose one. Moreover, in doing what it saw fit in individual cases (even finding crimes to fit the evidence), Guernsey's Court was only acting according to the principles its members might have observed in contemporary Normandy. *Ancien régime* France was generally short on substantive criminal law, and in the Norman *bailliage* courts, equity was continually applied alongside both the *Coutume* and existing royal laws 'to make judgments in which informed reason was brought to bear in default of (or even in spite of) the written law'.[147]

Up to the 1760s, therefore, the discretionary element in Guernsey's criminal practice was in no way out of step with its continental model. Nevertheless, Guernsey, France and, indeed, the whole of Europe were by then on the cusp of great change. The French *ancien régime*, on whose system local practices were partially based, had notably only three more decades to go, after which the country's criminal justice structures were comprehensively modernised. Guernsey's problems arguably began when its own society changed but its criminal justice system was not modernised. In Part II of this book, we will begin by investigating the nature of the changes Guernsey underwent in the eighty years between 1765 and 1844. Following this, we will discuss the personnel and organisation of the justice system in this period. We will then conclude with an analysis of the Court's *ad hoc* responses to the changing criminal landscape, and an examination of how these responses eventually led to the Royal Commission into Channel Island Criminal Law.

[146] A.J. Eagleston, *The Channel Islands under Tudor Government, 1485–1642* (Cambridge, 1949), pp. 81, 156–7.
[147] Z.A. Schneider, *The King's Bench: Bailiwick Magistrates and Local Governance in Normandy, 1670–1740* (Woodbridge, 2008), pp. 104–5. See also Carbasse, *Histoire du Droit Pénal*, pp. 241, 246, 250.

II
1765–1844: A Frolic of their Own

Map 4. Guernsey, 1814

From W. Berry, *The History of the Island of Guernsey* (London, 1815)

4

1765–1844: Background

In Guernsey, as elsewhere in the British Isles, the period between the 1760s and 1840s was characterised by significant population growth. From around 12,000 in 1728, the population rose to over 18,000 by 1800. By 1821, it stood at over 20,000 and by 1841 it had increased again to more than 26,000.[1] Much of the increase was generated by a rapidly growing St Peter Port. In 1728, this parish probably already accommodated about half the island's population. By 1841, with more than 15,000 residents, it accounted for 57 per cent of the total. At this point, St Peter Port (including its rural fringe) had a larger population than Durham or Gloucester (both c.14,150) and was similar in size to Canterbury (15,435).[2]

In 1765, Guernsey's economy had received a considerable fillip from the Isle of Man's eclipse as a smugglers' supply-base after its purchase by the British government.[3] The Isle of Man had hitherto been more important as an entrepôt for smugglers than Guernsey, but Guernsey found itself well-placed to step into Manx shoes, especially after the British government abandoned its attempt to establish a customs house in St Peter Port in 1767.[4] Deprived of their usual sources of contraband, British smugglers turned south in increasing numbers, and St Peter Port reached its zenith as an entrepôt in the last quarter of the century.[5] Ferdinand Tupper described St Peter Port

[1] For 1728 figures, see Chapter 1, nn. 25, 40; for 1800, Royal Court to William Stiles, 15.12.1800, GG, Royal Court General Letter Book (first series), vol. 1; for 1821, *Billet*, 15.9.1821; for 1841, 22.6.1841, GG, Royal Court General Letter Book (first series), vol. 5.

[2] Abstract of Areas, Houses and Persons, 1841 Census of Great Britain (accessed 20.5.2021 at http://www.visionofbritain.org.uk).

[3] A.G. Jamieson, 'The Channel Islands and smuggling, 1680–1850', in A.G. Jamieson (ed.), *A People of the Sea: The Maritime History of the Channel Islands* (London, 1986), p. 203.

[4] *Ibid.*, p. 207.

[5] G. Stevens Cox, *St Peter Port, 1680–1830: The History of an International Entrepôt* (Woodbridge, 1999), p. 23.

harbour in the 1790s as 'often crammed to the very mouth', with 'twenty or thirty vessels in the roadstead waiting to enter.'[6]

The expansion of the entrepôt greatly intensified St Peter Port's demand for labour, both skilled and unskilled, as well as for retailers, victuallers and other service-providers. Some of the demand was filled from the town's rural hinterland, but increasingly large numbers came from across the sea, most of them from south-west England.[7]

Another factor which impacted on Guernsey's economy was war. For more than twenty-five of the eighty years examined here, Britain was at war with France – during the American War of Independence between 1778 and 1783; the French Revolutionary War between 1793 and 1802; and the Napoleonic War between 1803 and 1814. These wars brought military personnel into the island in unprecedented numbers. Summing up in Victorian times, Ferdinand Tupper stated that 'upwards of 50,000 British troops were successively quartered in Guernsey alone from 1793 to 1814'.[8] In addition to this, there were periodic influxes of allied troops. In 1799/1800, Guernsey saw the arrival of about 6,000 Russian soldiers, who over-wintered in the island after suffering a defeat in the Low Countries.[9] In 1809, a contingent of Black Brunswickers spent a few months in the island.[10]

During the Napoleonic War, the military presence was complemented by a naval one, as Guernsey hosted a squadron of the Royal Navy. According to Ferdinand Tupper, this squadron was 'composed occasionally of some twenty pendants' [sic].[11] The number of sailors this represented would have depended on the size as well as the number of ships in the squadron. At peak periods, totals might have risen to around 1,000.[12]

---

[6] F.B. Tupper, *The History of Guernsey and its Bailiwick* (Guernsey, 1854), p. 439.

[7] Stevens Cox, *St Peter Port*, pp. 82–5.

[8] Tupper, *History of Guernsey*, p. 403. Large numbers were also quartered in Alderney.

[9] A. Day, 'A Russian army on Guernsey and Jersey', *The Review of the Guernsey Society* (Summer 1997), pp. 40–5.

[10] J. Duncan, *The History of Guernsey* (London, 1841), p. 179.

[11] Tupper, *History of Guernsey*, p. 397. 'Twenty pendants' probably represented the squadron at its largest; Alan Jamieson recorded a force of 'a dozen frigates, brigs and cutters' in 1803 (A.G. Jamieson, 'The Channel Islands and British maritime strategy, 1689–1945', in Jamieson (ed.), *People of the Sea*, p. 226).

[12] A sixth-rate naval frigate would have been crewed by about 150 men; brigs and cutters had smaller crews.

The presence of all these soldiers and sailors made a tremendous contribution to the revenues of Guernsey's retailers and victuallers, and the wars also gave Guernsey's shipowners an opportunity to participate in privateering. Some 235 letters of marque were issued in respect of Guernsey vessels between 1793 and 1801, and a further 602 between 1803 and 1814.[13] The Royal Court estimated the value of prizes taken by Guernsey privateers in the first period alone at around £900,000.[14]

Unsurprisingly, the wealth of St Peter Port's residents rose considerably in the half-century after 1765. In 1761, the aggregate value of property assessed for parish rates stood at £708,920, but by 1810, this figure had risen to £1,979,100.[15] The inflow of money generated considerable building work and slowly changed the fabric of the town. By 1775, the landward side of the harbour had acquired a new quay. By 1783, the collection of market stalls near the Town Church had been replaced by a paved marketplace in the former rectory garden, furnished on one side by covered *halles* for the butchers.[16] Both of these projects were largely privately funded, but from the 1790s onwards, parish funds were used to pave St Peter Port's lesser thoroughfares and provide public lamps.[17] The States also funded some major projects, including a new courthouse and prison, and the British government financed the construction of Fort George, a new garrison headquarters, built between 1780 and 1812. Finally, a wave of private house-building extended the town's built-up area to the west, north and south. The most extensive of these developments was the 'New Town', atop the escarpment to the west of St Peter Port, which was begun in 1792 and eventually comprised six streets containing churches, chapels and workshops as well as houses to suit a variety of budgets.[18]

---

[13] W.R. Meyer, 'The Channel Island privateers, 1793–1815', in Jamieson (ed.), *People of the Sea*, pp. 174–5.

[14] Royal Court to William Stiles, 15.12.1800, GG, Royal Court General Letter Book (first series), vol. 1

[15] IA, AQ 1003/01; AQ 1004/02.

[16] On these developments, see R. Hocart, *An Island Assembly: The Development of the States of Guernsey, 1700–1949* (Guernsey, 1988), pp. 5, 7.

[17] The register of Ordinances for the period 1787–1802 contains many authorisations for the paving of streets, as also one of 18.11.1797 providing for the erection of lamps at ratepayer expense (GG, *Ordonnances*, vol. 2).

[18] R. Hocart, 'The building of the New Town', *TSG*, 23 (1992), pp. 342–77.

Plate 11. St Peter Port in the 1790s
© The British Library Board, K.Top.55.63.b

In addition to these physical changes, the accumulation of wealth in late-eighteenth-century St Peter Port effected what Gregory Stevens Cox has called a 'consumer revolution' characterised by conspicuous acquisition and consumption.[19] Drapers, milliners and haberdashers opened shops offering the latest London fashions. Watchmakers and silversmiths opened new outlets for luxury goods. New leisure venues were also established where the well-heeled could show themselves off: the 'New Ground' at L'Hyvreuse, which was provided with gravel walks in the 1760s, and the Assembly Rooms, opened above the market *halles* in 1782, where dances were held for the native elite and their military and naval guests.[20]

The town's success also brought benefits to country parishioners. The growing demand for fresh produce boosted the incomes of farmers.[21] The urban building boom provided work for country stonemasons, carpenters, plasterers, glaziers, and other tradesmen. Even unskilled rurals found more outlets for their labour in the entrepôt and at sea. On top of all of this, a new quarrying industry was also starting up in the northern parishes of the Vale and St Sampsons, which contained important reserves of hard-wearing blue-grey granite useful for roadmaking. Small quantities of this had been exported to England from the late 1600s, mainly in the form of beach pebbles for street

---

[19] Stevens Cox, *St Peter Port*, pp. 60–1.

[20] *Ibid.*, pp. 119–20.

[21] R. Hocart, *The Country People of Guernsey and their Agriculture, 1640–1840* (Guernsey, 2016), pp. 160–3.

paving.[22] In the mid-1760s, the virtues of Guernsey granite were discovered in London, and the Royal Court received a request from Londoner John Gale for permission to open two quarries in the Vale for the production of paving stones.[23] An English agent, Mr Whitworth, was sent to Guernsey to oversee the work, and one of Guernsey's Jurats (perhaps Thomas Dobrée, known to have had interests in the stone trade) arranged with the French foreign minister for 150 experienced quarrymen to be dispatched from Normandy to quarry the granite.[24] In addition to these, skilled stone-cutters were sent over from England to make the paving stones.[25] Stone exports increased from a mere 568 tons in 1766 to a peak of 60,636 tons in 1773.[26] From the 1780s, the industry slipped into something of a lull, but this was not destined to be permanent. In the interim, it left the island with a considerably expanded contingent of immigrants.

So far, the account presented in this chapter has been one of steady economic progress. The positive trend was not however to continue uninterrupted. In the first two decades of the nineteenth century, the island experienced a series of setbacks which caused its economy to falter. The first of these, and perhaps the most serious, was the demise of the entrepôt. The initial blow came in 1803, when the introduction of the bonding system in the United Kingdom deprived St Peter Port of its role as a depository for dutiable goods destined for legal re-export.[27] Subsequent blows came in 1805 and 1807 after mounting revenue losses finally pushed Westminster to extend two anti-smuggling statutes to the Channel Islands, which deprived St Peter Port of its less respectable role as a smugglers' supply-base.[28]

[22] *Ibid.*, pp. 68–9.

[23] 30.7.1766, GG, *Jugements, Ordonnances et Ordres du Conseil*, vol. 10.

[24] Duc de Choiseul to Sir Stanier Porten, 26.8.1767, NA, SP 78/273/37. This was a period of peace between Britain and France.

[25] Tupper, *History of Guernsey*, p. 447.

[26] Hocart, *Country People*, p. 241.

[27] The bonding system was introduced by the 1803 Warehousing of Goods Act.

[28] In a report to the Treasury in 1800, a Customs Commissioner estimated that smuggling from Guernsey and Alderney injured the Revenue 'to the enormous amount of one million pounds per annum' (NA, T 64/153). The 1805 Smuggling Act banned the import into or export from the Islands of spirits, wines and tobacco in vessels of under 100 tons or in casks of less than 60 gallons or packages of under 450lb in weight. The 1807 Smuggling Act ordered that all vessels leaving the Islands were to obtain a customs clearance, and forbade vessels coming from the Islands to break bulk or alter cargo during their voyage (Jamieson, 'The Channel Islands and smuggling', p. 209).

With the very foundations of their trade removed from under them, many – though not all – of St Peter Port's leading shipowners and merchants withdrew from business, sold off their ships and warehouses, and invested the considerable proceeds in securities and real estate.[29] The minority who did not sell up continued to participate in privateering until the end of the Napoleonic War, and also became active in the 'licence trade', whereby permits for the exchange of essential commodities between Britain and France were issued by the British government from 1808, and for which St Peter Port became something of a base.[30]

Privateering and the licence trade were however insufficient to provide employment to all of St Peter Port's redundant entrepôt workers, with the result that many were compelled to leave. Emigrants included large numbers of native islanders. In 1806, 1807 and 1810 parties of Guernseymen left for North America, where they founded Guernsey County in Ohio and Guernsey Cove on Prince Edward Island.[31]

Major-General John Doyle, Lieutenant Governor between 1803 and 1816, helped to relieve unemployment in some measure by instigating infrastructure projects which were also militarily useful. Worried that the detached northern tip of Guernsey could be taken with comparative ease, Doyle persuaded the British government to fund the reclamation of the Braye du Valle in 1806. Once filled in, a military road was built over the former sea channel, and the costs of the project were recouped by selling the 300 reclaimed acres to private buyers.[32] The road over the former Braye was Guernsey's first proper metalled road. Doyle also instigated the building of Guernsey's second and third such roads in 1810, one between town and L'Erée, the other between town and Vazon, both points on the west coast vulnerable to enemy landing. These roads were partly funded by the British government and partly by the States.[33] Enthusiasm for road-building caught

---

[29] Duncan, *History of Guernsey*, p. 262.

[30] *Ibid.*, p. 261.

[31] A.G. Jamieson, 'The Channel Islands and overseas settlement, 1600–1900', in Jamieson (ed.), *People of the Sea*, pp. 281, 286.

[32] Hocart, *Country People*, p. 81.

[33] The new roads are clearly marked on Map 4 (at the beginning of this section), as is the infilled Braye du Valle.

on, and from 1812 onwards, the States instituted a road-building programme of their own.[34]

By these means, and also because the large garrison and naval squadron were still generating income, Guernsey's economy had kept going through the difficult period since 1803. However, a further shock awaited the island at the end of the Napoleonic War. No longer needed in peacetime, the naval squadron was withdrawn and the garrison was reduced to one regiment of between 200 and 300 soldiers.[35] The end of the war also put a final stop to privateering. All of this impacted seriously on the incomes of St Peter Port's retailers, victuallers and tradesmen, and it also cut the demand for produce from the countryside. Compounded with a harvest failure and food shortage in 1816/17, the economic reversal resulted in a second and more substantial wave of emigration. Between 1817 and 1819, some 1,310 people are known to have left Guernsey for North America, 792 on ships bound for Baltimore, 360 to Philadelphia, and the rest to Gaspé and Quebec.[36] In the dismal winter of 1818, a letter to a local newspaper contrasted the bustle of twenty years previously with today's empty warehouses, the 'tufts of grass' growing in the streets, and 'the heretofore strong and sturdy artisan [who] from want of employment … exhibits a miserable picture of meagre and squalid wretchedness'.[37]

These shocks notwithstanding, Guernsey's wealthy ex-merchants continued to live comfortably on their investment incomes, and their spending helped sustain the economy of both town and country through the worst of the downturn. From the early 1820s, the native *rentier* contingent were joined by British half-pay military and naval officers and others drawn by St Peter Port's growing reputation as a place where one might live 'genteelly' on a fixed income.[38] The presence of this relatively affluent and expanding class renewed the demand for goods and services, such that by the mid-1820s, the insular economy had substantially revived.

[34] Frederick Lukis, who lived between 1778 and 1871, informs us that, after this time, carriages, which had previously been unusable in rutted rural cart tracks, began gradually to make their appearance in Guernsey's countryside (F.C. Lukis, 'Reminiscences of Former Days in Connection with Guernsey', PL).

[35] The garrison strength remained at 200–300 for the rest of the period covered by this chapter.

[36] *Comet*, 21.9.1889.

[37] Letter from 'Amicus Sarniae', *Mercure de Guernesey*, 19.12.1818.

[38] Tupper, *History of Guernsey*, p. 432.

Recovery was assisted by a certain amount of pump-priming on the part of the States, which since 1814 had enjoyed a new income stream in the form of the *impôt*.[39] In 1818, the States purchased the marketplace previously built by private enterprise, and in 1822 opened a new covered meat market on the south-west side, later adding a new fish market.[40] Between 1825 and 1829, they rebuilt the island's Elizabethan grammar school.[41] In the late 1820s and 1830s, they funded improvements to major town streets and began installing underground sewers.[42] All these public works, together with the continued arrival of British *rentiers*, stimulated confidence on the part of private developers. Some 400 private houses were built in St Peter Port between 1819 and 1829, extending the suburbs to the west and south-west up Grange Road, Les Gravées, La Petite Marche, Mount Durand, and Mount Row.[43] These houses were complemented by new churches and chapels, as well as the Commercial Arcade, a privately built shopping centre in the heart of town, completed in the late 1830s.[44] St Peter Port also acquired a gasworks in 1830, after which gas was piped into town to light houses, churches and the principal streets.[45]

The post-war modernisation process continued with the introduction of up-to-date communications facilities. A scheduled steamship service to and from Southampton began in 1824, and by 1841 steamers were also serving the island from Weymouth, Plymouth and London.[46] The island's first regular omnibus service opened in 1837, with a horse-drawn bus plying three times daily between St Peter Port and St Sampsons (soon followed by much competition).[47]

Shorn of its role as an entrepôt, post-Napoleonic St Peter Port became a more purely residential town, while also developing its role as an administrative, retail, service and manufacturing centre for the whole island.

---

[39] See Introduction, p. 30.

[40] Hocart, *Island Assembly*, pp. 26, 173.

[41] For more on the rebuilding of Elizabeth College, see R.-M. Crossan, *The States and Secondary Education, 1560–1970* (Guernsey, 2016), pp. 9–12.

[42] Stevens Cox, *St Peter Port*, p. 137; G. Lenfestey, 'The development of public sewers in Guernsey, 1826–1966', *TSG*, 25 (2002), pp. 374–80.

[43] Stevens Cox, *St Peter Port*, p. 137. See also J. Jacob, *Annals of some of the British Norman Isles constituting the Bailiwick of Guernsey* (Paris, 1830), pp. 119–29.

[44] Stevens Cox, *St Peter Port*, pp. 127, 137.

[45] Anon., *The Stranger's Guide to the Islands of Guernsey and Jersey* (Guernsey, 1833), p. 100.

[46] Jacob, *Annals*, p. 436; L.L. Clarke, *Redstone's Guernsey Guide; or the Stranger's Companion for the Island of Guernsey* (Guernsey, 1841), pp. 132–3.

[47] W.J. Carman, *Channel Island Transport* (Guernsey, 1987), p. 8.

As well as the Royal Court and States, the town hosted the island's main post office and banks, law offices, shipping and insurance agents. It also housed the island's principal churches, assembly halls and libraries, as well as most of Guernsey's doctors and dentists. Its streets were lined with shops selling everything from baby clothes to pianos, as also, further out, with the workshops of cabinetmakers, upholsterers, clockmakers, tinsmiths, saddlers, coachbuilders and wheelwrights, all catering for the home market.

Plate 12. St Peter Port in the 1830s
Detail from 1832 Cochrane map, courtesy of the Priaulx Library

Another factor which contributed to Guernsey's economic revival in the 1820s and 1830s was the gradual resurgence of the shipping sector. Some of the shipowners who had not retired after the anti-smuggling Acts ventured into the South American carrying trade after the opening of Spanish and Portuguese colonies to foreign vessels. This trade mainly involved the transport of wines and spirits from Europe to Cuba, Brazil and Uruguay, followed by a return voyage with cargoes of coffee, sugar and animal hides.[48] In due course, this led to the shipowners' participation in the worldwide carrying trade. Even though the ships involved rarely called into Guernsey, they were Guernsey-owned and (largely) Guernsey-crewed. From 64 vessels in 1817, the fleet had grown to 134 vessels in 1841, by which time it was employing a workforce of 1,108.[49]

The revival of shipping stimulated the establishment of a local shipbuilding industry. From 1815, construction yards began to spring up along the east coast between St Peter Port and St Sampsons, producing ocean-going sailing vessels commissioned by Guernsey shipowners for use in long-distance trade.[50] At peak periods of construction, which included the years 1822–5 and 1836–42, this industry employed a local workforce in the region of 500.[51]

Quarrying also underwent a major revival in the post-Napoleonic period. The revival seems to have started in 1815, when Colonel John Lindsay acquired the lease of Herm and developed the island as a quarrying centre for whose stone he found important outlets in London.[52] The industry was further stimulated in the 1820s, when James McAdam, Surveyor to the Commission of Metropolis Roads, promoted the use of Guernsey stone for the new roadmaking process known as macadamisation.[53] In 1830, the firm of John Mowlem & Co. (which had been paving London's streets since 1823) acquired its first quarry in Guernsey, to be followed in due course by many

---

[48] Tupper, *History of Guernsey*, p. 444.

[49] *Comet*, 22.7.1858.

[50] E.W. Sharp, 'The shipbuilders of Guernsey', *TSG*, 27 (1970), p. 492.

[51] R.-M. Crossan, *Guernsey, 1814–1914: Migration and Modernisation* (Woodbridge, 2007), p. 24.

[52] Herm granite was used in the East and West India Docks, London Bridge, Blackfriars Bridge, Commercial Road, and Somerstown (S.K. Kellett-Smith, 'Quarrying and mining on Herm and Jethou', *TSG*, 17 (1961), p. 263).

[53] W.J. Reader, *Macadam* (London, 1980), pp. 77, 181–2, 185–6. James McAdam was the son of John McAdam who had invented macadamisation.

other major English quarrying firms.[54] Exports of Guernsey granite rose from a low point of 2,666 tons in 1810 to 82,752 tons in 1847.[55] The stone industry was highly manpower-intensive, so its revival was particularly welcomed for the employment opportunities it generated.

We saw earlier that the availability of employment had stimulated immigration to Guernsey in the second half of the eighteenth century. Some fifty years later, a second – and larger – wave of immigration was initiated by a similar circumstance. As in the earlier period, most post-Napoleonic immigrants came from south-west England. To begin with, they settled in town, where they worked as craftsmen, labourers and domestic servants. Here they were joined by a small contingent of traders and shopkeepers from Normandy. Later, with the growth of the quarrying industry, immigrants from England were also attracted to the Vale and St Sampsons. By 1851, first-generation English migrants formed over a third of St Peter Port's population and almost a quarter of that of the northern parishes.[56]

The impact of immigration on Guernsey's seven other country parishes was slight. Indeed, the pace of change was altogether slower here, with landownership patterns and ways of life almost unaltered since the previous period. Only two significant differences can be identified in the post-Napoleonic era. The first was that overseas emigration had opened up a new outlet for 'surplus' country parishioners, so far fewer of them moved to St Peter Port.[57] The second was that farmers who sold produce in town were forced to become more specialised. This was largely due to the French, who began exporting basic foodstuffs to Guernsey on a large scale after Waterloo.[58] As Guernsey farmers could not compete with the French on quantity or price, they were obliged henceforward to focus on quality, selling such items as fresh

[54] D. Lewer (ed.), *John Mowlem's Swanage Diary, 1845–1851* (Wincanton, 1990), pp. 18–19; P.J. Girard, 'Adolphus Bichard's reminiscences of the stone industry', *TSG*, 21 (1982), p. 206.

[55] T. Quayle, *General View of the Agriculture and Present State of the Islands on the Coast of Normandy subject to the Crown of Great Britain* (London, 1815), p. 329; NA, HO 98/88.

[56] Crossan, *Guernsey, 1814–1914*, pp. 71, 91–3, 122–3.

[57] In the 1851 census, natives of the country parishes comprised no more than 8 percent of the town parish's population (Crossan, *Guernsey, 1814–1914*, p. 209).

[58] A return of imports from 1847 showed that a wide array of basic comestibles were sourced from France, including poultry and livestock, fresh fruit and vegetables, butter, eggs, cider, and dried pulses (NA, HO 98/88).

eggs and dairy produce at premium prices.[59] In addition to this, the largest farmers were also exporting increasing amounts of produce to England, notably cauliflower and potatoes.[60] All of this helped the rural economy along, but it could by no means be described as booming. Tax returns for 1832 showed rural wealth lagging far behind that of the town. While St Peter Port's ratepayers owned £3,016,100 worth of property, those of the nine country parishes combined owned only £1,107,600.[61]

Turning now to less tangible matters. Religiously, linguistically, culturally and socially, the eighty years between 1765 and 1844 wrought a number of important changes. In terms of religion, the island became much more diverse. Its monolithic Anglicanism was first breached by the arrival of Quakerism in 1782, when Claude Gay, a Frenchman, founded a local congregation of Friends. Next to arrive was Methodism, brought to Guernsey in 1785 by missionaries from England and Jersey. Then came Roman Catholicism, reintroduced by *émigrés* fleeing the French Revolution in 1793. Congregationalism also gained a foothold from the end of the eighteenth century, and the Baptist denomination made its appearance in the early nineteenth century.[62]

Within Anglicanism itself there were also changes. Since the 1730s, Britain had seen the rise of the Evangelical movement, which, deriving its inspiration partly from Puritanism, was moralistic in outlook and concentrated on ethical themes.[63] One branch of the movement eventually crystallised into low-church Anglicanism, which, making its way to Guernsey, culminated in 1788 in the building of a proprietary church (Trinity Chapel) by a group of Evangelical Anglicans.[64]

Protestant Nonconformity spread most rapidly in the countryside, where it flourished on the roots of the old Calvinism. A French-speaking Wesleyan Methodist circuit was established at the turn of the nineteenth century which by 1840 had an active membership of over 1,000.[65] Francophone Baptist and

[59] Hocart, *Country People*, p. 201.

[60] *Ibid.*, 191–4.

[61] *The Guernsey and Jersey Magazine*, 1 (1836), p. 177.

[62] The arrival of all these denominations is recounted in Jacob, *Annals*, pp. 468–74.

[63] D.W. Bebbington, *Evangelicals in Modern Britain: A History from the 1730s to the 1980s* (London, 1989).

[64] Jacob, *Annals*, p. 134.

[65] M. Lelièvre, *Histoire du Méthodisme dans les Iles de la Manche, 1784–1884* (Paris, 1885), p. 430.

Independent congregations also saw strong growth in the countryside, and there was a rural Plymouth Brethren congregation from 1835.[66] In town, a smaller English-speaking Wesleyan circuit was established, many of whose members were immigrants. St Peter Port also acquired English-speaking congregations of Bible Christians from 1823 and Primitive Methodists from 1832.[67] Roman Catholicism also remained confined to town and restricted to non-natives. Jonathan Duncan, writing around 1840, stated that the Catholic contingent consisted mainly of French traders and seamen, soldiers from the garrison, and English and Irish genteel residents.[68] Between the 1790s and 1840s, these were served by a single chapel in a St Peter Port backstreet.

Linguistically, Guernsey saw far-reaching changes in our period. The presence of rising numbers of English people in St Peter Port from the 1760s increased town parishioners' familiarity with the English language. Semi-permanent Franco-British war from 1778 disrupted long-standing contacts with France, and reorientated the urban upper ranks more firmly towards England. From the late eighteenth century, commercial academies offering instruction in English began to proliferate in town, and growing numbers of better-off families sent their sons to boarding schools in England. As a result, the generation of upper-class townsmen who came to maturity in the 1820s and 1830s underwent a fundamental language shift. As a newspaper observed in 1835, 'the men of the last generation, whose vernacular tongue was the French, have been gradually gathered to their fathers, and their places filled up by a generation who have, for the most part, been nurtured and educated in the English language'.[69]

Further down the urban social scale, the process of anglicisation was given a powerful fillip in the post-Napoleonic period by the second wave of immigration from England. The majority of immigrants were of child-bearing age. Many arrived as couples or in family groups.[70] As early as 1839,

[66] T. Grass, *Two Centuries of Baptists in Guernsey: The Story of an Island Community* (Isle of Man, 2013), pp. 20–31; W.R. Chapman, *His Praise in the Islands* (1984; Guernsey, 1995 edn), p. 123.

[67] R.D. Moore, *Methodism in the Channel Islands* (London, 1952), pp. 86–90; Jacob, *Annals*, pp. 472–3. The Bible Christians also set up a small chapel in St Peters, but this does not appear to have lasted long (Duncan, *History of Guernsey*, p. 364).

[68] Duncan, *History of Guernsey*, p. 365.

[69] *Star*, 1.10.1835.

[70] Crossan, *Guernsey, 1814–1914*, pp. 78–80, 101–2.

according to a newspaper article, 61 per cent of pupils at St Peter Port's National School had English parents, compared with just 36 per cent whose parents were from Guernsey.[71] Three factors – the presence of large numbers of English-speaking immigrants; their production of large numbers of English-speaking children; and the reduction in *guernésiais*-speaking rural in-migrants to St Peter Port – soon brought about the same language shift among the urban lower orders as had earlier occurred among the elite. The *Comet* declared in 1848: 'a wonderful change has been effected during a quarter of a century in the town parish; the language of the people is no longer French, but English.'[72]

For the country parishes, it was more a case of indirect exposure to English. Immigrants to the country parishes were few in number (aside from the Vale and St Sampsons); however, rurals sold farm produce to English residents in the town market. At home, they encountered English residents on sightseeing excursions and leisure trips. The larger farmers who exported produce to England liaised with English shippers and buyers. Such contacts engendered a recognition on the part of rural parents that it was desirable for their children to learn English if they wished to get on, and in due course this stimulated a demand for instruction in the English language. Two private 'English day schools' were already operating in St Saviours by 1818.[73] By 1824, three of Guernsey's nine rural parish schools had begun to provide tuition in English, and by the 1840s, instruction in English came universally to be offered in all parish schools.[74] In 1847, the Reverend Daniel Dobrée, rector of the Forest and Torteval, was able to report that, at his own schools, as deep in the countryside as any in Guernsey, children 'at about twelve years of age, can almost invariably read English as well as they can French.'[75]

None of this however meant that Guernsey had completely lost touch with its francophone heritage. Rural children continued to speak *guernésiais* at home. Royal Court and States business continued to be conducted in French, and the native urban elite generally remained well-versed in that language.

---

[71] *Comet*, 14.2.1839.

[72] *Comet*, 28.12.1848.

[73] Digest of Parochial Returns made to the Select Committee on the Education of the Poor, Parliamentary Papers 1819 IX.

[74] Jacob, *Annals*, pp. 202–3; Crossan, *Guernsey, 1814–1914*, p. 257.

[75] *Second Report of the Commissioners Appointed to Inquire into the State of the Criminal Law in the Channel Islands: Guernsey* (London, 1848), p. 257.

The final subject we will examine here is social structure, which also underwent considerable change in our period, particularly in St Peter Port. Commercial success after 1765 brought a great increase in wealth, but it was unevenly spread. This uneven distribution both deepened the gulf between those at opposite ends of the social spectrum, and introduced hitherto unknown cleavages in its higher echelons. The late-eighteenth-century rise in St Peter Port's population seems primarily to have been due to a thickening of the lower social strata. This caused existing problems of poverty to grow in extent, and perhaps also in acuity. Labourers' wages were pitched at subsistence level, which meant that they were unable to accumulate cash reserves. In periods of unemployment or unusually high food prices, such families were at risk of hunger. Parochial relief was minimal, and the authorities' stock response in times of want was to procure and distribute emergency grain supplies. The frequency with which they did so in our period is indicative of the persistence of serious poverty, even at times when merchants and retailers appeared to be prospering.[76] The last such measure was passed in 1847, after the potato blight and poor harvest which affected all of western Europe in 1845–7.[77]

Higher up the social scale, St Peter Port's commercial success enriched a number of hitherto non-elite families. Within a short time, their increasing wealth unsettled the traditional elite, who responded by erecting barriers between themselves and the *parvenus*. One of their first initiatives was to lay claim to a superior title. Partly in order to distinguish themselves from English settlers, with whom they did not wish to share the title 'Mr', the native elite claimed the right to be designated *Ecuyer* or Esquire. The Royal Court formally accorded its own members this privilege in 1765, and within a few years most male members of the native elite were styling themselves thus.[78]

The traditional top tier drove the wedge in further by employing exclusionary tactics. These were at their most overt with regard to the Assembly Rooms, from which *nouveaux riches* and their families were

[76] The late 1760s and early 1770s saw a whole spate of food procurement measures, as did the years 1795, 1799/1800, 1811/12, and 1816/19 (Crossan, *Poverty and Welfare*, pp. 37, 56, 77, 104).

[77] Ord, 11.5.1847; *Star*, 14.5.1847.

[78] Stevens Cox, *St Peter Port*, p. 105; *Guernsey Merchants*, p. 98.

consistently blackballed.[79] Eventually, this gave rise to the labels 'Sixties' and 'Forties', which distinguished the sixty old-established families with admission to the Rooms and the forty upstart families whom they excluded.

By the 1820s, however, the so-called 'Forties' were becoming a force to be reckoned with. Most of them had remained in business after the 'Sixties' had retired in the post-smuggling period, and many now exceeded the 'Sixties' in wealth. To a certain extent, this was translated into political power. In 1822, in a contested Jurats' election, William Collings, a prosperous 'Forties' merchant, succeeded in having himself elected to the bench.[80] In this decade too, the 'Forties' infiltrated the Town Douzaine, and by the 1840s they completely dominated it.[81] This gave *nouveaux riches* an increased presence in the States after 1844 when a reform replaced the ten Constables' seats with fifteen Douzaine Deputies' seats, six of which were allocated to St Peter Port.[82]

Cumulatively, perhaps the greatest impact of changes between 1765 and 1844 was a certain loss of social cohesion. Pre-1765, islanders from all ranks and all parishes had by land large shared a common language, a common religion, a common culture, and even a common ancestry. This had smoothed the path of criminal justice in that islanders were imbued almost from birth with a sense of their own obligations and duties relative to those beneath and above them. Since the 1760s, however, Guernsey's increasing intercourse with the outside world had destroyed this homogeneity and replaced it with a host of ethnically, linguistically and culturally different sub-communities. Replacing old certainties with a degree of wariness and distrust, this radically transformed the Court's criminal practice. Over the next two chapters we will analyse the haphazard and often singular manner in which this transformation unfolded.

---

[79] By the Rooms' constitution, admission was confined to the elite families who had originally subscribed to their construction, and to the garrison officers with whom they liked to socialise. New subscribers were not admitted unless their names were proposed by the Master of Ceremonies and approved by two-thirds of the subscribers (Jacob, *Annals*, p. 155).

[80] R. Hocart, 'Elections to the Royal Court of Guernsey, 1821–1844', *TSG*, 19 (1979), pp. 500–2.

[81] Crossan, *Guernsey, 1814–1914*, pp. 188, 284.

[82] O in C, 27.12.1844.

5

1765–1844: Personnel and Infrastructure

Personnel

Bailiffs

Six men served Guernsey as Bailiffs between 1765 and 1844: Samuel Bonamy, William Le Marchant, Robert Le Marchant, Peter De Havilland, Daniel De Lisle Brock, and John Guille.[1] All were from Guernsey's traditional elite and all had previously served as Jurats. Only one of them had any legal education. The average age at which they were appointed Bailiff was fifty-two, and the average age at which they retired (or died) sixty-seven. The two longest-serving Bailiffs were William Le Marchant and Daniel De Lisle Brock, who held the post for twenty-nine and twenty-one years respectively.

The first Bailiff of our period was Samuel Bonamy. He was elected a Jurat at the age of thirty-six in 1744 and served as Bailiff from 1758 until his death at sixty-two in 1770. Bonamy was from a family prominent in the island since the 1300s, which had previously provided the Royal Court with at least six Jurats and a Lieutenant Bailiff. During the eighteenth century, the Bonamy family were much involved in commerce and shipping.[2] Whilst Bailiff in the 1760s, Samuel Bonamy was involved in resistance to the imposition of a British customs house in Guernsey,[3] but, aside from this, his tenure was unremarkable. Bonamy never married and left no descendants, so that his

---

[1] Appendix 1.
[2] G. Stevens Cox, *The Guernsey Merchants and their World* (Guernsey, 2009), pp. 174–5.
[3] A.G. Jamieson, 'The Channel Islands and smuggling, 1680–1850', in A.G. Jamieson (ed.), *A People of the Sea: The Maritime History of the Channel Islands* (London, 1986), p. 207.

branch of the family became extinct at his death, and no more Bonamys served as Jurats or Bailiffs.[4]

Uneventfulness was not a characteristic of the tenure of Bonamy's successor, William Le Marchant. Le Marchant, whose family had long occupied a leading position in Guernsey, was elected a Jurat at the age of thirty-three in 1754. He served as Receiver between 1764 and 1766, and was appointed Bailiff at fifty in 1771, retiring aged seventy-nine in 1800 after nearly three decades in office. Le Marchant was a merchant and shipowner, importing wine from Spain and Portugal, dealing in brandy, and supplying the Royal Navy with alcohol during the Seven Years War.[5] While not lacking in ability or intelligence, he had some notable character defects. Perhaps the worst of these was that he found it difficult to work collegially and allowed his personal feelings to obtrude into official duties. His years as Bailiff were marred by disputes with other Court members, and in 1775–7 and again in 1795–6, these resulted in a hiatus in Court sittings and a suspension of justice. The 1770s episode was triggered by Le Marchant's attempts to monopolise power and resulted in ten of the Jurats resigning *en masse*, only six of whom eventually resumed their seats. The 1790s episode centred around Le Marchant's personal feud with Jurat Peter De Havilland. In the course of this episode – in what Richard Hocart described as 'the most reckless outrage of his career' – the Bailiff pulled a knife in Court and threatened to use it on the Prévôt (who happened to be De Havilland's brother). Le Marchant was in due course convicted of assaulting the Prévôt in the exercise of his duty, fined 300 *livres tournois* (about £21 8s 8d) and condemned to fifteen days' imprisonment, which he was allowed to serve at home because of his age (he was seventy-five at the time).[6] Such intra-Court warfare and interruptions to justice were never to be repeated, but they set a lasting seal on Le Marchant's reputation as Bailiff.[7]

When William Le Marchant retired from office in 1800, he used his influence to secure his replacement by his younger son, forty-five-year-old

---

[4] W.C.L. De Guérin, *Our Kin: Genealogical Sketches, Pedigrees, and Arms of Sundry Families* (Guernsey, 1890), pp. 21–2.

[5] Stevens Cox, *Guernsey Merchants*, p. 194.

[6] 30.4.1796, GG, *Crime*, vol. 19.

[7] For a detailed account of these episodes, see R. Hocart, *Peter de Havilland: Bailiff of Guernsey: A History of his Life, 1747-1821* (Guernsey, 1997), pp. 14–19, 37–50.

Robert Porret Le Marchant.[8] Robert Le Marchant had become a Jurat in 1784 and Receiver ten years later, but, notwithstanding his father's ambitions for him, he had no interest in personal power. Frederick Lukis characterised him as being 'of weak powers of body & mind'.[9] In 1806, he withdrew permanently from the Court on health grounds, leaving his Lieutenant Bailiff (and cousin), Eléazar Le Marchant, to preside over proceedings. Possibly in deference to his father who lived till 1809, Robert Le Marchant did not however resign as Bailiff until 1810. When he eventually died in 1840, his branch of the family became extinct.

It is perhaps ironic that, after four decades of Le Marchant Bailiffs, the next incumbent should be Peter De Havilland, with whom William Le Marchant had feuded so bitterly. Peter De Havilland was the first Bailiff known to have a background in the law, although his legal training appears to have been minimal. Born into a mercantile family, he spent his adolescence learning the wine trade in the French town of Sète. On return to Guernsey, he decided to become an Advocate and attended the Royal Court for a year as an observer.[10] With this preparation and still only nineteen, he was sworn in as an Advocate on 17 April 1767. De Havilland did not however serve in this capacity for long, resigning from the Bar in 1777, probably because of his personal difficulties with the Bailiff. In 1785, De Havilland was elected a Jurat (his father having preceded him in this role between 1729 and 1770). After spending the next twenty-five years on the Jurats' bench, De Havilland was recommended by the Lieutenant Governor as a replacement for retiring Bailiff Robert Le Marchant, and, at the age of sixty-two, he was sworn in as Bailiff on 12 May 1810.[11]

One of Peter De Havilland's most notable achievements as Bailiff was to secure a proper salary for the post. Up to De Havilland's time, Guernsey's Bailiffs had received only a retainer of 30 *livres tournois* (about £2 2s) per year from Crown revenues, topped up by £100–£120 in Court fees. When De Havilland discovered soon after his installation that his Jersey counterpart was in receipt of a salary of £300 a year, he petitioned the Privy Council for

---

[8] Hocart, *Peter De Havilland*, p. 66. Although the Bailiffs were appointed by the Crown, initial recommendations were made by Lieutenant Governors, on whom influence could be exerted, persuasion exercised, favours called in, and so on.

[9] F.C. Lukis, 'Reminiscences of Former Days in Connection with Guernsey', PL.

[10] Hocart, *Peter De Havilland*, pp. 5–6.

[11] *Ibid.*, pp. 83–4.

the same sum for himself, as also proper salaries for the Law Officers and Greffier.[12] On 14 August 1813, the Privy Council granted De Havilland's request in respect of both himself and the other officers.[13] Bailiffs from Peter De Havilland onward (though retaining their supplementary income from Court fees) refrained from engaging in trade or other employments and worked entirely at their duties as Bailiff.

When De Havilland died in 1821, fifty-eight-year-old Daniel De Lisle Brock, a Jurat since 1798, was appointed to succeed him. Brock had been foremost among a group of Jurats opposed to the Bailiff's pay rise, for the reason, *inter alia*, that it might make incumbents more malleable to British government pressure.[14] Brock could not, however, have fitted this description less. He belonged to a family which had been relatively prominent in Guernsey since at least the sixteenth century, but was the first of that name to become a Jurat.[15] The son of a successful merchant and shipowner, Daniel Brock received his early education in Guernsey. He then went to Alderney to study under a Swiss clergyman, and completed his schooling in Richmond-upon-Thames. After a spell in the counting-house of his uncle, John Le Marchant, Brock spent several months in his early twenties travelling on the continent.[16] Resuming his commercial activities on return to Guernsey, he retained a keen interest in international politics. In the late 1780s, he became a member of the 'Liberty Club', which collectively owned a yacht named 'Liberty' in which club members made excursions to France to monitor events in the lead-up to the Revolution.[17] When, however, war with the new republic seemed inevitable in 1792, Brock had a letter published in the local newspaper disavowing any republican tendencies and pledging to defend his island against the Revolutionary regime:

> Everything which I hold dear in life – my family, friends, property – attaches me
> to my birthplace … I will repel the French, if they dare to attack us, as ardently

---

[12] Petition dated 19.9.1812, NA, PC 1/4022.

[13] NA, PC 1/4022.

[14] Hocart, *Peter De Havilland*, p. 90.

[15] Brock's mother, however, was a De Lisle, and there had been several De Lisle Jurats, notably his grandfather Daniel De Lisle, who served on the bench between 1742 and 1779, and was also a Lieutenant Bailiff.

[16] C.R. Dodd, *The Annual Biography* (London, 1843), p. 225.

[17] Lukis, 'Reminiscences'. Lukis is the main source of information on the 'Liberty Club', but see also J.P. Warren (ed.), *Extracts from the diary of Elisha Dobrée* (Guernsey, 1929), whose subject was a member.

as I wished them success against the tyrants who sought to oppress them ... I will demonstrate [my loyalty] by my obedience to the laws, my military service if there is war, and my efforts to preserve peace and concord in this cherished isle.[18]

Brock was to remain sincerely – and energetically – attached to the island for the rest of his life. On several occasions during his forty-four years as Jurat and Bailiff, he was deputed by the Royal Court and States to defend Guernsey's interests at Westminster.[19] He was also in large part responsible for pushing through the many civic improvements from which St Peter Port benefited in the 1820s and 1830s. When Daniel Brock died in 1842, the Lieutenant Governor, William Napier, wrote to the Home Secretary:

> The late Bailiff was a man of such remarkable intellectual power, knowledge and industry, and so devoted to his duties, that ... it would be impossible to find in the Island, and difficult anywhere else, a person of such capacity and aptitude.[20]

Much though Napier doubted that anyone could quite replace Daniel Brock, he nevertheless recommended fifty-four-year-old John Guille, Lieutenant Bailiff since 1835, as Brock's successor.[21] Guille had been brought up by his grandfather, a well-to-do country Jurat and Seigneur of the fief of St George. He became an officer in the island's militia at the age of seventeen, a Jurat at the age of twenty-one, and inherited his grandfather's fief at the age of thirty-one. Sworn in as Bailiff in January 1843, Guille successfully piloted the States through its first major reform in 1844. Unfortunately, he did not live long enough to accomplish anything else. Falling ill at the beginning of 1845, Guille travelled to Plymouth for medical treatment, only to die there in June of that year.[22] His tenure had lasted only twenty-nine months.

It should be noted in closing our account of this period's Bailiffs that none of them appear to have taken much interest in criminal justice. All seem to have been tolerant of the major defects in the island's administration of justice which had steadily grown more evident since the mid-eighteenth century. These defects, and the need to remedy them, prompted a major break with

[18] *Gazette de Guernesey*, 22.12.1792.
[19] J. Marr, *Guernsey People* (Chichester, 1984), pp. 16–17.
[20] Napier to Sir James Graham, 7.10.1842, NA, HO 45/213.
[21] Napier to Graham, 17.9.1842, NA, HO 45/213.
[22] *Star*, 9.5.1845.

the traditional mode of appointing Bailiffs after the death of John Guille. This will be addressed in Chapter 8.

Jurats

A total of fifty-five Jurats served between 1765 and 1844, of whom forty-four were elected within the period itself. As in the previous period, a majority of these forty-four came from St Peter Port, with just a handful from the countryside. Their average age at election was forty, as opposed to thirty-five in the previous period.[23] At least six of them were still only in their twenties when elected.

More than twenty of the Jurats who served in this period remained on the bench well into their seventies and eighties. Service once elected was still obligatory and for life, with the only means of obtaining a discharge a petition to the Privy Council, organised and paid for by the Jurat himself. An extra complication was added in 1778 when it was established that Jurats wishing to petition Council for their discharge must first have obtained the consent of the States.[24] In 1822, however, when eighty-six-year-old Pierre De Jersey expressed a wish to retire, the States, fully acquiescing in his decision, resolved to petition Council on his behalf, as also to pay all his costs. De Jersey was duly discharged, and the procedure adopted in his case created a precedent for all future discharges. Henceforth, whenever an elderly or incapacitated Jurat wished to retire, he would first apply to the States, and if that body assented to the application, the States would organise and fund the petition themselves. Seven more of the Jurats elected in this period retired by this method after 1822, and it was to become more common as time went on.[25]

As in the previous period, the staggered nature of Jurats' elections meant that there was usually a good balance between inexperience and experience.

[23] I have found birth dates for all but two of the Jurats elected in this period.

[24] This convention was established in relation to a discharge petition submitted by Jurat Eléazar Le Marchant which was opposed by the States. In the Order rejecting the petition, the Privy Council expressed its concurrence with the States' contention that this body should be consulted prior to a Jurat's submission of a petition for discharge (Act of 11.7.1778, G.E. Lee (ed.), *Actes des Etats de l'Ile de Guernesey, 1651–1780* (Guernsey, 1907); O in C, 11.6.1778).

[25] Orders in Council discharging Jurats are to be found in successive volumes of GG, *Ordres du Conseil et Actes du Parlement*.

The one notable exception came when the dispute with Bailiff William Le Marchant caused the departure of four long-serving Jurats in 1777. In 1780, only two of the twelve Jurats had served more than twenty years, and half the bench had served just three years or fewer. Within a few years, however, the balance was restored.

Also as in the previous period, a majority of the fifty-five Jurats who served between the mid-1760s and mid-1840s were from the island's traditional elite. They shared thirty-one surnames between them. The Le Marchants, of which there were no fewer than nine, continued to dominate the bench. There were also five Dobrées, four Careys, and three each from the Andros, Guille and De Havilland families. Consanguinity continued to prevail, and around the time of Waterloo, the genealogist and historian William Berry demonstrated how eleven of the men on the bench were related 'without the necessity of even tracing the Descent beyond the Great-Grandfather'.[26]

In the thirty years after Waterloo, the bench underwent a number of significant changes. Not only did several ancient elite families, including the Le Marchants, Fiotts, Bonamys and De Beauvoirs, disappear from it for good, but members of the 'Forties' succeeded in gaining seats for themselves: William Collings (whom we encountered in the last chapter) was elected in 1822, and his brewer cousin Frederick Mansell in 1830.[27] Finally, the 1840s saw the advent of an entirely new type of Jurat: Guernseymen from elite backgrounds who retired to the island after a professional career spent elsewhere. The first such Jurats were Thomas Fiott De Havilland and Thomas Andros, elected in 1842 and 1843 respectively. De Havilland had spent his career as a military engineer in India; Andros as a solicitor in London.[28] Men such as these brought a wider perspective to the bench. Andros was particularly useful for his legal experience – an asset in notably short supply, since, besides him, only three of the Jurats who served between 1765 and 1844 had any form of legal training.[29]

[26] W. Berry, *The History of the Island of Guernsey* (London, 1815), pp. 203–4.

[27] R. Hocart, 'Elections to the Royal Court of Guernsey, 1821–1844', *TSG*, 19 (1979), p. 500–4.

[28] *Comet*, 14.3.1853; *Star*, 26.4.1866.

[29] Peter De Havilland (1785–1810), Peter Le Cocq (1822–30) and Hilary Ollivier Carré (1829–67).

Law Officers

The first of the four Procureurs of our period, Jean De Sausmarez, served for thirty years from 1744.[30] For part of this time, he also served as Receiver. When De Sausmarez died at the age of sixty-eight in 1774, the Bailiff, William Le Marchant, secured the post for his own elder son, Hirzel. Hirzel Le Marchant does not appear to have had any legal training, and there is no record of his admission as an Advocate. He was sworn in as Procureur at the age of twenty-two in May 1774.[31] After a few years' service during which, according to Peter De Havilland, he covered himself 'with the complete execration of the public', Hirzel Le Marchant died aged forty-one in 1793.[32] The post then went to thirty-seven-year-old Thomas De Sausmarez, son of the former Procureur Jean De Sausmarez and a nephew of William Le Marchant. Thomas De Sausmarez had served a long apprenticeship as Comptroller (of which more in the next paragraph) and combined the post of Procureur with service as Guernsey's military Deputy Judge-Advocate. When he retired from both of these posts at the age of seventy-four in 1830, his place as Procureur was taken by forty-seven-year-old Charles De Jersey, who, like him, had served a long apprenticeship as Comptroller. From this point onwards, service as Comptroller came generally to be regarded as a prerequisite for promotion to Procureur.[33] De Jersey served more than twenty years as Procureur and retired aged sixty-eight in 1851.[34]

---

[30] Appendix 2.

[31] 17.5.1774, GG, *Ordres du Conseil et Actes du Parlement*, vol. 1.

[32] Hocart, *Peter De Havilland*, p. 44.

[33] With the notable exception of a period in the mid-nineteenth century, when the office of Comptroller was suspended for a number of years – more on this in Chapter 8.

[34] C. Long (ed.), *Sequel to the Annals of Guernsey by John Jacob, Esq.* (Guernsey, 1872), pp. 185–6.

Plate 13. Jean De Sausmarez
(Procureur, 1744–74)
© The Priaulx Library, Guernsey

Plate 14. Thomas De Sausmarez
(Procureur, 1793–1830)
© The Priaulx Library, Guernsey

Plate 15. Charles De Jersey
(Procureur, 1830–51)
Courtesy of Guernsey Museums &
Galleries (States of Guernsey)

The first of the eight Comptrollers of our period was Eléazar Le Marchant, step-son of Bailiff William Le Marchant.[35] He was appointed at the age of twenty-two in 1765, having been sworn in as an Advocate the previous year. When he resigned after nine years' service in 1774, the Comptroller's post went to the Bailiff's nephew, Thomas De Sausmarez (who, as we saw above, became Procureur in 1793).[36] Thomas was only eighteen on appointment and lacked legal training. Rather than take up his post immediately, he went to learn law in Rouen, where he attended the courts and law libraries.[37] On his return to Guernsey in 1777, De Sausmarez was simultaneously sworn in both as an Advocate and as Comptroller.[38]

De Sausmarez's successor as Comptroller in 1793 was thirty-five-year-old Jean Carey Métivier. Métivier had been sworn in as an Advocate in 1780 and elected Prévôt two years later. Métivier's father, a Huguenot clergyman, had taken refuge in the island in 1752 and married into the elite Carey family, thereby securing acceptance into Guernsey's higher ranks. Jean Métivier, who was not personally wealthy, owed his Comptrollership to his better-off brother-in-law, Jurat Jean Guille, who had successfully lobbied the Lieutenant Governor on his behalf.[39] Métivier however died after only three years in the role. Between his death and the end of our period, the office of Comptroller passed successively through the hands of five other men, all of whom save one were time-served Advocates. The first, seventy-five-year-old Pierre Coutart, was appointed as a mere stopgap after his predecessor's demise caught the Court and Lieutenant Governor unprepared.[40] Coutart was replaced after just a year by thirty-four-year-old Jean Condamine, his own son-in-law and the son of former Sergeant Jean-Jacques Condamine. Condamine, a draper by trade, was sworn in as an Advocate just a few months before his appointment and served as Comptroller for the next twenty-four years. Peter Le Cocq, who succeeded Condamine in 1821, was a highly

---

[35] This Eléazar is not to be confused with the Bailiff's nephew of the same name who was elected a Jurat in 1777.

[36] Richard Hocart informs us that the post was effectively purchased for Thomas De Sausmarez by his mother, Martha De Sausmarez, who was the Bailiff's sister. Mrs De Sausmarez paid her brother £200 and lent him a further £100 in return for recommending her son as the next Comptroller (Hocart, *Peter De Havilland*, pp. 13, 38).

[37] Long (ed.), *Sequel to the Annals*, pp. 19–21. Rouen did not have a university.

[38] 12.7.1777, GG, *Ordres du Conseil et Actes du Parlement*, vol. 2.

[39] Hocart, *Peter De Havilland*, p. 44.

[40] *Ibid.*, pp. 50–1.

experienced Advocate, having first been admitted to the Bar in 1794. However, he served only a year as Comptroller, being elected to the Jurats' bench in 1822. Next to fill the post was thirty-nine-year-old Charles De Jersey, the son of a former Jurat, who had himself been practising at the Bar for seventeen years. When De Jersey was promoted to the Procureur's post eight years later, the Comptrollership went to thirty-nine-year-old John De Sausmarez, son of the retiring Procureur and the last Law Officer appointed in our period. John De Sausmarez's career as a Law Officer ended in 1845 in unusual fashion. He had been a practising Advocate since 1815 and had doubtless hoped to follow his father into the Procureur's office. However, his career was cut short by an incident which seems to have forced him to resign. The episode concerned an alleged sexual assault by Comptroller De Sausmarez on Elizabeth Irving, the mistress of St Peter Port's National School. Andrew Irving, her husband, reported the incident to HM Procureur in May 1845, and the Ordinary Court was convened to determine whether or not there was a case for proceeding.[41] Although the Court returned a negative answer, John De Sausmarez submitted his resignation three months later.[42] After two years away from the Court, De Sausmarez was elected a Jurat in 1847 and served on the bench till his death in 1870.[43]

Law Officers' remuneration underwent a number of changes in our period. Prior to the late eighteenth century, both Procureur and Comptroller had received a small annual retainer and submitted separate accounts to the Receiver for each piece of work done for the Crown. This changed somewhat in 1785, when the Receiver agreed to pay the Procureur (only) a fixed sum of £40 per year from Crown revenues in lieu of separate fees.[44] A bigger change occurred in 1813, when Bailiff Peter De Havilland secured an improved package for the Law Officers at the same time as himself. From this point onwards, both the Procureur and the Comptroller were paid salaries in lieu of separate fees: £100 and £50 initially, but doubled to £200 and £100

---

[41] The assault was alleged to have taken place when Mrs Irving was consulting De Sausmarez on business.

[42] 22.5.1845, GG, *Crime*, vol. 31; De Sausmarez to Home Office, 8.8.1845, NA, HO 45/938.

[43] *Star*, 11.6.1870.

[44] Law Officers to Privy Council, 6.4.1835, Law Officers' salaries, 'Privy Council', vol. 2, Royal Court Library, IA.

in 1839.[45] Both nevertheless continued to do private work, and both continued to receive fees for non-Crown tasks performed for the Court and States.

Advocates

A total of twenty-four Advocates were admitted to the Guernsey Bar over the eighty years between 1765 and 1844.[46] This was eight more than between 1680 and 1764. Only eleven of these were admitted in the half-century between 1765 and 1814. After Waterloo, the pace picked up, and thirteen more were admitted between 1815 and 1844. In the pre-Waterloo period, about a third of new Advocates were from Guernsey's traditional elite, and the rest mainly from Huguenot families such as the Huberts, Coutarts, Métiviers and Jeremies, all of which had two or more representatives at the Bar. In the post-Waterloo era, Advocates from the traditional elite became rarer, and men from a greater variety of backgrounds filled the gaps, among them Carrés, Fallas, Champions, Radfords, and Galliennes.

Four of the twenty-four Advocates sworn in during this period went on to become Jurats; three became Greffiers; nine became Law Officers; two became Bailiffs; and one, John Jeremie junior, became a colonial officer and ultimately Governor of Sierra Leone. John Utermarck, the last Advocate to be sworn in during this period, was the first to follow the full *cursus honorum* from Advocate to Bailiff, becoming an Advocate in 1839, Comptroller in 1845, Procureur in 1851, and Bailiff in 1883.[47]

At no time during this period were any formal qualifications required of Advocates, who continued to be appointed by the Court as and when vacancies arose. In 1777, the maximum number of Advocates with rights of audience at the Bar was fixed by Ordinance at six.[48] This Ordinance followed the resignation of Advocate Peter De Havilland, and its preamble shows it was motivated by a wish not to spread Court business so thinly that 'persons

---

[45] O in C, 14.8.1813; Treasury Minute of 2.5.1839, Law Officers' salaries, 'Privy Council', vol. 2, Royal Court Library, IA.

[46] Appendix 3.

[47] Utermarck's grandfather, Rudolf, was a merchant from Hamburg who had married into an elite Guernsey family in 1779 (Stevens Cox, *Guernsey Merchants*, pp. 47, 209).

[48] Ord, 6.10.1777.

of condition' could not make decent money from the profession. As matters turned out, the Ordinance proved unnecessary, since there were seldom more than three or four practising Advocates at any time during the period dealt with here.

Most Advocates continued to receive their training in the form of apprenticeship, sometimes complemented with study visits to France. For those admitted between the 1770s and Waterloo, such visits were difficult, given Britain's semi-permanent warfare with France.[49] For Advocates sworn in post-Waterloo, trips to France were easier, and the presence of apprentice lawyers in Normandy is more clearly documented. Robert MacCulloch, sworn in as an Advocate in 1824, summarised his own legal education for the benefit of the Royal Commissioners of 1846:

> I was about fourteen years of age when I went as a clerk to an advocate here, and remained four or five years. After that, I spent about a twelvemonth in France, at Caen, attended the lectures there, and frequented the public libraries, where there were a quantity of books on the ancient Norman Law, the general principles of which I studied. On my return, I attended the office of the Procureur de la Reine about six or eight months.[50]

Although it does not appear from MacCulloch's account that he sat any formal examinations, some slightly later contemporaries did emerge from their French sojourns with paper qualifications. George Radford, who was admitted to the Bar in 1827, was a *Licencié en Droit*; Henry Tupper (admitted in 1830) and James Gallienne (admitted in 1838) were *Bacheliers en Droit*.[51] This became a popular option, and all Advocates sworn in from the 1840s had some form of diploma, albeit that the only subjects taught in nineteenth-century French law faculties – Caen included – were Roman Law and French Law.

---

[49] Charles De Jersey, who subsequently served as Comptroller and Procureur, undertook a study trip to France at the Peace of Amiens only to be taken prisoner when war resumed a few months later (Long (ed.), *Sequel to the Annals*, pp. 185–6; *Star*, 6.10.1874).

[50] *Second Report of the Commissioners Appointed to Inquire into the State of the Criminal Law in the Channel Islands: Guernsey* (London, 1848), p. 103.

[51] To graduate as a *bachelier* required a minimum of two years' study, and to graduate as a *licencié* three years.

Police

Guernsey's policing arrangements during the first three decades covered by this chapter were similar to those of the previous period. Each parish had two Constables who were responsible for all aspects of policing in their respective parishes, except St Peter Port, which since 1736 had an additional force of four unpaid assistant constables. Until the end of the eighteenth century, St Peter Port's assistant constables worked under the direction of the parish Constables and had no personal discretion. This changed in 1799 when the Royal Court passed an Ordinance giving assistants the same policing powers as the principal Constables.[52] The preamble stated that the change had been necessitated by the large increase in the town's population which made it difficult to maintain order. From this point on, assistant constables were able to search premises, make arrests and bring offenders before the Court entirely on their own initiative.[53] An Ordinance of 1801 attempted in addition to rationalise the organisation of urban policing. It divided St Peter Port into six cantons, each of which became the special responsibility of one of the parochial police officers (principal Constables included), who was to exercise surveillance over streets, public houses and sojourning strangers.[54]

Assistant constables continued to be chosen behind closed doors by the Town Douzaine. As the 'Sixties'/'Forties' breach widened in the early nineteenth century, this aroused suspicions that 'Sixties' Douzeniers were targeting 'Forties' members unfairly, and a parish meeting in 1824 voted in favour of allowing ratepayers to elect assistant constables from among themselves.[55] The Douzaine resisted this, and a committee of leading ratepayers was delegated to petition the Privy Council to enforce the change. The Council, declining to act in what they deemed a parish matter, simply referred it back to the Royal Court, which in turn expressed itself in favour of the *status quo*.[56] The Bailiff, Daniel Brock, was not however without sympathy for the petitioners. He suggested that problems might be solved if the parish could be persuaded to engage two permanent policemen on salaries

---

[52] Ord, 30.9.1799.
[53] *Second Report*, pp. xxvi–ii, 10, 142.
[54] Ord, 19.1.1801.
[55] *Indépendance*, 20.3.1824.
[56] Royal Court to Privy Council, 28.2.1825, GG, *Réponses au Conseil*, vol. 3.

amounting to £35 or £40 a year.[57] This is the first known mention of paid police in Guernsey, and it is interesting that it came from Brock. The Douzaine did not however act on his suggestion, and the matter was left in abeyance.

Aside from the mode of appointing assistant constables, there were other, more urgent, policing problems. Of particular concern was the very limited number of officers. In 1831, with a population of over 24,000, Guernsey had a total of only fourteen Constables and assistant constables, or one for every 1,720 inhabitants. The following year, this was somewhat alleviated by the appointment of unpaid volunteer 'special' constables, who were endowed with the same powers as assistant constables. The first specials were sworn in to help cope with the 1832 cholera epidemic. They were initially stood down when the epidemic ended, but after being reinstated in 1838 in the wake of several burglaries, they became a permanent feature of island life. By the 1840s, specials numbered about a dozen and were all based in town, where each was responsible for a particular district.[58] Our period thus ended with a police force around twenty-five-strong. It should be observed, however, that all of these officers were part-time, untrained and unpaid.

Infrastructure

Courthouse

At the start of the current period, the States spent 700 *livres tournois* (about £43) of their own money patching up the old *Cohue* at La Plaiderie, but nothing further appears to have been done to the building for the rest of the century.[59] By the 1790s, conditions in the courtroom were so bad that the States decided it was no longer a dignified venue for their meetings.

---

[57] Brock to Privy Council, 16.5.1826, NA, PC 1/4296.
[58] *Second Report*, pp. xxi, 119, 120; J. Duncan, *The History of Guernsey* (London, 1841), p. 499.
[59] Act of 23.9.1766, Lee (ed.), *Actes des Etats, 1651–1780*.

Resolving to take matters into their own hands, they petitioned the Privy Council in May 1792 for permission to sell the old *Cohue* and use the proceeds to buy land and build a new courthouse without further call on Crown revenues.[60] The Council having given their consent,[61] the States purchased a site to the west of the town's main built-up area, and construction work started in 1799.[62] Within a couple of years, the new Royal Court building was complete, and Chief Pleas were held there for the first time in January 1803.[63] In 1808, the Court passed a resolution formally making the running and maintenance of the new courthouse the responsibility of Crown revenues.[64]

The building had cost a total in the region of £7,000.[65] It was altogether on a larger scale than its predecessor, accommodating a large upper chamber for States' meetings and major trials, a smaller downstairs courtroom for the Ordinary Court, and an official 'Greffe' for the storage of Court records.[66] Between 1821 and 1824, the building was further enlarged. Withdrawing rooms were provided for Jurats, lawyers and witnesses; the Greffe was extended; drainage was improved; and stables were added.[67] Writing in the late 1820s, John Jacob described what he called Guernsey's *Palais de Justice* as comparable to 'any county court of law in England'.[68]

[60] Royal Court to Privy Council, 5.5.1792, GG, Royal Court General Letter Book (first series), vol. 1.

[61] O in C, 15.6.1792.

[62] J. Jacob, *Annals of some of the British Norman Isles constituting the Bailiwick of Guernsey* (Paris, 1830), p. 142.

[63] 17.1.1803, GG, *Ordonnances*, vol. 2.

[64] 20.2.1808, GG, *Ordonnances*, vol. 2. The old *Cohue* was sold to a merchant, after which it served multiple purposes (including as a broker's shop, auction room, and hotel). The building was eventually demolished in 1929 (E.F. Carey, 'La Plaiderie', *TSG*, 10 (1929), pp. 405–6).

[65] Jacob, *Annals*, p. 142.

[66] Prior to construction of the new premises, Court records had been kept at the Greffier's home.

[67] D.M. Ogier, *History of the Buildings of Guernsey's Royal Court* (Guernsey, 2004), p. 12.

[68] Jacob, *Annals*, p. 143.

Plate 16. Royal Court, 1830s
Courtesy of the Priaulx Library, Guernsey

Prison

Since Tudor times, Guernsey's prison had been located in Castle Cornet, on an islet half a mile off St Peter Port which was also the garrison headquarters. The prison consisted of three rooms, one of which was originally tenanted by the gaoler. By the 1780s, the gaoler had relinquished his quarters, and his former apartment appears to have been turned over to carceral use.[69] These premises, whose maintenance fell to Crown revenues, had long been found unsatisfactory. Disputes with the military over access were common, and the transport of prisoners in bad weather was difficult. In an effort to solve these problems, Guernsey's authorities had been lobbying unsuccessfully for the

---

[69] For the gaoler's departure, see Act of 20.1.1781, G.E. Lee (ed.), *Actes des Etats de l'Ile de Guernesey, 1780–1815* (Guernsey, 1910).

construction of a prison within the town since at least the seventeenth century.[70] In 1764, the States decided to approach the Crown once more, seeking the gift of a site for a new prison.[71] Again, their petition came to nothing, although they still appear to have held out the hope of a positive response as late as 1786.[72] Finally, the States resolved in 1799 to adopt an approach similar to that employed with the new courthouse. Offering to buy a site and build a new prison at their own expense, they proposed to finance the enterprise by means of a general tax.[73]

Gaol-building was in fashion in the late eighteenth century. Imprisonment had been gaining in popularity as a penal sanction during the Enlightenment – most particularly since the publication in 1764 of Cesare Beccaria's *Dei Delitti e Delle Pene*, which had emphasised the importance of rehabilitation over retribution. In France, the Revolutionaries' 1791 *Code Pénal* had introduced a penal system based primarily on imprisonment.[74] In England, prison reformer John Howard had published an influential report on prisons in 1777, which had resulted in the passage of the ground-breaking 1779 Penitentiary Act.[75] This Act proposed the building of two national prisons where a regime of work, religious instruction and night-time solitary confinement would be instituted in order to transform prisoners' social and religious outlook and send them back into the community as responsible citizens. Although the Act was never put into practice, it stimulated an extensive prison-building programme across England, and forty-five new local prisons were built in the last quarter of the eighteenth century.[76]

---

[70] Jersey had had one since 1693, when a gaol was built in St Helier to replace the old prison at Mont Orgueil Castle (P. Ahier, 'The house of correction in Jersey', *Annual Bulletin of la Société Jersiaise*, 20 (1971), pp. 286–7).

[71] Act of 17.9.1764, G.E. Lee (ed.), *Actes des Etats de l'Ile de Guernesey, 1651–1780* (Guernsey, 1907).

[72] Acts of 29.3.1786 and 20.1.1787, Lee (ed.), *Actes des Etats, 1780–1815*.

[73] Act of 13.6.1799, Lee (ed.), *Actes des Etats, 1780–1815*.

[74] J.-M. Carbasse, *Histoire du Droit Pénal et de la Justice Criminelle* (2000; Paris, 2014 edn), p. 441.

[75] J. Howard, *The State of the Prisons in England and Wales … and an Account of some Foreign Prisons* (Warrington, 1777).

[76] J.M. Beattie, *Crime and the Courts in England, 1660–1800* (Oxford, 1986), pp. 308, 571–6; H. Johnston, *Crime in England, 1815–1880: Experiencing the Criminal Justice System* (Abingdon, 2015), pp. 88–9.

The Privy Council granted the States permission to proceed with their gaol-building project when the new courthouse was completed in 1803.[77] It was not however until 1807 that the States acquired a site suitably close to the courthouse.[78] Construction began immediately, but the island was by then in the midst of the economic slump caused by the anti-smuggling Acts, and the proceeds of the general tax proved insufficient to cover costs. Supplementary sources of funding were found, but work was forced to proceed in fits and starts as one source dried up and another was sought.[79] By 1810, the prison was in a useable state and began to admit debtors and criminals on longer sentences.[80] In the meantime, the Castle gaol continued to be used for short-term prisoners. Finally, the Royal Court declared the new prison complete in August 1815 and turned over the rooms at the Castle to the military.[81] The town prison was put under the nominal supervision of the Prévôt, and it was laid down that two Jurats should inspect it each quarter.

John Jacob tells us that the prison eventually cost around £11,000,[82] but this is a surprisingly high figure, given that it was little more than basic stabling for human beings. The historian William Berry was putting it politely when he described it as 'certainly not on the best contrived plan, either for safety or convenience, that might have been adopted from the many admirable improved structures in England'.[83] (Berry was well-placed to know, having been briefly imprisoned himself in 1813.[84])

---

[77] O in C, 18.5.1803. This Order in Council included a provision for the new gaol to be run and maintained at Crown expense, as had been the case with the old one.

[78] For vicissitudes in the search for a site, see Acts of 20.8.1803, 15.11.1806, 19.3.1807, 23.4.1807, 25.8.1807, Lee (ed.), *Actes des Etats, 1780–1815*.

[79] Undated accounts in GG, *Réponses au Conseil*, vol. 3 show that, between 1808 and 1810, about £1,000 of lottery money was used for the prison. This was followed after 1810 by an element from the tax on taverns (Act of 22.10.1810, Lee (ed.), *Actes des Etats, 1780–1815*).

[80] The first person to be incarcerated there was Joseph Sibrel, sentenced to three months for assault in October that year (18.10.1810, GG, *Crime*, vol. 22).

[81] 4.8.1815, GG, *Ordonnances*, vol. 4. In October 1830, the Royal Court registered an act abandoning any right to, or jurisdiction over, the Castle prisons in future (28.10.1830, GG, *Ordonnances*, vol. 5).

[82] Jacob, *Annals*, p. 150.

[83] Berry, *History of Guernsey*, p. 146.

[84] For refusing to return an unpublished map lent to him by its maker (F.B. Tupper, *The History of Guernsey and its Bailiwick* (Guernsey, 1854), p. 19). This map may well be the one from which the map used at the beginning of Part II, above, was copied.

In its final form, the prison was a simple oblong block 96ft long by 33ft wide, consisting of two floors and a basement.[85] The basement contained four lock-ups destined for the use of the police. The ground floor, fronted by a veranda 8ft wide, contained five cells intended for debtors, each measuring 16ft by 9ft and equipped with fireplaces. The first floor, whose 8ft balcony echoed the veranda downstairs, contained ten cells of 9ft by 7ft in which the prison's criminals were to be accommodated, irrespective of their age or sex, and whether they had been convicted or were on remand. Only four of these ten cells had fireplaces. A windowless cell at the rear of the first floor was painted black in order to serve as a punishment cell, but the gaol had no sick bay, no chapel, no kitchen, nor day-room.

Plate 17. New prison, 1815
From W. Berry, *The History of the Island of Guernsey* (London, 1815)

The gaol was built with just one fixed privy. This was located on the ground floor and reserved for debtors. Criminals were to use buckets in their cells. Neither was the gaol provided with a well or piped water supply. Gutters

---

[85] The account which follows is based on *Third Report of the Committee of the Society for the Improvement of Prison Discipline* (London, 1821), p. 105; prison regulations dated 16.5.1818, GG, *Ordonnances*, vol. 4; Bailiff to Lieutenant Governor, 11.3.1836, GG, Royal Court General Letter Book (first series), vol. 5.

and downpipes fed rain from the roof into a tank from which it could be pumped into the yard. No bathroom or wash-house was installed within the gaol, so prisoners were obliged to wash themselves and their clothes at the outdoor pump.

Within the prison grounds was a dwelling house purpose-built for the gaoler, which took up fully one-fifth of the site. Between 1807 and 1856, the Barbets, father and son, served successively in this post.[86] Barbet senior was a plasterer, and his son a printer. Both left the prison daily to attend to their work. To begin with, no warders were employed. The gaoler's remuneration was on the same basis as previously. Besides free accommodation and a retainer of £13 a year, he made his money from fees,[87] and from selling food and drink to the prisoners, who were given a daily subsistence allowance of 9d from Crown revenues.[88] Although there was no cookhouse in the prison itself, the gaoler's wife prepared food for those prisoners who wanted it in the kitchen of her house. Alcohol was a monopoly reserved to the gaoler. Prisoners were banned from procuring it outside, and the gaoler was authorised to sell each inmate one pint of wine or a quarter-pint of spirits every day.[89]

Compared with contemporary English prisons, this regime was extremely outdated. Three statutes passed by Parliament between 1815 and 1835 had brought England's gaols into the modern age. In 1815, the Gaol Fees Abolition Act had put all gaolers on consolidated salaries and prohibited them from making money from fees or sales. In 1823, the Gaols Act had laid down that gaolers should not engage in other employments, and had additionally made it mandatory to separate different classes of inmate, as well as setting out a basic prison diet and establishing prisoners' right to fresh air and

---

[86] Stephen Barbet was first sworn in as gaoler in February 1807. His son, also named Stephen, replaced him in February 1833 and remained in post until his death in December 1856. The Barbet family, originally from Jersey, also supplied the Court with a number of Sergeants between 1790 and 1835.

[87] These now stood at 2s 6d every time a prisoner was admitted or released; 2s 6d each time a prisoner appeared in Court; 1s 6d for each quarterly change of straw in a prisoner's palliasse; and 3d for every day a prisoner spent in prison.

[88] The upkeep of debtors was the responsibility of their creditors. That of detainees in the police lock-ups fell to the parishes whose Constables or assistant constables confined them there.

[89] The only beverage available free of charge to prisoners was rainwater from the underground tank.

exercise. Finally, in 1835, the Prisons Act had introduced a new system of inspection, in which the whole of Britain was divided into four regions, with a Government Inspector appointed to each.[90]

It was not long before Guernsey's prison came under adverse scrutiny from across the Channel. The Quaker reformer Elizabeth Fry, who visited Channel Island prisons in 1833 and 1835, drew the attention of Home Secretary Lord John Russell to the poor conditions she had found there.[91] Russell in turn commissioned Dr Francis Bisset Hawkins, Inspector of Prisons for the South and West, to include Jersey and Guernsey on his 1836 inspection tour. Dr Hawkins's inspection of Jersey's gaol bore considerable fruit.[92] Echoing recommendations made by Mrs Fry, he proposed a number of improvements, including the addition of a separate house of correction and the institution of regulations based on the 1823 Gaols Act. Accepting most of Hawkins's proposals, Jersey's States built a house of correction adjacent to the existing gaol in the late 1830s, and put the whole establishment under the control of a new Prison Board, with a new financial arrangement and new rules sanctioned by the Home Office.[93]

Dr Hawkins made almost identical recommendations with regard to Guernsey, but, whether from shortage of funds or other reasons, Guernsey's authorities were not so compliant as their Jersey counterparts. An article in a local magazine commented: 'to model our prison on the system of a county gaol in England is preposterous; yet such seems to be the wish of Mr Hawkins … Surely we can manage our own affairs without the meddling interference of Mrs Fry and her co-adjutors?'[94] Thus the only changes which followed the Inspector's visit were the banning of spirits from the prison in 1836; the

---

[90] Johnston, *Crime in England*, pp. 89–91.

[91] K. Fry and R.E. Cresswell (eds), *Memoir of the Life of Elizabeth Fry*, 2 vols (London, 1847), 2, pp. 133–4, 173.

[92] Like Guernsey's gaol, Jersey's current prison was relatively new, built in St Helier at local expense between 1811 and 1815 to replace the prison of 1693 (Ahier, 'House of correction', pp. 286–7).

[93] C.A.R. Du Feu, 'Elizabeth Fry and the Jersey prison', *Annual Bulletin of la Société Jersiaise*, 20 (1970), pp. 180–91. The financial arrangement obliged Crown revenues to pay £300 annually towards the running and upkeep of the prison, with anything above this sum to be met by the States.

[94] *The Guernsey and Jersey Magazine*, 2 (1836), pp. 50–51.

institution of a prison chaplain in 1839; and the engagement of a prison doctor in 1844.[95]

As far as a house of correction was concerned, Guernsey's authorities considered that problem solved. The States had debated building such a house in 1828 and 1831, but had decided against it.[96] In 1832, however, St Peter Port's parochial authorities had opened what they called their 'house of separation'. Part of the Town Hospital and built on Hospital land, it had space for about twenty-five men and women, who were to spend their days at hard labour, dressed in a striped uniform and fed on vegetables and barley bread.[97] This house was primarily intended for refractory workhouse inmates, but the Court started using it to confine petty offenders almost as soon as it was opened. In essence, this was merely an extension of a policy already adopted by the Court. The Town Hospital's constitution accorded all town-resident Jurats *ex-officio* seats on the Hospital Board, which gave the Court considerable sway over the institution.[98] The Court had intermittently been sentencing petty offenders to Hospital detention since the 1790s, and by the 1820s such sentences had become fairly common, particularly for offenders with alcohol or other social problems.[99] St Peter Port's new house of separation proved a convenient substitute for a purpose-built house of correction, and the Court made regular use of it for the next twenty years. On occasion, Court registers even explicitly referred to the building as *la maison de correction*.[100]

Such were the structures which composed Guernsey's late eighteenth- and early nineteenth-century criminal justice system. In the next chapter we will turn our attention to the law and its implementation, and examine how these, too, evolved in response to social and demographic pressures.

---

[95] 3.10.1836, 21.1.1839, 29.1.1844, GG, *Ordonnances*, vols 6 & 7.

[96] *Billets,* 26.3.1828, 10.2.1831; *Comet,* 31.3.1828, 26.3.1829, 14.2.1831.

[97] R.-M. Crossan, *Poverty and Welfare in Guernsey, 1560–2015* (Woodbridge, 2015), p. 141.

[98] Crossan, *Poverty and Welfare*, pp. 120–1.

[99] The first such sentence was issued to Marie Le Cheminant in 1797 (5.8.1797, GG, *Crime*, vol. 20). By the 1820s, the Court was also sentencing offenders to detention in the Country Hospital. For further details, see Crossan, *Poverty and Welfare*, p. 140.

[100] See entry relating to Thomas Cole, 11.1.1838, GG, *Crime*, vol. 30.

6

1765–1844: Crime

This chapter follows a similar plan to Chapter 3, and is based on a study of the eighteen crime registers spanning the period between 1765 and 1844 (volumes 14–31). The quinquennia analysed in detail are 1780–4, 1800–4, 1820–4 and 1840–4. By the period dealt with here, crime registers followed a fairly consistent format, although entries remained perfunctory, and non-criminal matters (such as swearings-in of Vingteniers and the occasional Ordinance) continued to be recorded in them.

In this period, an average of 105 criminal cases were determined by the Royal Court each year. This was nearly three times the annual average in the period 1680–1764. In Chapter 3, we noted that the trend between 1680 and 1764 was essentially flat, with crime numbers at the end not dissimilar to those at the beginning. From 1765 until the end of the 1770s, this flat trend continued. The 1780s then saw a doubling of cases: from thirty-two per year in 1770–9 to sixty-four in 1780–9. This, among other things, reflected an increase in immigration. The upward trend continued over the 1790s with numbers reaching 122 a year in 1800–9. There was then a brief dip to seventy-nine per year in 1810–19, which was probably caused by emigration in the post-Napoleonic slump. Following Guernsey's economic recovery in the 1820s, numbers began to climb again, reaching an annual average of 125 in 1820–9 and further increasing to 176 per year by 1840–4. Figure 2 illustrates this progression.

Figure 2. Average number of criminal cases determined per year, 1765–1844

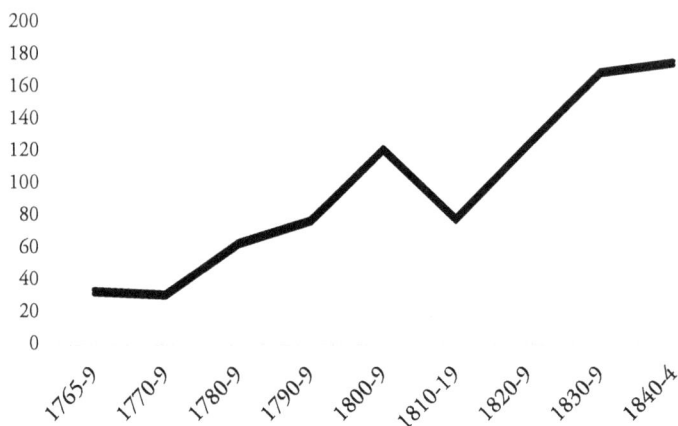

The ratio of purely procedural sittings to those which resulted in a verdict was much lower between 1765–1844 than in the previous period. In the quinquennium 1760–4, almost half of all sittings were purely procedural. This proportion had dropped to one-tenth by 1840–4. As the number of purely procedural sittings declined, so did the number of sittings held on a Saturday. In 1760–4, more than three-quarters of criminal sittings took place on Saturdays, but by 1840–4, this had declined to one-third, with Thursday now accounting for nearly 50 per cent of all criminal sittings.[1] Sittings were by this time also more evenly spread through the year.

In about half of cases in our four sample quinquennia, registers specified the parishes in which crimes had been committed. At 78 per cent, St Peter Port strongly predominated. At just 8 per cent, St Sampsons came a modest second, and the Vale came in third at 3 per cent.

Figure 3 divides all criminal cases determined over the four quinquennia into the major procedural categories set out in Chapters 2 and 3.

---

[1] We noted in Chapter 3 that emergency sittings of the Court were occasionally held on a Sunday. This practice continued in the period covered by the present chapter, but only until the 1820s. The last Sunday sitting appears to have taken place in 1821, when an inquest was hastily convened for a solider found dead in the harbour (14.1.1821, GG, *Crime*, vol. 24).

Figure 3. Distribution of criminal cases determined over 4 quinquennia, 1765–1844

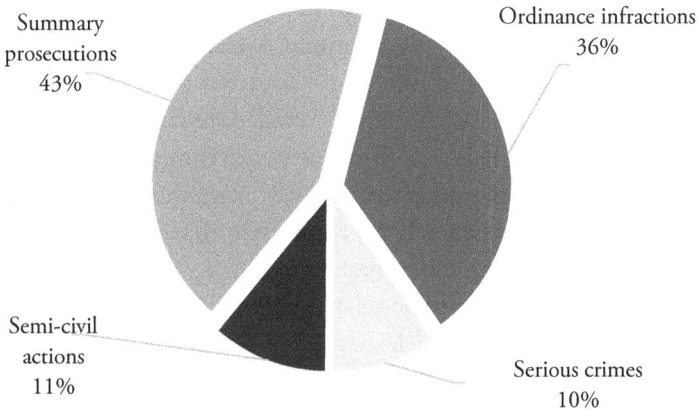

The balance between categories had significantly changed since the previous period. The biggest difference concerned summary prosecutions and semi-civil actions, which had effectively changed places, the former rising from 10 per cent to 43 per cent of cases, the latter dropping from 41 per cent to 11 percent. The proportion of Ordinance breaches also registered a decline, falling from 45 per cent of cases in 1680–1764, to 36 per cent in 1765–1844. Serious crime, by contrast, had increased – from 4 per cent of cases in the previous period to 10 per cent in the current period. In the following paragraphs we will look in detail at changes in the various categories.

Ordinance infractions

The Court's output of Ordinances in this period was unabated. As well as addressing novel issues and establishing rules for previously unregulated activities,[2] this was also a time when much past legislation was repealed and

---

[2] Such as inshore pilotage and harbour porterage (Ords, 22.10.1803, 7.4.1834).

re-issued in tidied-up form: the militia, highways, hunting, markets, taverns and traffic were all addressed by major consolidating Ordinances in this period.[3]

Output nevertheless bore little relation to prosecutions, since an astonishing two-thirds of all Ordinance-related cases in our sample quinquennia fell within just one area – breaches of militia rules. This was partly a product of the warfare which prevailed for more than twenty-five of the eighty years examined here. Wartime duties comprised frequent watches and training, and militiamen were routinely prosecuted for failing to attend. Punishment was usually a small fine, and some appear to have regarded this as preferable to sacrificing their time.

The predominance of militia-related prosecutions was also partly due to the comparative ease with which they could be effected. *Délateurs* willing to report breaches of hunting Ordinances might be hard to find, but in militia cases, the *délateur* was always the offender's superior officer. However, the concept of 'ease' only went so far, since the same cumbersome procedure was followed as of old, with prosecutions only possible in term-time and before the Full Court.

These two factors led in due course to congestion, and in 1796, the Court requested Privy Council guidance as to how the log jam might be relieved. The Council directed that, in future, prosecutions under militia Ordinances should take place both in and out of term, and that the Bailiff (or his Lieutenant) and just three Jurats should henceforth be deemed a competent Court.[4] This was highly significant in that it was the first major procedural modification of any sort to be effected in the period dealt with by this book.

The change in procedure, however important, applied to militia Ordinances only. All other Ordinance prosecutions had still to be conducted in the old time-consuming way. This led, in time, to a tendency to prosecute offences summarily notwithstanding the existence of an Ordinance,[5] which in part explains the reduced proportion of such prosecutions in this period. In a bid to revive the use of Ordinances, the States passed a measure at the very end of the period which became the second major modification of

---

[3] Ords, 3.10.1803, 8.10.1810, 30.11.1818, 6.10.1823, 17.1.1825, 16.1.1826.
[4] O in C, 24.2.1796.
[5] In 1843, for example, Isaac Lake was summarily prosecuted for allowing his horse to graze on the public highway notwithstanding that this was an offence already addressed by an Ordinance (24.8.1843, GG, *Crime*, vol. 31).

criminal procedure. In a law of 1844 relating to *les Procédures en cas d'Infractions d'Ordonnances* they made all Ordinance breaches of whatever sort triable both in and out of term by the Bailiff (or his Lieutenant) and just two Jurats, providing that the maximum fine was no more than 30 *livres tournois* (about £2 3s).[6]

Acts of Parliament

As in the previous period, there were comparatively few prosecutions under Westminster statutes between 1765 and 1844.[7] They fell into two main categories: prosecutions under the Mutiny Acts, and prosecutions under the Customs Acts. The Mutiny Acts were statutes regulating the conduct of soldiers and their relations with civilians. *Inter alia*, they made it an offence for civilians to assist soldiers to desert, to give them credit, or to purchase military equipment or clothing from them. First instituted in 1689, they were renewed annually, and copies were sent to Guernsey every year for registration by the Royal Court.[8] Their local use steadily increased as the garrison expanded. Typical of prosecutions under this statute were that of William Mauger who was fined £5 in 1800 after his wife bought a shirt from a soldier, and John Harris who was fined £20 in 1803 for helping a soldier to desert (fines levied under Westminster legislation were always denominated in sterling).[9]

Prosecutions under the Customs Acts proper began after Westminster extended anti-smuggling statutes to the Islands in the early 1800s and established a British customs presence there. They superseded prosecutions made in the previous period under the Acts of trade and navigation. Such prosecutions were brought in the joint names of the Chief Customs Officer and the Law Officers. They were generally not numerous. That said, in the late 1820s and early 1830s, there was a noticeable upsurge in customs-related

[6] O in C, 19.6.1844.

[7] As in Chapter 3, since prosecutions under these statutes were conducted in the same way as those under Ordinances, the few which occurred are included in our statistics on Ordinances, above.

[8] From the early 1700s, they were officially known as the Acts for Punishing Mutiny and Desertion and for the Better Payment of the Army and their Quarters.

[9] 22.11.1800, GG, *Crime*, vol. 20; 15.10.1803, GG, *Crime*, vol. 21.

prosecutions, almost all of which concerned tea. A typical example was that of Charles Batiste and five associates who in 1827 were all fined £100 (and had their cargo confiscated) for having been found carrying tea in the Channel contrary to the provisions of the 1825 Act for the Prevention of Smuggling.[10] At this period, the East India Company enjoyed a monopoly on the import of tea into Britain, and Batiste and his companions had been attempting to circumvent this. According to a letter in a local newspaper, the activities of Guernsey traders in this respect were brought to the notice of the East India Company by informants in 1824, and an order was sent to the island by HM Treasury to put a stop to them.[11] After 1833, when the East India Company's monopoly on tea imports ceased, such prosecutions also ceased, and customs-related prosecutions reverted to a trickle.

Semi-civil actions

We noted above that semi-civil actions declined from 41 per cent of criminal cases in the period 1680–1764 to just 11 per cent in the period dealt with here. The proportion comprised by actions for *nouvelle dessaisine* declined particularly sharply, and, by the end of our period, the action had ceased to be used. The last case seems to have occurred in 1840, when Sr Mathieu Tostevin was sentenced to restitution and costs after being actioned by Mr Charles Le Lacheur for cutting and removing brushwood from Le Lacheur's field.[12]

Causes en adjonction survived but underwent a major change of application. This change concerned their use in respect of assault. The first intimations of an incipient shift became apparent towards the end of the eighteenth century. An interesting document survives in Guernsey's Royal Court Library which seems to mark a pivotal moment. This was a pamphlet published in 1798 entitled *Examen d'une Question en Petit-Criminel*.[13] The anonymous author, who identified himself as a 'distinguished citizen', appears to have been publicly prosecuted for an assault after the injured party reported him to the authorities instead of seeking redress through *une cause*

---

[10] 9.6.1827, GG, *Crime*, vol. 26.
[11] H.D. Jeremie in *Comet*, 30.1.1832.
[12] 28.3.1840, GG, *Crime*, vol. 30.
[13] Royal Court Library, IA.

en adjonction. The author did not deny the assault, but insisted that it was a private matter between himself and the other party and thus not suitable for public prosecution. 'If such cases continue to be admitted,' he urged,

> there will no longer be any private transgressions, and the Crown's time will be entirely taken up with disputes between individuals as if they were crimes threatening the very existence of society … in a short while causes *en adjonction* of all kinds will cease, and every quarrel will be dealt with au grand criminel.

Mild exaggeration aside, the author had correctly foreseen the future. This was moreover a change which was occurring throughout Europe. In England, according to Professor Peter King, assault lost its essentially civil character some time between the American War of Independence and the beginning of the French Revolutionary War.[14]

In Guernsey, the change of attitude to assault (which came to encompass verbal as well as physical violence) increasingly restricted the use of *causes en adjonction* to defamation. They were particularly resorted to for this purpose after the advent of local newspapers.[15] Early-nineteenth-century editors had a comparatively relaxed attitude to what they published, and persons who considered themselves unfairly maligned reached for the *cause en adjonction* as the most expeditious remedy. The last few decades of our period were peppered with such actions, and in 1841, no fewer than four editors were brought before the Court in separate *causes* for defamation. Damages to the plaintiffs in these cases ranged between 12 and 200 *livres tournois* (17s 2d to £14 6s). As always, this was complemented by a smaller fine to *le Fisc*.[16]

Summary prosecutions

In the period 1680–1764, there were an average of only five summary prosecutions per year. In the period dealt with by this chapter, this rose to nearly fifty per year.[17] The increase was due to a combination of factors, all acting

---

[14] P. King, 'Punishing assault: the transformation of attitudes in the English courts', *Journal of Interdisciplinary History*, 27 (1996), pp. 52, 61.

[15] Guernsey's first known newspaper, *La Gazette de Guernesey*, appeared on 8.1.1791.

[16] 30.1.1841, 1.5.1841, 15.5.1841, 5.6.1841, GG, *Crime*, vol. 30.

[17] We should note that these figures are minima, since a summary prosecution was only recorded if it resulted in a conviction.

simultaneously. Accelerating immigration and population growth produced a very real rise in troublesome behaviour, as did the widening of the wealth gap and proliferation of opportunities for theft. This was to some extent compounded by changing subjective attitudes. Scholars such as Vic Gatrell have identified the late 1700s as a period when the British elite's tolerance of plebeian misbehaviour declined in the face of anxieties over social and political unrest.[18] There was also the growing influence of Evangelicalism, to whose imprecations against 'vice and immorality' local Jurats were not deaf.

All of these factors played a part in the late-eighteenth-century increase in public prosecution of assaults previously dealt with *en adjonction*. They also contributed to the major change in policing whereby, in 1799, St Peter Port's assistant constables were granted precisely the same powers as the principal Constables.[19] This was truly ground-breaking, in that any assistant constable could henceforth order a person to appear in Court entirely on his own initiative, simply by issuing them with a 'warning' to present themselves at the next judicial session. As a result of this change, summary prosecutions, already mounting, rose almost exponentially in the first decade of the nineteenth century. Their scope also broadened considerably as the traditional categories of assault, theft and disorderly conduct were joined by an increasingly varied miscellany of other minor misdeeds. In this decade, too, came the first identifiable summary prosecutions of children. In the spring of 1802, brothers William and Edward Berry, explicitly identified as 'minors', were sentenced to two days' imprisonment for throwing dirt at Elizabeth Le Gallez's washing and ill-treating Josué Mauger's children.[20] Rising numbers of convictions for such trivial mischief from the early 1800s are suggestive of sustained growth in juvenile prosecutions from this point on.

As the number of offences brought forward for summary prosecution rose, so did pressure on the Ordinary Court, which had traditionally disposed of such matters before the civil cases which formed the main business of their sittings. By the late 1820s and early 1830s, the volume of summary work had begun seriously to encroach on the time available for other business, and this prompted a change in the Court's mode of operation. A series of measures were adopted which reconstituted the criminal iteration of the Ordinary

[18] V.A.C. Gatrell, 'Crime, authority and the policeman-state', in F.M.L. Thompson (ed.), *The Cambridge Social History of Britain, 1750–1950*, 3 vols (Cambridge, 1990), 3, p. 243.
[19] Ord, 30.9.1799.
[20] 23.4.1802, GG, *Crime*, vol. 20.

Court in the new guise of the Police Court or *Cour de Police Correctionnelle*.[21] Firstly, summary criminal business was detached from the Court's other business and concentrated on Thursdays. Secondly, these Thursday sessions were extended throughout the year. Thirdly, the Court began to sit with no more than two Jurats in addition to the Bailiff (or Lieutenant Bailiff).[22] Fourthly, the Court's summary sentencing powers became more clearly defined.[23] Fifthly, police officers (Constables, assistant constables and special constables) were recognised as primarily responsible for bringing offenders to Court.[24] These five important changes, which were all in place by the mid-1830s, were introduced gradually, and purely by convention of the Court.[25]

By the quinquennium 1840–4, summary prosecutions comprised an unprecedented 62 per cent of the Court's criminal business, and the transformation which had begun in the second half of the eighteenth century was virtually complete. The wholesale move into summary mode simultaneously created and reflected a change in the Court's criminal clientele. The vast majority of people now standing in the dock were poor.

---

[21] The concept of the Police Court/*Cour de Police Correctionnelle* was based on British and French precedents. In France, *les tribunaux de police correctionnelle* had come into existence in 1790 when the Revolutionaries reorganised the criminal justice system. In England, police courts had grown organically out of the seven police offices introduced to London in the wake of the 1792 Gordon Riots (themselves modelled on the Bow Street police office in existence since 1739). At each of these offices, three stipendiary magistrates were appointed to despatch all criminal business arising in their districts. In due course, these police offices became known as police courts, and the concept was copied in provincial towns and cities (J.M. Carbasse, *Histoire du Droit Pénal et de la Justice Criminelle* (2000; Paris, 2014 edn), p. 437; J.M. Beattie, *Crime and the Courts in England, 1660–1800* (Oxford, 1986), pp. 65–6).

[22] Two Jurats had always been the minimum quorum for the Ordinary Court. However, it had seldom sat with two alone. In the quinquennia 1780–4 and 1800–4, it sat with two Jurats in only 4 per cent of summary cases. In the other 96 per cent of cases, it sat sometimes with three Jurats, sometimes with four, and sometimes with even larger numbers.

[23] These came to be recognised as the power to award up to one month's imprisonment (in part or whole on bread and water or in solitary confinement); the power to award small fines of up to 30 *livres tournois* (about £2 3s); the power to order a moderate whipping or birching; and the power to bind over individuals to be of good behaviour or keep the peace.

[24] *Second Report of the Commissioners Appointed to Inquire into the State of the Criminal Law in the Channel Islands: Guernsey* (London, 1848), p. 102.

[25] Other aspects of summary procedure remained unaltered. Sittings continued to be open to the public, and the accused remained entitled to representation by an Advocate. The Law Officers continued to act as prosecutors and to deliver their *conclusions* as to verdict and sentence. In its new Police Court guise, the Ordinary Court also continued to function as *une cour d'instruction*.

Indeed, a majority seem to have come from the most disadvantaged backgrounds: alcoholics, street girls, social misfits, and juveniles from difficult homes. In making this transition, Guernsey's criminal justice system had ceased being a service provided for 'us' and become a tool for dealing with 'them'.

Serious crime

In the period 1680–1764, crimes tried on indictment had amounted to just 4 per cent of the Royal Court's criminal business. By the period dealt with here, the proportion had risen to 10 per cent. Taking our sample quinquennia in aggregate, two-thirds of cases tried on indictment concerned property crime (up from one-half in 1680–1764); just over a fifth involved interpersonal violence (unchanged since 1680–1764); and the remaining tenth consisted of miscellaneous crimes, to which a number of novel offences had been added since the previous period.

In trials on indictment, registers usually recorded the accused's place of origin (a detail omitted in summary trials). Only 36 per cent of those indicted came from the Bailiwick of Guernsey; a further 50 per cent came from Great Britain or Ireland; 4 per cent came from France; and 3 per cent from Jersey. At almost two-thirds of the total, strangers to the island formed a clear majority of those indicted for serious crime. The category was also strongly male-dominated, with 90 per cent of serious offences in this period committed by males.[26]

To some extent, the predominance of male strangers in this category was related to the presence of British and allied troops, of whom, as noted above, more than 50,000 passed through Guernsey during the French Wars. Before proceeding, therefore, a few general words are in order in respect of the military. By and large, men who took the king's shilling were drawn from the most deprived classes in society, many enlisting through desperation, others tricked into enlisting when they were drunk or otherwise vulnerable. Further, owing to the policy of pardoning convicted felons in return for military life

---

[26] Summary prosecutions were slightly less male-dominated, with only 80 per cent of offences in the current period committed by males.

service, a significant proportion of British soldiers came with prior criminal records.[27] While all the regiments stationed in Guernsey contained their quota of these, some, such as the Royal African Corps and its sister regiment the Royal York Rangers, were entirely composed of pardoned offenders. These regiments were stationed in Guernsey intermittently between 1804 and 1808, and again in 1814.[28] Their members were responsible for many serious crimes and inspired mistrust throughout the community.

Plate 18. Satirical cartoon depicting British military recruits in 1780
© The National Army Museum/Mary Evans Picture Library

[27] This practice was first authorised by the 1705 Mutiny Act (J.A. Sharpe, *Crime in Early Modern England, 1550–1750* (1984; London, 1999 edn), p. 97).
[28] In 1807, the Royal African Corps changed its name to the Royal York Rangers. In 1808, the Royal York Rangers were divided into two separate regiments. One of these retained the York name, and the other re-emerged as the Royal African Corps (W.Y. Baldry, 'Disbanded regiments', *Journal of the Society for Army Historical Research*, 56 (1935), p. 233).

Interpersonal violence

Homicide

Some thirty-eight individuals were charged with killing another human being in the eighty years between 1765 and 1844. By this period, the wording of *actes d'accusation* (indictments) for any type of killing was fairly standardised – namely, that someone had *félonieusement tué, occis et meurtri* (killed, slain and destroyed) someone else, usually *dépourvu de la crainte de Dieu* (bereft of the fear of God) and *de propos prémédité* (premeditatedly).[29] Of the thirty-eight persons charged with homicide in this period, only eight were women. Five of these women were charged with killing their newborns; two were charged with attempted homicide (their intended victims not having died); and the eighth, suspected of a fatal stabbing, had the charges against her dropped. None of these women was capitally punished.

Of the thirty males charged with homicide, ten were found guilty of killing their victims intentionally. Nine of these men were hanged. Five of the remaining twenty were acquitted, and the other fifteen were found guilty of manslaughter. Sixteen of the men charged with homicide in this period were serving or former soldiers, and most of their offences were committed

---

[29] Use of the word *félonieusement* is interesting. The term *félonie* appeared several times in *Le Grand Coutumier* to designate the breach of fidelity owed to feudal superiors which was characteristically punished by forfeiture. This term was imported into England after the Norman Conquest, and by the early Middle Ages, serious crimes such as treason, murder and rape were designated 'felonies' on the principle that convicted 'felons' suffered capital punishment and thus forfeited their property. The word *félonie* was never used in this sense in France. At the beginning of the period covered by this study, it was not used in this sense in Guernsey either. In the mid-1600s, Thomas Le Marchant had defined *félonie* simply as 'a deliberate and premeditated action proceeding from hatred, malice, or the desire for vengeance' (T. Le Marchant, *Remarques et Animadversions sur l'Approbation des Lois et Coustumier de Normandie usitées ès Jurisdictions de Guernezé*, 2 vols (Guernsey, 1826), 2, p. 208). One of the first appearances of this term in Guernsey's crime registers occurred in 1726, when Rachel Moulin was charged with having *félonieusement commis le crime de meurtre* after the bones of an infant were found in her garden (18.3.1726, GG, *Crime*, vol. 10). For the first few decades thereafter the word was used sporadically but not consistently in connection with serious crimes. By the 1790s, however, the use of the words *félonie* and *félonieusement* had become routine, and, in a growing convergence with English notions, generally denoted serious crimes punishable by actual or civil death and confiscation.

during fights with fellow soldiers. The following section will look, in sequence, at males convicted of murder, males convicted of manslaughter, and males who were acquitted of homicide.

Three of the male-perpetrated murders of this period stand out as particularly interesting and/or significant, and we will focus on these. The first occurred in 1775 and concerned Nicolas Rougier.[30] Although the case was a fairly 'classic' one involving young men and alcohol, it is of interest because Rougier was the only native Guernseyman to hang for murder in our period. Rougier, in his twenties, was accused of fatally stabbing Jean Du Four, also in his twenties, in an altercation late one Sunday night outside a public house at le Bourg in the Forest. Both had been the worse for wear, particularly Rougier, who been drinking cider and *eau de vie* all day. Du Four had been stabbed three times: in the back, in the ear, and in the chest. The wound to his chest had severed an artery and caused a fatal haemorrhage. Rougier insisted that he had been too drunk to remember anything about the incident, but his guilt was confirmed by several other young men who were present during the altercation. Other witnesses testified that Rougier was a bad character and argumentative when drunk. His case was not helped by the fact that he had fled from the scene and lain low until found the next day. After investigations and a trial collectively lasting three months, Rougier was sentenced to be hanged. No application was made for clemency, and the execution was carried out within six days.[31]

We shall look next at a military murderer. The interest in this case lies in the fact that, unusually for a soldier, the victim was a woman rather than a man, and killed during a burglary rather than a fight. Robert Wilson was a twenty-seven-year-old private in the Royal York Rangers. He was also known as James Wood, under which name he had been convicted of a capital offence in England but reprieved in return for enlisting.[32] Early one morning in 1808, Wilson had entered the home of seventy-four-year-old Vale widow Olympe Henry with intent to commit a burglary. Apparently surprised in the act by Mrs Henry, he had cut the elderly woman's throat before leaving her house with cash and other stolen articles. Wilson was in due course apprehended and confessed in full to the burglary and fatal attack. His trial was quickly

---

[30] Exceptionally, the depositions in this case have survived intact. They are to be found in GG, Miscellaneous Books, no. 38.

[31] 1.7.1775, GG, *Crime*, vol. 15.

[32] He claimed to be connected with Jerry Abershaw, a notorious highwayman hanged in London in 1795 (*The Times*, 8.6.1808).

despatched, there was no appeal for mercy, and he was executed just three weeks after the crime had been committed.[33] Following the incident, Lieutenant Bailiff Eléazar Le Marchant wrote to the Privy Council via the Lieutenant Governor to request that no more convicts be sent to Guernsey under military colours.[34] His request was not granted.

While the outcomes of the Rougier and Wilson cases were in a sense predictable, the next one we shall consider had a highly unusual outcome. This case concerned Joseph Chapman (also known as 'Captain Melmoth'), who was a half-pay lieutenant in the 61st (South Gloucestershire) Regiment and a veteran of the Peninsular War.[35] He was separated from his wife, and had moved to Guernsey around 1818, where he lived on a private income. Prior to the homicide with which he was charged, he had been lodging at the house of William Brown at Les Banques. Chapman appears to have been a difficult character, given to heavy drinking and aggressive outbursts. There were allegations that he was engaged in a sexual relationship with Brown's fifteen-year-old daughter.[36]

In the evening of 15 November 1825, Lieutenant Chapman had a violent argument with William Brown, as a result of which Brown became fearful and asked a friend to stay in the house overnight. Early the following morning, when the friend had departed, Chapman came down from his room and shot Brown dead. Chapman admitted during his *interrogatoire* that he had indeed shot Brown but claimed that his pistol had gone off accidentally. His defence counsel, Robert MacCulloch, sought to exonerate him by contending that Chapman had acted while the balance of his mind was disturbed. The trial concluded on 28 January 1826. Five of the ten Jurats thought the murder was deliberate but committed while the accused was temporarily insane. The other five Jurats thought the killing accidental. The Bailiff, Daniel Brock, used his casting vote to support the insanity verdict, and the apparently 'unhinged' Chapman was consigned to the safe custody of a prison cell. Meanwhile, the Court wrote to the Privy Council to request guidance as to how to dispose of him.

---

[33] 28.5.1808, GG, *Crime*, vol. 22. According to a local newspaper, Wilson cut a defiant figure on the gallows, where he refused the ministrations of local clergymen (*Gazette de Guernesey*, 4.6.1808).

[34] Le Marchant to Lieutenant Governor, 16.5.1808, GG, Royal Court Letter Book (first series), vol. 2.

[35] The following account has been compiled from 19.11.1825, 28.1.1826, GG, *Crime* vol. 26; 30.8.1831, GG, *Crime*, vol. 28; *Star*, 31.1.1826; *Indépendance*, 4.2.1826, 11.2.1826.

[36] *Bath Chronicle & Weekly Gazette*, 24.11.1825.

This was an entirely unprecedented proceeding. In the past, when dealing with an offender who was clearly insane, the Court had acted as prescribed in Terrien,[37] and simply discharged the accused and handed him or her over to relatives to be kept in safe custody.[38] In the Chapman case, the Court's decision seems to have been based on Westminster's 1800 Criminal Lunatics Act, which allowed mentally ill offenders to be found 'not guilty by reason of insanity' while authorising their detention at His Majesty's pleasure.[39] In nineteenth-century Britain, insanity verdicts were far from uncommon in murder trials involving persons of Chapman's social standing. Professor Carolyn Conley has observed that 'the courts in Britain were not comfortable with murder convictions against middle- or upper-class defendants, and … used insanity verdicts to avoid executing the respectable.'[40]

A file on Lieutenant Chapman survives in the National Archives.[41] It appears that the Royal Court's request for instructions went missing, and no further action was taken by either the Privy Council or the Court for the next four years. By this time, Chapman's continued presence in Guernsey's gaol had become burdensome. The prison was not designed for long-stayers, and Chapman's maintenance was an unwelcome charge on Crown revenues. Early in 1831, the Home Secretary, Lord Melbourne, received a dossier from Guernsey containing testimonials from two local doctors as to Chapman's restored sanity, and a covering letter from Bailiff Daniel Brock which asserted:

> the Royal Court of Guernsey, in conformity with their sentence of 28th January 1826, are fully authorized to liberate the said Chapman on condition that he leaves the island for ever [but] the Court have hitherto been unwilling without the concurrence of His Majesty's Government to incur the responsibility of setting [him] at large, in England.[42]

---

[37] G. Terrien, *Commentaires du Droict Civil tant Public que Privé Observé au Pays & Duché de Normandie* (1574; Paris, 1578 edn), p. 496.

[38] For instances of this, see cases of John Leghorn, 25.8.1709, GG, *Crime*, vol. 7; Rachel De Carteret, 3.7.1770, GG, *Crime*, vol. 14; Pierre Girard, 5.7.1793, GG, *Crime*, vol. 19.

[39] J. Turner, P. Taylor, S. Morley & K. Corteen (eds), *A Companion to the History of Crime and Criminal Justice* (Bristol, 2017), p. 56.

[40] C.A. Conley, *Certain other Countries: Homicide, Gender, and National Identity in Late Nineteenth-Century England, Ireland, Scotland, and Wales* (Columbus, Ohio, 2007), p. 91.

[41] NA, HO 17/87/141.

[42] Bailiff to Lord Melbourne, 15.2.1831, NA, HO 17/87/141.

There is no trace in the National Archives file of explicit permission for Chapman's release, but in the summer of 1831, the Deputy Prévôt took the Lieutenant to Southampton and left him there, from which point Chapman disappeared from Guernsey's records for good.[43] Some time later, the Royal Commissioners on Channel Island Criminal Law questioned the correctness of the Court's decision to liberate Chapman. Advocate Peter Jeremie stated that his release was fully permissible because Chapman's 'insanity' had only ever been 'temporary'.[44]

Turning now to manslaughter. Eleven British soldiers were punished for manslaughter in our period. All the rank-and-file soldiers killed their victims in fights, and the officers killed their victims in duels. Four native male civilians were also punished for manslaughter. One killed his victim in a duel, and the remaining three caused someone's death in an accident.[45] We shall here consider only the twelve men who killed their victims in fights or duels.

We saw in Chapter 3 that, in assimilating Guernsey's manslaughter practice to that of England and Wales, the Court had adopted the standard seventeenth-century English sentence for manslaughter, namely branding followed by release. In the current period, there were three cases in which this punishment was applied: those of Private John McDougal in 1787, and Privates Ewan McDonald and James Charlesworth in 1798.[46] These were the last cases in which branding/release was used.[47] In the rank-and-file manslaughter cases which occurred after 1799, punishments ranged from life banishment to short gaol terms, calibrated according to the degree of culpability.

---

[43] 30.8.1831, GG, *Crime*, vol. 28.

[44] *Second Report*, pp. 224–5.

[45] The three accidental killings involved a militiaman whose gun went off unexpectedly during a parade (one month's imprisonment, 25.6.1800, GG, *Crime*, vol. 20); an unlicensed 'doctor' who prescribed a fatal dose of laudanum (three months, 3.2.1838, GG, *Crime*, vol. 30); and a thirteen-year-old boy who fired a deadly live round from a toy canon (one month, 1.2.1840, GG, *Crime*, vol. 30).

[46] 1.9.1787, GG, *Crime*, vol. 17; 3.2.1798, 17.2.1798, GG, *Crime*, vol. 20. In these three cases, crime registers actually spelled out that the soldiers sentenced to branding had been convicted of '*l'homicide appelé en anglais Manslaughter*'.

[47] Guernsey was here behind England and Wales, where imprisonment had become the usual penalty for manslaughter in the 1760s, and the branding of clergied offenders had been abolished in 1779 (Beattie, *Crime and the Courts*, pp. 88–9).

Duellists who killed were handled somewhat differently. Between the 1780s and 1840s, there were a number of duels in Guernsey which pitted the military against civilians.[48] Frederick Lukis attributed some of these to the fact that 'the officers of the Garrison sometimes gave themselves a higher bearing towards the Gentlemen & Militia of the Island than was proper'.[49] Three of the duels resulted in homicide charges, but only one man suffered a punishment. The man unlucky enough to be punished was twenty-five-year-old Advocate Thomas Andros, who was sentenced to four weeks' imprisonment in 1780 for shooting dead Kenneth Beauvais, an officer of the 78th (Highland) Regiment.[50] In 1795, surgeon James Taylor of the 92nd Regiment had the homicide charge against him dropped, even though he had admitted duelling with Major William Byng who was found dying of a gunshot wound at the New Ground.[51] In 1798, Lieutenant Charles Thompson of the 27th (Inniskilling) Regiment fled Guernsey after killing William Tupper in a duel, and, despite being found guilty *in absentia*, never suffered any penalty.[52] Royal Court crime registers contain no entries relating to fatal duels after 1798.

It was noted above that five of the men charged with homicide in the period 1765–1844 were acquitted. Of these acquittals, we shall look at only one. This case is particularly worthy of consideration for what it tells us about local attitudes. It concerned a seventeen-year-old Danish cabin boy named Wilhelm Fleckner who died in December 1844. The case began the previous month, when John Gardner, one of St Peter Port's assistant constables, was

---

[48] Duelling had been used by the British nobility and gentry as a way of upholding honour since the 1600s. The first duel-related entry in Guernsey's crime registers appeared in 1716, when an English officer was accused of issuing a challenge to a civilian but evaded prosecution by fleeing the island (18.4.1716, GG, *Crime*, vol. 8). There was then silence on duels until the 1780s.

[49] F.C. Lukis, 'Reminiscences of Former Days in Connection with Guernsey', PL. On this subject see also, P.K. Johnston, 'Duelling in Guernsey: T. Andros v. K. Beauvoir [sic]', *The Review of the Guernsey Society* (Summer 1976), pp. 44–6 and 'Four Guernsey duels', *The Review of the Guernsey Society* (Summer 1998), pp. 57–8.

[50] 11.11.1780, GG, *Crime*, vol. 16. The episode is recounted at length in *Star*, 16.6.1878. Andros was the father of the Jurat of the same name elected in 1843 (see Chapter 5).

[51] 14.3.1795, GG, *Crime*, vol. 19.

[52] 2.2.1799, GG, *Crime*, vol. 20. For a detailed account of this episode, see R. Hocart, *Peter de Havilland: Bailiff of Guernsey: A History of his Life, 1747–1821* (Guernsey, 1997), pp. 63–5.

called to the harbour to investigate reports that the cabin boy had been excessively beaten by the captain and mate of his ship. Gardner removed the seventeen-year-old from his vessel and took him up to the courthouse to obtain guidance as to how to proceed.[53] Here, however, he received the instruction to return the boy to the boat – apparently from William Mellish, one of St Peter Port's principal Constables, who was the consignee of the vessel's cargo.[54] Wilhelm Fleckner was subjected to further beatings on return to his ship. He then tried to commit suicide, after which he was bound to the ship's mast for several hours, ostensibly to forestall further attempts. After seeing the boy tied up, another port user, Philip Le Couteur, summoned a different assistant constable, George Payne, and insisted that the boy be taken off the boat. This time Fleckner was in such poor physical condition that he was taken to the Town Hospital.[55] When it became apparent that the boy was unlikely to survive, the Royal Court summarily tried – and acquitted – Constable Mellish and assistant constable Gardner for failing to perform their duty properly.[56]

On 7 December, Wilhelm Fleckner died in the Town Hospital.[57] On 9 December, Captain Hans Christensen was indicted for homicide, and on the following day the same charge was filed against mate Paul Bisscrop.[58] During the procedural stages of the men's trial, conflicting evidence was heard from doctors. Frederick Lukis and Marc Corbin, who carried out an autopsy on Fleckner, testified that the boy's body carried 'no signs of organic disease' and that, in their opinion, he had died from injuries caused by ill-treatment.[59]

---

[53] In the past, Guernsey's authorities had occasionally acted to protect crew members from violent officers. In 1806, for instance, the Court had ordered Norwegian cabin boy Christian Jorgen Neglin to be removed from his ship and sent home at the captain's expense when evidence emerged that he had beaten the boy excessively (12.4.1806, GG, *Crime*, vol. 21).

[54] *Star*, 21.11.1844.

[55] *Star*, 21.11.1844. Fleckner's arrival at the Hospital was recorded in its registers, where he was described as 'grievously injured' (17.11.1844, IA, DC/HX 130–01).

[56] *Star*, 2.12.1844.

[57] 7.12.1844, IA, DC/HX 130–01; *Star*, 12.12.1844.

[58] 9.12.1844, 10.12.1844, GG, *Crime*, vol. 31. The men's *actes d'accusation* spelled out that they had *félonieusement tué, occis et meurtri* Fleckner by (1) having beaten the boy with their fists and a piece of rope on several occasions between 2 and 17 November; (2) having confined the boy in a barrel on deck on several occasions between the same dates; (3) having tied the boy to a winch at the foot of the main mast and left him there between 2.00am and 7.00am on 17 November.

[59] *Star*, 10.2.1844. See also NA, HO 45/931.

A third medical man who had watched the autopsy, Nicholas Magrath, said that Fleckner may have had health problems whose exacerbation by rough handling had indirectly resulted in his death. Christensen's defence counsel John Utermarck (who later became Bailiff) used Magrath's testimony to support his contention that Fleckner had not died from ill-treatment and that his client was therefore not guilty of murder. The *Star* reported him as stating:

> the prisoner was accused of having committed murder, and nothing less. The Court must be satisfied that he was guilty of this crime, or it would not have the right to condemn him to a day's imprisonment. It must either pronounce an unqualified acquittal, or it must convict him of murder. [60]

Utermarck was just a young Advocate of twenty-six, but his contention (if correctly reported) is puzzling, because – like all other persons accused of causing a death – Christensen and Bisscrop were charged simply with homicide, and the Court had on countless previous occasions found such people guilty only of manslaughter and punished them accordingly. In the event, six of the ten Jurats sitting in judgment on Christensen and Bisscrop adopted Utermarck's view and voted for unqualified acquittals. [61] A simple majority sufficing to carry a verdict, both men were freed and left Guernsey for Denmark five days later. [62]

As noted above, only eight women were charged with homicide between 1765 and 1844. Of these, five were charged with killing their newborns, two were charged with attempted homicide, and the eighth had the charges against her dropped. The women accused of killing their newborns will be dealt with in the separate section on infanticide below, but we will first briefly consider the cases of the two women charged with attempted homicide. These were twenty-year-old Françoise Archenaux in 1834 and fourteen-year-old Mary Ann Dorrill in 1838. Both young women were domestic servants accused of trying to poison their employers. Françoise Archenaux had put arsenic into a bottle of her master's wine after having been given notice for striking one of his children. [63] Mary Ann Dorrill had put lead acetate into a

[60] *Star*, 10.2.1844.
[61] 8.2.1845, GG, *Crime*, vol. 31.
[62] *Star*, 13.2.1845.
[63] *Star*, 27.10.1834.

bottle of brandy after having been barred from going out unaccompanied.[64] While no one had suffered serious harm as a result of the girls' actions, the Court viewed them extremely seriously, not least because they breached the fundamental trust which masters placed in their employees. Françoise Archenaux's sentence came in triple form: she was firstly to spend two hours hatless in the cage with a notice inscribed '*Empoisonneuse*' above her head; then she was to spend three months in gaol (in solitary confinement on bread and water); and finally, she was to be banished in perpetuity on pain of hanging if she returned.[65] In Mary Ann Dorrill's case, the cage and imprisonment were omitted, but she, too, was sentenced to perpetual banishment on pain of hanging if she returned.[66] For Françoise, a Frenchwoman, banishment probably meant no more than a return home. For Mary Ann, who was Guernsey-born and hardly more than a child, banishment represented a far greater degree of hardship. Banished, however, she was.[67]

Infanticide

In the period dealt with here, five women and one man were brought to Court for killing their infants. As previously, they were charged simply with homicide, since there was no separate crime of infanticide in Guernsey. Of these six, only the man was hanged. Although his case was arguably the most interesting, we will begin by examining the cases of the five women.

The women brought to Court on suspicion of killing their infants in the period covered by this chapter were Marie Langlois (1771), Margaret Mackenzie (1817), Rachel Brehaut (1822), Elizabeth Robin (1826), and Sarah Elliott (1830).[68] In all of these cases, the softening trend detected in

[64] *Comet*, 17.6.1839.

[65] 25.10.1834, GG, *Crime*, vol. 29.

[66] 15.6.1838, GG, *Crime*, vol. 30.

[67] Mary Ann Dorrill eventually returned to Guernsey in 1848, blind and unable to maintain herself. Her original sentence was formally remitted, and she seems to have spent the next decades as a recipient of parochial poor relief (Bailiff to Home Secretary, 6.11.1848, GG, Royal Court General Letter Book (second series), vol. 3; O in C, 28.11.1848, GG, *Ordres du Conseil et Actes du Parlement*, vol 6).

[68] 29.6.1771, GG, *Crime*, vol. 14; 6.12.1817, GG, *Crime*, vol. 24; 13.7.1822, GG, *Crime*, vol. 25; 4.3.1826, GG, *Crime*, vol. 26; 23.10.1830, GG, *Crime*, vol. 28.

the 1750s continued. Rachel Brehaut was acquitted, and – despite John Utermarck's contention that it was impossible under Guernsey law to find a person guilty of anything less than the full offence with which he was charged – the other four were convicted only of concealment (as we saw in Chapter 3, Guernsey's Court had imitated English practice in bringing in verdicts of concealment from an early period).

Since the cases of the four women convicted of concealment shared many similarities, we will use the best documented – that of Margaret Mackenzie – to illustrate the way in which these cases were dealt with. Margaret was the unmarried servant of twenty-two-year-old newly qualified Advocate John Jeremie and his wife, and lived with them at their house in Smith Street. She was accused of having concealed her pregnancy, given birth secretly at night, killed her baby, then disposed of it in a tub in the yard which served as a privy. An autopsy had found the infant to be full-term and without signs of violence on its body. Margaret Mackenzie contended that the baby had been stillborn. The two medical men who performed the autopsy disagreed with one another as to whether or not the baby had breathed.[69] The trial came up for judgment in December 1817. Defence Advocate Charles De Jersey attempted to argue that, since Margaret Mackenzie was charged with homicide, homicide would have to be proved in due form, or she would have to be acquitted. He added that, even if it had been technically possible to find his client guilty of a lesser charge, a verdict of concealment would not be acceptable because no such crime existed in *L'Approbation* or Terrien. 'I expect Terrien to be adhered to,' De Jersey said; 'surely the Jurats … will not follow English law under present circumstances.'[70] Nevertheless, English law was followed, and Margaret Mackenzie was duly found guilty of concealment. She was sentenced to perform *amende honorable* at the bar of the Court, and thereafter to be banished for six years.[71]

The only man charged with killing a newborn in our period suffered a harsher fate. This was Marie Joseph François Béasse, a former French army officer in his thirties who had bought a large house in Guernsey after coming

[69] *Indépendance*, 20.12.1817.
[70] *Indépendance*, 10.1.1818.
[71] 6.12.1817, GG, *Crime*, vol. 24; *Indépendance*, 13.12.1817.

into an inheritance.[72] His housemaid, Sarah Elliott, who was originally from Exeter, had become pregnant by Béasse shortly after starting work for him.[73] Béasse, who was aware of his servant's pregnancy, had apparently intended to send the girl to England to give birth, but the baby had arrived sooner than expected. The birth took place at night, in Sarah Elliott's bedroom, with Béasse the only other person in the house. Allegations of foul play were soon made, as a result of which the back garden of Béasse's house was searched. A corpse was found and exhumed. The autopsy which followed revealed that the baby's digestive tract had been perforated by the insertion of a sharp instrument downwards through its mouth and upwards through its anus. Both parents were charged with killing the infant. However, when medical experts testified that Sarah Elliott could not have inflicted such damage in her post-partum condition, the principal burden of guilt fell on Béasse.

When the trials of Elliott and Béasse came to Court for judgment on 23 October 1830, the Law Officers recommended the death penalty for Béasse and a lesser penalty for Elliott whom they deemed guilty only of concealment. The ten Jurats sitting in judgment on the pair endorsed these recommendations unanimously.[74] Perhaps because the baby's killing was so cold-blooded and deliberate, there was no request for clemency in respect of Béasse. A petition to the Home Secretary from Béasse himself achieved nothing, and neither did a hasty visit to London by his defence Advocate, Peter Jeremie.[75] Under the watchful eyes of a detachment of fifty soldiers,[76] Béasse was hanged on Friday 5 November in front of a crowd of 'thousands'.[77] Sarah Elliott, like Margaret Mackenzie before her, was sentenced to perform *amende honorable* and banished for six years.[78]

---

[72] For biographical details on Béasse, see H. Juin (ed.), *Victor Hugo, Choses Vues: Souvenirs, Journaux, Cahiers, 1849–1869* (Paris, 1972), pp. 306–11.

[73] The account which follows is drawn from *Comet*, 25.10.1830, and a local broadsheet dated 5.11.1830 (PL).

[74] 23.10.1830, GG, *Crime*, vol. 28.

[75] NA, HO 17/26/132. Jeremie went on to become a lifelong opponent of the death penalty.

[76] Bailiff to Lieutenant Governor, 2.11.1830; Lieutenant Governor to Bailiff, 3.11.1830, GG, Royal Court General Letter Book (first series), vol. 4.

[77] 'Murder and execution in Guernsey sixty years ago', *The Guernsey Magazine*, 16 (October 1888), p. 83.

[78] Sarah Elliott was the last person to be sentenced to *amende honorable* in Guernsey. In France, *amende honorable* had been abolished as a judicial punishment in 1791 (B. Garnot, *Crime et Justice aux XVIIe et XVIIIe Siècles* (Paris, 2000), p. 23).

Abortion

Just two cases involving suspected abortionists came to the Royal Court's attention between 1765 and 1844. The first was that of William Hammill, a self-styled man-midwife from Plymouth who practised in Guernsey from around 1810. Advertisements in local newspapers vaunted his services as a modern alternative to 'old women in the country' and their 'emmenagogues', which never failed 'to destroy the strongest constitution'.[79] In 1822, Hammill was arrested during investigations into the case of Rachel Brehaut who was suspected of terminating her pregnancy or otherwise doing away with her infant.[80] Brehaut eventually stood trial for concealment and was acquitted for lack of proof,[81] but Hammill was permitted to abjure the island for two years rather than be prosecuted for any crime.[82]

Seven years later, a similar practitioner came to the notice of the Court, with similarly equivocal results. In June 1829, Thomas Beaugie of St Martins was arrested on suspicion of having terminated Anne Dumaresq's pregnancy by inserting an instrument into her uterus. Enquiries were made, but Beaugie was released when it became apparent that there was insufficient evidence on which to base a charge.[83]

Suicide

Guernsey saw an upsurge in suicides during the French Revolutionary and Napoleonic Wars. This was especially evident among soldiers, where precipitating factors might include such things as harsh discipline, bullying and alcohol abuse. In the second half of the eighteenth century, the Court began systematically to ascribe suicide to a temporary loss of reason and allow the burial of such people in consecrated ground. Thus the two soldiers who killed themselves within days of each other at Delancey Barracks in December 1797 were described as *dérangés dans leurs esprits* (disturbed in their mind),

---

[79] *Indépendance*, 15.11.1817.
[80] *Indépendance*, 15.6.1822.
[81] 13.7.1822, GG, *Crime*, vol. 25.
[82] 15.11.1822, GG, *Crime*, vol. 25. Abjuration will be discussed in the section on Punishment, below.
[83] 22.6.1829, 27.6.1829, GG, *Crime*, vol. 27.

and permission was given for a Christian burial.[84] This mirrored a more sympathetic attitude towards suicide all over western Europe. Reflecting on such matters in 1798, Jurat (and later Bailiff) Peter De Havilland noted 'in these enlightened times one cannot believe that any man would destroy himself unless he was deranged.'[85]

The single judicial sentence to the dragging and beach burial of a suicide victim in our period was issued in 1807. Its purpose, however, was to inflict symbolic punishment on a convicted criminal who, like John Kemp in 1753, had eluded actual punishment. Private John Hyles of the Royal York Rangers had been found guilty of burglary and was awaiting the second instalment of his 300 lashes when he was unexpectedly found hanged at the gaol. Apprised of his suicide, the Court ordered the hangman to drag his body on a hurdle to the beach at Mare Pirouin and throw it into a pit above the high water mark.[86] This was the last known occurrence of such a practice in Guernsey.[87]

In England and Wales, after the introduction of municipal and county police forces in the 1820s and 1830s, courts adopted the entirely novel practice of prosecuting persons who had tried to take their own lives but survived the attempt.[88] This practice, which was essentially a public order measure, was noted by Guernsey's authorities, and in due course it began to be imitated locally. During the current period, there were only two prosecutions for suicide attempts – those of William Tostevin in 1835 and Nicolas Brouard in 1841.[89] However, from the 1850s onwards (and entirely without legislation), the prosecution of people who had unsuccessfully attempted to take their own lives became a routine part of the Royal Court's practice.

---

[84] Both inquests were held on 5.12.1797 (GG, *Crime*, vol. 20). One had cut his throat and the other hanged himself.

[85] Hocart, *Peter De Havilland*, p. 68.

[86] 12.12.1807, 29.12.1807, GG, *Crime*, vol. 22.

[87] Traditional rituals surrounding suicides in England and Wales were abolished by the 1823 Burial of Suicides Act which decreed that all suicide victims should henceforth be interred in either a churchyard or private ground.

[88] S. Moore, 'The decriminalisation of suicide' (unpub. PhD thesis, London University, 2000), pp. 40–3. For more on English policing, see Chapter 8, n. 84.

[89] 24.4.1835, 6.8.1835, GG, *Crime*, vol. 29; 25.3.1841, GG, *Crime*, vol. 30.

Serious assault

Trials of assault on indictment remained as rare between 1765 and 1844 as in the previous period. Indeed, the expansion of the summary sphere meant that many assaults formerly dealt with on indictment – such as those on public officers in the execution of their duty – were now despatched by the Ordinary Court, so that the only assaults generally deemed grave enough to be tried on indictment were those where injuries were life-threatening.

In all assaults tried on indictment in our period, the accused was male. Usually the victim was also male. In the absence of precise definitions and gradations of violence, sentences for such assaults varied considerably. Better-off assailants generally received a large fine, as did Sr Ezechiel Robin in 1797 for brutally beating an officer's batman in one of his fields.[90] Lower-status assailants might, by contrast, be whipped and then banished, as was Demeraran sailor John Jacobs in 1809 for his savage attack on a fellow crewman.[91]

As in the previous period, the Court was remarkably tolerant of domestic violence. Cases such as that of William Warden described in Chapter 3 continued to arise and to be handled in precisely the same ways. In what was almost a replay of the Warden case, the Court ordered the arrest of John Murrant in 1773 after learning that his wife was close to death after a beating she said he had inflicted.[92] Nevertheless, when Mrs Murrant recovered without dying, John Murrant, like Warden before him, was released without charge. His wife's injuries appear to have counted for nothing, and he was not held to account for the assault of which she accused him. As in the previous period, such prosecutions were hampered by the ban on wives testifying against husbands in Court.

---

[90] Robin was fined 300 *livres tournois* or about £21 8s 8d (28.1.1797, GG, *Crime*, vol. 19).
[91] Jacobs was sentenced to fifty lashes and six years' banishment (8.7.1809, GG, *Crime*, vol. 22).
[92] 4.12.1773, GG, *Crime*, vol. 15.

Sexual crime

Thirty-four crimes of a sexual nature were prosecuted in the eighty years between 1765 and 1844, of which twenty-eight were offences against adult women and six against girls. Thirteen of these cases were charged as full rape, fifteen as attempted rape, and six as indecent assault.

All thirteen charges of full rape fell in the wartime period between 1778 and Waterloo. Although evidential barriers in rape cases remained high, eleven of the thirteen alleged rapists were convicted. The high conviction rate was almost certainly related to the fact that, in all but one instance, the alleged rapist was a British soldier and the victim a local woman.[93] The death penalty, eschewed as a punishment for rape in the previous period, was used four times in the period examined here: in respect of Privates Dennis Kelly and John Reilly of the 96th Regiment of Foot in 1781, and Privates Daniel Fell and Edward Davies of the 67th (South Hampshire) Regiment in 1810. The 1781 case was a particularly grim one. Kelly and Reilly were among a gang of soldiers who burgled the house inhabited by brothers Pierre and Abraham Collenette and their families. After the soldiers had ransacked the house and brutally beaten the two Collenettes, Kelly and Reilly raped the men's wives in front of them. The Lieutenant Governor asked the Court to apply for mercy for Kelly, but the Court refused to do so on the grounds that islanders had suffered so long from military violence that it was time to make examples of the perpetrators.[94]

The 1810 case was equally appalling. This involved the gang rape of Emilie Piesing in the town guardhouse. One evening when out walking, Mrs Piesing was dragged into the guardhouse from the street and raped six times. Four of her assailants were sentenced to whipping and banishment, Privates Fell and Davies were hanged, and the officer in charge, a Lieutenant Leabon, was court-martialled for failing to control his men.[95]

All twelve prosecutions of sexual crimes brought after Waterloo were either for attempted rape or indecent assault. This may have been because most of them concerned pre-pubescent children, who were not permitted to give evidence in Court, and the lower level of proof in such cases was felt to

---

[93] One Russian soldier was also accused of rape, but charges against him were dropped (23.1.1800, GG, *Crime*, vol. 20).

[94] 9.6.1781, 3.11.1781, 13.11.1781, GG, *Crime*, vol. 16.

[95] 7.7.1810, GG, *Crime*, vol. 22; *Mercure de Guernesey*, 14.7.1810.

facilitate conviction. This was in many ways to the advantage of offenders, since charges of attempted rape, though dealt with on indictment, were not normally laid *félonieusement*, and punishments rarely exceeded two months' imprisonment.

In one of these cases, which occurred in 1818, the Court hedged its bets by charging the man with having *félonieusement commis ou attenté de commettre le crime de rapt et viol*. The man in question was William Laurens, a native of Torteval, and his victim ten-year-old Mary Pritchard. The laying of the charge in this way suggests that the girl may well have been violated. However, when the case came to Court, the prosecution could offer no evidence of violence. Imputing consent to the ten-year-old, the Jurats therefore downgraded the offence, and Laurens, like the others, was imprisoned for two months.[96]

Unlike England, where all intercourse with girls under thirteen was regarded as criminal,[97] Guernsey had no age of consent. Questioned on the Laurens case by the Royal Commissioners in 1847, Procureur Charles De Jersey informed them that 'the child consented; but they punished the man nevertheless.' He went on to explain that Laurens had suffered two months' imprisonment even though 'the girl in question belonged to a family whose sisters were not very well behaved; and there is no doubt but that the child was consenting.'[98]

Guernsey's lack of a defined age of consent was compounded by a widespread view (not limited to the island) that young girls from poor backgrounds seldom remained innocent for long and might exercise a degree of agency in sexual cases. Something of this attitude lay behind the dropping of charges against William White for attempted *communication charnelle* with ten-year-old Margaret Elliott and eleven-year-old Elizabeth Newell in 1829, after the girls were found guilty of petty theft.[99]

All six prosecutions for indecent assault fell in the years after 1820. This was to some extent an improvement on the past, since prior to the 1820s, assaults of this nature were not prosecuted at all. The increase in such cases was directly related to the growing tendency to prosecute offences summarily.

[96] 27.6.1818, GG, *Crime*, vol. 24.
[97] L.A. Jackson, *Child Sexual Abuse in Victorian England* (London, 2000), p. 13.
[98] *Second Report*, p. 276.
[99] 17.10.1829, GG, *Crime*, vol. 27.

All indecent assaults between the 1820s and 1840s were dealt with by the Police Court, and punishments were light. The two last men convicted of indecent assault in our period were brothers Pierre and Thomas Thoumine, sentenced to just one week's imprisonment for an unspecified assault on a young girl on the public highway.[100]

There are no records in Guernsey's crime registers of any sexual assaults on males between 1765 and 1844, and registers are equally devoid of sodomy prosecutions. Unlike Jersey in this period, Guernsey still lacked a sodomy law.[101] The Royal Court appears, moreover, to have consciously adopted the policy of turning a blind eye to these matters. As Charles De Jersey told the Royal Commissioners, 'the Court are very unwilling to investigate such a case, and rather conceive that the investigation does more harm than the punishment would do good.'[102]

Property crime

The Guernsey Court's treatment of theft in this period continued to be governed by custom, and much the same kinds of offence were prosecuted on indictment as previously: robbery from the person; burglary; theft from a church; theft from a master or employer. Over the four quinquennia analysed for this chapter, property offences accounted for about two-thirds of all crimes prosecuted before the Full Court. This represented an increase on 1680–1764, when the proportion was just over one-half. The island had grown in prosperity, and opportunities for theft had multiplied. The wealth gap, too, had widened, and this had increased the temptation to steal.

Property crime – men

Some 87 per cent of those tried on indictment for property crime were adult men. Men were responsible for all the violent robberies in this period, and

---

[100] 22.12.1842, GG, *Crime*, vol. 31.
[101] Jersey's States had passed a law criminalising sodomy in 1800, under which at least one prosecution was brought in our period (*First Report of the Commissioners appointed to Inquire into the State of the Criminal Law in the Channel Islands: Jersey* (London, 1847), p. 67).
[102] *Second Report*, p. 276.

almost all the burglaries. Such crimes increased in frequency during the French Revolutionary and Napoleonic Wars, and many of the perpetrators were British soldiers. As in the case of rape, punishments handed down to soldiers for such offences could be harsh. In contrast with the previous period when hanging was not used to punish property crime, no fewer than fifteen death sentences were handed down for such crimes in the period covered here – all of them to British soldiers. Of these fifteen soldiers, eight were actually executed and seven were granted pardons. The pardons, which were issued by the Privy Council on the recommendation of the Royal Court, were in all seven cases made conditional on the recipients' life service in an infantry regiment. Some of those who were pardoned obtained mercy for themselves at the expense of their companions. One such was Matthew Wyborn of the 56th (West Essex) Regiment, who with mess mates Robert Blackburn and Thomas Welch had burgled Pierre Perrin's house in the Clos du Valle in 1806, attacking Perrin with a bayonet and threatening to cut his wife's throat. Blackburn and Welch were hanged within days of the trial, but an Order in Council was received pardoning Wyborn for having 'been induced to discover his accomplices under a promise … to save his life'.[103]

The last recorded hangings for property crime in Guernsey were those of William Cox and Adam Shellard of the 82nd (Prince of Wales's Volunteers) Regiment in 1813. These men had attacked Margueritte Simon and her servant as they made their way home late at night from the Alderney military canteen which Mrs Simon tenanted. Aware that the women were carrying the canteen takings, the soldiers ambushed them from the roadside, knocked them both to the ground and made off with the cash. In a small island like Alderney, it was not long before the men were arrested and sent to Guernsey for trial. No mercy was solicited for either of the soldiers, and both were executed in a double hanging on 16 July 1813, less than a week after they had been convicted.[104]

After Cox and Shellard, there were no further executions in Guernsey for property crime. Instead, floggings and banishment, which had continued as a punishment for lesser burglaries and robberies, were used in respect of all serious property offences. This regime pertained for a quarter of a century. In

---

[103] 13.12.1806, 14.1.1807, GG, *Crime*, vol. 21.
[104] 10.7.1813, GG, *Crime*, vol. 23; *Mercure de Guernesey*, 17.7.1813; *Gazette de Guernesey*, 17.7.1813.

the mid-1830s, however, an entirely new penal option became available. This was transportation.[105] In 1838, transportation was used for the first time as a sentence for robbery, after Pierre Pécqueur, a twenty-three-year-old farm worker from Normandy, was found guilty of throwing Rachel Le Prevost to the ground at le Camp du Roi and stealing over £30 in coins and banknotes. To begin with, Pécqueur was simply sentenced to 200 lashes and perpetual banishment.[106] Almost as an afterthought, however, the Court decided to apply to the Privy Council to have Pécqueur transported. The response was positive, and an Order in Council was received the following month transporting Pécqueur to Van Diemen's Land for life.[107] Within a few years of this episode, transportation became the Court's preferred sentence in serious property cases.

Property crime – women

Women did not usually engage in burglary or highway robbery; their serious property offences lay generally in thefts from masters and mistresses, from shops, or from institutions such as the Town Hospital. Nevertheless, there was one female burglary during our period which illustrates the special circumstances under which women might carry out such a crime. The culprit in this case was Catherine Le Ray, the wife of a blacksmith who had fallen on hard times.[108] Before her marriage, Mrs Le Ray had worked as a servant for Catherine Priaulx in Sausmarez Street, St Peter Port. She used her knowledge of Mrs Priaulx's house to enter the premises one Sunday evening in 1831, when the occupants were at church. Mrs Le Ray made her way in over the garden wall and through the back door, which was unlocked. Once in the house, she broke into a bureau and a secretaire where she knew her ex-mistress kept money, and made off with a considerable sum in banknotes and coins. According to a newspaper account of her trial, Procureur Charles De Jersey observed that 'it could scarcely be credited that so much wickedness should

---

[105] Transportation was first used in an 1835 counterfeiting case which will be explored below. It will be further discussed in the section on Punishment at the end of this chapter.
[106] 12.5.1838, GG, *Crime*, vol. 30.
[107] 20.6.1838, 15.8.1838, GG, *Crime*, vol. 30.
[108] This account is compiled from 3.12.1831, GG, *Crime*, vol. 28; *Comet*, 5.12.1831; *The Guernsey Magazine*, 22 (1894), pp. 723–4.

be met with in a person of her sex'.[109] He nevertheless did not recommend flogging, as she had an infant at the breast, but suggested she should be exposed in the cage and banished instead. HM Comptroller agreed, and the Court eventually settled on three years' banishment and four hours in the cage, divided into two two-hour sessions. The role of Catherine's husband in this episode is unclear. He does not appear to have instigated the crime, but he did use some of the stolen cash to pay creditors. Nevertheless, since, by customary law, accomplices were liable to the same punishment as the principal in a crime, he received an identical sentence to his wife, and they both appeared in the cage together, with placards above their heads inscribed with their names and their crime.

Miscellaneous serious offences

This residual category accounted for 11 per cent of offences tried on indictment across our sample quinquennia, representing an average of four or five prosecutions per year. Some of these were of crimes which had been brought before the Court many times before, such as counterfeiting and 'witchcraft'. Others concerned entirely novel matters, such as workers' strikes and combinations. Evolving attitudes and changing circumstances obliged the Court to find innovative ways of dealing with offences in both categories.

Counterfeiting

The first case of counterfeiting to come before the Royal Court in our period was that of Stuart Kelly in 1781. Kelly, a private in the 83rd (Glasgow Volunteers) Regiment, was charged with making a French *six-livre* piece (worth about 8s 8d).[110] Unsure how to deal with the matter, the Court seems to have consulted *L'Approbation des Lois*. Unfortunately, this flawed document contained an error in its section on coining, stating that, although the offence was cognizable by the Royal Court, judgment and sentencing were matters

---

[109] *Comet*, 5.12.1831.
[110] 16.6.1781, GG, *Crime*, vol. 16. The Kelly case is also covered in 'Judicial Proceedings', vol. XIII, Royal Court Library, IA.

for the King in Council.[111] This was incorrect, since according to the fifteenth-century *Précepte d'Assise*, sentencing alone (not judgment) was a matter for the Privy Council.[112] Accordingly, the Court went through all the preliminary stages of a trial *au grand criminel* but stopped short of judgment. In July 1781, they instead sent all the trial papers to London and requested that the Sovereign in Council pass judgment on the evidence.[113] This, however, the Council declined to do, directing the Court to pass a verdict itself, and then submit it 'for His Majesty's royal determination thereupon.'[114] On 8 December, the Court found Stuart Kelly guilty as charged. They passed no sentence, but as the standard punishment in such cases was hanging, they recommended Kelly to mercy on account of his previous good character, his unforced confession, and his assertion that he had only made the coin *par badinage* (for a lark).[115] This was communicated to the Privy Council, which, in light of the Court's representations, responded in January 1782 with an Order for Kelly's unconditional release.[116]

In the next coining case, which occurred in 1810, the Court properly followed the procedure outlined in *Le Précepte d'Assise* and passed a verdict but not a sentence. Mary McLaughlin, wife of a Corporal in the Royal Engineers, was found guilty in the summer of that year of having silvered a quantity of *liards* to give them the appearance of English silver sixpences.[117] In referring Mrs McLaughlin for sentencing, the Court recommended her to mercy on the basis that she had made a full and unconstrained confession, that this was her first offence, and that she had conducted herself 'with

---

[111] T. Tramailler (ed.), *Approbation des Lois, Coutumes, et Usages de l'Ile de Guernesey* (1715; Guernsey, 1822 edn), p. 24.

[112] H. De Sausmarez, 'Guernsey's Précepte d'Assise of 1441: translation and notes', *Jersey & Guernsey Law Review* (June 2008).

[113] Royal Court to Privy Council, 28.7.1781, GG, Royal Court General Letter Book (first series), vol. 1.

[114] O in C, 28.9.1781, GG, Royal Court General Letter Book (first series), vol. 1.

[115] 8.12.1781, GG, *Crime*, vol. 16.

[116] 12.12.1781, GG, *Crime*, vol. 16; O in C, 2.1.1782, GG, Royal Court General Letter Book (first series), vol. 1.

[117] Eight *liards* (also known as 'doubles') were worth one penny. *Liards* were the commonest coin in circulation in Guernsey. John Jacob described them as 'formed of various sizes, thicknesses and materials, some of them being old English farthings, some Dutch or Flemish, other French or Spanish, many of them only very thin pieces of plain copper' (J. Jacob, *Annals of some of the British Norman Isles constituting the Bailiwick of Guernsey* (Paris, 1830), pp. 410, 416).

'propriety' during her detention. As had been the case with Private Kelly, the Council responded with an Order for Mrs McLaughlin's unconditional release.[118]

There followed a further four counterfeiting cases between 1814 and 1829, in which – owing perhaps to the low value of the coins involved – the Royal Court took the unprecedented step of sentencing the guilty parties without any prior reference to the Privy Council.[119]

The last two prosecutions of our period, which occurred in 1834/5, concerned coins of significantly higher value and were treated in the traditional way. In December 1834, Frenchmen Pierre Poidevin (40) and François Noyon (37) were found guilty of manufacturing a substantial number of French 2 franc and 5 franc pieces.[120] As per *Le Précepte d'Assise*, the verdict was followed by a referral to the Privy Council for sentencing, and the Council responded the following March with an Order transporting both Frenchmen to Australia for seven years.[121] This was the first use of transportation in Guernsey. The men were delivered to the Superintendent of Convicts of the York hulk at Gosport, and sent out to New South Wales two months later.[122]

In a curious footnote to these cases, Comptroller John Utermarck informed the Royal Commission in 1847 that a coining case would only be referred to Council for sentencing if it involved 'coin of the realm, and that counterfeiting a foreign coin would be tried and punished here'.[123] Utermarck must have been alluding to a new policy (or making up policy on the hoof), because all the cases which had hitherto been referred to the Privy Council had concerned foreign coin alone.

[118] 14.7.1810, 17.10.1810, GG, *Crime*, vol. 22; Royal Court to Privy Council, 20.7.1810, GG, Royal Court General Letter Books (first series), vol. 2.
[119] In 1824, Henry Barge was sentenced to two months' imprisonment and banished for six years for silvering *liards* just as Mary McLaughlin had done fourteen years earlier (20.3.1824, GG, *Crime*, vol. 26). In 1828, Pierre Vimont was sentenced to one month's solitary confinement for manufacturing a quantity of *liards* from scratch (8.11.1828, GG, *Crime*, vol. 27). In 1829, Michael and Mary Brannagan served a month in gaol and were banished for six years for manufacturing false French *dix-sous* pieces (24.10.1829, GG, *Crime*, vol. 27).
[120] 13.12.1834, GG, *Crime*, vol. 29.
[121] O in C, 4.3.1835.
[122] See www.convictrecords.com.au, where Noyon is referred to as 'Noyou'.
[123] *Second Report*, p. 277.

Forgery

Prosecutions for this offence – usually in respect of bills of exchange or banknotes – became almost as numerous as prosecutions for coining in this period, as the circulation of such instruments increased. No particular statute governed forgery in Guernsey, but local punishments were harsh.[124] In 1774, Daniel Brouard was sentenced to 100 lashes and six years' banishment for forging a bill for 200 *livres tournois* (£14 6s).[125] In 1806, Thomas Bell was sentenced to 100 lashes and perpetual banishment for forging a bill for £20 sterling.[126] Following the introduction of transportation in the 1830s, forgery joined counterfeiting as a crime for which offenders could be transported. In 1841, Henry Laporte Smith, a forty-nine-year-old widower with a large family, was sentenced to seven years' transportation for having altered a number of bills of exchange which enabled him to draw several hundred pounds from the Guernsey Commercial Banking Company and other banks.[127] He was conveyed to Tasmania in 1842 and lived there until his death at eighty-five in 1877.[128]

'Witchcraft' (as fraud on the credulous)

Belief in the supernatural remained entrenched in Guernsey in our period, and locals were an easy prey to fraudsters. The Royal Court attempted to check the activities of self-proclaimed mystics and shamen by sporadic prosecutions. As in the previous period, there were prosecutions for fortune-telling.[129] There were also a number of prosecutions for what we might term 'faith' healing.[130] In addition to these, *désorcellement*, which was not prosecuted at all in 1680–1764, formed the subject of four separate Court cases. *Désorceleurs* made a profession of removing spells which people believed had been cast on them for

---

[124] In England and Wales, the 1728 Act for the Prevention and Punishment of Forgery had made forgery of banknotes a capital crime.

[125] 14.5.1774, GG, *Crime*, vol. 17.

[126] 6.12.1806, GG, *Crime*, vol. 21.

[127] 4.12.1841, GG, *Crime*, vol. 31.

[128] For further detail on Mr Laporte Smith's life in Tasmania, see www.convictrecords.com.au.

[129] See, for instance, 17.9.1785, GG, *Crime*, vol. 17.

[130] 7.4.1818, GG, *Crime*, vol. 24; 6.4.1838, GG, *Crime*, vol. 30.

malevolent purposes. The *désorceleurs* prosecuted in this period were Nicolas Roussel, Anne Marquis, Louis D'Orléans and Jean Lainé, all of whom had charged fees for their services.[131] Their prosecution was significant in that, from the early nineteenth century onwards, *désorcellement* became the main focus of the Court's prosecution of 'witchcraft'.

All four *désorceleurs* of our period were punished by exposure in the cage, with or without a fine and/or banishment, according to the sums they had pocketed. The highest-profile case was that of Louis D'Orléans, an itinerant curse-lifter from Normandy, who was charged in 1837 with seven counts of obtaining money from rural parishioners by such means. D'Orléans' method was to make wax figurines of individuals supposed to have cast spells on his clients and burn them on the fire. As usual in such cases, very few people came forward to testify against the Frenchman (fearing, perhaps, that he had ways of exacting retribution). Nevertheless, he was found guilty and sentenced to an hour's exposure in the cage followed by six years' banishment.[132] The editor of the *Comet* bemoaned the leniency of D'Orléans' punishment but hoped that the spectacle would make rural parishioners 'wash their hands for ever' of 'those quacks which infest the country'.[133] As we shall see in Chapter 9, events would prove him wrong.

Libel

As in the previous period, the only libels which were publicly prosecuted between 1765 and 1844 were, as the Royal Commissioners were informed in 1847, 'atrocious libels against public functionaries'.[134] These functionaries were almost invariably Court members acting in their official capacity. The incidence of such cases was greater over the current period than it had been between 1680 and 1764, primarily because of the advent of local newspapers, which, as noted above, began to appear in 1791. The trend towards more frequent prosecution may also have been stimulated by an awareness of

---

[131] 2.3.1805, GG, *Crime*, vol. 21; 13.2.1813, GG, *Crime*, vol. 23; 4.2.1837, GG, *Crime*, vol. 29; 20.9.1841, GG, *Crime*, vol. 30.

[132] 4.2.1837, GG, *Crime*, vol. 29.

[133] *Comet*, 6.2.1837.

[134] *Second Report*, pp. 103, 187.

developments in England, where Fox's Libel Act of 1792 had encouraged the state prosecution of political libels.[135]

Unsurprisingly, most of Guernsey's criminal libel cases in this period involved newspaper proprietors and editors (often the same person), who were prosecuted for the publication of defamatory statements in readers' letters as well as in their own editorials and articles. In October 1819, Henry Brouard, proprietor of *Le Mercure de Guernesey* and the *Star*, was found guilty of defaming Lieutenant Governor Henry Bayly in an issue of the *Star*, and sentenced to deposit a surety in the sum of £100 against his future good conduct.[136] In April 1823, Nicolas Mauger, proprietor of the *Gazette de Guernesey*, was fined 300 *livres tournois* (about £12 6s) for publishing an attack on the Court after they rejected a petition demanding restrictions on foreign hawkers.[137] Although libel continued to be publicly prosecuted into the second half of the nineteenth century, prosecutions of this kind declined from the 1830s.

Bigamy

As noted in Chapter 3, the Royal Court had attempted to prosecute a bigamist in 1758 by charging him with perjury, but the attempt proved abortive when the man escaped before his trial. In 1798 and 1801, the Court tried again. On these occasions, bigamy was prosecuted as a crime in its own right, but both prosecutions failed for lack of proof.[138] Between 1804 and 1840, there were a further five prosecutions of bigamy, four of which resulted in convictions. The first successful prosecution was that of Sr Jeremy Holloway (alias Hutton) in 1804. Found guilty of contracting a marriage in Guernsey while his first wife was still alive in England, Holloway was

---

[135] T.F.T. Plucknett, *A Concise History of the Common Law* (1929; Boston, 1956 edn), pp. 500–1.

[136] 1.10.1819, GG, *Crime*, vol. 24. On this case, see also *Second Report*, p. 128.

[137] 19.4.1823, GG, *Crime*, vol. 25; A. Bennett, 'A history of the French newspapers and nineteenth-century English newspapers of Guernsey' (unpub. MA dissertation, Loughborough University, 1995), pp. 14–15.

[138] The alleged bigamists were John Winscombe (21.6.1798, GG, *Crime*, vol. 20) and Andrew Knee (25.7.1801, GG, *Crime*, vol. 21).

sentenced to one hour in the pillory and six years' banishment.[139] There then followed Marguerite Rougier, who was sentenced to two hours in the cage and three weeks' imprisonment for bigamy in 1821; John Skroder, sentenced to one month's imprisonment and six years' banishment in 1830; and Pierre Le Patourel, who was imprisoned for four weeks and banished for two years in 1839.[140]

Most cases of bigamy arose from the impossibility of obtaining a divorce, and many of those punished for it had resorted to second marriages for understandable reasons.[141] Marguerite Rougier was left alone and unsupported after her first husband (from whom she had met with ill-treatment) deserted her.[142] John Skroder was judicially separated from his wife who had started a new life in Jersey and left him to bring up their children alone.[143] Charles De Jersey, acting as defence counsel for Marguerite Rougier, said that 'people of her kind believe they can remarry without greatly sinning. There are a great many people in precisely this situation.'[144]

Questioned by the Royal Commissioners in 1847 as to whether, in the absence of a positive statute, bigamy was prosecuted 'under your general common law jurisdiction', Advocate Robert MacCulloch answered affirmatively.[145] Elsewhere during Commission proceedings, Procureur Charles De Jersey invoked the notion of a 'general common law jurisdiction' to cover every other offence not mentioned in *L'Approbation* or Terrien over which the Court now found itself adjudicating. 'We consider ourselves very much as the Scotch consider themselves,' De Jersey asserted; 'in that … the Royal Court have an authority to punish every crime, though we may not have a positive law or statute on that point.'[146] In referring to Scotland, De Jersey was alluding to the power exercised by the Scottish High Court of

---

[139] It seems, however, that Holloway escaped before his punishment could be carried out (17.7.1804, 11.8.1804, 18.8.1804, GG, *Crime*, vol. 21).

[140] 16.1.1821, GG, *Crime*, vol. 24; 8.5.1830, GG, *Crime*, vol. 28; 2.3.1839, GG, *Crime*, vol. 30.

[141] In Guernsey, spouses could be separated by act of Court, but divorce with the possibility of remarriage was not available until 1946 (R.-M. Crossan, *A Women's History of Guernsey, 1850s–1950s* (Benderloch, 2018), pp. 97–9, 104–8).

[142] *Indépendance*, 27.1.1821.

[143] *Comet*, 10.5.1830.

[144] *Indépendance*, 27.1.1821.

[145] *Second Report*, p. 281.

[146] *Ibid.*, p. 226.

Justiciary to try any behaviour that was *malum in se* (obviously wrong or wicked) regardless of whether a law existed or not.[147] This notion would be repeatedly invoked in Guernsey as the range of novel crimes the Royal Court dealt with continued to increase over subsequent decades.

Worker combinations

Worker combinations had long been regarded by the Court as *malum in se*. The first attempt to prosecute a combination had occurred in 1754, when eight *traîneurs* or sledmen were charged with conspiring to induce other *traîneurs* to suspend work unless they were given a pay rise.[148] This may well have been influenced by an awareness of developments in Britain, where anti-combination legislation was first passed in 1749.[149] During the period covered here, the Royal Court took action against worker combinations on a further six occasions. In 1797, cooper David Dorey was prosecuted for conspiring with workmates to force a merchant to stop importing barrels from England.[150] In 1802, another cooper, Thomas Mahy, was prosecuted for inducing colleagues to strike for better wages.[151] In 1804, fourteen ships'

---

[147] At this time, the flexibility of Scottish criminal law, which was comparatively short on positive statutes, was attracting praise in sections of the English legal press (L. Farmer, *Criminal Law, Tradition and Legal Order: Crime and the Genius of Scots Law, 1747 to the Present* (Cambridge, 1997), pp. 136-7).

[148] 9.3.1754, GG, *Crime*, vol. 13. For reasons which are unclear, the charges in this case were dropped.

[149] In 1749, the Frauds by Workmen Act made it illegal for workers in certain industries to combine to raise wages. In 1799 and 1800, the 1749 statute was superseded by two more stringent Acts which became known as the Combination Acts. The first of these was repealed by the second, which remained in force for a quarter of a century. On pain of up to three months' imprisonment, the 1800 Act made it illegal for workmen to meet or encourage others to meet, or to refuse to work with others, for the purpose of increasing their wages or reducing their working hours. This Act was replaced in 1825 by the Combinations of Workmen Act which imposed criminal sanctions for picketing and other methods of persuading workers to suspend their labour. The 1825 Act remained in force until 1871, when trade unions were finally legalised (J.V. Orth, 'The English combination laws reconsidered', in F. Snyder & D. Hay (eds), *Labour, Law and Crime: An Historical Perspective* (London, 1987), pp. 123–4).

[150] 21.10.1797, GG, *Crime*, vol. 20.

[151] 2.11.1802, GG, *Crime*, vol. 21.

carpenters were prosecuted for combining to raise pay rates.[152] In 1825, four journeymen bakers were prosecuted for parading the effigy of a 'scab' workmate through the streets.[153] In 1832, ropemaker Nicholas Richards was prosecuted for attempting to induce colleagues not to work for less than 2s 6d per day.[154] Finally, in 1841, seven journeymen shoemakers were prosecuted for trying to organise a boycott of low-paying masters.[155] Some of these cases were tried summarily and others on indictment. Punishments took the form of fines, prison terms of up to four weeks, and orders to find bail or leave.[156]

The 1841 shoemakers' case was discussed in 1847 by the Royal Commission. The Commissioners asked Advocate Robert MacCulloch if the men's offence lay specifically in combining rather than simply expressing a wish for higher wages. MacCulloch replied that it did. The Commissioners continued, 'Suppose a set of masters were to unite to say that they would not give more than a certain amount of wages; would that be treated in the same way?' 'Yes; it ought,' answered MacCulloch. The Commissioners pressed him: 'Would it?' MacCulloch replied 'It would not be so likely, perhaps.'[157] The fact of the matter was that the Jurats, most of them from mercantile backgrounds, had effectively functioned as a masters' combination throughout.

Punishments

Analysis of our four sample quinquennia enables us to rank punishments between 1765 and 1844 in order of precedence.[158] Imprisonment was used in 49 per cent of criminal cases. Banishment, transportation and other forms of ejection were next at 30 percent; then came fines at 18 per cent,

---

[152] 8.10.1804, GG, *Crime*, vol. 21.
[153] 17.8.1825, GG, *Crime*, vol. 26.
[154] 24.1.1832, GG, *Crime*, vol. 28.
[155] 2.6.1841, GG, *Crime*, vol. 30.
[156] Orders to find bail or leave will be discussed in detail below.
[157] *Second Report*, p. 285.
[158] The figures which follow are exclusive of semi-civil actions and prosecutions under Ordinances, which could only be punished by fine.

corporal punishment at 5 per cent, and lastly capital punishment at 0.8 per cent. Sentences usually combined more than one form of punishment (which explains why percentages add up to more than 100).

Capital punishment

Greater recourse was had to the death penalty in 1765–1844 than in 1680–1764. In the earlier period, six executions took place in Guernsey, four of women and two of men. In the current period, there were nineteen executions, all of men. Of these nineteen men, two were convicted of rape, eight of burglary or robbery (in two cases aggravated by rape), and nine of murder. Fourteen of the men who suffered the death penalty were soldiers, two were sailors, and three were civilians. Just one of the executed men was a native of Guernsey.

As in the previous period, the Prévôt, Sergeant, Greffier, *Bordiers* and Law Officers were all obliged to be present at hangings (which always took place on a Friday), and Court members continued to be given a dinner at Crown expense every time an execution took place.

The first hanging of our period – that of Nicolas Rougier in 1775 – saw the gallows moved from its traditional location in St Andrews to a site on the east coast between St Peter Port and St Sampsons. The move was made because Rougier's execution was being held close to harvest time, and crops in surrounding fields were in danger of being trampled.[159] A contemporary diarist recorded that Rougier was hanged at the half-tide mark on the beach at Hougue à la Perre.[160] The St Andrews site was not used again, and all the executions in our period took place at Hougue à la Perre.

[159] 5.7.1775, GG, *Crime*, vol. 15.
[160] 14.7.1775, Journals and Correspondence of Charles Mollet, PL.

Plate 19. Hougue à la Perre at high tide, 1832
© Priaulx Library, Guernsey

The gallows was a fairly ad hoc structure, erected and dismantled when required, and regularly renewed. In the mid-1850s, French writer Victor Hugo was shown the apparatus used to hang Marie Joseph François Béasse. It was made of wood painted an iron-grey colour, and seems to have consisted of two uprights and a crossbeam. The uprights were planted in the sand and braced with supporting timbers so that they would not move. The crossbeam was mounted on top of them, and three ropes were hung from it. One in the middle was the noose, left slack around the criminal's neck, and two others suspended a board several feet up on which the criminal stood. The hangman's task lay in severing the ropes so that the board fell away and the criminal was left to swing. Béasse's hangman, John Rooks, had never performed a hanging before, and Hugo tells us that he took so long to cut the ropes that outraged spectators were on the verge of stoning him.[161]

---

[161] Juin (ed.), *Victor Hugo, Choses Vues*, pp. 365–6.

Plate 20. Hanging of Marie Joseph François Béasse, 1830 [162]
By kind permission of HM Greffier

John Rooks was Guernsey's last hangman and unusual among the thirteen who held the office between 1765 and 1844 in that he was Guernsey-born. Aside from John Whitehead who was English and John Christie who was Irish, all the other hangmen in this period were French.[163] Most were criminals who consented to take the job in return for acquittal or release. Rooks accepted the job of hangman to avoid punishment for returning prematurely from a period of abjuration.[164] By 1835, he was on a retainer of 15s weekly, with extra payments for whippings, cagings and hangings, and free accommodation.[165]

---

[162] 23.10.1830, GG, *Crime*, vol. 28.

[163] Appendix 4.

[164] 16.10.1830, GG, *Crime*, vol. 27; *Star*, 18.10.1830.

[165] Hangmen were accommodated in a house called 'Gresley's Forfeiture' until it was sold in 1798. Between 1798 and 1833, they were housed in lodgings rented at Crown expense. In 1833, the dwelling and 13 acres belonging to Béasse in Ruettes Brayes were sold, and part of the proceeds were used to purchase a new house and garden for Rooks in the St Johns area of town (O in C, 6.3.1833, GG, *Ordres du Conseil et Actes du Parlement*, vol. 5).

Corporal punishment

Like the gallows, the cage and the pillory were regularly renewed. When St Peter Port's new marketplace was opened in the late eighteenth century, a freshly-built combined cage-and-pillory was erected in the north-west corner.[166] As shown in figure 4, the space-saving structure incorporated a pillory above, cage below, and rings either side of the door for securing criminals' limbs during whippings. This contraption was in use for almost forty years.

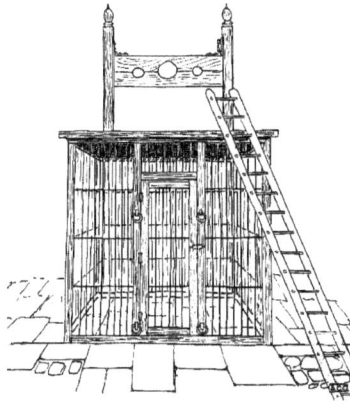

Figure 4. Combined cage, pillory and whipping post
Courtesy of the Priaulx Library, Guernsey

When the new covered meat market opened in 1822, the cage-cum-pillory was taken down and replaced with a mobile cage which was only brought in when required. Frederick Lukis tells us that this cage was octagonal in shape.[167] Victor Hugo (who saw it at the same time as the gallows) informs us that it was made of wood painted iron-grey.[168]

---

[166] Lukis, 'Reminiscences'.
[167] *Ibid.*
[168] Juin (ed.), *Victor Hugo, Choses Vues*, p. 366.

Plate 21. Mobile cage, 1822–41 [169]
By kind permission of HM Greffier

Unlike the cage, the pillory element of the old structure was never replaced, and Guernsey's use of *le carcan* was discontinued. One of the pillory's last uses came in 1814, when soldier Archibald MacMaugh was sentenced to one hour in *le carcan* as punishment for attempted rape. [170] The octagonal cage, however, continued intermittently to be wheeled into the marketplace until 1841. Its final use came in the autumn of that year, when James Bailey was sentenced to sit in it for an hour for having misrepresented his assets and liabilities in a bankruptcy case. [171] Once the cage and the pillory were abandoned, their place in the penal repertoire was taken by sentences of imprisonment in solitary confinement or on bread and water. [172]

Whipping was the commonest form of corporal punishment between 1765 and 1844. It was particularly common between the 1760s and Waterloo, which also saw an increase in the number of lashes to which offenders were sentenced. In the early 1700s, thirty lashes had been a common sentence for men, and twenty for women. The number rose progressively after 1750, reaching a peak late in the century, when maxima of 500 lashes were reached for males, and 100 for females, although such large

---

[169] 27.5.1758, GG, *Crime*, vol. 14. This drawing, from a crime register, was clearly added long after the register entry, which preceded the mobile cage by sixty-four years.

[170] 7.5.1814, GG, *Crime*, vol. 23. The pillory was by this time falling out of favour all over western Europe. In England, a statute of 1816 restricted its use to a narrow range of offences, and it was formally abolished as a judicial punishment in 1837 (Beattie, *Crime and the Courts*, p. 616).

[171] 4.9.1841, GG, *Crime*, vol. 30. Bailey was also sentenced to two months in gaol.

[172] Prison Report, 26.11.1850, GG, Royal Court General Letter Book (second series), vol. 4.

numbers of lashes were usually administered over more than one session. After Waterloo, the number gradually declined. This appears to have resulted from a change in sentiment regarding judicial violence which reached the island via Britain.[173] The change in sentiment also led to the cessation of flogging for women. In England, the judicial whipping of females ceased in 1817 and was formally abolished in 1820. In Guernsey, the last woman to be sentenced to a whipping was Bertranne Du Chemin of St Saviours, who received twenty lashes for stealing clothing from the Country Hospital in 1819.[174] Although judicial whipping remained in use for males in both Britain and Guernsey until the twentieth century, it ceased to be performed in public in England around 1830.[175] In Guernsey, men continued to be flogged in the marketplace until 1845.

Ear-cropping and branding were other corporal punishments carried out for the last time in the course of our period. The final instance of ear-cropping occurred in 1795, when Frenchman Jacques Le Bâtard was punished for burglary by having his right ear cut off in addition to receiving 500 lashes and being banished for life.[176] The branding iron was employed for the last time in 1799 – on Private James Charlesworth who was convicted of the manslaughter of a fellow soldier in a fight.[177]

Imprisonment

Sentences to imprisonment became noticeably more frequent in the early 1780s, after the gaoler's quarters at the Castle were turned over to carceral use. This development coincided with a trend towards the greater use of imprisonment in western Europe generally, and it was further promoted by the growth in summary prosecutions. By the quinquennium 1800–4, some

[173] Historians have attributed the change in British sentiment to the cumulative influence of penal reformers such as Cesare Beccaria, John Howard and Elizabeth Fry, as well as Evangelicals such as William Wilberforce and Hannah More (Beattie, *Crime and the Courts*, p. 614).
[174] 6.11.1819, GG, *Crime*, vol. 24.
[175] For a chronology of corporal punishment in the United Kingdom, see www.corpun.com/ukjur4.htm.
[176] 11.7.1795, GG, *Crime*, vol. 19.
[177] 2.2.1799, GG, *Crime*, vol. 20. We should however note that neither of these punishments had been used more than a handful of times since 1680.

28 per cent of convicted offenders were receiving prison terms as all or part of their sentences. In 1820–4, after the opening of the new prison, this proportion rose to 55 per cent.

Sentences served in Guernsey's prison were short and sharp. Taking all four quinquennia together, 22 per cent of prison sentences were for less than one week; 69 per cent were for between one and four weeks; and only 9 per cent were for more than one month. In the period dealt with here, the Royal Court never handed down a sentence in excess of three months. Only 14 per cent of gaol sentences in our sample quinquennia were handed down to females. This reflected their proportion among the ranks of criminals generally.

Banishment

Banishment was used to punish serious crime. In the absence of facilities for extended imprisonment, it remained a useful expedient for ridding the island of criminals long-term. It was normally preceded by another punishment, usually whipping in the earlier part of our period, or a short gaol term in later years. Between 1765 and 1844, a majority of those banished were adult male non-natives. Nevertheless, banishment was also occasionally used with females, children, and native islanders.

Banishments of more than seven years (which entailed forfeiture) were rare: there were only five such cases across our sample quinquennia. Just over half of banishments were for six years, with the remainder for periods of between one and five years. Returning prematurely from banishment began to be treated as a crime in this period, and those who did so were harshly punished. When William Newell was found guilty of returning half-way through a six-year banishment in 1818, he was sentenced to twenty lashes and a further three years' banishment in addition to the three remaining from his original sentence.[178]

By the end of our period, many Guernseymen evinced strong opposition to banishment, which had by now been dropped as a judicial punishment in most of western Europe. William Maillard, the editor of the *Comet* and a prominent Methodist, was among the most outspoken of campaigners:

---

[178] 21.2.1818, GG, *Crime*, vol. 24.

this mode of punishment ... has always appeared to us to be one of the most fruitful sources of evil connected with our penal laws; and the most afflictive ... But this is not all. That it has been followed ... by the most fatal results to various individuals is a fact as appalling as it is true. And indeed how can it be otherwise when men are driven from their homes, their families, and their connexions without the means of subsistence, and compelled to wander up and down in a strange land like vagabonds.[179]

Maillard's editorial was written in 1830. Despite his and many other people's misgivings, banishment was to persist as a penal sanction in Guernsey for nearly the next hundred years.

Transportation

As noted above, transportation was added to the Royal Court's penal repertoire in 1835. It proved a useful complement to banishment, being reserved for crimes which might in earlier years have attracted the death penalty, while banishment was used in slightly less serious cases. In the period covered here, Guernsey's transportees were sentenced either to seven years' transportation or life transportation, both of which incurred forfeiture of property.

By 1835, transportation had been used in Britain for well over a century. It had begun in earnest with the 1717 Transportation Act, which had established a system for transporting offenders to North America. This ran successfully for sixty years but ceased when the newly founded United States stopped accepting convicts in the 1770s. Following a period of experimentation, a new Transportation Act passed in 1784 had substituted Australia for America as the convicts' destination.[180] Guernsey's Court had first shown an interest in transportation in 1795. In June of that year, the Court had sentenced Privates John Mullins and Allan Ramsay of the Irish Rangers to be hanged for highway robbery.[181] However, rather than proceed immediately to execution, the Court had written to the Privy Council asking

---

[179] Editorial in *Comet*, 13.12.1830.
[180] Beattie, *Crime and the Courts*, pp. 503–4, 548, 596, 599.
[181] 13.6.1795, 27.6.1795, GG, *Crime*, vol. 19.

if the soldiers could be transported to New South Wales instead. The Court added:

> we require some rule therein, and as we believe a late like case of punishment of convicts from Scotland to be equally new, the referring to that instance might lead to establish some mode herein, both for this and the Island of Jersey, whose magistrates would be equally glad to have it in their power to more efficaciously execute their sentences of banishment than merely sending convicts out of their island, as is done in both, to go where they list.[182]

At this point in time, the Privy Council were more interested in preserving the strength of the army than in extending transportation to the Channel Islands, and they simply granted Mullins and Ramsay pardons on condition of lifetime military service.[183] The Royal Court made no further such requests. In 1806, the military authorities began using transportation as a sentence for court-martialled garrison members, of which seven were despatched to Australia between that year and 1833.[184] In 1835, the Privy Council itself introduced civilian transportation to Guernsey, unsolicited and without legislative preparation, by peremptorily ordering the transportation of two counterfeiters referred to them for sentencing.[185] Something similar had already happened in Jersey in 1821.[186] The counterfeiters' transportation created a precedent of which Guernsey's Court was not slow to avail itself, not least because the only expense involved was that of conveying the convicts to the hulks, with the British government bearing the rest of the costs. All future civil sentences to transportation were given effect by Orders in Council for which the Royal Court applied separately in respect of each transportee.[187]

---

[182] Royal Court to Privy Council, 24.7.1795, GG, Royal Court General Letter Book (first series), vol. 1. Scotland had been incorporated within the national system for transporting criminals by means of special statutes: one of 1766 extended the provisions of the 1717 Transportation Act, and another of 1785 those of the 1784 Transportation Act (I. Donnachie, 'Scottish criminals and transportation to Australia, 1786–1852', *Scottish Economic and Social History*, 4 (1984), pp. 21–38).

[183] 13.2.1796, GG, *Crime*, vol. 19.

[184] Australian Convict Transportation Registers, 1791–1868, accessed at Ancestry.co.uk, 31.7.2021.

[185] See section on Counterfeiting, above.

[186] *First Report*, pp. 112, 239.

[187] These were all recorded in the registers of *Ordres du Conseil et Actes du Parlement*.

Other forms of ejection

Banishment and transportation were punishments which only the Full Court was entitled to inflict. In time, a variant of these evolved for the use of the Ordinary Court. As Advocate James Gallienne informed the Royal Commissioners in 1847,

> although the Police Court has no power of imprisoning a person beyond one month, it has the means, indirectly, of banishing a person from the Island for life. The mode adopted is by obliging the party to find bail for his future good conduct or quit the island.[188]

The sums required in bail were calculatedly beyond the means of working people, and in the majority of cases, individuals could not find the money and were duly ejected.[189] This seems to have grown out of a practice which began in the 1720s of ordering strangers to deposit a sum with the Crown Officers as a surety against their requiring parochial poor relief, in default of which they were not permitted to remain in the island.[190] Over the next two decades, such orders were adapted to serve as a penal sanction. In 1745, an order to find bail or leave was used to deal with two soldiers suspected of theft but against whom there was insufficient proof to secure convictions.[191] In 1747, an order to find bail or leave was appended to Bartholomew Shoemaker's thirty-six lashes for stealing silverware.[192] By the quinquennium 1780–4, orders to find bail or leave were issued in 10 per cent of cases which

---

[188] *Second Report*, p. 62. This is not to be confused with a more benign practice whereby persons might be ordered by the Court to bind themselves, on the strength of a pecuniary security or promissory oath, not to repeat an offence, not to molest a particular individual, or just generally to keep the peace. This practice (as opposed to orders to find bail or leave) came into use with the decline of *causes en adjonction* and the related procedure of *trêves*. It was almost certainly calqued on the power exercised by English JPs and Judges to bind a person over to be of good behaviour for a specified term. In the period dealt with here, this more benign form of bind over was infrequently used, but in the decades after 1845, it became a staple of the Police Court.

[189] As with banishment, the ejected person's passage to England, Jersey or France was paid from Crown revenues (*Second Report*, p. 152).

[190] One of the first such orders was issued to Frenchman Louis Allary in 1724 (17.10.1724, GG, *Crime*, vol. 10).

[191] 13.7.1745, GG, *Crime*, vol. 12.

[192] 31.1.1747, GG, *Crime*, vol. 12.

came before the Ordinary Court. By 1800–4, this proportion had grown to 45 per cent. At this point and for at least the next forty years, the Court essentially used these orders as a convenient way of ridding the island of people who were, or were likely to become, troublesome and/or burdensome.

Orders to find bail or leave were issued to people of both sexes and all ages. Immigrants to the island were particularly vulnerable, but such orders were also occasionally given to natives.[193] Most frequently, they were used as punishment for an actual offence, but they could also be given to people merely suspected of offending,[194] or indeed simply on account of a deviant lifestyle.[195] There was no appeal against an order to find bail or leave, the term of exile was indefinite, and returning to the island was treated as a crime.[196] Between 1800 and 1849, the Ordinary Court expelled more than 900 suspected or convicted offenders from Guernsey by means of orders to find bail or leave.

Another of the Court's self-invented expedients in this period was abjuration. This allowed a person standing trial to apply to the Court (usually at the pleading stage) for permission to quit the island for a specified term rather than continue with proceedings. It seems to have been tenuously based on a provision in *Le Grand Coutumier* enabling crime suspects who sought sanctuary in a church to abjure the country within eight days rather than stand trial.[197]

---

[193] See, for instance, 26.2.1811, GG, *Crime*, vol. 22.

[194] In 1829, for example, William Butler was ordered to find £200 or leave on suspicion of stealing goods from his employer, but no proof of the offence was sought or obtained (4.4.1829, GG, *Crime*, vol. 27).

[195] In 1816, Neil and Mary Donnelly were ordered to find £100 or leave for being 'frequently drunk, always quarrelling, and a nuisance to the neighbourhood' (2.1.1816, GG, *Crime*, vol. 23).

[196] In 1847, Comptroller John Utermarck claimed that one year was considered to be the time limit during which a person ordered to leave in default of finding bail was liable to punishment if he returned (*Second Report*, p. 152). Evidence from crime registers however belies his claim: John Lally, who was ordered to find bail in the sum of £20 or leave for a theft in April 1841, was imprisoned for one week and then re-ejected when he returned in April 1843 (30.4.1841, 27.4.1843, GG, *Crime*, vol. 31).

[197] J.A. Everard (tr), *Le Grand Coutumier de Normandie* (Jersey, 2009), pp. 330–2. Darryl Ogier has recorded instances of sanctuary and abjuration in the sixteenth century (D.M. Ogier, *Reformation and Society in Guernsey* (Woodbridge, 1996), pp. 21–2, 56–7). Terrien, on pp. 518–520 of his *Commentaires* stated that the practice was no longer used in Normandy, and *L'Approbation* (p. 25) confirmed that this was also the case in Guernsey.

The procedure was first resurrected in its modern guise in 1790, when the Court permitted Jean Pezet to abjure the Bailiwick for three years rather than proceed with his trial for making 'threatening and inflammatory statements against the inhabitants of Alderney'.[198] Though this modern form of abjuration was at first infrequently resorted to, it became relatively common after Waterloo. Between 1815 and the end of the period dealt with here, it was used on more than forty occasions, with natives as well as strangers.[199] Crimes in respect of which abjuration was permitted included serious assaults, sexual offences and burglary. In 1839, James Pratt was permitted to abjure for five years to avoid standing trial for an unspecified sexual assault against Miss Henrietta Patey.[200] In 1844, teenagers James Cohu and Henry Du Four were allowed to abjure for five and four years respectively to avoid prosecution for burgling Caroline Delancey's house in the Grange.[201] The last use of abjuration occurred in April 1845, when Nicholas Watson of St Peter Port was permitted to abjure the island for three years to avoid prosecution for a string of metal thefts.[202] Two months later (as we shall see in Chapter 8), there was a change of Bailiff, and abjuration was never used again.

Conclusion

Guernsey's criminal justice system changed almost out of recognition between 1765 and 1844. The island had begun the period with a small population, where control over the citizenry was largely exercised informally and face-to-face. Recourse to the Court for public order purposes was rare, and, aside from prosecuting serious crime, the criminal justice system served essentially to provide a dispute-resolution service for those who could afford the costs.

---

[198] 9.1.1790, GG, *Crime*, vol. 18. It was understood that Pezet would stand trial if he returned within the three-year period, but if he returned after that time the offence would be considered purged.

[199] In contrast to offenders undergoing banishment or ordered to find bail or leave, abjurors paid their own passages (*Second Report*, p. 152).

[200] 15.6.1839, GG, *Crime*, vol. 30.

[201] 27.4.1844, GG, *Crime*, vol. 31.

[202] 12.4.1845, GG, *Crime*, vol. 31.

By the end of the period, Guernsey was a much larger, more disparate and more complex community, and the criminal justice system had become a tool for maintaining public order. Over the course of this transition, offences began to be prosecuted which had never been prosecuted before; novel punishments were invented; a new iteration of the Court was created – and all of this was done *ad hoc*, without statutory enactments. This had increased the degree of arbitrariness in the Court's proceedings, and in some cases, it had resulted in inequity.

It was against this background that, in 1842, Guernsey acquired a new Lieutenant Governor with an interest in criminal matters. This was fifty-seven-year-old Major-General William Napier. Napier was born in Ireland in 1785 to the daughter of the Duke of Richmond and the son of Lord Napier of Merchiston.[203] After retiring from active service in 1819, he devoted the next twenty years to writing a six-volume history of the Peninsular War, in which he had served with distinction.[204] The final volume of his history was published in 1840, and when Sir James Douglas retired as Lieutenant Governor of Guernsey in 1842, Napier's contribution to military history was rewarded with his appointment as Douglas's successor.

Plate 22. Sir William Francis Patrick Napier (1785–1860) by W.H. Egerton
© National Portrait Gallery, London

---

[203] L. Stephen (ed.), *Dictionary of National Biography* (London, 1885), pp. 82–7.
[204] W.F.P. Napier, *History of the War in the Peninsula and in the South of France from the Year 1807 to the Year 1814*, 6 vols (London, 1828–40).

William Napier had forged a reputation as a reformer long before his arrival in Guernsey. He had supported the Reform Bill in the early 1830s, shown sympathy with the Chartists, and involved himself in Radical politics.[205] David Hannay, who wrote a brief biography of Napier, attributed his politics to his Irish childhood:

> the state of Ireland and of the poorer Irish account[ed] for some part of his intense sympathy with the sufferings of the people and his boundless scorn for the ineptitude of their callous rulers everywhere … he was a double-minded man: democratic and humanitarian sentiments were combined in him with all the instincts of an aristocrat.[206]

William Napier's 'double-mindedness' set him on a collision course with the Royal Court. Not long into his tenure, he wrote to John Roebuck, 'I am not well or comfortable here [but] I am doing what I can to effect good, and though I have little hope of doing much, the pursuit of good is something in life.'[207] Specifically, Napier had identified the Royal Court as the 'inept and callous rulers' and was about to do battle with them on behalf of the 'suffering people'.

The battle began in 1844 over a number of incidents Napier perceived as abuses of justice, and in which he attempted directly to intervene.[208] This was an error of judgment on his part, not least because it made the Royal Court, who were sensitive to encroachments on their autonomy, assume a defensive posture which stymied any possibility of reform during his tenure.

Throughout his Governorship, Napier kept up a correspondence with the Home Secretary, Sir James Graham, detailing the abuses he had identified and his growing frustrations with the Court.[209] He was also in touch with

---

[205] Although offered several parliamentary seats, Napier had declined to stand for Parliament himself, and instead campaigned on behalf of Radicals such as John Roebuck, who was MP for Bath during Napier's Governorship (H.A. Bruce, *Life of Sir William Napier, K.C.B.,* 2 vols (London, 1864), 1, pp. 346–9).

[206] D. Hannay, 'Sir William Napier', *Macmillan's Magazine*, 86 (1902), p. 210.

[207] Bruce, *Sir William Napier*, 2, p. 83.

[208] These incidents will not be detailed here, but are retold from Napier's point of view in Bruce, *Sir William Napier*, 2, pp. 87–131, and from the Royal Court's point of view in H. Tupper, *Observations of Advocate Tupper of Guernsey Explaining Recent Events and Grievances* (Guernsey, 1844).

[209] This is preserved in NA, HO 45/399, HO 45/931, HO 45/930 and HO 45/090.

people in Jersey who were agitating for reform there. In the early part of 1845, Napier and others (including his friend Roebuck) began pressing Graham for the institution of a Parliamentary Select Committee into Channel Island criminal law. While the Home Secretary felt that the Islands' lack of parliamentary representation made a Select Committee inappropriate, he nevertheless acknowledged the persuasiveness of Napier's evidence and stated his willingness to initiate a Royal Commission instead.[210] In June 1845, Graham set the process in motion with a letter to the Lord President of Council, and within little over a year, a team of Royal Commissioners had embarked on their mission.[211]

William Napier left Guernsey in September 1847 and was not present when the Royal Commissioners arrived to take their evidence in that island.[212] He had, however, primed them in advance with sixty-five pages of notes on Guernsey's Royal Court.[213] A comparison of these notes with the Commissioners' eventual Report shows that much of their line of questioning was prompted by Napier himself.

Napier's influence was not, however, limited to the Royal Commission. At the height of his clash with the Court in 1845, Guernsey's Bailiff, fifty-six-year-old John Guille, fell ill and died. As was usual in such cases, Napier was consulted on a suitable successor, and his input led directly to the appointment as Bailiff of the English barrister Peter Stafford Carey. The revolutionary nature of Carey's appointment cannot be understated, and neither can his effect on Guernsey's criminal justice system. As well as setting a new standard for Bailiffs, Carey went on to engineer a major re-orientation of the law. The circumstances of Carey's appointment – and the nature of his response to the Royal Commission's Report – will be examined at length in Chapter 8.

---

[210] Graham to Napier, 2.5.1845, NA, HO 45/930.
[211] Graham to Lord Wharncliffe, 10.6.1845, NA, PC 1/2247. The Commissioners began their work with a visit to Jersey in August and September 1846.
[212] Formally resigning his office early in 1848, Napier was knighted in 1849 and promoted Lieutenant General in 1851.
[213] NA, HO 45/090.

III
1845–1929: A New Direction

Map 5. Guernsey, c.1890
Courtesy of the Priaulx Library, Guernsey

7

1845–1929: Background

Part III of this book will cover the period from 1845 to the end of the 1920s. This period saw a continuation of the population growth which had marked our previous period. From 26,649 in 1841, Guernsey's population grew by over a third to reach 40,588 in 1931.[1] Increases were registered at every census save that of 1921, when, through the effects of war and emigration, the island's population fell by about one-tenth. This fall was Guernsey's first since the post-Napoleonic slump. Nevertheless, growth resumed strongly from the mid-1920s, and within a decade the island's population had recouped most of its wartime losses.

As in the previous period, much of the growth in population was attributable to immigration. Censuses show that immigrants, in the sense of non-natives, never comprised less than one-fifth of the island's population between 1841 and 1901. Until the end of the century, the majority of incomers came from south-west England, with an additional trickle from Normandy and a brief influx of Irish between 1847 and 1853. The last years of the century, however, saw an unprecedented rise in arrivals from Brittany, as Bretons sought refuge from the agricultural depression afflicting their province. Such were their numbers that, by 1901, French-born immigrants and their families accounted for just under one-tenth of Guernsey's population.

Most English migrants settled, as previously, in St Peter Port, while French migrants settled primarily in the country parishes, where they found work in farming, horticulture and quarrying. This, together with improvements in the rural economy, spelled the end of the town's historic role as the engine of population growth. By 1891, accelerating population growth in the country parishes had reduced St Peter Port's share of

---

[1] Unless otherwise stated, population statistics in this section are derived from the decennial censuses, sources for which are given in the Bibliography. These data are also available online at www.histpop.org. Statistics relating specifically to immigration are from R.-M. Crossan, *Guernsey, 1814–1914: Migration and Modernisation* (Woodbridge, 2007), pp. 40–139.

Guernsey's inhabitants to 48 per cent, and this proportion continued to fall over subsequent decades.[2]

At our starting-point in the mid-1840s, the island's economy was based on four main sectors: shipping, shipbuilding, quarrying, and agriculture. All of these sectors experienced major change between 1845 and 1929 – some negatively, others positively. Shipping and shipbuilding were in the first category. Guernsey shipowners' participation in worldwide trade declined from the late 1840s as they were displaced by larger players, and over the next twenty years, shipowners focused on niche markets, notably the Azores fruit trade and the Costa Rica coffee trade, of which the Le Lacheur family enjoyed a virtual monopoly for several decades. From the 1850s onwards, Guernsey-registered vessels also took an increasing share of the local stone and coal trade, which spared shipowners the worst effects of international slumps caused by the Crimean and American Civil Wars.[3]

As an employer of labour, Guernsey's nineteenth-century shipping industry was at its all-time peak around 1861, when it gave work to nearly 1,200 men and boys.[4] Within fewer than twenty years, however, the workforce had shrunk by a third, with numbers continuing to decline thereafter.[5] This decline stemmed largely from the fact that local shipowners had failed to invest in modern steam technology and iron ship construction, which meant that, during the 1870s and 1880s, their traditional sailing ships were displaced from long-distance markets by more cost-effective iron-hulled steamships. By 1890, the international business of local shipowners had largely disappeared. Nevertheless, owners managed to keep some of their aging ships in action a while longer by transporting stone and coal between England and Guernsey. Gradually, however, the bulk even of this was ceded

---

[2] Numerically, St Peter Port's population peaked at 18,264 in 1901. The 1901 peak was not then exceeded until 2015, when parish population reached 18,585. By this time, however, St Peter Port accommodated just 29.7 per cent of Guernsey's population (States of Guernsey, *Guernsey Facts and Figures, 2016*, accessed 24.5.2021 at www.gov.gg/data).

[3] A.G. Jamieson, 'Voyage patterns and trades of Channel Island vessels, 1700–1900', in A.G. Jamieson (ed.), *A People of the Sea: The Maritime History of the Channel Islands* (London, 1986), pp. 381, 399–400; F.B. Tupper, *The History of Guernsey and its Bailiwick* (Guernsey, 1854), p. 444.

[4] 26.1.1865, IA, AQ 40/04.

[5] *Comet*, 8.3.1879. See also Crossan, *Guernsey, 1814–1914*, p. 23.

to non-Guernsey carriers, and by the first decade of the twentieth century the local shipping industry had lost its economic significance.[6]

A similar trajectory was followed by the shipbuilding industry, which grew up to supply the needs of local shipowners and shared the fortunes of its sister-industry. Like shipping, shipbuilding peaked in the 1860s, when some forty ships were built in the island, providing employment for many hundreds of skilled workers.[7] However, the island's small shipbuilders lacked the resources to embark on iron ship construction, and as the demand for wooden sailing ships dried up, the shipbuilding business declined. In the 1880s, only three ships were built at the rapidly dwindling number of yards, and by the turn of the twentieth century, shipbuilding had followed shipping into economic insignificance.[8]

The eclipse of shipping and shipbuilding was in a measure counterbalanced by growth in the stone trade. This industry grew rapidly after 1847, when contractors secured the right to break stone for London's streets *in situ*, thereby providing work to a large casual force of stone-crackers.[9] By 1878, according to a letter in a local newspaper, the industry employed a workforce of nearly 2,000 with annual take-home pay in the region of £95,000.[10] Such a large sum made a significant contribution to Guernsey's economy. However, unlike shipping and shipbuilding, which were controlled by local entrepreneurs, the stone trade was dominated by large English firms which meant that the primary profits went off-island.[11]

---

[6] A.G. Jamieson, 'Channel Island shipowners and seamen, 1700–1900', in Jamieson (ed.), *People of the Sea*, pp. 326–33.

[7] E.W. Sharp, 'The shipbuilders of Guernsey', *TSG*, 27 (1970), pp. 496–502.

[8] *Ibid.*, pp. 496–502.

[9] *Comet*, 4.2.1847. Stone for macadamising had formerly to be broken within 20 miles of London.

[10] *Comet*, 8.3.1879.

[11] English firms included major players such as John Mowlem & Co., A. & F. Manuelle, Wm Griffiths, Nowell & Robson, and E. & H. Beevers (Crossan, *Guernsey, 1814–1914*, pp. 27–8).

Plate 23. Stone-crackers, 1898
© Priaulx Library, Guernsey

The quarrying industry continued to expand throughout the nineteenth century and beyond. It peaked in 1913, when 453,947 tons of granite were exported, in both cracked and dressed form. This figure was never replicated, and – with bitumen-based tarmac superseding macadam for roadmaking after World War I – the trajectory thereafter was progressively downwards. By 1929, annual exports had sunk to just 172,132 tons, and the workforce had declined to about 350.[12]

By this point, however, another major industry had become established. This was commercial horticulture, which had developed slowly on the foundations of insular farming. Its beginnings can be traced to 1853, when, paradoxically, farming was in the doldrums, with exports depressed by the harvest failures of 1846–7.[13] That same year, the States embarked on an ambitious and much delayed project to enlarge St Peter Port harbour.[14] Rural representatives in the States had initially opposed the project in the belief that it would benefit only St Peter Port merchants. However, these harbour improvements ultimately revolutionised farmers' fortunes.

---

[12] P.J. Girard, 'Adolphus Bichard's reminiscences of the stone industry', *TSG*, 21 (1982), p. 208; *Census 1931: Jersey, Guernsey and Adjacent Islands* (London, 1933).
[13] Crossan, *Guernsey, 1814–1914*, pp. 55–6.
[14] E.W. Sharp, 'The evolution of St Peter Port harbour,' *TSG*, 18 (1967), p. 232.

Plate 24. St Peter Port harbour during construction work
© Priaulx Library, Guernsey

Hot-house grapes had been grown in Guernsey since the eighteenth century and small quantities of these had been exported to England for almost as long.[15] With the advent of steamships, exports were to some extent held back by the fact that, prior to the harbour's enlargement, steamers were unable to enter it, and were loaded from tenders in the roads. New internal berthing facilities became available in 1864,[16] and these, combined with the possibility of rapid rail transit from the south coast of England to the wholesale market in Covent Garden, stimulated an increase in the export of grapes. By coincidence, the British market for grapes and other culinary luxuries was expanding at this time, as developments in transport and food-chilling technology facilitated the import of cheap staples from the New World.[17] Increasing numbers of Guernsey farmers

[15] P.J. Girard, 'The Guernsey grape industry,' *TSG*, 15 (1951), pp. 126–44.
[16] Sharp, 'St Peter Port harbour', p. 236.
[17] J. Burnett, *Plenty and Want: A Social History of Food in England from 1815 to the Present Day* (1966; London, 1989 edn), p. 118.

sought to capitalise on the rising demand by building glasshouses on their land. As early as 1875, the *Comet* described 'expanses of glass … where but a short time ago not an inch of that product was seen.'[18] Making the most of their new glasshouses, farmers grew melons and cucumbers alongside grapes, and these, too, found a ready market in England.

In the early 1880s, British consumers developed a taste for a new luxury food – the tomato, and farmers soon experimented with this. Within a few years, tomatoes had become just as profitable as grapes, and many growers switched to tomatoes as their main crop.[19] In 1887, more than 1,000 tons of tomatoes were sent from Guernsey to Covent Garden, returning a profit to growers of £30,600.[20] In 1891, Guernsey's Chamber of Commerce, which had recorded statistics for horticultural exports beside those for shipping and stone since 1877, finally conceded that growing had outstripped its two rivals and become the island's 'staple industry'.[21]

Encouraged by commercial success, Guernsey's horticulturalists sought to expand their range of exports, and by the early 1900s they had added a flourishing trade in bulbs and cut flowers to their repertoire.[22] Cattle also became a commercial commodity in the late nineteenth century, when the recognition of the 'Guernsey' as a distinct breed stimulated a market for live cattle exports.[23]

By the 1890s, there were three distinct classes of horticulturalist. Native farmers, who incorporated greenhouses and bulb fields into their holdings while continuing with mixed farming as before; British horticultural entrepreneurs who set up large-scale commercial vineries in the island (mainly in the Vale and St Sampsons); and a myriad of small local growers who in a previous age might have sought a living at sea, or in a shipyard or quarry. A small plot sufficient for four or five greenhouses was all that was needed to maintain a family, and in a positive economic climate, loans and

---

[18] *Comet*, 17.3.1875.

[19] E.A. Wheadon, 'The history of the tomato in Guernsey,' *TSG*, 12 (1935), p. 339.

[20] 13.3.1888, IA, AQ 40/04.

[21] 19.3.1891, IA, AQ 44/05.

[22] P.J. Girard, 'Development of the bulb and flower industry in Guernsey', *TSG*, 13 (1939), pp. 284–97.

[23] B.C. De Guerin, *History of Agriculture on the Island of Guernsey* (Guernsey, 1947), pp. 74, 79.

mortgages were easy to come by.[24] As a result, the total number of landholdings rose to 2,506 by 1887, with the average area of a holding 'only a minute fraction over 4⅔ acres'.[25]

With nearly all horticultural holdings producing a reasonable profit, the wealth gap between town and country also declined. As the twentieth century dawned, country parishioners were taxed on real and personal property collectively worth £3,019,400 while town parishioners were taxed on £3,143,725.[26] This was a huge transformation from seventy years previously, when, at £1,107,600 and £3,016,100 respectively, country-dwellers' property had been worth just a third of that of their urban counterparts.[27]

Agriculture/horticulture became increasingly vital to Guernsey's economy as our period drew to its end. According to the 1931 census, farming and growing occupied as many as 38 per cent of Bailiwick working males over the age of fourteen, about a fifth of them on their own account.[28] In addition to those directly employed, the horticultural sector also gave work to large numbers in allied trades, such as carpenters, glaziers, box-makers and hauliers.

[24] As an English observer noted, 'to industrious beginners, the local banks are very liberal in the way of advancing money, often taking the known character of the applicant as their sole security' (H. Rider Haggard, *Rural England*, 2 vols (London, 1902), 1, p. 78).

[25] W.E. Bear, 'Glimpses of farming in the Channel Islands', *Journal of the Royal Agricultural Society of England*, 24 (1888), pp. 387–9.

[26] Average annual figures for the first few years of the twentieth century from *Billet*, 5.7.1905.

[27] See Chapter 4, n. 61.

[28] *Census 1931: Jersey, Guernsey and Adjacent Islands* (London, 1933).

Plate 25. Greenhouse workers, early twentieth century
© Priaulx Library, Guernsey

By the end of our period, tourism had also become a significant contributor to Guernsey's economy. It had begun in the 1820s with the introduction of steamer services from England, but remained for a long time the preserve of a small number of specialised travellers. With the growth in mass tourism after World War I, the island started to attract larger volumes of holiday-makers. It never developed facilities associated with English coastal resorts, such as pleasure piers and amusement arcades, but efforts were nevertheless made by Guernsey's States and Chamber of Commerce to advertise the island in the United Kingdom. Some 1,260 'summer visitors' were enumerated in the 1921 census, which was a large enough number to have generated a reasonable financial return and a welcome measure of employment.[29]

Although Guernsey's economy followed a generally positive trend between 1845 and 1929, the trajectory was not uniformly smooth, nor the benefits evenly spread. As in all communities, there was a substantial layer of poor people at the base of the social pyramid who suffered more than others when economic problems struck. For most of the period between the 1840s

---

[29] *Census 1921: Jersey, Guernsey and Adjacent Islands* (London, 1924). This census was taken in June.

and 1920s, Guernsey's only export market was the United Kingdom. This made the island vulnerable to downswings in the British trade cycle. Guernsey experienced three significant downturns in the period dealt with here. The first fell in the 1860s and early 1870s when a trade slump in Britain set off by the American Civil War sharply reduced the demand for stone and caused considerable local unemployment. The second fell between 1902 and 1908, when another British trade slump, this time associated with the Boer War, reduced demand not only for stone but also for horticultural produce, causing a number of bankruptcies among growers, and joblessness among farm workers and greenhouse hands. The third and last major downturn which afflicted Guernsey in our period was caused by the slump of the early 1920s which, exacerbated by the 1926 General Strike, reduced demand for horticultural exports at a time when the labour market was struggling to accommodate a flood of demobilised servicemen. In anticipation of a jobless total around 500 in the winter of 1926/7, the States released the substantial sum of £3,000 to institute make-work schemes for the unemployed.[30]

In 1926, Guernsey's States had only very recently become proactive in alleviating unemployment. The first time they had taken such action was in 1919, when they set aside £2,000 to fund a temporary work scheme for returning servicemen.[31] Prior to this, unemployed workers had few options. Parochial poor relief was ungenerous, and most non-natives were ineligible for it, so that pressure was generally released through emigration from the island, willing or not.[32] The States were also late in instituting a social security safety-net. The United Kingdom had had a Workmen's Compensation Act since 1906, an Old Age Pensions Act since 1908, and a National Insurance Act since 1911. Guernsey saw only two such measures in the period covered by this book – a Workmen's Accident Compensation Law in 1924 and an Old Age Pensions Law in 1926 – both of them rudimentary in comparison with their British counterparts.[33] These measures had been made possible by

---

[30] *Billet*, 27.10.1926. For more on all these downturns, see R.-M. Crossan, *Poverty and Welfare in Guernsey, 1560–2015* (Woodbridge, 2015), pp. 38–9.

[31] *Billet*, 21.5.1919.

[32] Crossan, *Poverty and Welfare*, pp. 60–95.

[33] For the genesis and content of these laws, see Crossan, *Poverty and Welfare*, pp. 241–7.

the boost given to States' finances by income tax, which superseded the *impôt* as the main source of States revenue in 1920.[34]

Turning now to changes in the built environment. We noted above that construction work on the new St Peter Port harbour had begun in 1853. The harbour was largely complete by 1869, by which time the enclosed area had increased to 30 hectares. Building work then continued intermittently atop the quays and piers, adding such amenities as stores, offices, waiting rooms, a restaurant, an abattoir, a lifeboat house, and a pond for model yachts. Between 1926 and 1929, the harbour underwent a second round of major structural work, when a 200ft jetty was built in its north-eastern corner to enable modern (deeper-draught) steamers to berth.[35]

The smart quays of the new harbour completely transformed St Peter Port's frontage, encouraging parallel changes in other respects. In 1871–3, a broad new thoroughfare – St Julian's Avenue – was laid out westwards from the north arm of the harbour to improve communication with the western parishes.[36] In 1879, St Peter Port's market complex was extended by a new covered vegetable market in High Victorian style.[37] In 1883, Guernsey's first public library was opened in St Peter Port's former Assembly Rooms, followed by a second public library six years later.[38] In 1900, a power station was built on the northern outskirts of St Peter Port, and electric lighting was introduced to the town. In 1903, the Royal Court House and the Greffe were extended, and in 1912–13 a new States Office was built on St Peter Port's North Esplanade.[39]

After a mid-Victorian lull, St Peter Port's housing stock also expanded. In the late nineteenth century, dwellings were built for the middle and working classes along such streets as Rosaire Avenue, Dalgairns Road, Coronation Road and Norman Terrace on the town's western and north-western fringes. These were followed in the inter-war period with more exclusive developments at the

[34] O in C, 20.12.1919.

[35] Sharp, 'St Peter Port harbour', pp. 236–7, 244–6.

[36] Anon., 'St Julian's Avenue – a centenary', *The Review of the Guernsey Society*, 28 (1972), p. 3.

[37] C.E.B. Brett, *Buildings in the Town and Parish of St Peter Port* (Guernsey, 1975), p. 33.

[38] These were the Guille-Allès and Priaulx Libraries respectively (J. Marr, *The History of Guernsey: The Bailiwick's Story* (1982; Guernsey, 2001 edn), pp. 467–8).

[39] R. Hocart, *An Island Assembly: The Development of the States of Guernsey, 1700–1949* (Guernsey, 1988), p. 75.

Ville au Roi and Village de Putron on the town's southern and south-western fringes.[40] In the mid-1920s, St Peter Port also saw the construction of some of Guernsey's first social housing – States' maisonettes in the Gibauderie and a housing estate at Collings Road.[41]

Plate 26. Aerial view of St Peter Port, early 1930s
© Priaulx Library, Guernsey

The island's country parishes also experienced considerable development between 1845 and 1929. At first, this was mainly concentrated in St Sampsons, from whose harbour most of Guernsey's stone was exported.

---

[40] R. Clarke, 'Growth of the Village de Putron', *TSG*, 22 (1990), pp. 798–805.
[41] *Billets*, 2.2.1923, 21.5.1924.

Between the 1860s and 1880s, the States organised the redevelopment of the port, rebuilding several quays and installing a harbour office.[42] In parallel with these improvements, the major stone companies built extensive stores, stables, offices and stone-cracking yards in the harbour vicinity. New housing sprang up nearby to accommodate workers and managers, and shops were established to provide for their domestic needs.

Both St Sampsons and the Vale underwent further changes after the introduction of large-scale vineries later in the century. Glass began to overspread the old patchwork of green fields, and suburban-style villas and worker's housing sprouted up between ancient cottages and farmhouses. Just before World War I, French geographer Camille Vallaux described the northern parishes as 'a strange and immense industrial garden ... a landscape made of glass as far as the eye can see.'[43]

Plate 27. Workers' housing in the Vale, 1907
© Priaulx Library, Guernsey

---

[42] E.W. Sharp, 'The evolution of St Sampson's harbour,' *TSG*, 18 (1968), pp. 310–12.
[43] Vallaux, *Archipel de la Manche*, pp. 100, 103.

Plate 28. 'A landscape made of glass as far as the eye can see'
© Priaulx Library, Guernsey

By the end of the nineteenth century, Guernsey's seven other parishes also found themselves in the throes of physical transformation, opened up by the expanding road network which by 1890 covered 225 miles.[44] In the 1880s, four modern militia arsenals were built in St Peters, the Castel, St Andrews, and St Sampsons.[45] At around the same time, St Martins and St Andrews, which bordered St Peter Port to the south and west, acquired a fringe of middle-class residences spilling over from town. In the inter-war period, ribbon development set in in the rural parishes, with new villas and bungalows springing up along major roads, often with small attached vineries. Social housing also made its appearance in the country parishes, with small estates built in the Castel and St Sampsons in 1923, and in St Martins in 1924.[46]

Our period also saw a number of major improvements to Guernsey's communications infrastructure. In 1858, a telegraph cable was laid between Guernsey and England.[47] In 1880, tram tracks were laid between St Peter

---

[44] Hocart, *Island Assembly*, p. 67.

[45] *Ibid.*, p. 63.

[46] *Ibid.*, p. 100.

[47] This was however beset with breakages, and the link only functioned properly when a new cable was laid in 1870 (Tupper, *History of Guernsey* (1874 edn), p. 492).

Port and St Sampsons, and steam trams began to run along the seafront from 1881.[48] In 1898, the States inaugurated their own Telephone Service.[49] In 1919, Guernsey's first island-wide motor bus service was established.[50] In the 1920s, the island entered both the civil aviation and wireless broadcasting eras, when a regular seaplane service was established between Guernsey and England, and BBC broadcasts began to be received on local sets.[51]

Militarily, changes were fewer and slower. Notwithstanding the receding threat of Franco-British war, Westminster kept Guernsey garrisoned throughout our period.[52] Relations with the civilian population remained variable. On the one hand, the island's retail and hospitality sectors greatly valued military trade (assessed in 1898 as worth £20,000 annually).[53] On the other hand, soldiers continued to cause law and order problems. Reflecting on a serious assault by a soldier in 1871, the *Comet* observed, 'the sight of a red coat at night in the suburbs of the town causes a feeling of mistrust, only relieved by the disappearance of its object.'[54] Towards the end of the nineteenth century, drunken brawls between groups of soldiers and locals seem to have become a regular Saturday night fixture in town.[55]

Militia service remained as unpopular in some quarters as it had always been. An article in the *Star* in 1868 mooted the militia's abolition in light of the diminishing threat from France:

[it] is an annoyance, a nuisance, and an injury, and we now wake up and enquire whether there is any necessity for it; whether, while it is a heavy tax on individuals, it is of any use to Guernsey or to England?[56]

---

[48] W.J. Carman, *Channel Island Transport* (Guernsey, 1987), pp. 11, 14.

[49] A.R. Bennett, *History of the States of Guernsey Telephone System* (London, 1926), p. 10.

[50] Carman, *Channel Island Transport*, p. 24.

[51] Marr, *History of Guernsey*, p. 416.

[52] Between the 1840s and 1870s, troops in the garrison numbered 250–300; between the 1880s and early 1900s, they numbered around 500. Following World War I, garrison strength was cut to less than 200, and the garrison was permanently withdrawn in 1939. Garrison statistics were supplied in most census abstracts (references in Bibliography).

[53] *Star*, 25.6.1898.

[54] *Comet*, 22.11.1871.

[55] For examples of serious affrays, see *Star*, 9.12.1886, 13.6.1901.

[56] *Star*, 21.11.1868.

In the late 1860s, there were some 4,468 men on the militia's active list, and 1,156 on the reserve.[57] This represented as much as two-thirds of Guernsey's male population aged between sixteen and sixty and constituted a significant burden on local men. This burden was partly relieved when the active force and first reserve were both slimmed down to 1,000 in 1900, and it was decreed that men undergoing training would be paid a daily allowance, with conscription only resorted to if there were insufficient volunteers.[58]

Guernsey's militia continued under this regime until World War I. The conflict, however, brought major changes. In 1916, the militia was suspended for the first time in its history. Islanders' immunity from compulsory British military service was also suspended, and wartime conscription was introduced for men aged between eighteen and forty-one.[59] Rather than enrol these Guernsey conscripts into existing regiments, a new unit was created for them under the name of the 'Royal Guernsey Light Infantry (RGLI)', which was funded by the British Exchequer. The first conscripts left for training in England in June 1917, and saw subsequent service in France. Some 2,280 soldiers, mostly Guernseymen, eventually served with the RGLI, which fought as part of the British 29th Division. The regiment sustained heavy casualties at the battles of Cambrai (November 1917) and Lys (April 1918). Large numbers of Guernseymen also served in the Royal Navy.[60] The total death toll among Guernsey servicemen in the First World War has never been calculated, but one contemporary put it at a possible '900 or more'.[61] If men who fought under French colours, and emigrants enrolled in Dominion and US forces are included, the actual figure may be upwards of 1,500. The RGLI was disbanded in 1919. Two years after its disbandment, Guernsey's militia was revived in smaller form, only to be disbanded for good nineteen years later.[62]

Politically, the second half of the nineteenth century was a torpid time. Having undergone a major reform in 1844, the States' constitution remained

---

[57] Report on Channel Island Militias, 9.8.1869, NA, HO 45/9492/5006.

[58] *Loi relative à la Milice de Guernesey*, O in C, 13.12.1900. See also Hocart, *Island Assembly*, p. 69.

[59] In 1915, some 500 volunteers, many of them militiamen, had already left Guernsey to join the 6th Royal Irish Regiment and the 7th Royal Irish Fusiliers.

[60] Including my grandfather, who survived the sinking of his ship at the Battle of Jutland.

[61] A.C. Robin, 'The population of the Bailiwick of Guernsey', *TSG*, 16 (1955), p. 55.

[62] E. Parks, *The Royal Guernsey Militia* (Guernsey, 1992), pp. 23–4.

undisturbed for the next fifty years. Pressure for wider representation nevertheless mounted over time and eventually became insistent during the 1890s. Bowing to public pressure, the States passed a new Reform Law in 1899 which saw a tentative move in a democratic direction. The law expanded States membership by giving a seat to HM Comptroller and adding nine new 'Deputies of the People', to be elected by island ratepayers.[63] More radical changes were enacted in a second Reform Law of 1920, which not only doubled the number of Deputies but abolished the ratepayer franchise and replaced it with universal franchise for men over twenty and women over thirty.[64] Equalisation of male and female voting ages was not achieved during the period covered by this book.[65] Jurats, Rectors and Law Officers remained entitled to their *ex-officio* seats until 1948.

Alongside these practical changes, less tangible religious, social and cultural transformations were taking place. Roman Catholicism increased its presence to levels not seen since the Reformation. The small French-speaking Catholic chapel established in St Peter Port in the 1790s was joined by a much larger English-speaking church designed by Augustus Pugin and opened under the name of St Joseph's in 1851.[66] A rather more modest chapel was opened at Delancey in St Sampsons in 1879 to serve the Irish stone-working community. In 1890, this was joined by the French-speaking chapel of Saint Magloire, which served Breton stone-workers and their families.[67] Three further French-speaking chapels were opened in the first decade of the twentieth century – La Chaumière in the Castel, Ker Maria in the Vale, and Saint Yves in the Forest – by French religious orders driven from France by their government's anti-clerical policies.[68]

Meanwhile, Protestantism was also undergoing changes. In 1865, St Stephen's Anglican church opened in St Peter Port for worship in the Puseyite tradition.[69] The Salvation Army established itself locally in 1881;

---

[63] O in C, 8.8.1899.

[64] O in C, 13.10.1920.

[65] Provision was made for equal franchise in a law of 1939, but it was not used in a States general election until 1945. For more detail, see R.-M. Crossan, *A Women's History of Guernsey, 1850s–1950s* (Benderloch, 2018), pp. 201–3.

[66] J. Crozier (ed.), *Catholicism in the Channel Islands* (Guernsey, 1951), p. 33.

[67] C. Chauvel, 'The contribution made to the Christian life of the island', *The Review of the Guernsey Society* (winter 2006–7), pp. 88–9.

[68] *Ibid.*, pp. 89–90; Crossan, *Guernsey, 1814–1914*, pp. 137–9.

[69] A.E. Croucher, *A Short History of St Stephen's Church, Guernsey* (Guernsey, 1983), p. 7.

Christian Scientists arrived in 1904, and Jehovah's Witnesses in 1926.[70] In general terms, the period saw a continuation of the retreat of Anglicanism *vis-à-vis* Nonconformity. A census of church attendance in 1893 revealed that 57 per cent of attendances were of Nonconformist churches and chapels, with a further 9 per cent of Roman Catholic places of worship. Anglican places of worship accounted for just 34 per cent of the island's attendances.[71]

Socially, while Guernsey remained strongly hierarchical, considerable change had occurred among the island's highest echelons. By the end of the nineteenth century, the old 'Sixties'/'Forties' divide had disappeared, and so had many of the 'Sixties' families themselves.[72] According to French writer Henri Boland, only one 'Sixties' family had hung on to its ancient status: 'that of the Careys', he wrote in 1904, 'whose influence is paramount'.[73] This was a mild exaggeration, but the next chapter of our study will demonstrate its essential truth. As for the other 'Sixties', they had mostly been supplanted in their traditional positions by a newly influential cohort of successful businessmen and growers, both local and non-local. According to Boland, wealth had endowed these new men 'with a prestige that poverty ha[d] stripped from the others.'[74]

Culturally and linguistically, the period between 1845 and 1929 was one of growing anglicisation. The process had begun long before 1845, but spread more widely during this period. English was made the medium of instruction in Guernsey's rural parish schools in 1850, which gave a huge boost to country pupils' knowledge of English.[75] This equipped them to make the most of the popular press which was now becoming available. England's first mass-circulation daily, the *Daily Telegraph*, was launched at the price of a

---

[70] Marr, *History of Guernsey*, p. 55.

[71] The results were summarised in *Comet*, 15.7.1893. For further analysis, see also Crossan, *Guernsey, 1814–1914*, pp. 193–5.

[72] Twentieth-century Guernsey accommodated few De Havillands, Bonamys or Dobrées, later generations of which had gradually dispersed as their forefathers' entrepôt fortunes ran out. For an instructive account of the De Havillands' last years in Guernsey, see R. Hocart, *Peter De Havilland: Bailiff of Guernsey, A History of his Life, 1747–1821* (Guernsey, 1997), pp. 126–7.

[73] H. Boland, *Les Îles de la Manche* (Paris, 1904), p. 135. Henri Boland lived in Guernsey between 1883 and 1889, during which period he edited *Le Bailliage* newspaper.

[74] Boland, *Îles de la Manche*, pp. 134–5.

[75] R.-M. Crossan, 'The retreat of French from Guernsey's public primary schools, 1800–1939', *TSG*, 25 (2005), p. 861.

penny in 1855 and made its way to Guernsey on the regular steamer services. In 1860, Guernsey acquired its own penny paper in the form of the *Mail and Telegraph*, which – by no coincidence – was also in English.[76] In reading such material, growing numbers of islanders at all social levels became familiar with English preoccupations, English fashions, English attitudes, styles and perspectives, imbibing large doses of English culture almost unconsciously as they read.

Personal contacts with the English also multiplied as the nineteenth century wore on. Tomato-, grape- and flower-growers liaised with buyers and agents in England. Guernsey teams travelled to shooting matches and cycling competitions in England.[77] English banks, such as the Capital and Counties, set up Guernsey branches, as did English chain stores, such as Boots. Cumulatively, this eroded much of Guernseymen's distinctive identity while psychologically integrating them into the British and imperial mainstream. So thoroughly British in outlook had even rural islanders become by 1913 that the Frenchman Camille Vallaux was driven ruefully to reflect:

> in the final analysis, I would find Guernsey's peasantry more congenial if they were less intent on imitating English habits in so many respects. Their anglomania is at odds with their lively feeling of independence.[78]

In the decade or so after Vallaux wrote, the process of anglicisation was ratcheted up even further – not only by the patriotic feelings aroused in the First World War, but also through the BBC broadcasts which delivered home counties perspectives directly into Guernsey living-rooms.

Linguistically, however, anglicisation had not gone so far. Vallaux was obliged to concede in 1913 that Guernsey's south-western parishes were 'still on the whole more Franco-Norman than English'.[79] The presence of French-speaking immigrants in these parishes may even have served to buttress the position of *guernésiais*. As late as the end of the 1920s, although virtually all

---

[76] A. Bennett, 'A history of the French newspapers and nineteenth-century English newspapers of Guernsey' (unpub. MA dissertation, University of Loughborough, 1995), pp. 77–8.

[77] In 1882, Guernsey's militia began sending teams to National Rifle Association competitions (*Comet*, 22.7.1882). By the 1890s, Guernsey was also sending representatives to National Cyclists Union events (*Comet*, 13.2.1897).

[78] C. Vallaux, *L'Archipel de la Manche* (Paris, 1913), p. 134.

[79] *Ibid.*, p. 92.

country parishioners could speak English, the south-west still accommodated significant numbers for whom *guernésiais* was a first language.

By 1929, few areas of insular life remained untouched by radical change: the economy, transport, communications, the built environment, as well as the island's cultural and social make-up. Whether Guernsey's criminal justice system had kept pace remains, however, to be seen. As always, we will begin our investigation in the next chapter by examining the system's personnel, infrastructure, and legislative underpinnings.

8

1845–1929: Personnel, Infrastructure, Legislation

Personnel

Bailiffs

When John Guille died in June 1845, just twenty-nine months after his appointment as Bailiff, Lieutenant Governor William Napier declined to support the candidacies of any local contenders for the post.[1] Instead, he strongly advised the Home Office to seek out 'an English barrister of learning and firmness … to bring the practice of the Royal Court to a legal and just course.'[2] The vacancy soon came to the notice of forty-two-year-old English barrister Peter Stafford Carey, and Carey appears spontaneously to have approached the Home Office to volunteer his services. In his own words:

> if I had been altogether a stranger to the Island of Guernsey, I should never have thought of taking the office of Bailiff. I am of a Guernsey family, and though I had never been there for any length of time, I had always kept up my connection with the Island. The circumstances of the time appeared to call for an appointment somewhat out of the ordinary course … Under these

---

[1] Jurat Hilary Ollivier Carré, HM Procureur Charles De Jersey and St Peter Port Douzenier Carré Tupper had all expressed a wish to be considered (*Star*, 12.6.1845, 19.6.1845).
[2] Napier to Home Office, 8.6.1845, NA, HO 45/213.

circumstances I made a tender of my services. They were accepted and I received the appointment of Bailiff.[3]

Before entering office, Carey met with the Home Secretary, Sir James Graham. As he later observed, Graham was at pains to impress upon him that Guernsey's criminal law 'was in a very defective state, and … required great alteration'.[4] With this message firmly imprinted on his mind, Carey was sworn in as the new Bailiff on 18 July 1845.

Carey had been born in Guernsey in 1803 to Peter Martin Carey, a member of a local brewing dynasty, and Frances Stafford, an English clergyman's daughter. His grandfather, Pierre Carey *'de la brasserie'*, had served as a Jurat between 1719 and 1744. Carey had left Guernsey in early childhood and was brought up and educated in England. He graduated MA from Oxford University in 1829 and was called to the Bar at Lincoln's Inn in 1830. Prior to his arrival in Guernsey, Carey had served as Recorder of Dartmouth from 1836, and Judge of the Borough Court of Wells from 1838. Simultaneously, he had also worked as part-time Professor of English Law at University College, London.

Knowing that Jurat Hilary Carré had aspired to the Bailiff's post, Peter Stafford Carey appointed him Lieutenant Bailiff, both as a conciliatory gesture and also because he valued his knowledge and experience. Carré served in this role until 1867 (when he resigned from the bench to become Greffier). Carey himself served as Bailiff for thirty-eight years. Knighted in 1862, he retired at the age of eighty in 1883 and died in 1886.[5] His achievements in relation to the criminal justice system will be detailed below.

---

[3] Carey to Lord Palmerston, 8.6.1854, NA, HO 45/5188.
[4] Carey to Lord Palmerston, 27.7.1854, NA, HO 45/5188.
[5] For a biography, see *Star*, 19.1.1886.

Plate 29. Peter Stafford Carey presiding over the States, c.1865
© Priaulx Library, Guernsey

Peter Stafford Carey's successor was John Utermarck, the first of Guernsey's Bailiffs to have followed the full *cursus honorum* from Advocate to Comptroller and thence from Procureur to Bailiff. Unlike Carey, Utermarck had no experience of English law. Having served a legal apprenticeship in Guernsey, he had attended Caen University and graduated *Docteur en Droit.*[6] In its brevity, John Utermarck's tenure mirrored that of his predecessor-but-one, John Guille. Appointed at the age of sixty-five in August 1883, Utermarck died unexpectedly only ten months later. In his obituary, the *Star* observed that he had 'long been maturing ... several reforms and ameliorations.'[7] Some of Utermarck's ideas for reform are to be found in his submission to the Royal Commission of 1846–8.[8] His tenure was however too short to bring any of them to fruition.

Utermarck was replaced in October 1884 by seventy-six-year-old Edgar MacCulloch. A Jurat since his thirties, MacCulloch had devoted his entire

[6] *Star*, 28.8.1883.
[7] *Star*, 21.6.1884.
[8] *Second Report of the Commissioners Appointed to Inquire into the State of the Criminal Law in the Channel Islands: Guernsey* (London, 1848), pp. 43–5

adult life to public office.[9] He also had extensive experience of presiding over the Royal Court and States, having served intermittently as a temporary Lieutenant Bailiff since 1851 and taken over permanently from Hilary Carré when the latter became Greffier in the late 1860s. In addition to this, he had served twice as *Juge Délégué* or interim Bailiff. By recommending MacCulloch for the office of Bailiff, Lieutenant Governor Henry Sarel was no doubt acquiescing to the local view that he had earned it by his many years of conscientious service.[10] Unfortunately, the appointment came too late in MacCulloch's life. He was forced by incapacity to withdraw from the States and Court in 1892, but refused to relinquish his office until reaching the age of eighty-seven in 1895, stimulating local discontent and criticism in the press.[11] As a result of this episode, it was laid down after MacCulloch's departure that all future Bailiffs should retire at seventy.[12] MacCulloch's main achievements in the criminal justice field focused on juveniles. In the 1850s, he had been involved in setting up a local reformatory, and, as Bailiff in the 1880s and 1890s, in establishing procedures for the admission of Guernsey adolescents to English reformatories.

Following MacCulloch, no more non-lawyers were appointed Bailiff. The next incumbent, Thomas Godfrey Carey, was the first of many Advocates appointed to the office as the culmination of a long career. Carey became Bailiff at the age of sixty-three in 1895. Like John Utermarck before him, he had served a local apprenticeship and studied at Caen, where he graduated *Docteur en Droit*. Admitted to the Guernsey Bar in 1854, he had succeeded Utermarck as Procureur in 1883 without first becoming Comptroller. While in office, he helped pilot the 1899 *Loi relative à la Réforme des Etats* through

[9] Edgar MacCulloch's great-grandfather, originally from Scotland, had come to Guernsey via the Isle of Man c.1766, and married into the local elite. He was the first cousin of Advocate Robert MacCulloch, and the great-nephew of Thomas De Sausmarez, HM Procureur 1793–1830. A lifelong bachelor, he was also known for his interest in antiquarian studies. For biographies of MacCulloch, see R. Hocart, 'Sir Edgar MacCulloch', *TSG*, 21 (1983), pp. 274–7; G. Rowland, 'Sir Edgar MacCulloch', *TSG*, 26 (2007), pp. 224–9.

[10] A writer to the *Star* in 1884 observed that such an appointment would only be 'graceful … considering … his long and devoted labours in the interest of the island' ('PATRIOT', *Star*, 10.7.1884).

[11] See, for instance, *Le Bailliage*, 1.12.1894, 15.12.1894, and G.A. Robinet de Cléry, *Les Iles Normandes, Pays de Home Rule* (Paris, 1898), pp. 120–2.

[12] MacCulloch, who had been knighted in 1886, died in 1896.

the States. Carey received a knighthood in 1900, retired in 1902, and died in Guernsey four years later.[13]

Carey's replacement, Henry Giffard, although also a lawyer, differed from his predecessor in two important respects. Firstly, he was not from Guernsey's traditional top drawer.[14] Secondly, he was English-trained. Born in Guernsey in 1838, he had graduated MA from Oxford in 1863 and was called to the Bar at Lincoln's Inn in 1865.[15] Following a successful career as an equity lawyer, he returned to Guernsey in 1899, where he was elected unopposed to the Jurats' bench.[16] After less than three years as a Jurat, he was appointed Bailiff at the age of sixty-three in 1902. A dyed-in-the-wool civil lawyer, Giffard had little interest in the criminal law. Although Guernsey's first sexual offences law was passed on his watch,[17] his main focus while in office was tax reform.[18] Knighted in 1903, Giffard retired at seventy in 1908. He died nineteen years later at his family home in the Vale.[19]

Henry Giffard was the last of Guernsey's Bailiffs to have served as a Jurat. His successor, William Carey, was appointed directly from the ranks of Advocates, without having first served as a Law Officer. Guernsey-trained and Caen-educated, Carey became Bailiff at the comparatively young age of fifty-five. As well as preparing the ground for the introduction of Guernsey's first salaried all-island police, he oversaw the passage of important laws on sexual offences and abortion. Carey died in office at the age of sixty-two in 1915.[20]

---

[13] One of Carey's sons, Lionel Slade Carey served as a Jurat, and another, Cecil Carey, as an Advocate.

[14] Giffard's grandfather, also Henry, had raised the family's status in the early nineteenth century by a well-judged purchase of land reclaimed from the Braye du Valle.

[15] *Star*, 1.7.1927.

[16] He had previously also ventured into English politics, having stood (unsuccessfully) as Tory candidate for eastern Cambridgeshire in the General Election of 1892 (*Gazette de Guernesey*, 25.11.1899).

[17] See Chapter 9, n. 129.

[18] In 1901, Giffard instituted the States' first permanent Finance Committee as well as annual States' budgets (*Billet*, 30.10.1901). His tax reform efforts centred on the reduction of Guernsey's dependence on indirect taxation, but did not meet with success.

[19] *Star*, 1.7.1927.

[20] Carey received a knighthood in the New Year's honours which preceded his death in July 1915 (*Guernsey Weekly Press*, 31.7.1915). His son, Allan Carey, followed in his footsteps as an Advocate.

William Carey was replaced by Edward Chepmell Ozanne, an almost exact contemporary of Carey's who had been serving as a Law Officer since 1877. Like Henry Giffard, Ozanne was not from Guernsey's top drawer. His father, homeopath John Ozanne, had died young, leaving his mother with a large family to bring up alone.[21] Having gained a *Licence en Droit* from Caen in 1874, Edward Ozanne was sworn in as an Advocate the same year, and laboriously worked his way through the offices of Comptroller and Procureur to become Bailiff. As well piloting Guernsey through the worst years of World War I, Ozanne oversaw the passage of several ground-breaking laws, not least the Children's Law of 1917, the Income Tax Law of 1919 and the States' Reform Law of 1920. Having been knighted during the course of a Royal Visit in 1921, Ozanne retired the following year and died in 1927 at the age of seventy-five.[22]

Ozanne's successor, Sir Havilland De Sausmarez, had by far the most illustrious credentials of any Bailiff of our period. Guernsey-born and very much top-drawer, he was educated at Cambridge and called to the Bar at the Inner Temple in 1884.[23] Starting out as a barrister on England's South-Eastern circuit, he joined the Foreign Office Judicial Service in 1892 and served for nearly thirty years as a judge in British extra-territorial courts from Zanzibar to Shanghai.[24] Knighted in 1905, he retired from the Foreign Service in 1920 and returned to his home island. Seen as an ideal choice for Bailiff, De Sausmarez was appointed to the office aged sixty-one in 1922 and served until 1929. He pushed through a significant change to the Royal Court's criminal procedure in 1923 and helped create the post of stipendiary magistrate in 1925.[25] Following his retirement, De Sausmarez lived on in Guernsey until 1941.

[21] 'John Ozanne, 1816–1864', accessed 5.10.2020 at www.sueyounghistories.com/2008-10-17-john-ozanne-1816–1864.

[22] *Guernsey Weekly Press*, 23.10.1915; *Star*, 16.3.1927.

[23] This account is drawn from *Star*, 12.12.1922 and G. Rowland, 'Sir Havilland De Sausmarez, Bt, *TSG*, 26 (2007), pp. 229–37.

[24] British extra-territorial courts dealt with civil and criminal cases in which British subjects were involved. The law they administered was, so far as circumstances admitted, English law.

[25] These two reforms will be examined in detail below.

Plate 30. Sir Havilland De Sausmarez
© Priaulx Library, Guernsey

The last Bailiff to be appointed during our period was Arthur Bell. Another swing of the pendulum brought the office back to a locally trained and Caen-educated Advocate who had spent his career in Guernsey. Bell, who had previously served as Comptroller and Procureur, was appointed Bailiff at the age of sixty-one in 1929.[26] Bell's mother was a Carey, and his father, Colonel William Bell, had served for many years as Secretary to the Lieutenant Governor. Arthur Bell died in office in 1935 and did not oversee any major reforms while serving as Bailiff. During his thirty-four years as a Law Officer, however, he had helped draft most major laws of the early twentieth century, including a number of substantive criminal laws.

For almost all of the Bailiffs of this period, remuneration was a major bone of contention. Since the death of Guernsey's last Governor in 1835, surplus Crown revenues had been remitted to the Imperial Exchequer, with HM Treasury in ultimate control of the purse strings. When Peter Stafford Carey became Bailiff in 1845, his salary from Crown revenues stood at £300, where it had been fixed in 1813.[27] Although Court fees increased his total

---

[26] *Star*, 1.8.1929. Bell was the third Bailiff to have followed the full *cursus honorum*. The next would be Ambrose Sherwill, appointed in 1946.
[27] We should note, by contrast, that Lieutenant Governors of this period drew a salary of £1,700 ('Channel Islands Finance' (HM Treasury, 1909), p. 61, Royal Court Library, IA).

emoluments to c.£450, he deemed this insufficient for what was now a full-time job, and submitted two formal applications for a pay rise. He was turned down on both occasions.[28] In refusing Carey's second application, HM Treasury suggested that the States should themselves contribute towards Carey's salary, since much of the Bailiff's work was now done for that body.[29] Out of pride or propriety, however, Carey never put such a proposition before the assembly.

The next Bailiff to request a pay rise was Thomas Godfrey Carey. His first attempt, on entering office in 1895, received no response. Carey tried a second time in 1899, having heard that the salary of Jersey's Bailiff had recently been increased to £400. The Treasury replied on this occasion that it would be willing to sanction a rise to £400 if the States agreed to commute the Bailiff's Court fees into a single direct payment from themselves.[30] The assembly agreed, the fees were commuted, and from 1901, the Bailiff's total emoluments rose to £1,000: £400 from Crown revenues in respect of judicial duties, and £600 from the States in respect of civil duties.[31]

A further application came from Edward Chepmell Ozanne in 1919. Ozanne applied not only for himself but the whole judicial establishment, complaining that, despite large unspent surpluses on Crown revenues, HM Treasury had been so slow to sanction spending increases that Guernsey's entire judicial apparatus had become 'cramped and crippled'.[32] On this occasion, the Treasury agreed to augment the Law Officers' salaries, but negotiated an alternative arrangement for the Bailiff by which his £400 from Crown revenues remained unchanged, but his salary from the States was increased to £1,400, so that by 1921, Ozanne was in receipt of a total of £1,800.[33] When Sir Havilland De Sausmarez took office in 1922 (perhaps in recognition of his private income), the States element was reduced by £300.[34]

---

[28] Correspondence relating to these applications is preserved in NA, HO 45/5188 and HO 45/6268.

[29] Treasury to Home Office, 31.7.1856, NA, HO 45/6268.

[30] For correspondence on this matter, see NA, HO 45/10143/B18108.

[31] Bailiff to Lieutenant Governor, 9.5.1919, NA, HO 45/10978/B15797.

[32] Bailiff to Lieutenant Governor, 7.5.1919, NA, HO 45/10978/B15797. Annual surpluses on Crown revenues had increased from c.£250 in the 1850s to c.£2,500 in the years after World War I.

[33] Bailiff to Lieutenant Governor, 18.2.1920, 2.7.1921, NA, HO 45/10978/B15797; *Billet*, 1.12.1920.

[34] *Billet*, 6.12.1922.

Jurats

A total of fifty-nine Jurats were elected to the judicial bench between 1845 and 1929. This represented an increase of over a third on the number elected during the previous period. The increase was in large part due to a reduction in the terms served by Jurats. The average tenure of Jurats elected between 1845 and 1929 was sixteen years, compared with twenty-two years in the period between 1680 and 1844. One reason for this was the growing tendency for Jurats to be granted their discharge by Order in Council: over half of those elected between 1845 and World War I relinquished their seats by this means in the course of our period.[35] Another cause of the reduction in terms was the increase in the age at which Jurats were elected. The average age at election in this period was fifty-two, compared with forty in the previous period. In the past, many men had been elected at young ages merely because of their social status.[36] As the traditional elite faded away, choices became more meritocratic, with most incumbents elected on the basis of their lifetime's achievements.[37] About a third of Jurats in this period were retirees from military or colonial service elected on their return from decades abroad. A further third consisted of men elected after a successful local career in business or a profession. The last third was made up of well-to-do farmers and growers, many elected after years of parochial office-holding. The proportion of rural Jurats in this period was higher than previously. This arose partly from the fact that a knowledge of French remained essential for Court work, which gave country-dwellers, almost all of whom were fluent French speakers, a degree of preference over urban or ex-colonial candidates whose grasp of the language was deficient.

While the increased turnover among Jurats produced a succession of relatively unseasoned benches, this was to some extent compensated for by Jurats' greater diversity of experience. The bench was also improved by the

---

[35] Some thirty-five Orders in respect of our period are recorded in the volumes of *Ordres du Conseil et Actes du Parlement* at the Greffe. No statutory retirement age for Jurats was set until 1950, when Jurats were permitted to leave the bench at seventy. Any Jurat wishing to retire before that age still had to seek Privy Council permission.

[36] Only one man was elected in his twenties in the current period: John T.R. De Havilland, elected aged twenty-nine in 1881.

[37] We should note that open voting in Jurats' elections was replaced by secret ballot in 1899 (*Loi relative au Scrutin Secret*, O in C, 7.10.1899).

larger than usual number of Jurats who had either studied law or practised as lawyers. There were a total of eight among those elected in this period, who were distributed fairly evenly over time and between them served a total of 175 years on the bench.[38]

Plate 31. Jurats, 1896
© Priaulx Library, Guernsey

Back row, left to right: Colonel Alfred Collings (49); John De Garis (age unknown);
Dr William MacCulloch (47); Brigadier-General Hubert Le Cocq (63);
Major-General Ferdinand B. Mainguy (57); John N. Brouard (55, retd master mariner);
Edward Chepmell Ozanne (44, HM Procureur)
Front row: Major-General De Vic F. Carey (65); John T.R. De Havilland (44);
John L. Mansell (80, retd banker); Thomas Godfrey Carey (64, Bailiff);
John R. Tardif (72, retd Ecrivain); William Le Ray (71, farmer);
Nicholas Domaille (60, grower).

[38] John De Sausmarez, 1847–70; Henry Tupper, 1857–75; John T.R. De Havilland, 1881–1907;
Henry Giffard, 1899–1902; Julius Bishop, 1904–32; John Tardif, 1878–1904;
John Le Mottée, 1851–96; and William Cohu, 1884–90 (the last three had worked as
Ecrivains, whose role will be discussed in the section on Advocates, below).

Stipendiary magistrate

Until the mid-1920s, Jurats were responsible for determining cases in both the Full Court and the Police Court, where they sat in twos and threes under the presidency of the Bailiff or his Lieutenant. This changed in September 1925, when they were replaced in the Police Court by a single stipendiary magistrate on the United Kingdom model.[39] The possibility of a paid Police Court magistrate had first been mooted by the Royal Commissioners who visited Guernsey in 1847.[40] The matter had been debated inconclusively by the States on several occasions since that time, but was not finally resolved until after Sir Havilland De Sausmarez became Bailiff in 1922. De Sausmarez considered the obligation to preside at Police Court sittings a poor use of his time, and it was one of the first issues he dealt with. A *projet de loi* proposing the institution of a salaried magistrate responsible for both the Police Court and a new Petty Debts Court was put before the States, and on 19 July 1924, seventy-seven years after the Royal Commissioners had first suggested it, the States approved the establishment of a stipendiary magistrate.[41]

La Loi ayant rapport à l'Institution d'un Magistrat en Police Correctionnelle et pour le Recouvrement des Menues Dettes set out the duties of the new officer.[42] In his role *en Police Correctionnelle*, the Magistrate was to exercise broadly the same powers and perform the same functions as the Ordinary Court in its capacity as the Police Court. Sitting alone (and without the assistance of the Law Officers), he was to hold inquests and try criminal and quasi-criminal cases liable to (or which he felt merited) a maximum of two

---

[39] The first stipendiary magistrates were appointed to London police courts in 1792. By 1813 they had spread to Salford and Manchester. The 1835 Municipal Corporations Act allowed any provincial boroughs which so wished to appoint their own stipendiaries, after which their numbers increased considerably. Scotland's first stipendiary magistrate was appointed in Glasgow in 1876 (C. Emsley, *Crime and Society in England, 1750–1900* (1987; Harlow, 1996 edn), p. 14; D.G. Barrie & S. Broomhall, *Police Courts in Nineteenth-Century Scotland*, 2 vols (Farnham, 2014), 1, pp. 161–2).

[40] *Second Report*, p. xl. The title the Commissioners suggested for this paid officer was 'Vice-Bailiff'.

[41] Correspondence between the Law Officers and Home Office on this subject is preserved in NA, HO 45/24658.

[42] O in C, 17.3.1925.

months' imprisonment and/or fines of up to £10.[43] He was also to act as a committing court in cases beyond his personal jurisdiction, admitting the accused to bail or remanding him in custody pending Full Court trial.[44]

What had formerly been the Police Court now became generally known as the Magistrate's Court, and the Ordinary Court's duties were restricted to civil matters. Technically speaking, the Ordinary Court shared jurisdiction over minor offences and petty debts with the Magistrate's Court until 1954, but after the appointment of the new stipendiary, this jurisdiction was never exercised.[45]

The successful candidate for the newly created post was Henry Casey, a forty-one-year-old barrister from London, who was sworn in as Guernsey's first paid Magistrate on 5 September 1925. The son of a manufacturing tailor of Irish descent, Casey had been educated at Cambridge and called to the Bar in 1909. During World War I he had served as a Major in the Royal Artillery and had won the Military Cross.[46] The States voted him an annual salary of £400, which was to come entirely from States' revenues. Casey occupied the post of Magistrate between 1925 and 1940, and again between 1945 and 1957 (having left Guernsey during World War II to serve as Judge-Advocate in the RAF). In 1946, he added the post of Judge in Matrimonial Causes to his portfolio of offices, and in 1952 he was appointed Lieutenant Bailiff.[47] Casey retired at the age of seventy-two in 1957 and died in Cheltenham four years later.

---

[43] He was also to try offences whose penalties exceeded these limits but which statutes prescribed should be dealt with summarily. Treason, homicide, rape, arson, theft with violence, piracy, fraud and perjury were specifically excluded from his jurisdiction.

[44] This finally achieved the Royal Commissioners' recommendation that decisions whether or not to commit a person for trial should not be made by the same Court members who would later sit in judgment on him (*Second Report*, p. xxix).

[45] The Ordinary Court's concurrent jurisdiction was abolished by The Magistrate's Court (Guernsey) Law 1954, with the exception of Sark and Alderney cases (D.M. Ogier, *The Government and Law of Guernsey* (2005; Guernsey, 2012 edn), p. 94). On its non-exercise, see F. Gahan, 'The law of the Channel Islands, IV: criminal law in Guernsey', *Solicitor Quarterly*, 2 (1963), p. 155.

[46] *Star*, 13.8.1925.

[47] *Guernsey Evening Press*, 24.6.1957.

Plate 32. Magistrate Henry Casey
Guernsey Weekly Press, 29.8.1925

Law Officers

As we saw in Chapter 5, John De Sausmarez, HM Comptroller since 1830, resigned in August 1845, shortly after the Royal Court had dismissed allegations of sexual misconduct against him. His place as Comptroller was taken the following month by John Utermarck, then a young Advocate of twenty-seven.[48] The Procureur at this time was Charles De Jersey, who had been appointed at the same time as De Sausmarez had become Comptroller. After serving alongside Utermarck for six years, De Jersey relinquished the office of Procureur in 1851 at the age of sixty-nine. His retirement precipitated what has usually been characterised as the attempt to suppress the office of Comptroller, although the episode was more the product of random events than a concerted plan to dispense with the office.

We noted above that the Royal Commissioners had recommended that a paid officer should be appointed to preside over the Police Court. Following Charles De Jersey's retirement as Procureur, Lieutenant Governor John Bell

[48] Appendix 2.

wrote to the Home Office proposing John Utermarck as De Jersey's successor, and also suggesting that the vacated post of Comptroller be left unfilled, so that the annual salary of £100 attached to this post could be used to pay the new Police Court magistrate (or Vice-Bailiff, as the Commissioners had termed him).[49] Apprised of this, John Utermarck stated his readiness to perform both Law Officers' duties on condition that he be paid an additional £50 from Crown revenues. This arrangement was approved by all interested parties, including Bailiff Peter Stafford Carey, and Utermarck was duly sworn in as Procureur in July 1851.[50]

Plate 33. John De Havilland Utermarck
By kind permission of the Royal Court

For some years, Court business continued with a single Law Officer.[51] Over time, however, parochial Douzaines grew frustrated at not having a choice of Law Officer to handle their legal affairs, and in 1857 they petitioned

---

[49] Lieutenant Governor to Home Office, 7.6.1851, 'Suppression of the Office of Comptroller', 'Privy Council', vol. 3, Royal Court Library, IA.
[50] Home Office to Bailiff, 3.7.1851, 'Suppression of Office of Comptroller', IA.
[51] Advocate Robert MacCulloch acted as *Contrôle Délégué* in the two major murder trials of the period, and from time to time, a *Contrôle Délégué* was sworn in to act for the defence in *causes en adjonction* (Bailiff to Lieutenant Governor, 12.2.1857, NA, HO 45/6390; Lieutenant Governor to Bailiff, 23.10.1858, GG, Royal Court General Letter Book (second series), vol. 8).

the Home Secretary for the reinstatement of the Comptrollership. The Home Office consulted the Bailiff on this, but when Carey replied that the Royal Court did not need a permanent second Law Officer, the Home Office took no action.[52] Supporters of reinstatement did not, however, allow matters to rest here, and after a further round of lobbying from Guernsey, the Privy Council consented to hold a formal hearing into the subject in April 1861.[53] Evidence presented to them at this hearing seems to have persuaded the Council that a second Law Officer might be desirable after all, and an Order reinstating the Comptrollership was issued the following August.[54]

When the office was revived, the post of Comptroller was first offered to twenty-nine-year-old Thomas Godfrey Carey. Carey turned it down, because the salary had been cut from £100 (the sum paid to Utermarck when he was Comptroller) to a mere £50.[55] The Home Office's second choice was fifty-four-year-old Peter Jeremie, the son of Advocate John Jeremie and brother of future Jurat Frederick Jeremie. Jeremie, who had served as *Contrôle Délégué* in 1858 and personally petitioned the Privy Council for reinstatement of the Comptrollership, accepted the post.[56]

After ten years as Comptroller Peter Jeremie died in 1871, and the Comptroller's post was offered to fifty-three-year-old Advocate James Gallienne. Although in two minds about the salary, Gallienne accepted the offer. When his request for an increase was turned down in 1872, however, he seems to have resolved not to remain in the post any longer than necessary. A more lucrative opportunity arose in 1874 in the form of a vacancy for Greffier. Gallienne lost no time in applying for it, and when his application met with success, he resigned the Comptrollership. Unfortunately, no one could be found to replace Gallienne as Comptroller on so low a salary, so the post remained unfilled. In 1877, however, twenty-five-year-old Edward

---

[52] Bailiff to Lieutenant Governor, 12.2.1857, NA, HO 45/6390.

[53] Documents relating to the hearing are preserved in NA, HO 45/9293/7221.

[54] O in C, 9.8.1861. The idea of a paid Police Court magistrate had in the meantime fallen by the wayside.

[55] Carey to Home Office, 5.10.1861, NA, HO 45/9293/7221. The £50 was in fact the extra sum allocated to the Procureur in 1851 for performing the duties of two Law Officers. The Procureur's salary itself reverted to £200.

[56] Jeremie's petition is recorded in 'Suppression of Office of Comptroller', IA.

Chepmell Ozanne wrote to the Home Office to volunteer his services, and made it quite clear that he was happy to accept the ungenerous pay.[57] Ozanne was sworn in as Comptroller at the end of 1877.

In 1883, long-serving Procureur John Utermarck was finally appointed Bailiff, and Thomas Godfrey Carey was appointed to replace him as Procureur. For the next twelve years, Thomas Godfrey Carey and Edward Ozanne served alongside one another as Procureur and Comptroller. When Carey in turn became Bailiff in 1895, Ozanne was promoted to the office of Procureur, and the Comptroller's post was filled by twenty-seven-year-old Advocate Arthur Bell. Bell and Ozanne served together as Law Officers for a further twenty years. Finally, in 1915, Edward Ozanne reached the top of the ladder, and was appointed Bailiff after more than thirty-seven years as a Law Officer. Bell then succeeded him as Procureur, and thirty-one-year-old Advocate William Foote became Comptroller.

Plate 34. Thomas Godfrey Carey
Courtesy of Guernsey Museums & Galleries (States of Guernsey)

---

[57] Ozanne to Lieutenant Governor, 11.10.1877, NA, HO 45/9293/7221.

Plate 35. Edward Chepmell Ozanne
By kind permission of the Royal Court

Plate 36. Arthur Bell
© Priaulx Library, Guernsey

By 1915, the Law Officers' salaries had remained unchanged for over half a century, with the Procureur still on £200 and the Comptroller on £50, though the workload of both had increased considerably. When the new Comptroller William Foote died unexpectedly of pneumonia in 1919, there were fears that the inadequate salary would again make the Comptrollership unfillable, and it was at this point that Edward Ozanne applied for pay rises for the whole judicial establishment.[58] HM Treasury agreed increases from Crown revenues of £100 for both Law Officers, and an arrangement was negotiated with the States whereby the Law Officers' fees for non-Crown Court and States work were commuted into annual payments from States' revenues of £1,100 and £300 respectively.[59] This put the Procureur on a yearly total of £1,400 and the Comptroller on £450. In return, the Procureur was required to give up private work and devote himself full-time to his Law Officer's duties. The Comptroller was permitted to continue supplementing his salary with private work until he too became full-time in 1940.

Advocates

Twenty-six Advocates were sworn in by the Royal Court between 1845 and 1929.[60] Twelve of these eventually became Law Officers, seven became Bailiffs, and one became a Jurat. The Advocates of our period came from an unprecedentedly diverse range of backgrounds. Some, such as Peter Le Ber and Theophilus De Mouilpied, came from farming families. Others, such as Harold Randell, had fathers who worked as Ecrivains. William Foote and Ambrose Sherwill's forebears had been butchers.

All of this period's Advocates had a university education, and all but two had obtained their qualifications in France. In the 1870s, a number of young Advocates (Edward Ozanne, Amelius Corbin, William Carey and William Lainé) complemented their French studies with short uncertificated legal

[58] See n. 32, above.
[59] *Billets*, 3.11.1920, 8.12.1920. See also file note dated 9.5.1921, and Bailiff to Lieutenant Governor, 2.7.1921, NA, HO 45/10978/B15797.
[60] Appendix 3.

courses in England.[61] William Moullin, admitted in 1874, qualified as an English barrister and eschewed study in France altogether.

The only other Advocate of our period not to have studied in France was Wyndham Yates Peel, who was admitted in 1896. Peel, the great-grandson of former British Prime Minister Sir Robert Peel, was also unusual in that he was not Guernsey-born. He had been educated at Cambridge and admitted to the Bar at the Middle Temple in 1884. Having bought property in Guernsey in the early 1890s and taken up residence in the island, he applied for a vacancy at the insular Bar which came up in 1895.[62] At this time, no regulations governed admissions, and there was nothing to disqualify Peel from submitting an application. Despite some misgivings, the Court admitted him in February of the following year.[63]

The property acquired by Peel appears to have been a vinery.[64] At this period, relations between Guernsey's authorities and British commercial horticulturalists had reached a low point. In the early 1890s, the latter had formed a 'British Growers' Association' to campaign for the redress of their grievances, and Wyndham Peel had become their leader. What these growers objected to most was the compulsion to perform unpaid militia service.[65] Public meetings of British residents in February and April 1896 were followed by a letter to the Home Secretary soliciting exemption from service,[66] and a petition to this effect was addressed to Guernsey's Royal Court.[67] The Royal Court declined to act on the British residents' petition, and the Home Secretary also declared himself unable to assist. Prominent British vinery owners then launched a campaign of civil disobedience by ostentatiously

[61] *Star*, 15.8.1874; 30.10.1875, GG, *Ordonnances*, vol. 11.

[62] 14.12.1895, GG, Royal Court General Letter Book (second series), vol. 15.

[63] 8.2.1896, GG, *Ordonnances*, vol. 14.

[64] He had purchased it jointly with his brother Edmund Peel.

[65] According to the law then in force, any British subject within the age limit for service who was engaged in employment or business in Guernsey was liable to militia service after residence of a year and a day. The British Growers conceptualised this as taxation without representation, since, they claimed, the inability of most of them to speak French excluded them from insular government, which was conducted in the French language. For more on this episode, see R.-M. Crossan, *Guernsey, 1814–1914: Migration and Modernisation* (Woodbridge, 2007), pp. 205–7.

[66] Wyndham Peel to Home Secretary, 27.2.1896, NA, HO 45/10072/B5960A.

[67] The text of the petition, which was dated 30.5.1896 and contained 226 signatures, is to be found in GG, *Requêtes*, 1864–1907. See also *The Guernsey Times*, 6.6.1896.

absenting themselves from militia drill. Many were tried in Court, where Wyndham Peel made a speciality of defending them.[68] For several months, Peel's behaviour was tolerated by the Court. However, their patience ran out in December 1896 when, at a Christmas dinner given by the British Growers' Association, Peel insulted them in a speech, which he later attempted to justify in the newspapers.[69] The Royal Court reacted by suspending him.[70]

By this time, the Court had in any case taken action to ensure that the admission of someone like Peel would not be repeated. Ten months after admitting him, they had passed an Ordinance which, for the first time, regulated admissions to the Guernsey Bar.[71] Repealing the Ordinance of 1777 which restricted the number of Advocates, the 1896 Ordinance opened the Bar to any native of the Bailiwick (or other British subject who had lived in Guernsey for at least five years since the age of ten) on condition that the applicant held either (a) a *licence en droit* from a French university, or (b) a *baccalauréat en droit* from a French university plus a certificate showing him to be an Utter Barrister of one of the English Inns of Court.[72] In addition to either (a) or (b), the applicant had also to have passed an examination in Guernsey law set by a committee composed of the Bailiff, a Law Officer and an Advocate. The practical effect of this Ordinance was to make study in France compulsory for all future Advocates, while paradoxically also encouraging qualification as English barristers for those who wished to shorten their studies in France. In the early twentieth century, George Ridgway, Ambrose Sherwill, Alan Carey and William Arnold all complemented French diplomas with qualifications as English barristers.

In 1896, Norman law did not form part of the curriculum of any French law faculty. Two years later, however, Caen University introduced a course leading to the new qualification of *Doctorat ès Lois* which, experimentally, incorporated a small amount of teaching on Norman law. A prospectus survives in a Royal Court Letter Book, accompanied by a note to the effect

---

[68] For examples of trial reports, see *Le Baillage*, 27.6.1896 and 4.7.1896.

[69] *Guernsey Mail and Telegraph*, 24.12.1896; *Star*, 26.12.1896. For a detailed account of the Christmas dinner incident, see also Robinet de Cléry, *Les Îles Normandes*, pp. 266–73.

[70] 4.1.1897, GG, *Ordonnances*, vol. 13.

[71] Ord, 5.10.1896.

[72] The *licence* sufficed on its own, because it required a full three-year course of study. The *baccalauréat* was a lower-level diploma which took only two years – hence the necessity to complement it with a barrister's qualification.

that the course was devised with Channel Island students in mind.[73] In 1906, a new Bar Ordinance added the qualification of *Doctorat* to the list of options available to aspiring Advocates.[74] In 1908, Caen launched courses entirely focused on the Norman *Coutume* which led to the qualifications of *Certificat d'Etudes de Droit Normand* and *Diplôme d'Etudes Supérieures de Droit Normand*.[75] Originally conceived as a stepping stone to the *Doctorat*, the *Certificat d'Etudes* course was modified over time and eventually became the favoured option for Guernsey students.

Court dress

Court dress, in the form of wigs and gowns, was adopted in seventeenth-century England in order to add an air of solemnity to judicial proceedings. In Guernsey, by contrast, Court members attended sittings in their everyday clothes until the mid-nineteenth century. In a sequence of events initiated by John Utermarck, this changed in the early 1850s. Shortly after becoming Procureur, Utermarck wrote to the Home Office requesting permission to appear in Court in the silk gown worn by British QCs. The Home Office responded positively and suggested that all Guernsey Bar members should perhaps wear gowns and wigs.[76] Advocates were consulted and, although all of them (save Peter Jeremie) accepted the idea of gowns, they unanimously rejected that of wigs. Instead, they asked if they might adopt the *tocques* worn by French lawyers.[77] The Home Office was not initially in favour of French-style headwear, but seem to have accepted the idea after Peter Stafford Carey explained that he himself had worn a *tocque* when presented to the Queen, and no objections had been raised.[78] In January 1853, an Ordinance laid

---

[73] Bailiff to Dean of Caen Law Faculty, 22.8.1898, GG, Royal Court General Letter Book (second series), vol. 15.

[74] See Appendix 5 for the substance of this and subsequent Bar Ordinances.

[75] H. Nézard, 'Allocution, séance d'ouverture', *Travaux de la Semaine d'Histoire du Droit Normand tenue à Guernesey du 8 au 13 Juin 1938* (Caen, 1939), pp. 38, 40.

[76] Lieutenant Governor to Bailiff, 9.12.1852, GG, Royal Court General Letter Book (second series), vol. 5.

[77] Advocate Robert MacCulloch to Bailiff, 31.12.1852, GG, Royal Court General Letter Book (second series), vol. 5.

[78] Bailiff to Lieutenant Governor, 12.1.1853, GG, Royal Court General Letter Book (second series), vol. 5.

down that there should be Court costume for all Bar members: a black silk gown for the Procureur and black stuff gowns for the Advocates – all topped off with French-style *tocques*.[79] A few months later, a second Ordinance was passed specifying variations on this theme for the Bailiff, Greffier, Prévôt, Sergeant and Deputy Sergeant.[80]

Ecrivains

As noted in earlier chapters, there existed alongside Guernsey's Advocates a body of 'Law Agents' who produced legal documents such as wills, deeds and contracts, but had no rights of audience at the Bar. These Law Agents had never had any statutory recognition, and in 1867 some twenty-seven of them petitioned the Court for this gap to be filled. In response to their request, the Court passed an Ordinance which established *le Corps des Ecrivains*.[81] The Ordinance accorded thirteen named Law Agents the status of Ecrivain and licensed them to prepare certain legal documents. It also provided the *Corps* with its own disciplinary structures and admission procedure. In addition to this, the Ordinance laid down that, after natural attrition had reduced the Ecrivains to eight, their numbers should henceforth be kept at that level, with new admissions only permitted when a vacancy arose.

Ecrivains functioned under these structures for nearly fifty years. In 1914, however, the Court decided that new admissions to the *Corps* should cease, with the seven remaining Ecrivains allowed to continue practising until they died or retired.[82] The last of Guernsey's Ecrivains retired in 1971, leaving Advocates' firms with a complete monopoly of paper-based work in addition to their monopoly of audience at the Bar.[83]

---

[79] Ord, 17.1.1853.

[80] Ord, 11.7.1853.

[81] Ord, 6.7.1867. See also T.F. Priaulx, 'Le Corps des Ecrivains', *Quarterly Review of the Guernsey Society*, 37 (1981), pp. 34–6.

[82] Ord, 1.3.1914. This Ordinance also established a 'chamber of discipline' composed of HM Procureur and two Advocates, to exercise a supervisory role over both Ecrivains and Advocates.

[83] Jersey also had a body of Ecrivains (though their role differed slightly from that of their Guernsey counterparts). Unlike in Guernsey, these still exist today, admitted by virtue of a local examination. They do work similar to that of an English solicitor and have rights of audience only in Jersey's Petty Debts Court.

Police

At the beginning of the period covered by this chapter, Guernsey was policed entirely by unpaid and untrained amateurs. This state of affairs was criticised by the Royal Commissioners, who recommended the establishment of a permanent paid force along the lines of that already in existence in England.[84] The Commissioners had made a similar suggestion in respect of Jersey, and in 1852 Jersey's States passed a law instituting a ten-man paid police force in St Helier.[85] Guernsey voices had been calling for a local paid force since at least the 1820s. These calls intensified in the wake of the Commissioners' visit, and on 13 April 1853, perhaps encouraged by Jersey's move, a St Peter Port parish meeting finally approved the establishment of a four-man salaried force for the town parish, for a trial period of one year only.[86]

On 28 May 1853, John Williams (46), William Jesse (42), John Le Goubey (32) and Bernard Elliot (29) were sworn in as St Peter Port's first paid assistant constables.[87] They were issued with uniforms modelled on those of the Metropolitan Police, and given a suite of rooms at the St Peter Port Constables' Office in Manor Street. At the end of the trial period, it was decided that paid police should become a permanent fixture. For almost thirty years thereafter and despite periodic calls for enlargement, the size of the force remained set at four. In 1881, the force was expanded to six.[88] In 1902, it was further expanded to twelve.[89]

In the late nineteenth century, the country parishes also began to employ paid assistant constables. The Vale was the first to employ one in 1894,

[84] *Second Report*, p. xxviii. England's first paid police were the Bow Street Runners, created in 1749. At their height, the Runners numbered fewer than seventy. In 1829, police numbers were greatly expanded when the Metropolitan Police Act introduced 3,000 paid constables to London's streets. In 1835, the Municipal Corporations Act allowed provincial boroughs to raise their own salaried forces, and in 1839 the Rural Constabularies Act did the same for the shires. The 1856 County and Borough Police Act made paid police obligatory for all local authorities which had not yet established a salaried force (C. Emsley, *Crime, Police, and Penal Policy: European Experiences, 1750–1940* (Oxford, 2007), pp. 63, 66–7, 99, 112, 216, 220–1, 225, 228, 232).

[85] *Réglement ordonnant l'Organisation d'une Police Salariée*, O in C, 29.12.1853.

[86] 13.4.1853, IA, AQ 0966/01; *Comet*, 15.4.1853.

[87] *Comet*, 30.5.1853.

[88] 15.6.1881, 17.1.1902, IA AQ 0967/01.

[89] *Gazette de Guernesey*, 25.1.1902.

followed over the next two years by St Sampsons and St Martins.[90] On the eve of World War I, the island had about sixty police officers of various sorts, some full-time and salaried, but most part-time and unpaid. These consisted of the twenty elected parochial Constables, about thirty special constables, and a total of eighteen salaried assistant constables (twelve in St Peter Port, two in the Castel, and one each in the Vale, St Sampsons, St Martins and St Andrews).[91]

The fragmented nature of policing militated strongly against co-ordination, and by the start of the First World War, calls for a States' all-island police force were becoming insistent. Jurat Henry Tupper had been among the first to call for a unitary States' police force when serving as States' Supervisor (States' Treasurer) in 1870.[92] Tupper had envisaged the role of a States' force as primarily to enforce Ordinances and prevent frauds on the *impôt*. Plans to introduce such a force were debated by the States in 1891 and 1896 but foundered on rural representatives' hostility to the loss of parochial policing duties.[93] Attempts by the Royal Court to resurrect the matter in 1901 and 1913 proved equally unavailing.[94] The issue was, however, forcibly returned to the agenda when Britain declared war on Germany in August 1914 and almost immediately extended emergency regulations to the island, raising urgent questions as to how these regulations could be policed.[95] On 17 August, Lieutenant Governor Major-General Henry Lawson wrote to Bailiff William Carey:

> I confidently appeal to you in the interests of the Empire and for the credit and security of the Island to take steps at once to provide an adequate organization capable of taking the actions … which have been laid down by HM Government.[96]

[90] 'A Policeman for the Vale', *The Guernsey Magazine*, 22 (1894), p. 701; *Star*, 7.3.1896.
[91] 30.10.1914, NA, HO 45/24671.
[92] *Billets*, 23.3.1870, 6.3.1896.
[93] *Billets*, 23.9.1891, 6.3.1896; *Star*, 24.9.1891, 7.3.1896.
[94] *Gazette de Guernesey*, 26.10.1901, 1.2.1913.
[95] The regulations took the form of the Aliens Restriction Orders and Defence of the Realm Regulations (see 18.8.1914 and 22.8.1914, GG, *Ordres du Conseil et Actes du Parlement*, vol. 12).
[96] NA, HO 45/24671.

The introduction of an all-island force was urgently tabled for discussion in the States, and, at the meeting of 30 October 1914, the assembly voted in favour of a States' force by a margin of twenty-nine votes to sixteen.[97] It took a further four and a half months to settle the detail, but Guernsey's first all-island police force finally took up regular duties on 14 March 1915.[98]

The twenty-two-strong force, based in St Peter Port, was composed of an inspector, two sergeants, two corporals and seventeen constables (some of them on secondment from St Peter Port's parochial force, which continued to exist in tandem). Routine oversight was the responsibility of a newly constituted States Police Committee, and the force (funded from States' general revenue) was under the ultimate control of the Law Officers.[99] It was complemented by more than 300 special constables enrolled for emergency war service from November 1914 onwards.[100]

The Bailiff, William Carey, must have been confident of a positive vote in the States, since he had secured a head for the new force before their debate even took place. Early in September 1914 he had written to Frank Elliott, an Assistant Commissioner of the Metropolitan Police with family links to Guernsey, asking him to 'dig up some retired Inspector'.[101] Elliott arranged to advertise the position internally. A number of candidates applied for the post, and Elliott vetted them personally, eventually recommending fifty-one-year-old Edwin Green, who had previously served as Chief Inspector of Dockyard Police at Devonport and Chatham.[102] Green was swiftly offered the Guernsey Inspector's post and brought over to the island to begin planning the new force. He was formally sworn in as Inspector of the States' Police in January 1915.[103]

[97] *Billet*, 30.10.1914; *Star*, 31.10.1914.
[98] The force officially came into being on 31 January 1915, and underwent a short period of training before commencing operations (IA, PC 181-01).
[99] *Billet*, 13.1.1915, 6.10.1915, 10.11.1915.
[100] 21.11.1914, 28.11.1914, 5.12.1914, GG, *Ordonnances*, vol. 18; *Star*, 14.10.1930.
[101] W. Carey to F. Elliott, 1.9.1914, NA, MEPO 2/1821.
[102] Born in Devonport in 1863, Green had worked in a copper mine on leaving school. In 1884, he joined the Metropolitan Police and worked his way up the ranks.
[103] 30.1.1915, GG, *Ordonnances*, vol. 18.

Plate 37. Police Inspector Edwin Green
Star, 14.10.1930

In his letter to Frank Elliott, the Bailiff had expressed the hope that the Inspector's post would in due course become permanent. Four months after the Armistice, the States instructed their Police Committee to draw up a scheme for a permanent States force, and resolved to retain the existing force until six months had elapsed following the formal declaration of peace.[104] In August 1919, the Committee came back with their plan, and it was approved by a clear majority.[105] The new force was instituted by a law of December 1919.[106] Under this law, the Island Police Force was to replace the parochial Constables and assistant constables in all their police functions. The force was to be under the supervision of a nine-man committee appointed by the States, three of whom were to be replaced each year on a rota basis, and for which Jurats and Law Officers were ineligible. The States ratified the re-appointment of Inspector Green, and the new force came into existence on 10 April 1920 with a combined strength of thirty: one inspector, five sergeants and twenty-four constables.[107] Following the inauguration of the force, a police station was established near the courthouse in St James Street, where Inspector Green held sway until his retirement at the age of sixty-seven in 1930.[108]

---

[104] *Billet*, 19.2.1919.

[105] *Billet*, 5.8.1919; *Guernsey Weekly Press*, 9.8.1919.

[106] *Loi ayant rapport à la Police Salariée pour l'Ile Entière*, O in C, 20.12.1919.

[107] *Billet*, 3.3.1920; 27.4.1920, IA, PC 181-03. Jersey did not acquire a States all-island paid police force until 1951 (R.G. Le Herissier, *The Development of the Government of Jersey, 1771–1972* (Jersey, 1973), p. 179).

[108] *Star*, 8.9.1929, 14.10.1939.

Plate 38. Guernsey Police Force, 1926
By kind permission of the Island Police

Plate 39. Police Station, St James Street
Island Archives Service, Guernsey

Infrastructure

Prison

The 'house of separation' created at the Town Hospital in 1832 was used to confine criminals for only the first five years of our period, as the parish decided in 1851 to convert it into a lunatic asylum.[109] This diverted many of the petty offenders formerly held there to the prison proper (though the Court continued until the 1950s to sentence offending alcoholics, vagrants and prostitutes to terms in the ordinary wards of both Town and Country Hospitals).[110] One of the house of separation's main *raisons d'être* had been that it provided facilities for hard labour. Five years after its closure, two cranks were purchased for the town gaol and an Ordinance was passed permitting the Court to sentence offenders to hard labour there.[111]

The prison's daily population fluctuated either side of twenty for the rest of our period (with an additional 200–300 persons passing yearly through the police lock-ups). Conditions in the prison were slow to change. In 1849, Lieutenant Governor Sir John Bell raised concerns over the state of the gaol with the Royal Court, prompting the Court to commission three Jurats to produce a report, which was eventually forwarded to the Privy Council in 1854, together with a petition praying that measures might be taken to put the prison 'on a more satisfactory footing'.[112] The Council responded to the petition with a suggestion that the States should take it upon themselves 'either wholly or in part' to make the first outlay.[113] The States then purchased a piece of land contiguous to the prison with a view to extending the facility. However, as funds were tight, nothing further was done for a number of years.

---

[109] R.-M. Crossan, *Poverty and Welfare in Guernsey, 1560–2015* (Woodbridge, 2015), p. 142.

[110] *Ibid.*, p. 164.

[111] Ord, 6.12.1856 permitted the Court to sentence men only to hard labour. Ord, 3.1.1884 introduced hard labour for women.

[112] The petition, report, and ancillary correspondence are reproduced in Guernsey Museum, GUELI:GMAG 2004.50.23, pp. 3–10, 23–5.

[113] GUELI:GMAG 2004.50.23, p. 12.

Eventually, in 1860, the prison's Chaplain and Medical Officer sent a critical report on the institution to the new Lieutenant Governor, Major-General Marcus Slade, which prompted him to raise the matter with the Home Secretary, Sir George Lewis. Lewis in turn commissioned John Perry, HM Inspector of Prisons for the Southern District, to carry out an official inspection (the first since Dr Hawkins's in 1836).[114] Perry inspected the prison in the early spring of 1861. His report was scathing.[115] Perry's most stringent criticisms focused on discipline, decency, and facilities for solitary confinement. In respect of the first, he observed that, even though a warder had now been engaged to assist the gaoler,[116] the hard labour element of sentences was left unenforced and prisoners spent most daylight hours unsupervised on the first-floor balcony, from whence they would spit on the heads of visitors to the debtors below. In respect of the second, he expressed disgust at the continuing obligation on female prisoners to wash outdoors in full view of the men. And in respect of the third, he declared his astonishment that, owing to lack of space, prisoners undergoing 'solitary confinement' were held two or three to a cell. In Perry's estimation, no meaningful improvements to the regime could be effected until the prison was extended. He added, however, that it was unlikely that the required work would be done unless the British government assisted with funding.

Guernsey's authorities capitalised on Perry's comments to send a further petition to the Privy Council.[117] This time the Council referred the matter to HM Treasury, which offered to part-fund an extension from Crown revenues on condition that the States bound themselves to bearing part of the cost.[118] At this point, however, the States' finances did not admit of such a commitment. The *impôt* currently in force was one which had been approved in 1849 and had already been extended for seven years beyond its expiry date. Realising that nothing could be done until a new *impôt* had been granted, the

---

[114] GUELI:GMAG 2004.50.23, pp. 18–21, 22, 26–7, 44)

[115] A copy of the report dated 22.4.1861 can be found in GG, Royal Court General Letter Book (second series), vol. 8.

[116] The current gaoler was John Le Goubey, one of St Peter Port's original paid constables, in post since 1856.

[117] GUELI:GMAG 2004.50.23, pp. 53–6; *Billet*, 21.1.1863; *Comet*, 24.1.1863.

[118] Home Office to Lieutenant Governor, 18.2.1863, GG, Royal Court General Letter Book (second series), vol. 9.

Bailiff, Peter Stafford Carey, did not put the Treasury's proposal before the States, and several more years of inaction ensued.

A new *impôt* was granted in 1871. Once it was in force, Peter Stafford Carey re-contacted the Treasury and negotiated a contribution of £1,000 from Crown revenues towards the long-mooted extension. He then put a motion before the States to approve a matching contribution.[119] The motion was duly approved, and work on the project at last began. The prison extension was completed in the spring of 1876.[120] Improvements included a separate cell block for females with its own wash-house and bathroom; a purpose-built chapel; a fixed water supply; a prison kitchen; and a stone-breaking yard with five stalls for prisoners. The final cost came in at £3,500, of which the States had no choice but to pay the lion's share, as the Treasury refused to increase its original offer.[121]

If the prison's buildings had been improved, the same could not be said of its regime. In the spring of 1886, the Home Office sent another Prison Inspector, Colonel Frederick Hankin, to compile a third report on Guernsey's gaol.[122] Gaoler Le Goubey, now sixty-five, was still in charge and his remuneration still fee-based. His wife had recently been appointed matron on £10 annually, and there were two male warders on 15s a week, one of whom was Le Goubey's son-in-law. Paid 14d daily from Crown revenues for each prisoner, the Le Goubeys bought the inmates' food themselves, and Mrs Le Goubey cooked it in the kitchen of their house (they did not use the prison kitchen installed in 1876). 'Of course,' Hankin observed, 'no arrangement could be worse'.

Although new washing facilities had been installed in the prison, Hankin reported that convicted prisoners never took baths. He further remarked that there were no sheets on prisoners' beds, and it was 'very doubtful' that their blankets were ever washed. No lighting was provided in prisoners' cells after dark. Both the gaoler and warders had keys to the female cells and could let themselves in and out at will.

[119] *Billet*, 2.10.1872.
[120] *Billet*, 30.6.1876.
[121] Bailiff to Lieutenant Governor, 24.4.1876, NA, HO 45/9320/16929.
[122] Hankin's report is in NA, HO 45/9595/94762. There is a copy in a letter from the Home Office to the Lieutenant Governor, dated 28.5.1886, in GG, Royal Court General Letter Book (second series), vol. 13.

Like Perry twenty-five years earlier, Colonel Hankin observed that the labour portion of prisoners' sentences was 'a dead letter'. The stone-breaking stalls installed in 1876 had never been used except as roosts for Le Goubey's fowls, and Le Goubey had turned the stone-breaking yard into his vegetable garden. 'Discipline in Guernsey jail is absolutely non-existent', Hankin commented; 'so long as prisoners do not escape, the authorities seem content.'[123] Hankin felt that chronic underfunding was at the root of the problem. 'The whole question … is one of money,' he remarked; 'all expenditure is provided from the Crown Revenues of the Island, and if the Treasury will accord sanction for the disbursement of funds, the Prison may be put in order.'

No extra funding was however forthcoming, and the prison continued its ramshackle existence over the next several decades. John Le Goubey retired in 1890 and was replaced as gaoler by former warder Peter Renouf.[124] Only one further significant change occurred in our period. This arose in 1907, when, largely as a result of pressure from Lieutenant Governor Barrington Campbell, an Ordinance was passed which finally put an end to the gaoler's fee-based remuneration (almost a century after it had been abolished in England).[125] The gaoler, matron and warders were all put on fixed salaries (the gaoler on £100 a year), and prisoners were henceforth maintained directly from Crown revenues. While removing the gaoler's incentive to skimp on rations to increase his own profit, this measure nevertheless failed to improve prisoners' conditions in any meaningful way.

We might add by way of a coda that the prison long remained the Cinderella of Guernsey's criminal justice system. In 1947, an agreement was reached with the British government whereby the whole of the Crown revenues were assigned to the States in return for the latter's assumption of

---

[123] Hankin was clearly not informed that escapes from the prison were fairly frequent – such as that, for instance, of William Falla in 1874 (19.12.1874, GG, *Ordonnances*, vol. 11). He was probably also unaware that lax surveillance had led to several deaths in the cells, including those of Nicolas Le Page in 1867, John Desperques in 1870, and Maria Male in 1880, all of whom succumbed to hypothermia after having been left unattended in unheated cells while in a vulnerable condition (19.1.1867, GG, *Crime*, vol. 39; 24.12.1870, GG, *Crime*, vol. 41; 16.10.1880, GG, *Crime*, vol. 43).

[124] *Guernsey Advertiser and Weekly Chronicle*, 4.1.1890.

[125] Lieutenant Governor to Bailiff, 3.4.1905, Bailiff to Lieutenant Governor, 12.9.1905, GG, Royal Court General Letter Book (second series), vol. 17; Ord, 2.11.1907.

financial responsibility for the Crown establishment. At this point, prison funding became solely a States matter, but this did little to improve either the fabric or the running of the institution. In 1976, the Home Office Prison Department Inspectorate were called in following an outbreak of disturbances. Their report, like those of their nineteenth-century predecessors, was scathing, highlighting lack of professionalism, inadequacy of staff training, and poor physical conditions in the 165-year-old building.[126] At length, a decision was taken to build a new prison in St Sampsons. The new facility was opened in 1989, and in 2003, the old town prison was demolished.

Plate 40. Cell, Guernsey Prison, 1970
© Priaulx Library, Guernsey

---

[126] *Billet*, 25.5.1977.

Reformatory and other juvenile provision

As we saw in Chapter 6, juvenile criminality seems first to have impinged on the consciousness of Guernsey's Court in the early nineteenth century. A similar awakening seems to have occurred at this time throughout western Europe.[127] One response was the establishment of specialised penal institutions for juveniles. In France, after a period of experimentation with juvenile prisons, a national network of *colonies pénitentiaires* was set up to which juvenile offenders could be sentenced directly by the courts. These were based on the farm colony founded in 1840 at Mettray, which combined manual work with basic schooling and strict discipline.[128] Developments in France attracted the attention of British social reformers such as Mary Carpenter, who in the late 1840s mounted a campaign for similar institutions in Britain. In 1853 and 1854, Miss Carpenter opened what she called 'reformatory schools' for boys and girls in Bristol. She was also called to give evidence to the 1852 Parliamentary Select Committee on Criminal and Destitute Children, whose report led to the passage in 1854 of The Reformation of Youthful Offenders Act. Substantially influenced by Miss Carpenter, the statute provided for under-sixteens to be confined in government-certified reformatories for periods of between two and five years following a prison sentence. Ten new certified reformatories were opened in 1855, and a further seventeen in 1856.[129]

In 1856, under the aegis of Bailiff Peter Stafford Carey, a group of concerned Guernseymen founded a private reformatory of their own, funding it through voluntary subscriptions. To begin with, the institution only took boys at risk of offending (rather than offenders themselves). After a few months, however, the Bailiff negotiated an agreement with HM Treasury whereby prison fees in respect of juveniles might be paid direct to the reformatory instead of the gaol,[130] and an Ordinance was passed which

---

[127] P. King, 'The rise of juvenile delinquency in England, 1780–1840: changing patterns of perception and prosecution', *Past & Present*, 160 (1998), pp. 116–66.
[128] G. Wright, *Between the Guillotine and Liberty: Two Centuries of the Crime Problem in France* (Oxford, 1983), pp. 80, 89–91.
[129] D.D. Gray, *Crime, Policing and Punishment in England, 1660–1914* (London, 2016), pp. 188–9.
[130] Bailiff to Lieutenant Governor, 20.7.1857, Treasury to Home Office, 2.9.1857, NA, HO 45/6393.

allowed the Court to sentence any boy of fifteen and under convicted of an imprisonable offence to a term of up to six months in the reformatory.[131]

Guernsey's reformatory ran fairly successfully on this basis for a couple of years, and at times accommodated over twenty youngsters. This, however, was more than its resources could bear and by 1861, the institution was in trouble. Subscriptions had fallen away, and prisoner maintenance fees from Crown revenues were insufficient to cover all the institution's costs. After an existence of just seven years, the reformatory closed on 15 May 1862, and its remaining inmates were returned to their parents.[132] The States paid off the defunct institution's debts.[133]

After the reformatory's closure, the Court had no choice but to send juvenile offenders it wished to imprison to the town gaol. This changed somewhat with the passage of *la Loi relative à la Servitude Pénale* in 1870, which made it possible to sentence juveniles as well as adults convicted of serious crimes to long terms in English convict prisons.[134] In 1872, George Glover (12), Isaac Maindonald (14) and Martin King (14) were all sentenced to five years' penal servitude for burglary.[135] This presented the British authorities with a problem, since British courts did not sentence children to penal servitude. The Privy Council solved the difficulty by commuting the boys' sentences to five years in a government-certified reformatory.[136] This procedure was repeated in later cases, so that, despite the demise of Guernsey's own reformatory, some local juveniles still continued to access the more rehabilitative regime provided in such institutions in England.

In 1879, the States approved a *projet* entitled *Loi sur les Ecoles dites "Certified Reformatory Schools"* which proposed to give the Royal Court power to commit juveniles of both sexes directly to English reformatories and have their transport costs and fees defrayed from Crown revenues. The *projet* was

---

[131] Ord, 13.12.1859. Ord, 24.3.1860 raised the maximum term to one year, and made parents liable to contribute up to 2s weekly for the maintenance of their offspring. Ord, 1.10.1860 provided the reformatory with a formal constitution.

[132] 10.5.1862, GG, *Ordonnances*, vol. 9.

[133] *Billet*, 16.7.1862.

[134] O in C, 19.7.1870. This law and its genesis are discussed in detail in the section on Punishment, Chapter 9.

[135] 22.6.1872, GG, *Crime*, vol. 41.

[136] 29.7.1872, GG, *Ordres du Conseil et Actes du Parlement*, vol. 8. Glover went to the Hertfordshire Reformatory, Maindonald to the Bedfordshire Reformatory, and King to the Roman Catholic Reformatory at East Ham.

initially refused sanction by the Privy Council on HM Treasury's objection that such an arrangement might saddle Crown revenues with unpredictable costs.[137] After some negotiation, however, the Treasury eventually assented to a compromise whereby the new law would run for a trial period of five years only, and the costs borne by Crown revenues would be limited to £75 yearly.[138] The *projet* was redrafted to incorporate these restrictions and ratified by an Order in Council of 1880.[139] The new law allowed Guernsey's Court to commit under-sixteens of both sexes to certified reformatories in England for terms of between two and five years after they had served a local prison sentence of not less than ten days. Reformatory fees would be met from Crown revenues up to a limit of 6d per child per day (although all or part of this could be recouped from parents). Any excess not met by these means would be paid out of harbour revenues.

The law worked smoothly, and when the five-year trial period expired in 1885, the States applied to the Privy Council to have it extended for a further five years.[140] Unfortunately, there had recently been a general election, and the new incumbents at the Treasury were intent on reducing expenditure.[141] The trial period was not extended, and the children currently in English reformatories were sent home in the spring of 1886.

The States tried again in 1889. This time, they offered to defray the whole cost of sending children to English reformatories from the States' own funds.[142] HM Treasury raised no objections, but the Home Office decided that the scheme could not go ahead until Westminster had passed a new statute to provide for committals from Guernsey.[143] Guernsey's authorities waited a further six years for the passage of the required statute. Finally, in 1895, The Act for Enabling Children to be Sent from the Channel Islands to Reformatory or Industrial Schools in Great Britain received royal assent, following which Guernsey's second *Loi sur les Ecoles dites "Certified*

---

[137] *Billet*, 1.10.1879.
[138] Treasury to Receiver General, 14.11.1879, NA, T 1/16938.
[139] O in C, 6.9.1880.
[140] Lieutenant Governor to Home Office, 5.11.1885, NA, HO 45/9578/83489.
[141] Treasury to Home Office, 13.11.1885, NA, HO 45/9578/83489.
[142] Lieutenant Governor to Home Office, 12.7.1889, NA, HO 45/9811/B6950. This represented the first major departure from the principle that the Crown should pay the running costs of Guernsey's criminal justice system.
[143] Home Office to Lieutenant Governor, 7.11.1889, NA, HO 45/9811/B6950.

Reformatory Schools" also received its Privy Council sanction.[144] Its provisions were identical to those of the first law, save that it was not time-limited.

In 1917, Guernsey's 1895 Reformatory Schools Law was repealed and replaced by a piece of legislation known locally as the Children Law or Children Act.[145] This law set twelve as the minimum age at which children could be sentenced to English reformatories, and laid down that younger offenders should be sent to 'industrial schools' – a less punitive type of institution which had not come within the compass of previous laws.[146] Perhaps most significantly, however, the 1917 Children Act also made it illegal to sentence any under-sixteen to imprisonment in the town gaol.

A few years after the Children Act, the States passed *la Loi ayant rapport aux Faibles d'Esprit.*[147] Based on Westminster's 1913 Mental Deficiency Act and aimed primarily at young people, this enabled the Court to send individuals guilty of imprisonable offences who exhibited 'a permanent mental defect and strong vicious or criminal tendencies' direct to English mental health institutions at States' expense. In England and Wales, orders under the 1913 Mental Deficiency Act were frequently used against unmarried mothers deemed 'moral imbeciles' on account of their conduct.[148] A similar use was undoubtedly envisaged locally.[149] However, the only order made under the *Faibles d'Esprit* Law by the criminal Court in our period was in respect of a nineteen-year-old male sent away as a 'moral imbecile' after exposing himself in a public garden.[150]

Until 1928, Guernsey had no special penal provision for juveniles who were aged over sixteen at the time of conviction. This was rectified by the passage that year of *la Loi pour pourvoir à la Détention de Jeunes Délinquants*

---

[144] O in C, 11.5.1895.

[145] *Loi ayant rapport à la Protection des Enfants et des Jeunes Personnes*, O in C, 24.1.1917. This was based on the United Kingdom's 1908 Children Act.

[146] Following United Kingdom practice, the 1917 Children Act also allowed the Court to send non-offending under-fourteens to industrial schools if their parents neglected them or could not control them. After the passage of this law, Guernsey's crime registers recorded all instances where youngsters were despatched to such schools, whether the children had been convicted of an offence or not.

[147] O in C, 26.7.1926.

[148] H. Johnston, *Crime in England, 1815–1880: Experiencing the Criminal Justice System* (Abingdon, 2015), p. 133.

[149] *Billet*, 20.2.1924.

[150] 21.6.1928, GG, *Crime*, vol. 59.

dans une Borstal Institution.[151] The Borstal training system, designed for older teenagers, had been in operation in Britain since 1901.[152] Guernsey had not originally sought to participate in this scheme, but local youths sentenced to penal servitude since the early 1900s had on occasion ended up in English Borstals. Cognizant of this, Westminster included a provision in its 1925 Criminal Justice Act making it possible for juveniles from Crown Dependencies to be detained in a Borstal institution, and in 1926 the Home Office informed Guernsey that, if it wished to make use of this facility, it would have to pass its own enabling legislation.[153] The 1928 Borstals Law accordingly allowed Guernsey's Court to sentence 16-to-21-year-olds convicted of offences liable to at least one month's imprisonment to Borstal institutions for terms of between two and three years. As had by now become a well-established practice, the States undertook to pay all transport and maintenance costs from their own funds.

Legislation

This section will deal chiefly with legislative changes made in the wake of the Royal Commission into Channel Island Criminal Law. We noted in Chapter 6 that the Royal Commission had been largely instigated by Major-General William Napier who served as Guernsey's Lieutenant Governor between 1842 and 1848. The Commissioners were appointed in 1846, but did not visit Guernsey until the autumn of 1847, having taken evidence in Jersey first. They were Thomas Ellis (51), a barrister and law reporter, and Thomas Bros (43), also a barrister.[154] Prior to their visit, the Commissioners requested the Bailiff, Law Officers, Prévôt, Greffier, Jurats and Advocates to submit written answers to three sets of questions which they later used as a basis for *viva voce*

---

[151] O in C, 22.3.1928.

[152] The first detention centre of this kind had been established on an experimental basis at Borstal in Kent in 1901. After seven years, the experiment was deemed a success, and Westminster's 1908 Prevention of Crime Act sanctioned the establishment of similar institutions across the United Kingdom (Emsley, *Crime, Police, and Penal Policy*, p. 231).

[153] NA, HO 45/17337.

[154] Ellis and Bros were accompanied by a third barrister, Charles Clark, who acted as Secretary to the Commission.

examination. Ellis and Bros were highly skilled lawyers and, in their examination of Court members, they clearly brought out gaps and anomalies in the insular system. They were, however, strongly anglocentric. The recommendations they made in their report were thus essentially aimed at making Guernsey's criminal justice system conform to the English model with which they were familiar.[155] Some of these recommendations were adopted in the decade following the Commissioners' visit. Others were adopted later in the century. Some, however, were never adopted at all.

Peter Stafford Carey was appointed Bailiff in June 1845 with a specific brief to reform Guernsey's criminal justice system. The first changes which followed the Commissioners' visit were all instigated by him. As an English barrister, Carey's views in some respects coincided with those of the Royal Commissioners. However, having already spent two years at the head of Guernsey's judiciary by the time of their visit, he had a better idea of what would work locally than they did. In his written submission to the Commission, he had listed his own six main priorities for reform.[156] These formed the basis of the reforms he effected in the course of his tenure.

Carey turned his attention first to Alderney, where reform of the court system had become a matter of urgency. Here, the court's lack of criminal jurisdiction had put it under severe stress as hundreds of construction workers arrived in the island to work on a government-commissioned naval harbour of refuge.[157] Preservation of public order had become difficult, and in desperation, the court had unofficially arrogated to itself the power to try petty offenders and sentence them to short terms in the island's lock-up.[158] At Carey's instigation, this situation was regularised by two laws which granted the Alderney court powers to try all breaches of the peace, simple thefts, and master-servant matters, and award prison sentences of up to one month and fines of up to £5.[159] A further law of 1851 authorised the construction of a new Alderney courthouse and prison (at the Alderney

---

[155] These recommendations are summarised in Appendix 6.

[156] *Second Report*, p. 13.

[157] The Alderney court was restricted to the preliminary investigation of crimes and their onward referral for trial in Guernsey. For more on the harbour project, which began in January 1847, see Crossan, *Guernsey, 1814–1914*, pp. 112–16.

[158] *Second Report*, pp. 183, 195.

[159] O in Cs, 11.8.1848, 9.3.1850. These powers were modelled on those of Guernsey's Police Court, which, paradoxically, was not regulated by any statute.

States' expense), and laid down that maintenance and running costs should be defrayed from Alderney's Crown revenues.[160]

All the other changes instigated by Peter Stafford Carey concerned Guernsey. Most of these related to procedural matters, since Carey eschewed any major changes to substantive law (notwithstanding that the Royal Commissioners had urged the enactment of an entirely new insular criminal code).[161] Aside from a minor law on fraudulent appropriation,[162] Carey's only significant foray into the substantive domain came in 1856, in the form of *la Loi relative à l'Application des Peines tant au Criminel qu'en Police Correctionnelle.*[163] Primarily designed to introduce a hard labour element to prison sentences, the 1856 law also defined and set out penalties for thirty-eight minor offences (some of them modelled on Westminster's 1824 Vagrancy Act).[164] This law, as amended, was to remain in force for more than 120 years.[165]

Carey's reforms in the matter of criminal procedure were far wider-ranging than his ventures into substantive law. He began in 1849 with *la Loi relative aux Témoins et aux Saons et aux Reproches contre iceux.*[166] This broke new ground in allowing pre-pubescent children (i.e., girls under c.12 and boys under c.14) to give sworn evidence in Court, provided the Court felt they understood the nature of an oath. It also lifted the limit on the number of witnesses permitted to give evidence in trials, and reduced the long list of

---

[160] O in C, 14.11.1851.

[161] *Second Report,* pp. xv, xvii. Why Carey avoided substantive enactments is unclear. He may have considered it constitutionally unwise to tamper with the law as found in *L'Approbation* and Terrien. He may have been overwhelmed by the sheer scale of the task. It is also possible that he may have appreciated the flexibility which the dearth of substantive criminal law afforded Guernsey's Court.

[162] *La Loi sur l'Appropriation Frauduleuse de Meubles et Effets* (O in C, 21.7.1876) filled a gap in existing law by laying down that someone who had fraudulently appropriated moveable goods entrusted to him by a third party would be deemed guilty of theft and liable to the usual punishment for theft.

[163] O in C, 24.6.1856.

[164] The offences are listed in Appendix 7.

[165] It was finally repealed and replaced by The Summary Offences (Bailiwick of Guernsey) Law 1982.

[166] O in C, 21.5.1849.

recusable witnesses to members of the accused's immediate family only. A supplementary law of 1853 restricted recusability to spouses alone.[167]

Next, Carey addressed the recording of prosecution witnesses' statements in committal proceedings. In England, these were taken down in writing, but this had never been the practice in Guernsey. An Ordinance of 1850 remedied the matter by laying down that the Greffier (or one of his clerks) should take down witness statements at such hearings.[168] If the Court decided to commit the accused for trial, copies of the statements would then be supplied to the Bailiff, Law Officers and defence Advocate. This Ordinance also introduced the English practice of opening criminal trials with a speech by the prosecution which set out the facts to be proved against the accused – again not something previously done in Guernsey.

Having secured the recording of preliminary evidence, Carey then introduced his most far-reaching reform to date: the abolition of the French-style trial *au grand criminel* or *à l'extraordinaire*. This was achieved by the 1850 *Loi relative à la Procédure en cas de Félonie et de Levées de Corps*,[169] which dispensed with the three formal *in camera* stages (examination of prosecution witnesses, *recolement* and *confrontation*) and replaced them with the real-time oral examination and cross-examination of witnesses in open court. This meant that the procedural distinction between trials on indictment *à l'extraordinaire* and *à l'ordinaire* had been abolished,[170] and that henceforth, only committal proceedings would be held *in camera*.[171] 'By the combined operation of these several measures of reform,' Carey informed the Home Secretary in 1854, 'the course of proceedings in criminal cases has gradually assimilated itself to what it is in an English Court.'[172]

Nevertheless, there remained one element of criminal proceedings which had no English analogue. This was the *interrogatoire*, whereby, after an *acte d'accusation* had been framed, the prisoner was brought before the Ordinary Court, *in camera*, without counsel or knowledge of the evidence against him,

[167] As noted in Chapter 2, the number of witnesses on either side was previously limited to twelve, and the list of recusable witnesses extended to cousins, special friends, known enemies, deaf and blind people, and many others.

[168] Ord, 2.2.1850. See also *Billet*, 7.12.1849.

[169] O in C, 12.12.1850. See also *Billet*, 4.10.1850.

[170] See Chapter 2, pp. 78–81 for more on this distinction.

[171] The law also laid down that inquests should be held in open court.

[172] Carey to Lord Palmerston, 27.7.1854, NA, HO 45/5188.

to hear the *acte* read out and submit to questioning by the Law Officers (his answers being later read out at the trial). The Royal Commissioners had criticised the *interrogatoire* as disadvantageous to the accused, but Peter Stafford Carey had opposed their objections, countering that experience had imbued him with the conviction that 'the truth told by a man in answer to questions ... without his having heard the evidence which suggested them, gives great weight to that part of his statement which is otherwise incapable of proof.'[173] Carey thus disregarded the Commissioners' recommendation in this respect, and the *interrogatoire* survived his tenure as an integral part of the committal procedure.

In *la Loi relative aux Preuves* of 1865, Carey further amended the rules of evidence.[174] As well as refining provisions first set out in the laws of 1849 and 1853 *relatives aux Témoins et aux Saons*, the 1865 law significantly relaxed the ban on spouses testifying against one another. Henceforth, wives would be permitted to testify against husbands charged with deserting or neglecting their families, and both spouses would be allowed to give evidence in proceedings relating to violence committed or threatened against them by their spouse. Though only permissive (spouses were not compellable), these measures went some way towards removing structural barriers to convictions in cases of domestic abuse.

At around the same period, Carey also oversaw the drafting and passage of an extradition law. Prior to this, Guernsey had had no extradition legislation, and although the British authorities had been able to effect the extradition from Guernsey of persons wanted in the United Kingdom,[175] it had not been possible to extradite people from the United Kingdom to Guernsey, nor from Jersey to Guernsey and *vice versa*. This problem was largely remedied by the 1867 *Loi relative à l'Extradition des Accusés en cas de Crime*, which instituted mechanisms for extraditing persons from the United Kingdom to Guernsey, and from Guernsey to Jersey.[176] It did not, however,

---

[173] *Second Report*, pp. xxix–xxx, 174.

[174] O in C, 29.6.1865.

[175] Before the 1840s, this had been done by means of Orders in Council relating to the individuals concerned (NA, PC 1/3463), and after this date, by procedures laid down in British statutes (NA, HO 45/7969).

[176] O in C, 26.6.1867.

establish a procedure for extraditing persons from Jersey to Guernsey, for which Jersey legislation was required but seemingly never enacted.[177]

Peter Stafford Carey also oversaw the introduction of facilities for extradition between Guernsey and foreign countries. These were instituted by Westminster's 1870 Extradition Act, whose local registration was superintended by Carey in 1871.[178] The 1870 Act was Britain's first modern extradition statute, and it was based on treaties with other countries, in respect of which Orders in Council were issued applying the Act. A series of such Orders were recorded at the Greffe from 1871 onwards.

Having accomplished most of his criminal justice reforms in the first two decades of his tenure, Peter Stafford Carey's third and final decade as Bailiff was quiet in terms of reform. The quiet spell continued through the tenure of Edgar MacCulloch, with reform only resuming after Thomas Godfrey Carey's appointment as Bailiff at the end of the century. Carey and the later Bailiff Sir Havilland De Sausmarez then oversaw a number of further significant procedural changes.

The first of these occurred around the turn of the century and concerned the manner in which verdicts were rendered in criminal trials. In their end-of-trial speeches, Jurats had traditionally confounded their views on guilt or innocence with suggestions for punishment. This was criticised by the Royal Commissioners, who recommended that the Jurats should first establish a verdict before they discussed punishment,[179] but the Commissioners' recommendation had never been implemented. In the event, changes in the mode of judgment and sentencing were effected consensually rather than by legislation. Early on during Thomas Godfrey Carey's tenure as Bailiff (and possibly at his instigation), Court members agreed among themselves to divide the final phase of trials into three distinct stages. Firstly, Jurats would establish a verdict by majority vote; secondly, they would listen to the Law Officers' sentencing recommendations; and thirdly they would debate and

---

[177] See jerseyeveningpost.com/news/2017/10/16/jersey-suspects-cannot-be-extradited-to-Guernsey (accessed 13.10.2020).

[178] For Carey's negotiations with the Home Office concerning the Act, section 17 of which applied specifically to the Bailiwick, see NA, HO 45/9314/14702.

[179] *Second Report*, p. xxxii.

vote on these recommendations.[180] This sequence henceforth became standard procedure.

The final procedural changes of our period occurred under Sir Havilland De Sausmarez, and were instituted in two laws passed within months of each other in 1923. The first was *la Loi relative aux Preuves au Criminel*, which was substantially based on Westminster's 1898 Criminal Evidence Act.[181] This law finally made it possible to compel a wife to testify against her husband in proceedings relating to violence committed by him against her, or where he was charged under specific sexual offences legislation. Even more significantly, it also changed the accused's input into his own trial. Previously, the accused had only been permitted to make an unsworn statement in Court, his evidence being provided in the form of his *interrogatoire*. The new law revolutionised this by allowing accused persons, for the first-ever time, to stand in the dock and give their own evidence under oath.

De Sausmarez's second law concerned the *interrogatoire* itself, still in place more than seventy-five years after the Royal Commissioners had urged its abolition. Like the Commissioners, De Sausmarez considered it anomalous and wished to see it changed.[182] This change was effected by *l'Ordonnance relative à la Procédure en Matières Criminelles et en Matières d'Enquêtes* of May 1923.[183] The new Ordinance did away with the old-style *interrogatoire* and put the accused in a more equitable position in committal proceedings. Henceforth, he or she (and an Advocate if so desired) could be present at the session where the evidence of prosecution witnesses was recorded, and might also cross-examine them. Further, once the *acte d'accusation* had been framed, instead of being questioned on it unassisted by counsel, the accused could now be accompanied by an Advocate, and, before responding, had compulsorily to be cautioned that he 'was not obliged to say anything, but that whatever he said would be taken down in writing and might be used in evidence against him'.[184] Having responded or not – as he chose – the accused

---

[180] An account of an assault case in *Gazette de Guernesey*, 6.7.1900 spells out this sequence in detail, as do later newspaper articles.

[181] O in C, 29.1.1923.

[182] See *Star*, 25.1.1923 for De Sausmarez's criticism of the *interrogatoire* in a burglary trial a month after his swearing-in.

[183] Ord, 5.5.1923.

[184] Peter Stafford Carey had apparently begun administering this caution from the start of his tenure, but there was no legal compulsion to do so until now (*Second Report*, p. xxiii).

then had the option to call witnesses in his defence, whose evidence would be recorded in the same way as that of prosecution witnesses.

This, broadly speaking, was the position the reform process had reached by the close of our period. It is important to note in concluding that not one of the reforms implemented since the Royal Commission had been achieved through imposition or coercion. While the process itself was initiated by Westminster, its successful implementation was down to the expertise of Bailiffs – legally qualified Guernseymen who, while knowledgeable as to the mechanics of reform, were also sensitive as to its acceptability. In the next and final chapter, we will examine how these reforms played out in practice, and how changes in procedure were complemented by changes in substantive law.

9

1845–1929: Crime

This chapter is based on an analysis of the twenty-nine crime registers spanning the period between 1845 and 1929 (volumes 31–60). The quinquennia studied in detail are 1860–4, 1880–4, 1900–4 and 1920–4.[1] The chapter will follow a slightly different format from Chapters 3 and 6. The first part will consist of general observations on the nature and distribution of the Royal Court's criminal business. The second part will look in detail at both Police and Full Court offences, and the third part will focus on modes of punishment.

General

Across the whole of our period in aggregate, an average of 291 criminal cases were determined by the Royal Court each year. This was about three times the annual average in 1765–1844, and eight times the annual average in 1680–1764. However, as the following figure illustrates, crime levels underwent major fluctuations over time:

---

[1] Crime registers remained perfunctory throughout this period, but they contained less extraneous material than previously. Swearings-in of Vingteniers ceased to be recorded in crime registers in 1874, and after this date, extraneous material consisted mainly of orders for the removal of paupers.

Figure 5. Average number of criminal cases determined per year, 1845–1929

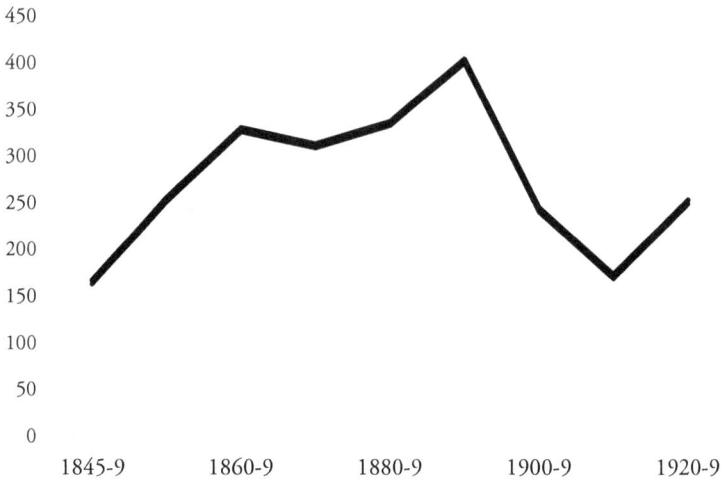

Between 1845 and 1869, numbers were on a steady upward trend, with a peak at the end of the 1860s. There was then something of a lull in the 1870s, after which numbers began rising again in the 1880s, reaching a second and much higher peak in the 1890s. At the turn of the twentieth century, numbers suddenly plunged, with the fall sustained throughout the Edwardian period. The bottom of the trough was reached during World War I, after which crime numbers rose sharply, and continued to climb beyond the end of our period. Broadly speaking, the two nineteenth-century peaks were associated with immigration, and the wartime trough with the absence of young men at the Front.

Figure 6 divides criminal cases over the four quinquennia into their principal categories:

Figure 6. Distribution of criminal cases determined over 4 quinquennia, 1845–1929

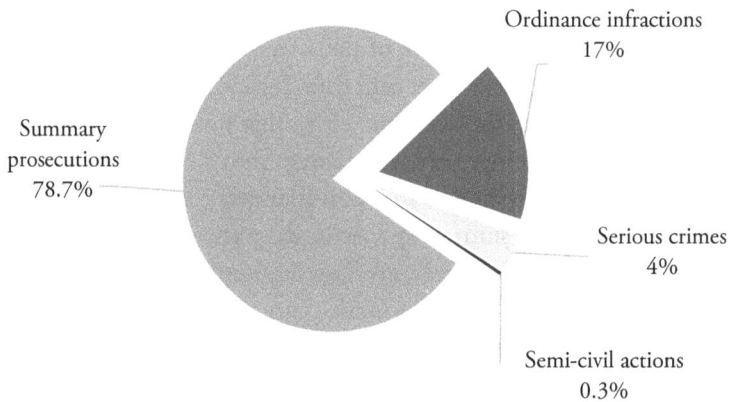

The salient feature of this period is the growth in summary prosecutions – up from 43 per cent of cases in 1756–1844 to nearly 79 per cent in 1845–1929. This growth was primarily at the expense of semi-civil actions (*causes en adjonction*), which, at 0.3 per cent of cases, no longer formed a significant category of criminal business. It also had an effect on prosecutions under Ordinances, which dropped from 36 per cent of cases in 1765–1844 to a mere 17 per cent in the current period. Serious crime, at 4 per cent of cases, had reverted to the proportion for which it had accounted in 1680–1764, having fallen from 11 per cent in the war-beset years of the intervening period.

With four-fifths of the Court's criminal business now handled summarily, the proportion of purely procedural sittings declined to just 8 per cent of criminal sittings (from 27 per cent in 1765–1844). The average number of Jurats present at sittings fell to just three, and most sittings now took place on Thursdays, which until 1925 was the allotted day for the Police Court. After the appointment of a stipendiary magistrate in 1925, police cases ceased to be dealt with on Thursdays and were instead heard on Mondays, Wednesdays and Fridays. The period 1845–1929 saw no Sunday sittings.

Most crime registers of this period recorded the name of the parish in which offences had been committed. The position had not significantly changed from that foreshadowed in 1765–1844: 72 per cent of crimes were committed in St Peter Port; St Sampsons was next at 9 per cent; and the Vale came third at 4 per cent. As in the previous period, the accused's birthplace was given in trials on indictment only. Just over a third of those indicted came from the Bailiwick of Guernsey, with non-natives accounting for the remaining two-thirds (37 per cent of these were from the United Kingdom; 9 per cent from France; and 7 per cent from Jersey). Police Court records did not specify offenders' birthplaces, but a hint that non-natives were also over-represented among summary offenders came from a set of Criminal Returns for the late 1840s which showed that non-islanders comprised around 70 per cent of those convicted summarily.[2] As in the past, many of the non-native offenders were soldiers. However, civilians accounted for a rising proportion of non-local offenders as the nineteenth century progressed, especially after the increase in migration from France.

Ordinance infractions

In the quinquennium 1860–4, prosecutions under Ordinances comprised just 6 per cent of the Royal Court's criminal business. This marked the extreme point of a downward trend which had set in with the formalisation of the Police Court in the 1830s. The Court's right to prosecute an offence summarily notwithstanding the existence of an Ordinance was asserted in evidence given to the Royal Commission.[3] This practice had been encouraged by the fact that summary proceedings were more expeditious than prosecutions under Ordinances, in addition to which many older Ordinances had been lost or forgotten.[4] In 1846, in a bid to recover some of the lost Ordinances, Peter Stafford Carey commissioned Advocate Robert MacCulloch to begin collecting and collating old Ordinances with a view to publishing them in a series of volumes to be paid for out of harbour dues.[5]

---

[2] 'Statistical Papers, 1847–52', Royal Court Library, IA.
[3] *Second Report of the Commissioners Appointed to Inquire into the State of the Criminal Law in the Channel Islands: Guernsey* (London, 1848), p. 281.
[4] The most important pre-1772 Ordinances were in the registers labelled *Jugements, Ordonnances et Ordres du Conseil,* and those from after 1772 were in *Ordonnances.* Others, however, were scattered about elsewhere, including crime registers.
[5] 14.11.1846, GG, *Ordonnances,* vol. 7.

The first volume, containing major Ordinances issued between 1533 and 1800, was published in 1852. Volume 2, covering 1801–40, was published in 1856, and volume 3, covering 1841–60, in 1864. This seems to have helped reinvigorate the Court's use of Ordinances, and from this point, prosecutions under Ordinances slowly began to increase. In 1876, *la Loi relative à l'Infraction des Ordonnances* allowed all Ordinance breaches to be tried by the Police Court save where the minimum fine exceeded 150 *livres tournois* (about £10 14s).[6] This gave an even more powerful boost to Ordinance-related prosecutions, so that by the quinquennium 1920–4, such prosecutions had risen to 26 per cent of criminal business.

As in the past, the vast bulk of prosecutions under Ordinances fell into a limited number of categories. In our first two quinquennia, some 60 per cent of Ordinance-related prosecutions were of militia offences (the easiest to detect and prosecute). A further 20 per cent were of liquor-licensing offences, and the rest were mainly of offences pertaining to traffic, streets and highways. This balance however radically changed in the last two quinquennia. Militia offences virtually disappeared after 1900 when a new militia law subjected embodied militiamen to the Army Act and brought their offences under military jurisdiction.[7] The prosecution of liquor-licensing offences also fell away as tighter surveillance of public houses increased licensees' adherence to rules.[8] The main category of Ordinance-related prosecutions in both 1900–4 and 1920–4 was an entirely new one: cycling and motoring offences. The two seminal Ordinances in this regard were *l'Ordonnance relative aux Vélocipèdes* of 1880 and *l'Ordonnance relative aux Automobiles* of 1902. Both were based on Westminster legislation and laid down basic road rules for cyclists and drivers and standards for their vehicles.[9] In our final quinquennium, such offences collectively accounted for an unprecedented 70 per cent of all Ordinance-related prosecutions.

[6] O in C, 12.2.1876. Fines continued to be specified in *tournois* in some (but not all) new Ordinances until the closing decades of the nineteenth century. Thereafter, they were denominated in Guernsey pounds.

[7] *Loi relative à la Milice de Guernesey*, O in C, 13.12.1900.

[8] In 1893, the States instituted an Inspector of Public Houses (O in C, 26.8.1893). This role was assumed by Police Inspector Green in 1916, and devolved to the force more generally in 1922 (*Billet*, 28.3.1917; O in C, 3.3.1922).

[9] Ords, 5.4.1880, 3.5.1902.

Guernsey's first prosecution of a motoring offence occurred in 1904, when Dr Henry Porter D'Arcy Benson, a local GP with a high-class clientele, was fined £1 under *l'Ordonnance relative aux Automobiles* for ignoring Mrs Henrietta Allez's pleas to slow down when passing her pony carriage.[10] The case caused a minor sensation. The *Star* reported that the Court's public gallery was overcrowded, 'ladies belonging to the elite of the island being in the majority.'[11] The novelty however soon wore off as prosecutions became more numerous. In 1904, only persons with the means of a Dr Benson could afford to purchase a motor vehicle. By 1929, costs had come down and Guernsey hosted more than 3,000 motor vehicles.[12] Prosecutions escalated, and by the 1930s, motoring offences accounted for well over half not just of Ordinance-related prosecutions but the whole of the Royal Court's criminal business.

Acts of Parliament

As in previous periods, only a small number of prosecutions were made under Westminster statutes between 1845 and 1929. The procedure by which such offences were tried followed that used for Ordinances, and as virtually all Ordinance infractions were brought within the ambit of the Police Court in 1876, the same applied to breaches of Westminster legislation.[13]

In our first two quinquennia, most cases fell under just three statutes: the 1844 Merchant Seamen Act, the 1853 Customs Consolidation Act, and the annual Acts for Punishing Mutiny and Desertion.[14] The first of these statutes dealt with seamen who had breached their contract with the master of a ship, for which the penalty was invariably a short prison term.[15] The second statute was used to punish attempts to smuggle dutiable goods into the United Kingdom, and in these cases, punishment took the form of a fine set at about

[10] The pony shied and went off at a gallop, pulling the carriage and its terrified occupants behind it (17.11.1904, GG, *Crime*, vol. 53).

[11] *Star*, 19.11.1904.

[12] *Star*, 1.7.1929.

[13] Prosecutions under Acts of Parliament are included in the statistics on Ordinances, above.

[14] The latter were replaced in 1879 by the Army Discipline and Regulation Act, later known as the Army Act and also renewed annually.

[15] As Andrew De Jausserand, sentenced to three weeks in 1861 for refusing to join the ship on which he had contracted to serve (18.4.1861, GG, *Crime*, vol. 37).

twice the value of the goods in question.[16] The third statute was mainly used, as previously, to punish civilians who bought military equipment from soldiers or helped them to desert. From 1876, it was additionally used to prosecute British soldiers who had made a false declaration when enlisting.[17]

In our last two quinquennia, changing conditions brought other Westminster statutes to the fore. One such statute was the 1908 Post Office Act, to which (as amended) insular postal employees were subject until Guernsey achieved postal independence in 1969. Typical of prosecutions under this statute was that of the postman imprisoned for six weeks in 1921 for purloining large numbers of letters and concealing them at his home.[18] Following the advent of radio broadcasting in the 1920s, prosecutions were also made under Westminster's Wireless Telegraphy Acts. Guernsey's first such prosecutions occurred in March 1928, when six men and a woman were all fined £2 for operating wireless sets without a licence.[19]

Semi-civil actions

As we noted above, at just 0.3 per cent of cases across the quinquennia sampled for this chapter, semi-civil actions no longer formed a significant category of criminal business. The year 1840 had seen the last action for *nouvelle dessaisine*, and by 1845, the number of *causes en adjonction* had dwindled to a trickle. By this point, moreover, actions *en adjonction* were almost exclusively used to prosecute defamation. Until 1861, this could include spoken as well as written defamation. A new law passed in that year however restricted the use of *causes en adjonction* to written defamation (libel) only, by laying down that spoken defamation (slander) should henceforth be

---

[16] Most offences were quite minor, typically perpetrated by the crew of steamers plying between Guernsey and England. Now and again, however, a major smuggling operation was detected. One such occurred in 1870, when John and Frederick Le Lacheur were both fined £100 for attempting to leave Rocquaine Bay with 2,262lb of tobacco on board their boat (28.11.1870, GG, *Crime*, vol. 41).

[17] One of the first to be prosecuted for this offence was Private Henry Gilmore, imprisoned for two months in May 1876 for having made a false declaration before a JP when enlisting in Hampshire four years earlier (25.5.1876, GG, *Crime*, vol. 42).

[18] 17.3.1921, GG, *Crime*, vol. 57.

[19] 30.3.1928, GG, *Crime*, vol. 59.

dealt with purely civilly.[20] This replicated the situation in England and Wales, where slander had been dealt with civilly for centuries. The 1861 law effectively prolonged the existence of *causes en adjonction* for many decades, but in far smaller numbers and with a much narrower scope than had been the case formerly. The limited number of libel cases dealt with *en adjonction* after 1861 will be discussed in detail in the section on Libel, below.

Summary prosecutions

Summary prosecutions accounted for 79 per cent of the Royal Court's criminal business across our four quinquennia in aggregate. This represented an average of 216 cases per year. At the beginning of the current period, what could and could not be prosecuted summarily was a matter of custom rather than legislation, and, broadly speaking, any offence punishable by a fine of up to £3 or a prison term of up to one month could be tried summarily. This situation changed somewhat in 1856, when *la Loi relative à l'Application des Peines* defined and prescribed sentences for thirty-eight separate summary offences.[21] Other offences such as theft and assault (which formed the vast bulk of Police Court work) were however left statutorily undefined throughout our period.

From the 1870s, Police Court work was increased by the proliferation of new regulatory laws enshrined in Orders in Council, most of which permitted summary prosecution of the offences they created. These laws regulated such matters as the licensing of dogs and firearms, the storage of explosives and petrol, infant vaccination, compulsory education, Sunday trading, and much

---

[20] *Loi relative aux Causes présentement poursuivies au Petit Criminel*, O in C, 5.8.1861. The law also created an option for dealing civilly with libels, and specified that the defence in *causes en adjonction* should now be open to all Advocates, and the fine to the Crown should no longer be smaller than the damages to the plaintiff. On the 1861 law, see also J. Barclay, 'The defamation action in Guernsey: past, present and future', in G. Dawes (ed.), *Paris 1259: Studies in the History and Law of Continental and Insular Normandy* (Guernsey, 2016), pp. 255–7.

[21] O in C, 24.6.1856. The list was further added to in 1878 and 1896. See Appendix 7.

more, breaches of all of which could be prosecuted in the Police Court.[22] Police Court work was further increased in the Edwardian period when new sexual offences laws were passed under which summary prosecutions could also be made.[23]

More than three-quarters of summary prosecutions over the sample quinquennia fell into just three categories – disorderly conduct, assault and theft. Disorderly conduct in its manifold forms accounted for 33 per cent of summary prosecutions. At 27 per cent, assaults of various kinds (verbal, physical, sexual) came next; and property offences (theft and related offences such as receiving) came last at 18 per cent. The remaining 22 per cent of summary prosecutions comprised a wide gallimaufry of misdeeds, some of them defined by law, others not. They included *inter alia* appropriating goods from shipwrecks, forming workmen's combinations, begging, and attempting suicide.

Some 85 per cent of summary offenders were male, with the proportion fairly constant over time. There was also a high incidence of recidivism. Some 14 per cent of Police Court trials in our four quinquennia were of individuals who had stood trial more than once, and certain individuals had Police Court appearances spanning as many as forty years.[24]

Serious crime

Across our four sample quinquennia in aggregate, 70 per cent of cases tried on indictment concerned property crime; 17 per cent involved interpersonal violence; and the remaining 13 per cent consisted of miscellaneous crimes, some of which, such as counterfeiting and forgery, had long been prosecuted in Guernsey, and others, such as blackmail and criminal sabotage, were new to the Court. While the aggregate proportions in each category were broadly

[22] *Loi sur les Chiens*, O in C, 4.6.1870; *Loi sur les Permis de Port des Armes de Chasse*, O in C, 26.6.1879; *Loi par rapport aux Substances Explosives*, O in C, 23.8.1883; *Loi relative aux Huiles ou Essences Minérales ou Végétales*, O in C, 4.7.1893; *Loi relative à la Vaccination des Enfants*, O in C, 14.8.1896; *Loi relative à l'Education Primaire Obligatoire*, O in C, 17.9.1900; *Loi interdisant l'Ouverture des Magasins le Dimanche*, O in C, 22.3.1911.
[23] These will be discussed in the relevant sections below.
[24] Such as Thomas Torode, already on his thirtieth appearance when sentenced to prison on a drunk and disorderly charge in 1857 (5.9.1857, GG, *Crime*, vol. 35; *Comet*, 7.9.1857).

similar to those in 1765–1844, the actual number of crimes tried on indictment fell steadily over the course of the current period. Beginning at an average of around twenty cases a year in the 1840s, they had fallen to a mere five cases a year in the 1920s. Overall, males were responsible for 90 per cent of serious crimes, but this proportion increased towards the end of our period, as the number of females prosecuted on indictment underwent significant decline. In 1860–4, 15 per cent of trials on indictment concerned females, but by 1920–4 the figure had fallen to 4 per cent.

Recidivists came before the Full Court less often than before the Police Court. There were, however, some repeat sex offenders and a larger number of re-offending thieves. William Falla probably held the record in this respect: born in St Saviours in 1850, Falla received the first of his four sentences for burglary in 1868 and the last in 1911, having spent thirty-five years in prison in between.[25]

Juveniles

For most of our period, children aged fourteen and under accounted for about a third of the Bailiwick's population.[26] They were thus a more conspicuous element within the community than today, especially since many were not in school.[27] Some 6 per cent of offenders across our sample quinquennia were recorded as juveniles. This should however be taken as a minimum, since the recording of children's ages was by no means systematic.

Guernsey's age of criminal responsibility was somewhat vague. In 1847, Advocate Henry Tupper told the Royal Commissioners that it depended on the discretion of the Court whether or not a particular child was deemed criminally responsible.[28] In the period between 1845 and 1929, it was not

---

[25] 11.7.1868, GG, *Crime*, vol. 40; 20.2.1875, GG, *Crime*, vol. 42; 13.6.1896, GG, *Crime*, vol. 50; 3.6.1911, GG, *Crime*, vol. 55; *Gazette de Guernesey*, 10.6.1911.

[26] The precise proportions at each census were as follows: 1851 – 32 per cent; 1861 – 32 per cent; 1871 – 35 per cent; 1881 – 31 per cent; 1891 – 33 per cent; 1901 – 31 per cent; 1911 – 29 per cent; 1921 – 27 per cent (census references in Bibliography). By contrast, in 2019, 0–15-year-olds made up just 16 per cent of Guernsey's population (States of Guernsey Annual Electronic Census Report, 30.1.2020, accessed 26.6.2021 at www.gov.gg/population).

[27] Education did not become compulsory in Guernsey until 1900.

[28] *Second Report*, p. 217.

unusual for children as young as seven or eight to be brought before Guernsey's Court, where they were dealt with precisely in the same way as adults. Guernsey's age of criminal responsibility was finally fixed at ten in 1967.[29]

At least three-quarters of incidents for which children were prosecuted were fairly harmless: apple-scrumping; playing football in a prohibited place; letting off fireworks in the street. The remainder chiefly comprised acts of vandalism and minor thefts and assaults. Most children were prosecuted in the Police Court, although a small number were tried on indictment, typically for housebreaking, sexual offences or arson.

Punishments of juveniles covered the full spectrum from small fines to transportation.[30] The imprisonment of under-sixteens in the town gaol was fairly common until 1917, when it was outlawed by the Children Act.[31] While children's prison sentences usually ranged between two days and two weeks, it was not unheard of for a juvenile to be sentenced to one or more months. As we saw in Chapter 8, reformatories were also used from the 1850s, but only for serious or persistent offenders. For boys (but never girls) birching was a frequent punishment throughout our period.[32]

Girls formed only 8 per cent of recorded juvenile offenders. This may partly have been because boys were likelier to be out on the streets. The offence with which girls were most often charged was theft, usually from employers or mistresses. Recidivism was notably high among juveniles, and many boys who were prosecuted as juveniles later returned as adults. A substantial proportion of juvenile offenders had parents and siblings who also appeared regularly in Court, and some children figured in registers as victims as well as offenders, generally of parental violence or sexual assault.

---

[29] By the Children and Young Persons (Guernsey) Law of that year. This followed England and Wales, where the age of criminal responsibility had been set at ten by the Children and Young Persons Act of 1963.

[30] The minimum age at which a child could be transported was fourteen (D.D. Gray, *Crime, Policing and Punishment in England, 1660–1914* (London, 2016), p. 187). In 1849, sixteen-year-olds Robert Gahagan and Richard Collins were sentenced to ten and seven years' transportation respectively for a burglary of a shop in the High Street (8.12.1849, GG, *Crime*, vol. 33).

[31] *Loi ayant rapport à la Protection des Enfants et des Jeunes Personnes*, O in C, 24.1.1917.

[32] This will be more fully discussed in the section on Punishment, below.

Plate 41. Juveniles near the market, 1870
© Priaulx Library, Guernsey

Crimes and their perpetrators

Interpersonal violence

This section will deal collectively with offences tried both summarily and on indictment. Offences involving some form of interpersonal violence accounted for about one-fifth of the Royal Court's entire criminal business across our four sample quinquennia. These offences covered the full spectrum from verbal insults to homicide. Most were fairly trivial, and some 97 per cent of cases were dealt with by the Police Court. We will however begin our survey with the most serious category of offence.

Homicide

We noted in earlier chapters that the Royal Court had long adopted the English murder/manslaughter distinction: as Comptroller John Utermarck told the Royal Commissioners in 1847, 'precisely the English doctrine' was followed in such cases.[33] As previously, all cases were charged simply as homicide, and the decision as to whether they amounted to murder or manslaughter was left to the Jurats.[34] In previous periods, crime registers had sometimes explicitly recorded 'manslaughter' verdicts (using the English term). In the period between 1845 and 1929, this was not repeated, so the only indication came in the form of the sentence: only wilful murder incurred the death penalty, and any lesser punishment indicated that the Court had judged the crime to fall short of that offence.

There were forty-two homicide charges in the years 1845 to 1929 (thirty-seven for the full offence and five for attempts). In thirty-three of these cases, the accused was male, and in nine cases the accused was female. At 43 per cent of the total, a manslaughter verdict (or a lesser verdict such as concealment of pregnancy) was the commonest outcome. Acquittals were next at 38 per cent, and in only 7 per cent of cases (relating to three people) was the accused found guilty of murder.

Two factors mark out this period as distinctive from the past. The first is that just under half of victims were female, as opposed to almost all male as previously. The second is that eight of the forty-two charges were in respect of offences which had not formerly been prosecuted in Guernsey. Of these, three were for causing a person's death by dangerous driving; four were for causing a child's death through neglect; and one was for causing the death of a patient through professional negligence.[35] In the following paragraphs, we will focus on the most interesting of the

---

[33] *Second Report*, p. 271.

[34] While *actes d'accusation* continued to indict the accused in homicide cases with having *félonieusement et dépourvu de la crainte de Dieu de propos prémédité tué, occis et meurtri* their victims, it is nevertheless noticeable that, as our period progressed, the words *dépourvu de la crainte de Dieu* and/or *de propos prémédité* tended increasingly to be omitted when it was plain that a death had been caused accidentally or unintentionally.

[35] See Appendix 8, which groups all forty-two cases by sex and type.

forty-two cases, addressing separately those in which the accused was male and those in which the accused was female.

Males charged with homicide

The three people found guilty of murder in our period were all men: John Tapner (1854), and Nugent Loughnan and Timothy Kelly (1856). The case of John Tapner is well known, but we will briefly recapitulate it. Tapner was an Englishman in his thirties who worked as a clerk for the garrison.[36] He was married to a local woman, with whom he had three sons, but had been having an affair with her younger sister, by whom he had an infant daughter. For a time, he had rented a room for his mistress in the house of seventy-year-old widow Elizabeth Saujon.[37] As well as an awareness of the valuables Mrs Saujon kept at her home, Tapner also had a grudge against the widow for her 'ill-natured remarks' about his female friend.[38] Struggling to sustain his complex domestic arrangements on a clerical salary, Tapner was in debt, and appears to have decided to solve his difficulties by robbing Mrs Saujon.[39] The seventy-year-old was found dead at her home on 19 October 1853. Her body had been partially destroyed by burning, though a wound to her head was still visible. Her apartment had been ransacked. An inquest concluded that Mrs Saujon had met her end through violence and commissioned further inquiries.[40] A detective was brought over from London, and Tapner was arrested within a week.[41] On 19 November 1853, John Tapner was charged with

---

[36] This account is based on Anon., *Procès de Jean Charles Tapner, Condamné à la Peine de Mort par Arrêt de la Cour Royale de Guernesey à la Date du 3 Janvier 1854 pour Crime d'Assassinat suivi de Vol et de Tentative d'Incendie* (Guernsey, 1854); F.W.B. Bouverie, *The Eleventh Hour* (Guernsey, 1854); and the Priaulx Library's Tapner family file.

[37] By coincidence, Mrs Saujon (*née* Simon) was the widow of French publican André Saujon who had been a witness in the 'Melmoth' murder case of 1825 (see Chapter 6).

[38] Bouverie, *Eleventh Hour*, p. 84.

[39] Tapner earned £120 a year (*Procès de Jean Charles Tapner*, p. 15). Equating to about £2 6s a week, it was at the lower end of the clerical scale.

[40] 20.10.1853, GG, *Crime*, vol. 34.

[41] Lieutenant Governor to Home Office, 25.10.1853, NA, HO 45/4889.

having killed Elizabeth Saujon by a blow to the head, set fire to her body, and stolen a long list of effects from her home.[42] He denied the charge.

After a trial lasting thirteen days in which more than sixty witnesses were heard, the twelve Jurats unanimously found Tapner guilty (even though evidence was purely circumstantial), and in early January 1854 he was sentenced to hang.[43] Local feeling on Tapner ran high in certain quarters, not least because the Victorian campaign against capital punishment was at its height,[44] and Victor Hugo, a prominent French writer and abolitionist then living in Jersey, took an interest in Tapner and published an open letter in a local newspaper appealing for mercy on his behalf.[45] More than 600 islanders signed a petition to the Home Secretary, Lord Palmerston, requesting that Tapner's sentence be commuted.[46] Palmerston however declined to take action, and Tapner was hanged on 10 February 1854. In the interval between sentencing and execution, Tapner appears to have admitted his guilt.[47] A public subscription was raised to send Mrs Tapner and her three sons to Australia.[48]

---

[42] 19.11.1853, GG, *Crime*, vol. 34.

[43] 3.1.1854, GG, *Crime*, vol. 34.

[44] J. Gregory, *Victorians against the Gallows: Capital Punishment and the Abolitionist Movement in Nineteenth-Century Britain* (London, 2012), p. 1.

[45] *Gazette de Guernesey*, 14.1.1854. In France, abolitionism was totemic for the liberal republican left to which Hugo belonged, but the reverse for the conservative regime of Napoleon III from which he had sought refuge in the Channel Islands. Hugo's involvement in the Tapner case will be further discussed in the section on Capital punishment, below.

[46] *Gazette de Guernesey*, 21.1.1854; A. Hugo, *Victor Hugo: A Life by One who has Witnessed It*, 2 vols (London, 1863), 2, p. 208.

[47] Tapner to Bailiff, 3.2.1854, GG, Royal Court General Letter Book (first series), vol. 8; Bouverie, *Eleventh Hour*, p. 72.

[48] *Star*, 11.2.1854.

JOHN CHARLES TAPNER,
AS HE WAS SEEN   THE NIGHT HE COM-
MITTED THE BARBAROUS MURDER OF
MRS. F SAUJON.
Executed February 10, 1854.

Plate 42. Poster commemorating John Tapner's execution
Courtesy of the Priaulx Library, Guernsey

The case of Nugent Loughnan and Timothy Kelly was more complex than Tapner's and, in many respects, more interesting. Loughnan (21) and Kelly (17) were Irish navvies employed in the construction of the naval harbour in Alderney. One night in the autumn of 1856 they had attempted to enter a house where Frenchman Jean Langlois sold liquor. Langlois had refused to let them in and, accompanied by one of his lodgers, went out of the house to see them off. Loughnan and Kelly resisted their ejection, and in the ensuing struggle, Langlois was stabbed in the thigh, piercing his femoral artery, and his lodger in the chest, piercing his heart. Both later died of their wounds.

In this case, it was difficult to argue that the killing was deliberate and premeditated. However, Procureur Utermarck, citing English authorities, argued that it was 'not necessary that there should be absolute premeditation to constitute the crime of murder … if one person kills another without considerable provocation, the law infers it was committed with premeditation.'[49] In Utermarck's view, the use of a knife showed that Loughnan and Kelly had set out to inflict grievous injury, and since this had been done in the absence of what he deemed 'sufficient' provocation, they must therefore be guilty of murder.

Loughnan's defence Advocate, James Gallienne, invoked the modern French *Code Pénal*, which distinguished three types of homicide: *assassinat* (intentional killing with premeditation); *meurtre* (intentional killing without premeditation); and *homicide simple* (unintentional killing). Only the first was a capital offence in French law, which as Gallienne said, 'made the act a secondary crime where there might be an intention to do bodily harm but no intention to kill'. On this basis, he asked the Court if it would 'follow the law which was most severe, or would it take that which, while it avenged society by punishing crime, made a wise discrimination in its degrees?'

Peter Stafford Carey, summing up after a trial of six days, stated that the 'ancient' French law was the only French law ever followed in Guernsey and he doubted that it had made such subtle distinctions. In any case, he insisted, it had long been superseded by English law, beginning, as far as murder and manslaughter were concerned, with the Orders in Council of the 1690s. The *Code Pénal* was therefore irrelevant and English practice must be followed to the letter. Unless the Jurats could detect any extenuating circumstances, the verdict must be murder and the sentence death.

The ten Jurats present at the trial reached the same conclusion in the cases of both Loughnan and Kelly: eight were for murder and the death penalty; two for manslaughter and transportation. As always, a simple majority sufficed to convict, and both young men were found guilty of murder.[50] Nugent Loughnan's execution was scheduled for 16 January 1857. However, given that Timothy Kelly was only seventeen and therefore a minor, no date was set for his execution, and his case was referred to the Home Office for further instructions. After the trial, Kelly unexpectedly and alarmingly claimed that the wounds which killed the two men had been inflicted solely by himself.[51] This became public knowledge, and a petition to the Home Office was organised on Loughnan's behalf. Just days before he was to be

---

[49] *Star*, 25.12.1856. The account which follows is also from this source.
[50] 19.12.1856, GG, *Crime*, vol. 35.
[51] *Star*, 3.1.1857.

hanged, a letter was received from the Home Secretary ordering his execution to be stayed.[52] Two months later, warrants under Her Majesty's Sign Manual commuted Loughnan's sentence to four years' penal servitude, and that of Timothy Kelly to transportation for life.[53] Kelly was conveyed to an English prison to await departure for Australia, but Loughnan was kept in Guernsey's gaol pending a further Home Office review of his case.[54] The review was carried out, and ultimately, Loughnan's four years were commuted into a free pardon.[55] After Loughnan and Kelly, no further death sentences were issued in Guernsey until 1935.

In thirteen of the remaining male homicide cases, the accused was convicted of manslaughter only, and in a further thirteen, he was acquitted of any wrongdoing. In seventeen of these cases, the victim was also a male and, as in the past, met his end in a fight or other violent incident. In an unprecedented nine cases, however, the victim was female. The nine cases involving female victims are particularly worth examining, not only because there were no such cases in the previous two periods, but also for the light which they shed on the values of the Court.

We will look first at some of the men who were acquitted of killing women. The most thought-provoking of these cases are those where the victim was a wife. Three men were acquitted of the murder of their wives in this period: Daniel Statt, Andrew Brehaut and William Kaines, in 1856, 1857 and 1880 respectively. All three had previous records of domestic violence. There were serious injuries to all the deceased women's bodies, and these all appeared to have been inflicted at a time when the women were alone at home with their husbands, or accompanied only by infants. Circumstantial evidence such as that used to secure Tapner's conviction was eschewed, and in the absence of proof to the contrary, the men were all deemed innocent. In Statt's and Brehaut's cases, although the Court acknowledged that the wives had probably died of their injuries, they argued that there was no conclusive proof that it was their husbands who had inflicted them.[56] In William Kaines's case, Jurats accepted neighbours' accounts of beatings

---

[52] Home Secretary to Bailiff, 9.1.1857, GG, *Crime*, vol. 35; *Star*, 10.1.1857.
[53] 7.3.1857, GG, *Ordres du Conseil et Actes du Parlement*, vol. 7.
[54] *Star*, 9.6.1857.
[55] Order dated 7.12.1857, GG, *Ordres du Conseil et Actes du Parlement*, vol. 7.
[56] 18.10.1856, 18.11.1856, GG, *Crime*, vol. 35; *Comet*, 17.11.1856, 20.11.1856; 18.5.1857, 30.5.1857, GG, *Crime*, vol. 34; *Comet*, 1.6.1857.

overheard shortly before Mrs Kaines's demise, but decided that her death was caused by her 'precarious' state of health rather than the beatings themselves (Mrs Kaines was known to drink, and the presumption was made that alcohol had weakened her health).[57]

Turning now to some of the male-on-female manslaughter verdicts. Five men were convicted of manslaughter in respect of a wife or cohabitee in our period, and one in respect of an unrelated woman. An examination of three of these cases will give something of a flavour of how such matters were handled. The first case concerns the unrelated female victim. This was a young married woman named Mary Ann Hornby, in the early stages of pregnancy at the time of her death.[58] Her mother ran a seamen's lodging house in St Peter Port, and Mary Ann was in the kitchen of the house with her sisters one evening in 1871 when a drunken English sailor, thirty-year-old Thomas Stevens, burst in looking for some friends. The friends were not there, but Stevens 'began to offer some familiarity' to Mrs Hornby. She resisted his advances, and a struggle ensued in which Stevens struck her several times and dragged her out into the street by her hair, where he knocked her to the ground and fell on top of her. When Stevens left off, a neighbour escorted the injured Mrs Hornby back to her own lodgings. Feeling unwell, Mrs Hornby took to her bed as soon as she got home. She died a few hours later. The immediate cause of Mrs Hornby's death was identified as convulsions, but a post-mortem examination showed clear evidence of injuries to her body. Stevens was arrested and charged with her murder. At his trial, defence counsel Thomas Falla contended that 'even if it were admitted that Mrs Hornby's death had been caused by his violence, the circumstance was purely accidental … and it was quite probable that [the convulsions] had been brought on by the excitement of her temper which had been proved very irritable.' Agreeing with Falla that the cause of Mrs Hornby's convulsions was unclear, the Jurats sentenced Stevens to just three months.[59]

The second manslaughter case concerned Mary Chick, a woman in her thirties who was living with older man Nicolas Brouard in the room he occupied in St Peter Port's Bouillon Lane. On the night of her death,

---

[57] 16.7.1880, GG, *Crime*, vol. 43; *Star*, 17.7.1880.
[58] This account is taken from *Star*, 17.1.1871.
[59] 16.1.1871, GG, *Crime*, vol. 41.

Brouard's son Joseph, a seaman ashore between voyages, was also in the room. The trio had been drinking gin together before retiring to sleep, Joseph on the floor and the couple in the bed. In the morning, Mrs Chick was found dead in the bed with a large wound to the right side of her head. A post-mortem examination found that she had died of a blood clot to the brain. No one else had been in the room overnight, but a log next to the fireplace was found to have human hair on it. Both Nicolas and Joseph Brouard were charged with Mrs Chick's murder. Joseph, who claimed to have been asleep the whole night, was acquitted. His father, however, was found guilty of manslaughter and sentenced to life transportation.[60] It is hard to understand how the Jurats could have thought the man guilty of anything other than murder, but their verdict may have been influenced by Mrs Chick's drinking and the fact that she was living with a man who was not her husband.

Our last manslaughter case prompts similar questions. In 1861, forty-year-old Thomas Geake shot his wife dead outside their house. The couple lived in Alderney, where Geake was employed quarrying stone for the harbour works. Geake was due to attend a funeral on the morning of his wife's death, but had been drinking. Notwithstanding his wife's attempts to stop him going, he set off for the funeral in an intoxicated state. On the way there, he discovered that she had not mended a slit in the thigh of his best trousers, so he returned. As he approached their house, he berated his wife and threw stones at her, and she answered him back from the garden. Geake then fired his gun at her, saying 'I'll show you'.[61] All this was witnessed by a neighbour, who was only ten or twelve yards distant. HM Procureur John Utermarck had argued for a verdict of murder and the death penalty, but only three of the eleven Jurats at the trial agreed, and Geake was sentenced to life transportation.[62] As in the Brouard case, it is difficult to understand how Geake's actions could have been seen as anything other than murder, but perhaps the Jurats felt that there was something exculpatory in the wife's incivility to her husband, or even in her inattention to domestic duties.

---

[60] 26.4.1858, GG, *Crime*, vol. 35; *Comet*, 29.4.1858.
[61] Where Geake got the gun is unclear, but it may have been kept in an outhouse.
[62] 2.12.1861, GG, *Crime*, vol. 37; *Comet*, 2.12.1861.

Females charged with homicide

Four of the nine females charged with homicide/attempted homicide between 1845 and 1929 were accused of killing their newborns, and their cases will be dealt with in the section on infanticide, below. Of the remaining five females, one was acquitted, three were convicted of manslaughter, and one was convicted of attempted murder. The four convictions will form the subject of the next paragraphs.

The attempted homicide case took place in 1894 and concerned fourteen-year-old Phoebe Woodland. Phoebe was accused of having tried to poison her father, pub landlord Alfred Woodland, by putting oxalic acid in a cup of tea she had made for him. Detecting a strange taste in the tea, Woodland had put it aside, and eventually sent it to a chemist for analysis. Phoebe's defence counsel, Theophilus De Mouilpied, described Woodland as 'a brute' whose violent behaviour had already driven his wife and some of their children to leave home.[63] Phoebe said she had resorted to the poison in response to the ill-treatment she had received from him. There was no attempt to enquire into the nature of the ill-treatment, and instead, the fourteen-year-old was sentenced to two years' imprisonment.[64]

Two of the female manslaughter convictions were associated with parental neglect. Homicide charges in such circumstances were a novelty of the late nineteenth century. In February 1894, eight-year-old Frank Le Lievre died of tuberculous peritonitis weighing only 20lb. His parents, who were extremely poor (the father earned only 17s a week), were accused of causing his death by failing to provide him with sufficient food and failing to summon timely medical help. Both were found guilty as charged and sentenced to six months' imprisonment.[65] Three years later, the parents of eleven-month-old Wilfred Clarke, who died weighing only 6lb, were similarly charged. They too were very poor, the father earning just 22s a week. This time, however, the mother

[63] *Star*, 25.8.1894.
[64] 25.8.1894, GG, *Crime*, vol. 49. Five years later, Phoebe's father, whom a newspaper described as 'addicted to drink', was himself imprisoned for attempting suicide (14.8.1899, GG, *Crime*, vol. 51; *Gazette de Guernesey*, 26.8.1899).
[65] 20.2.1894, 4.4.1894, GG, *Crime*, vol. 49; *Gazette de Guernesey*, 24.2.1894, 7.4.1894.

was known to drink, and she alone was sentenced to serve six months while her husband was acquitted.[66]

The last female manslaughter conviction concerned professional negligence. It is particularly interesting because of the contrast it highlights with the Court's earlier handling of such cases. In 1900, sixty-one-year-old midwife Maria MacPherson was sentenced to three years' penal servitude after she was convicted of causing the death of a patient through her reckless mismanagement of a delivery.[67] Refusing to summon a doctor in a case of transverse presentation, she had kept pulling on the baby's arm until it was 'hanging by only a thread from the vagina', causing internal injuries to the mother. The injuries became infected, and death from acute peritonitis followed a few days later.[68] Some fifty years earlier, midwife Mary Old had appeared before the Court in similar circumstances. Relentlessly pulling on the arm of a baby that would not follow, she had ruptured the mother's bladder, again causing a fatal infection. This was not, however, charged as homicide. Mrs Old was sentenced to just one month's imprisonment for 'felonious negligence'.[69] In 1900, Guernsey's authorities were more alert than previously to the dangers of unqualified midwives, and the Court clearly wished to make an example of Mrs MacPherson.

Infanticide

The four women charged with killing their newborns in this period were Elizabeth Jeffrey in 1850, Charlotte Simmonds in 1852, Susan Harris in 1867, and Violet Gallichan in 1901.[70] Elizabeth Jeffrey was a married woman who had been admitted to the Town Hospital with her infant after unexpectedly giving birth at home. Two days later, the infant had been found dead in the lying-in ward with nine suspicious pinprick punctures in its abdomen. Medical evidence failed to establish a link between the punctures

---

[66] 8.4.1897, 8.5.1897, GG, *Crime*, vol. 50; *Gazette de Guernesey*, 10.4.1897, 15.5.1897; *Star*, 13.4.1897.

[67] 16.6.1900, GG, *Crime*, vol. 51. Mrs MacPherson was the only woman to be sentenced to penal servitude in our period.

[68] 15.5.1900, 16.6.1900, GG, *Crime*, vol. 51; *Star*, 15.5.1900, 19.6.1900.

[69] 14.9.1848, 4.11.1848, GG, *Crime*, vol. 32.

[70] The name of the last woman has been changed.

and the baby's death, and Mrs Jeffrey was acquitted.[71] Charlotte Simmonds was a twenty-two-year-old laundress who lived alone with five younger siblings. She had been unaware of her pregnancy and had given birth in a bedroom shared with her sister. Simmonds had cut her baby's umbilical cord with a knife but failed to tie it, and the infant died of blood loss. She too was acquitted after the Court decided that there was no proof of a criminal intention.[72] Susan Harris was a twenty-four-year-old domestic servant who secretly gave birth at her employer's house, and whose baby was later found in a box belonging to Harris with a skull fracture and injuries to its windpipe. In this case, the evidence seemed damning, but the Court was nevertheless lenient. On the basis that the injuries might have been 'inflicted unknowingly' in the aftermath of birth, Harris was found guilty of manslaughter only and sentenced to three months' imprisonment to be followed by six years' banishment.[73] Violet Gallichan, who lived with her parents in St Peter Port, was alleged to have given birth secretly in her bedroom, left her baby without nourishment, and put it out with the rubbish once it had died (the corpse was found at the rubbish dump). Here, too, the Court was lenient. The young woman was found guilty of concealment only and imprisoned for two months.[74]

As well as the four cases charged as homicide, four cases of suspicious infant death were charged simply as concealment, which had long been tacitly accepted as an offence in Guernsey. These cases concerned Eliza Page in 1850, Ann Russell in 1857, Elizabeth Chennells in 1871, and Harriet Guille in 1890. In none of these cases could it be established that the infants had actually lived, so a charge of homicide was inappropriate. All four women were found guilty as charged. Eliza Page and Elizabeth Chennells were both imprisoned for two weeks, Ann Russell for one month, and Harriet Guille for two months.[75]

After Violet Gallichan in 1901, no further cases, either of concealment or neonaticide, came before the Royal Court in what remained of our period. During the early twentieth century, the development of psychological and

[71] 28.9.1850, GG, *Crime*, vol. 33; *Comet*, 30.9.1850.
[72] 24.2.1852, GG, *Crime*, vol. 33; *Comet*, 26.2.1852.
[73] 31.12.1866, 2.2.1867, GG, *Crime*, vol. 39; *Star*, 5.2.1867.
[74] 19.10.1901, GG, *Crime*, vol. 52; *Gazette de Guernesey*, 26.10.1901.
[75] 21.12.1850, GG, *Crime*, vol. 33; 7.12.1857, 28.12.1857, GG, *Crime*, vol. 35; 31.5.1871, 12.8.1871, GG, *Crime*, vol. 41; 26.7.1890, GG, *Crime*, vol. 47.

psychiatric explanations of human behaviour fostered increasing recognition of a link between infanticide and post-partum psychosis. In England and Wales, the Infanticide Act of 1922 made it possible for a woman accused of killing her infant to claim as a defence for a year after childbirth that the balance of her mind was disturbed by parturition or lactation. In Guernsey, no special legislation was ever passed concerning infanticide, but, here too, modern understandings made the authorities increasingly reluctant to bring prosecutions in such cases.

Abortion

Guernsey's Royal Court had long regarded abortion as criminal, and – even though no law proscribed it – had punished or attempted to punish it on several occasions between 1680 and 1844. There was only one major prosecution of this nature in the period covered by the current chapter. This concerned French druggist Edmond de Renty and his wife Aglaé Pottier. In March 1899, de Renty appeared before the Royal Court for having terminated the pregnancies of six named women. His wife was charged with terminating a further three. The couple's activities had only come to light because one of their patients had become unwell following a termination and had to be admitted to hospital. Acknowledging at the trial that Guernsey, unlike England and Wales, had no law prohibiting abortion, HM Procureur Edward Ozanne suggested that the Royal Court could nevertheless 'create a precedent'.[76] He proposed that Edmond de Renty be sentenced to twelve months' imprisonment and ten years' banishment, and his wife to three months' imprisonment and a similar period of banishment. The Court agreed (though not unanimously) and the couple were sentenced as suggested. None of their patients were prosecuted.[77]

For more than a decade after the de Renty case, Guernsey's authorities were content to let matters rest here. It was only during the Edwardian period that the possibility of a written abortion law was addressed. The proposal

---

[76] *Gazette de Guernsey*, 18.3.1899. Abortion had first been criminalised in England and Wales by Lord Ellenborough's Act of 1803. The matter was further addressed in the Offences against the Person Acts of 1828, 1837 and 1861 (B. Brookes, *Abortion in England, 1900–1967* (1988; Abingdon, 2013 edn), pp. 24–6).

[77] 11.3.1899, GG, *Crime*, vol. 51; *Gazette de Guernsey*, 18.3.1899.

originated from the Royal Court during a phase of legislative catch-up which seems to have been initiated by Law Officers Edward Ozanne and Arthur Bell. The Law Officers turned for a model to the 1861 Offences against the Person Act (the most recent English enactment on the subject) and drew up a *projet de loi* which was little more than a translation into French of sections 58–60 of the Act. The *projet* was nodded through by the States and, duly ratified by Privy Council, became the 1910 *Loi sur l'Avortement*.[78] There were no prosecutions under this law until 1936,[79] and just a small handful of prosecutions over subsequent decades. At the end of the twentieth century, abortion was decriminalised by the Abortion (Guernsey) Law 1997, whose provisions were based on Westminster's 1967 Abortion Act.[80]

Suicide

It was noted in Chapter 6 that, in emulation of English practice, Guernsey's Court had begun prosecuting people for attempting suicide in the 1830s. In Guernsey, such attempts were always tried summarily, whereas in England attempted suicides involving adults could only be tried on indictment until 1925.[81] Numerous islanders were prosecuted for attempting to take their own lives between 1845 and 1929. A short prison term of between two days and a month was the standard punishment until the mid-1920s. In 1855, twenty-three-year-old George Mills was sentenced to three weeks for trying to hang himself in his employer's stable.[82] In 1878, prostitute Judith Hamilton was imprisoned for two days after she tried to drown herself in St Peter Port harbour.[83]

The arrival of stipendiary magistrate Henry Casey in 1925 changed matters somewhat. Casey's attitude to suicide was informed by his experience

---

[78] O in C, 7.11.1910.

[79] 3.4.1936, GG, *Crime*, vol. 64.

[80] Abortion was also decriminalised in Jersey in the same year.

[81] S. Moore, 'The decriminalisation of suicide' (unpub. PhD thesis, London University, 2000), p. 42.

[82] 15.11.1855, GG, *Crime*, vol. 34.

[83] 9.11.1878, GG, *Crime*, vol. 43. She was also ordered to deposit 40s against her good behaviour for six months or leave the island. Prostitutes frequently figured in Court for suicide attempts.

in England, where by this time, courts would generally refer attempted suicides for treatment or put them under probation.[84] In what remained of our period, Casey dealt with eight cases of attempted suicide.[85] His usual approach was to bind over the person concerned to be of good behaviour for six months, or consign them to one of Guernsey's hospitals. In England and Wales, suicide was decriminalised by The Suicide Act 1961. In Guernsey, although suicide had also ceased to be punished as a criminal offence by this time, it was not formally decriminalised until the passage of The Homicide and Suicide (Bailiwick of Guernsey) Law 2006.

Assaults (non-sexual)

All but 3 per cent of non-lethal physical or verbal assaults were dealt with by the Police Court in the period covered here. They were typically punished by a short prison term or small fine. In 86 per cent of Police Court cases, the perpetrators were male. Some three-quarters of male assaults were on other males, and occurred spontaneously during bar-room quarrels or street altercations. The remaining quarter were on females and often took place in the home.[86]

In the 14 per cent of assaults for which females were summarily prosecuted, the victim was also a female, commonly a neighbour, co-worker or other close associate. Few female assaults involved actual blows, most stopping at insults or threats. Numbers of summarily prosecuted assaults dropped from 361 in 1861–4 to just seventy-eight in 1920–4. The main reason for this appears to be that the Court simply stopped prosecuting the most trivial incidents. This affected females more than males, so that in 1920–4, only four of the accused in the seventy-eight summary cases were female.

Numbers of assaults prosecuted on indictment, by contrast, changed little. In 1860–4, five serious physical assaults were tried by the Full Court. In 1920–4, eight assaults were tried in this forum. Aside from the severity of the injuries, the commonest reason for prosecuting an assault on indictment was

[84] Moore, 'Decriminalisation of suicide', pp. 81–2.

[85] 1.5.1926, GG, *Crime*, vol. 58; 28.7.1926, 8.10.1926, 17.8.1927, 29.8.1927, 28.9.1928, GG, *Crime*, vol. 59; 29.11.1929, 13.12.1929, GG, *Crime*, vol. 60.

[86] These will be considered in a separate section on domestic violence, below.

the use of a dangerous weapon. Further factors might be evidence of premeditation, or a record of violent offending on the part of the perpetrator.[87]

All but one of the physical assaults tried on indictment in our period were perpetrated by men. The sole female-perpetrated assault was Betsey Maindonald's attack on a St Saviours Constable in 1893. Mrs Maindonald had set upon the Constable with a knife and a sabre when he entered her cottage against her will. She was sentenced to six months' imprisonment.[88] This was a comparatively light punishment. Males found guilty of serious physical assaults might serve up to five years' penal servitude. Some of the heaviest sentences were issued in the early twentieth century. In 1900, an Alderney man well known to the Court was sentenced to three years for a knife attack on a stranger at night.[89] In 1902, another habitual offender (whose father and brothers were also regulars in Court), got three years for stabbing an acquaintance.[90] In 1905, two brothers in their twenties were sentenced to five and three years respectively when they drunkenly pulled a knife on a policeman, slicing through helmet, hair and skin to the man's skull.[91]

Domestic violence

Prosecutions for domestic violence were more frequent in this period than in any previous period. However, they still represented only 16 per cent of all assault prosecutions. Not only was it was taken for granted that men sometimes hit their spouses, but the difficulty of proving a spousal assault deterred prosecution. For the first twenty years of our period, the law continued to prohibit wives from giving evidence against husbands. In 1865,

---

[87] It was normal practice to read out a list of the accused's previous convictions to Jurats before they voted on a verdict and sentence. In England and Wales, this would have happened only after judgment had been rendered.

[88] 20.5.1893, GG, *Crime*, vol. 48.

[89] 30.6.1900, GG, *Crime*, vol. 52; *Gazette de Guernesey*, 6.7.1900. This man had already served fifteen years for previous offences.

[90] 17.5.1902, GG, *Crime*, vol. 52. This man had been sentenced to five years' penal servitude for robbery with violence in 1894, as well as having been convicted of several assaults in the Police Court.

[91] 17.7.1905, GG, *Crime*, vol. 53; *Star*, 18.7.1905. The brothers had already served time for burglary, assault, and disorderly conduct.

the prohibition was lifted, but only on a permissive basis, so that wives could not be compelled to testify if they chose not to.[92] This remained the situation for most of our period, with spouses only made compellable in domestic cases in 1923.[93]

Nine-tenths of spousal assaults between 1845 and 1929 were dealt with summarily, and sentences were light – two weeks' imprisonment at the most. In 1861, John Ingram was sentenced to just ten days for repeatedly kicking his wife in the head.[94] In 1874, Thomas Duquemin got four days for throwing hot soup at his wife and punching her in the mouth and chest.[95]

Until 1890, there was nothing to stop convicted wife-beaters from returning to exact retribution on their wives once released from prison. This situation was somewhat ameliorated by the passage in 1890 of *la Loi relative à la Séparation de Mari et Femme en Police Correctionnelle*, which was based on Westminster's 1878 Matrimonial Causes Act.[96] The new law permitted the Police Court to order the immediate separation of a wife from her husband (with maintenance) on convicting him of an assault on her.[97] This measure did not, however, have as salutary an effect as might have been hoped, since maintenance orders were rarely enforced, and penury drove many wives back to abusive husbands.

The Court rarely prosecuted domestic abuse on indictment, and there were just seven Full Court cases in the twenty years covered by our quinquennia. The leniency shown to summarily prosecuted husbands was, moreover, equally in evidence with those prosecuted on indictment. Whereas men convicted of serious assaults on other men might be sentenced to penal servitude, not one such sentence was handed down to an abusive husband, even when dangerous weapons were used. One year's imprisonment (sometimes with banishment) was the maximum sentence for serious spousal assault, and two or three months were the norm. In 1893, a French sailor was sentenced to a year's imprisonment and banished for three years for stabbing

---

[92] *Loi relative aux Preuves*, O in C, 29.6.1865.
[93] *Loi relative aux Preuves au Criminel*, O in C, 10.2.1923.
[94] 8.4.1861, GG, *Crime*, vol. 37.
[95] 24.9.1874, GG, *Crime*, vol. 42; *Star*, 26.9.1874.
[96] O in C, 30.6.1890.
[97] For the first such separation, see 19.7.1890, GG, *Crime*, vol. 47.

his wife in the chest.[98] In 1902, a Guernseyman was also imprisoned for a year (without banishment) for beating his wife with an iron poker.[99]

Assaults on children

In about 3 per cent of physical assaults in our sample quinquennia, the victim was identified as a child. Prior to the mid-nineteenth century, violence against children had scarcely ever been prosecuted, reflecting the traditional view that adults in charge of minors had a duty to 'correct' them. From the 1850s, such prosecutions became more common. The increase was undoubtedly related to the 1849 relaxation of the ban on pre-pubescent children testifying in Court,[100] but it also had to do with subtler changes in attitudes towards children and childhood. For the first few decades after 1850, punishments can only be described as token. The two-day prison sentence given to Mary Edgecumbe for abusing her eight-year-old in 1853 was not atypical, although the little girl's 'body, from the neck to the legs, exhibited one continuation of cuts and bruises'.[101]

From the 1880s, there was a hardening of judicial attitudes. This was almost certainly influenced by developments in Britain, which saw the foundation of the NSPCC in 1883 and the passage of The Prevention of Cruelty to Children Act in 1889.[102] The Royal Court prosecuted its first case of child neglect in 1883, and punishments for assaults on children thereafter grew more stringent.[103] In 1894, a man was imprisoned for two months for kicking his daughter while drunk.[104] In 1904, another man was imprisoned for four months for ill-treating his step-children.[105]

---

[98] 2.10.1893, GG, *Crime*, vol. 48; *Star*, 3.10.1893.
[99] 16.8.1902, GG, *Crime*, vol. 52; *Gazette de Guernesey*, 23.8.1902.
[100] *Loi relative aux Témoins et aux Saons et aux Reproches contre iceux*, O in C, 21.5.1849.
[101] 8.9.1853, GG, *Crime*, vol. 34; *Comet*, 8.9.1853.
[102] H. Hendrick, *Child Welfare: England, 1872–1989* (London, 1994), pp. 53–5.
[103] The neglect prosecution concerned the Reverend Basil Blogg Babington, who was charged with failing to properly clothe and feed a ten-year-old in his care. Babington was ordered to deposit a security of £30 against repetition of the neglect, and the St Andrews Constables were instructed to keep a watch on the child (22.11.1883, GG, *Crime*, vol. 44; *Star*, 24.11.1883).
[104] 12.11.1894, GG, *Crime*, vol. 49.
[105] 11.2.1904, GG, *Crime*, vol. 53.

In 1917, Guernsey passed its first Children's Law.[106] This was based on Westminster's landmark 1908 Children Act and made it an offence for any adult who had custody of a child aged under sixteen to assault, ill-treat, neglect, abandon or expose that child to danger on pain of a fine of up to £100 and/or imprisonment for up to two years, in addition to which the child could be removed from the adult's custody. Prosecutions increased markedly after this, most particularly in cases of neglect.

Public concern for child welfare continued to mount in the years following the passage of the Children's Law, and in 1924, Guernsey established its own branch of the NSPCC.[107] At the end of its first year in operation, the Society reported that its Inspector had attended 187 cases of child neglect and/or ill-treatment.[108] While most of these cases were dealt with out of Court,[109] the existence of broad scope for prosecution undoubtedly facilitated their resolution.

Sexual assaults

The years between 1845 and 1929 saw an average of one or two prosecutions of sexual assaults each year, which was a distinct increase on previous periods. This increase had arisen essentially because of the growth in summary prosecutions. About two-thirds of all sexual offences brought to Court in our period were summarily prosecuted. In the first half of the period, Police Court sentences for sexual assaults were pitifully low, typically a small fine or one or two weeks' imprisonment.[110] From the turn of the twentieth century, many sexual assaults were punished by the maximum available to the Police Court.[111] This, arguably, was because many should not have been prosecuted summarily at all. In 1905, a nineteen-year-old shop assistant was summarily sentenced to two months for sexually assaulting a toddler. In 1929, a labourer

---

[106] *Loi ayant rapport à la Protection des Enfants et des Jeunes Personnes*, O in C, 24.1.1917.

[107] *Star*, 17.1.1924, 5.7.1924. The Guernsey branch became independent in 1927, changing its name to the Guernsey Children's Aid Society (*Guernsey Weekly Press*, 7.5.1936).

[108] *Star*, 29.7.1925.

[109] Only twelve cases of child assault or neglect were prosecuted by the Court in this year.

[110] See, for instance, 19.10.1861, 23.11.1861, 5.12.1861, GG, *Crime*, vol. 37.

[111] The maximum prison term available to the Police Court was increased from one to two months by O in C, 17.11.1888.

was sentenced to two months for the sexual abuse of his nine-year-old daughter.[112]

The maximum punishment for sexual assaults tried on indictment in our period was fourteen years' transportation (there was no repeat of the previous period's death sentences). A total of forty-two such assaults were dealt with by the Full Court between 1845 and 1929. They were all charged as rape or attempted rape. Seventeen of the Full Court cases concerned adult women, and twenty-five concerned girls aged sixteen and under. We shall look first at the cases involving adult women.

Of the seventeen men charged with sexual offences against adult women, just seven were convicted of full rape. Four were convicted of attempted rape, and six were acquitted of any wrongdoing. By the period dealt with here, Guernsey's rape law was fully assimilated to that of England and Wales. As Peter Stafford Carey told the Royal Commissioners, the Royal Court operated on 'exactly the same principle as English law'.[113] As in England, the Court's default position was to allow men accused of rape the full benefit of any doubt. The 'cautionary instruction' coined by English jurist Sir Matthew Hale was routinely heard by nineteenth-century Jurats: 'rape is an accusation easily to be made and hard to be proved, and harder to be defended by the party accused, tho' never so innocent'.[114] To no less a degree than in previous periods, prosecutions succeeded only when the woman was of known good character and there was clear evidence of both violence and resistance.

The first successful rape prosecution of our period will serve as an example of the conditions required for a successful prosecution. This incident, which occurred in 1852, involved a respectable Alderney pub landlady and (not uncoincidentally) a soldier. The victim, Elizabeth Smith, had been tricked by the soldier, Private Henry Pope, into leaving her pub in search of her husband around 9.00 one October night. Pope had followed Mrs Smith at a distance and attacked her when she reached a secluded spot. The rape was brutal, and the woman pregnant. Signs of a struggle were visible at the scene of the attack,

[112] 6.5.1905, GG, *Crime*, vol. 53; 22.4.1929, GG, *Crime*, vol. 60.
[113] *Second Report*, p. 276.
[114] M. Hale, *History of the Pleas of the Crown*, 2 vols (London, 1736), 1, p. 634. Newspaper accounts of rape trials in this period often reported references to Hale's dictum – see, for instance, *Guernsey Evening Press*, 23.10.1903.

as were marks around the victim's throat. Screams were heard at the time; and the soldier, whose presence in Mrs Smith's pub had been noted by other soldiers, was late returning to barracks. Mrs Smith positively identified Pope, and was called as the principal witness at the subsequent trial. A newspaper account reported Bailiff Peter Stafford Carey as advising the Jurats that their verdict would depend

> on the amount of credit attached to the evidence of the principal witness. If they found it worthy of credence, there could be little question of the perfect establishment of the accusation; if they doubted the good faith of that evidence, they should give the prisoner the benefit of the doubt ... the woman was of good character and good feeling ... her deposition had left an impression of truthfulness.[115]

In this case, Mrs Smith's previous good character and her demeanour in the witness box convinced all except one of the Jurats, and Pope was sentenced by majority vote to fourteen years' transportation.[116]

As an illustration of how outcomes could differ if some aspect of a victim's character or conduct were found wanting, we will cite the case of Rosanna Smith. This Mrs Smith, described by the *Star* as 'a middle-aged and unprepossessing looking woman', had gone to lie down in a stone-yard near Pont Renier in St Peter Port after drinking heavily one day in 1846.[117] Three soldiers happened upon her while she was lying semi-conscious, and took advantage of her. The newspaper stated that 'the details of the assault [could] not be repeated'. Eventually, Mrs Smith was rescued by three passers-by who heard screams and entered the yard to find her 'covered with blood, her clothes torn and disordered'. Their entrance frightened the soldiers away, after which a doctor was called, and Mrs Smith was taken to hospital, where she remained several days. The three soldiers, who returned late to barracks, one of them with blood on his clothing, were later arrested and charged with attempted rape. Notwithstanding that they had been seen by Mrs Smith's rescuers, all three soldiers were acquitted on the grounds that there was

---

[115] *Comet*, 11.11.1852.
[116] 10.11.1852, GG, *Crime*, vol. 34.
[117] *Star*, 17.8.1846.

'insufficient proof' of their culpability to warrant convictions.[118] In this case, Rosanna Smith's drunkenness and antecedents went decidedly against her.

Another case, which occurred in 1921, involved a twenty-two-year-old woman described in press reports as profoundly deaf and 'below average intelligence'.[119] The twenty-two-year-old had been waiting for her mother outside a shop in St Peter Port, when a man had approached her and taken her by the arm. Although the man was unknown to the girl, he behaved in a friendly way and persuaded her to walk with him through town, where he stopped several times to buy her chocolate and a golliwog. He later continued their walk to Fort George, where he was alleged to have taken her into the moat and raped her. The man's defence counsel, Harold Randell, did not attempt to deny that intercourse had taken place, but contended that the man had 'rightly or wrongly ... assumed from the outset that he had the consent of the girl, who, though meeting him for the first time, accompanied him to such an out-of-the-way spot.' The Jurats appear to have accepted this assumption as understandable and took no account of the young woman's vulnerability. Six of the seven Jurats voted to exonerate the man, and he was acquitted of the charge.[120]

Turning now to child victims. All but two of the twenty-five men tried on indictment for sexual offences against girls in our period were charged with attempted rape rather than the full offence. As noted previously, however, the fact that an assault was charged as attempted rape did not mean that an actual rape had not occurred, merely that it had been deemed easier to secure a conviction on a lesser charge. This was particularly true of child cases, owing mainly to difficulties regarding the admissibility of child testimony.[121] There were nine successful prosecutions for the attempted rape of a girl between 1845 and the early twentieth century, but only one successful prosecution of an actual rape.

[118] 15.8.1846, GG, *Crime*, vol. 32.
[119] The following account is based on *Star*, 19.10.1921, 20.10.1921 and *Guernsey Weekly Press*, 22.10.1921.
[120] 19.10.1921, GG, *Crime*, vol. 57.
[121] It may even also have been influenced by a widespread nineteenth-century belief that the full rape of a pre-pubescent girl was physically impossible (A.S. Taylor, *Elements of Medical Jurisprudence* (1836; London, 1849 edn), p. 635).

The sole man convicted of full child rape was twenty-one-year-old Thomas Godfrey in 1862. Godfrey, a seaman, was staying between voyages at a lodging house in St Peter Port's Pier Steps. He was accused of raping eight-year-old Elizabeth Burley when she came to the house to make a delivery one morning when Godfrey was alone there. Godfrey's conviction was exceptional, particularly since the child's evidence was ruled inadmissible owing to her inability to understand the nature of an oath. It was only secured because, unusually, Godfrey had made a full confession. He was sentenced to seven years' transportation.[122]

In the only other nineteenth-century prosecution for the full rape of a child, the man was acquitted. The alleged rapist was Private John Reid and his victim fifteen-year-old Mary Ann Mackenzie. The alleged rape took place in the summer of 1865 in a room at Mary Ann's mother's house in the Strand, St Peter Port. Another woman, Alice O'Brien, was charged with aiding and abetting the rape. 'Although the commission of the act with which the prisoner was charged was fully proved,' the *Star* reported, 'the Court being unanimously of the opinion that the girl was a consenting party, acquitted the prisoner.'[123] Reid's abettor, Alice O'Brien, was also acquitted.

Consent was an issue which continued to dog child cases throughout the nineteenth century. Six of the attempted child rape charges of our period failed on this issue, and in the nine prosecutions which resulted in convictions, the notion of consent was used to mitigate sentences.[124] One example will stand for the rest. In 1871, William Stephens, a retired master mariner working as a porter at the Town Hospital, was charged with attempting to rape eight-year-old Harriet Hine and nine-year-old Sarah Glove on multiple occasions in his lodge at the Hospital. According to newspaper reports, Stephens' assaults on the girls were carried out 'with, as it appears, the *willing assent of the wretched little creatures*, the prisoner bribing

---

[122] 5.9.1862, GG, *Crime*, vol. 37; *Comet*, 6.9.1862.

[123] 11.8.1865, GG, *Crime*, vol. 39; *Star*, 12.8.1865.

[124] The longest sentence for the attempted rape of a child in the nineteenth century was nine months (24.6.1893, GG, *Crime*, vol. 48). Four sentences ran only to two months (8.8.1846, GG, *Crime*, vol. 32; 1.9.1850, GG, *Crime*, vol. 33; 14.10.1871, GG, *Crime*, vol. 41; 10.7.1897, GG, *Crime*, vol. 50), three to three months (23.9.1851, GG, *Crime*, vol. 33; 9.5.1885, GG, *Crime*, vol. 45; 5.6.1893, GG, *Crime*, vol. 48), and one to six weeks (17.1.1881, GG, *Crime*, vol. 43).

them with small presents of money, sweetmeats, pictures, &c.' Defence Advocate Thomas Falla argued that Stephens should not be subjected to a severe sentence since he had never used any violence 'and that what had happened had been *with the children's consent.*'[125] Falla's arguments clearly won over the Jurats, since Stephens, though found guilty, was sentenced to just two months' imprisonment.[126]

From a modern perspective, it seems shocking that little girls of eight and nine could be thought capable of 'consenting' to sexual acts perpetrated on them by adults (especially if we bear in mind that such children could be deemed of 'insufficient understanding' to testify on oath). However – as we saw in Chapter 6 – Guernsey had no statutory age of consent. In England and Wales, the age of consent stood at twelve at the time of Stephens' prosecution.[127] A few years later, it rose to sixteen. This milestone was achieved by the 1885 Criminal Law Amendment Act, which also applied to Scotland and Ireland. In 1895, Jersey passed its own version of the Criminal Law Amendment Act which also set the age of consent at sixteen.[128]

Guernsey showed no haste to follow suit, and for thirty-six years after the Stephens case, consent continued to be used as a defence in child cases. Finally, in 1907, Law Officers Ozanne and Bell produced a *projet de loi* also based on the Criminal Law Amendment Act, which was ultimately ratified as *la Loi relative à la Protection des Femmes et Filles Mineures.*[129] This new law made sexual intercourse with girls between thirteen and sixteen (and 'female idiots and imbeciles' of any age) punishable by imprisonment for up to two years, and sexual intercourse with girls aged under thirteen liable to a term of penal servitude at the discretion of the Court. Attempted sexual intercourse with under-thirteens was punishable by up to two years' imprisonment.[130]

Arguably the most important innovation of the 1907 law was to introduce the concept of 'statutory rape', in which the question of consent was

---

[125] *Star*, 14.10.1871. My italics.
[126] 14.10.1871, GG, *Crime*, vol. 41.
[127] L.A. Jackson, *Child Sex Abuse in Victorian England* (London, 2000), p. 13.
[128] *Loi (1895) appliquant à cette Ile Certaines Provisions du Criminal Law Amendment Act.*
[129] O in C, 6.7.1907.
[130] For more on this law and a similar law of 1914 which repealed and replaced it, see R.-M. Crossan, *A Women's History of Guernsey, 1850s–1950s* (Benderloch, 2018), pp. 129–31.

immaterial. Thus when a thirty-year-old man was tried for violating an eleven-year-old at her parents' home in Mill Street in the autumn of 1910, the child's consent, or lack of it, was not even considered. HM Procureur Edward Ozanne reminded Jurats that the law under which the case was being tried criminalised all under-age sex irrespective of circumstances. The man was found guilty as charged and sentenced to seven years' penal servitude.[131]

Just as Guernsey had no statutory age of consent until the twentieth century, it also had no law proscribing incest. The legislative gap concerning incest was filled in 1909. Action was precipitated by a case which came to the attention of Guernsey's authorities in January that year. The wife and teenage daughters of a forty-seven-year-old father of six came forward with multiple allegations against the man after one of the girls became pregnant. According to a press report of the trial, Procureur Edward Ozanne drew Jurats' attention to the fact that, since incest was not a crime under Guernsey law and the girls were not under age, the man could only be tried for rape. There was, however, no obvious violence, and debate ensued as to whether rape necessarily involved force, and whether that force could be moral as well as physical.[132] The consensus appears to have been that it could, and the man was found guilty as charged and sentenced to ten years' penal servitude.[133] By coincidence, the Westminster parliament had just the previous year passed its own Punishment of Incest Act. This provided a template for Guernsey's Law Officers, who drafted a *projet* copied almost verbatim from the English law. In August 1909, *la Loi pour la Punition d'Inceste* was sanctioned by the Privy Council.[134] The new law made any male who had sexual intercourse with a female he knew to be his mother, sister, daughter or grand-daughter punishable by up to seven years' penal servitude, with females over sixteen

---

[131] 31.10.1910, GG, *Crime*, vol. 54; 12.11.1910, Crime, vol. 55; *Gazette de Guernesey*, 19.11.1910. This should be contrasted with William Laurens' two-month sentence for a similar crime in 1819 (Chapter 6, p. 199).

[132] *Gazette de Guernesey*, 9.1.1909. The prosecution of an incestuous offence as rape was not unprecedented. In 1885, a man had been sentenced to three months and twenty lashes for the attempted rape of his minor daughter, and in 1894 another man was sentenced to five years' penal servitude for the attempted rape of his fifty-seven-year-old mother. In these cases, however, the offence was clearly compounded with violence (9.5.1885, GG, *Crime*, vol. 45; 17.11.1894, GG, *Crime*, vol. 49).

[133] 6.1.1909, GG, *Crime*, vol. 54.

[134] O in C, 3.8.1909.

liable to the same penalty if they consented to such an act. The first prosecution under this law occurred in 1928.[135]

Male-on-male sexual crime

No male-on-male sexual offences were prosecuted in Guernsey prior to the period covered here. Guernsey had no statutes on the subject, and (as already noted) Procureur Charles De Jersey told the visiting Royal Commissioners in 1847, 'the Court are very unwilling to investigate such a case, and rather conceive that the investigation does more harm than the punishment would do good.'[136]

In England and Wales, the death penalty for sodomy, first instituted in 1533, was removed by the 1861 Offences against the Person Act, sections 61–3 of which made the active participant in an act of anal intercourse with another male liable to a maximum penalty of penal servitude for life, while also making attempted sodomy, and any male-on-male indecent assault, punishable by up to ten years' penal servitude. In 1885, the Criminal Law Amendment Act went further by making it a crime punishable by up to two years' imprisonment for any male person to 'engage in, procure, or attempt to procure the commission of any act of gross indecency' with another male in a public or private place – a deliberately catch-all enactment which effectively criminalised all homosexual acts, consenting or not.

In 1898, and still without a law, Guernsey's Court broke with centuries of tradition and prosecuted its first male-on-male sexual assault. In November that year, a thirty-seven-year-old vagrant was tried before eleven Jurats for sexually assaulting a schoolboy in the toilets at St Peter Port's Candie Gardens. He was sentenced to six months' imprisonment and twenty-four lashes of the cat o'nine tails.[137] Over the course of the next ten years, there

---

[135] 28.8.1928, GG, *Crime*, vol. 59. Prosecutions under this law were rare. For later cases, see 29.3.1947, 18.11.1950, 1.7.1955, GG, *Crime*, vol. 72.

[136] *Second Report*, p. 276.

[137] 26.11.1898, GG, *Crime*, vol. 51; *Gazette de Guernesey*, 3.12.1898. The boy was a pupil at Elizabeth College, Guernsey's version of a public school. It is interesting to note that his name was suppressed in newspaper reports at a time when female sexual assault victims' names were still routinely published.

were two further prosecutions of sexual assaults by men on boys. The first of these, which occurred in 1907, was perpetrated by a Town Hospital inmate on a seven-year-old, and the second, in 1908, by a sailor on a fourteen-year-old. Both assaults incurred two-month prison sentences.[138]

In the absence of any relevant statute, all three of these prosecutions were carried out under the Court's general criminal jurisdiction. The passage of the 1907 *Femmes et Filles Mineures* Law highlighted a legislative gap regarding young boys, and in 1910, Law Officers Ozanne and Bell produced a *projet de loi* relating to sodomy and male-on-male sexual assaults. This *projet* was not based on Westminster's most recent enactment on the subject (the 1885 Criminal Law Amendment Act), but on the 1861 Offences against the Person Act, sections 61–3 of which it replicated almost word-for-word. It was approved by the States with little debate and ratified by the Privy Council as *la Loi relative à la Sodomie* in 1911.[139]

The first prosecution under the new law came in 1914. It concerned the same Town Hospital inmate who had been tried for indecently assaulting a seven-year-old in 1907, and was now being tried for assaulting a ten-year-old. Full advantage was taken of the new law's punitive provisions, and the man was sentenced to three years' penal servitude.[140] Three further prosecutions followed over the next few years. All involved serious assaults by adult men on young boys, and all attracted sentences of five years' penal servitude.[141]

Unlike the 1885 Criminal Law Amendment Act, *la Loi relative à la Sodomie* did not criminalise all homosexual acts, and Guernsey's authorities used only it against predatory paedophiles. In 1927, however, a case occurred where there was no juvenile victim but which the police and Law Officers nevertheless wished to see prosecuted. This case concerned a twenty-two-year-old hotel waiter accused of committing an indecent act with a soldier late one night on a St Peter Port street. The soldier was never identified, and since no crime could be proved under the 1911 Sodomy Law, the waiter was prosecuted under the Royal Court's general criminal jurisdiction and

[138] 8.8.1907, 2.4.1908, GG, *Crime*, vol. 54.
[139] *Billet*, 7.12.1910; O in C, 25.5.1911.
[140] 26.9.1914, GG, *Crime*, vol. 55.
[141] 29.1.1921, 4.6.1921, GG, *Crime*, vol. 57; 6.2.1925, GG, *Crime*, vol. 58.

sentenced to one month's imprisonment.[142] This was Guernsey's first prosecution for a consensual homosexual act. In order to fill the newly perceived gap, the 1911 law was repealed in 1929 and replaced by a second *Loi relative à la Sodomie*. The 1929 law re-enacted previous provisions pertaining to sodomy and indecent assault, but – significantly – also incorporated an article replicating word-for-word the section of the Criminal Law Amendment Act which dealt with 'gross indecency'.[143]

A cursory inspection of crime registers between the 1930s and 1950s reveals only a small number of prosecutions of adult males for consensual homosexual acts.[144] In England and Wales, consensual homosexual acts carried out in private by men over twenty-one were decriminalised by the 1967 Sexual Offences Act. Similar legislation followed in Scotland in 1980 and Northern Ireland in 1982. In Guernsey, the Sexual Offences (Bailiwick of Guernsey) Law of 1983 brought Guernsey into line with the United Kingdom by decriminalising homosexual acts within the same parameters.[145]

Property Crime

Across our four quinquennia in aggregate, property crime (theft and allied offences) accounted for 16 per cent of criminal cases determined by the Royal Court, thus comprising the second largest category of the Court's criminal business after offences of interpersonal violence. Aside from a minor law of 1876 on fraudulent appropriation, no Guernsey statutes addressed the subject of theft until the passage of the 1958 Larceny Law.[146] There were thus no

---

[142] 21.1.1927, GG, *Crime*, vol. 59.

[143] *Loi relative à la Sodomie* (O in C, 7.5.1929). It further added a clause stipulating that consent was to be no defence when an indecent assault had been carried out on a boy under sixteen.

[144] Notably, 19.3.1955, GG, *Crime*, vol. 72; 12.8.1957, 9.9.1958, GG, *Crime*, vol. 73.

[145] This law was enacted on Home Office advice when it emerged (after a court case which had forced the change in Northern Ireland) that Guernsey's 1929 law was in breach of article 8 of the European Convention on Human Rights which provided for the right to respect for private and family life. Correspondence between the Law Officers and Home Office on this matter is preserved in NA, HO 284/336.

[146] O in C, 7.1.1958.

statutory definitions of different kinds of theft, so Law Officers and Jurats assessed the gravity of such offences at their own discretion. Between 1845 and 1929, 83 per cent of property offences were dealt with summarily and 17 per cent on indictment. We will look at each category separately, beginning with the first.

Property crime accounted for nearly one-fifth of all summary prosecutions over our four quinquennia. The items involved in Police Court cases were typically of low value, purloined opportunistically and without violence to persons or forced entry to property. In 17 per cent of summary theft cases, the accused was female (a somewhat higher proportion than the 14 per cent tried summarily for assault). Among the items most commonly stolen by females were food, clothing, household linen and domestic utensils. Poverty was a well-known incentive for this type of crime. Male thieves also stole food and clothing, but also heavier items such as coal, tools, metal, wood and other construction materials. The standard Police Court punishment for both male and female thieves was imprisonment, often for periods which now seem quite disproportionate to the value of the stolen goods. In 1848, Mary Winter was imprisoned for four weeks for stealing a piece of cheese and a dish.[147] In 1851, Marie Torode got three weeks for stealing a small quantity of bacon.[148] In 1888, William Moore was imprisoned for a month for stealing a 2lb loaf from a baker's van.[149] In 1894, Nicolas Lenfestey also got a month for taking cabbages out of a field.[150] The severity of punishments for petty theft abated after World War I, with sentences of two and four days becoming more common for such minor offences.

As in previous periods, the property offences tried on indictment consisted of burglaries, robberies and other forms of aggravated theft. Property offences were more liable to be tried on indictment than any other category of offence, accounting for 70 per cent of Full Court cases across our four quinquennia. As Professor Vic Gatrell has observed, law-makers and enforcers tended to

---

[147] 17.2.1848, GG, *Crime*, vol. 32.
[148] 6.3.1851, GG, *Crime*, vol. 33.
[149] 15.3.1888, GG, *Crime*, vol. 46.
[150] 1.2.1894, GG, *Crime*, vol. 48.

treat most severely what they themselves most feared.[151] This figure nevertheless masks considerable changes over time. Property crime dealt with on indictment peaked in the earlier part of our period and declined as time went on. In 1860–4, it accounted for as much as 85 per cent of the Full Court's criminal business, and equated to about seventeen cases a year. By 1920–4, however, the proportion had dropped to 35 per cent, and cases dealt with on indictment averaged just under two a year.

Females formed 12 per cent of those indicted for property crime in this period. One group of female thieves who often figured in the Full Court were prostitutes who stole valuables such as snuff boxes, cigarette cases and watches from clients' pockets. In 1889, for instance, Louise Cortier was imprisoned for six weeks for stealing François Saliot's silver watch and chain when they were in a room together in Cornet Street.[152] Most female thieves were however indicted for stealing from their employers. One of the most serious cases involving a woman was that of Mary Saint in 1891. Mrs Saint was convicted of burgling a shoe shop in the High Street, for whose owner she worked as a domestic servant. Together with a female accomplice, she stole sixty-four pairs of boots and shoes, three pairs of gaiters, and three pairs of slippers. Her sentence, to eight months' imprisonment, was the longest given to any woman tried on indictment for a property offence in our period.[153]

Men indicted for property crime tended to commit graver offences and hence attracted harsher punishments. Just over three-quarters were punished with sentences of up to eighteen months' local imprisonment, sometimes accompanied by whipping or banishment. The remaining quarter were sentenced to either transportation or penal servitude, which were the usual punishments for a serious burglary or robbery. Here, the underlying trend was also one of declining severity. Between 1845 and 1870, the standard sentence for a serious robbery or burglary was between seven and fifteen years' transportation. In 1849, for example, discharged soldiers John Navin and Michael Dugan were each sentenced to fifteen years' transportation, and their

---

[151] V.A.C. Gatrell, 'The decline of theft and violence in Victorian and Edwardian England', in V.A.C. Gatrell, B. Lenman & G. Parker, *Crime and the Law: The Social History of Crime in Western Europe since 1500* (London, 1980), p. 243.

[152] 17.8.1889, GG, *Crime*, vol. 46.

[153] 1.6.1891, GG, *Crime*, vol. 47. Her accomplice was sentenced to three months.

accomplice John Winfrey to ten, for a nocturnal robbery of pedestrians on the public highway in the Vale and St Sampsons.[154] In 1870, sentences of penal servitude replaced those of transportation, and at first, the average term of penal servitude for serious property crime was also seven years. From the 1880s, however, five years became standard, and from the turn of the twentieth century, sentences further declined to three years. Thus the two soldiers who burgled Bachmann's Jewellers in St Peter Port in 1901 received this relatively short term for a haul of considerable value – diamond rings, gold bracelets, pearl necklaces, silver cigarette cases – which earlier in our period would certainly have seen them spend the rest of their lives in Australia.[155]

By this time, not only had sentencing policy softened, but perceptions of what constituted a 'serious' property offence had also begun to change. This process accelerated after Henry Casey was appointed Police Court Magistrate in 1925. Casey was given discretion as to which cases he would deal with himself and which he would refer to the Full Court.[156] Although thefts involving violence were specifically excluded from his brief, thefts involving forcible entry to premises were not.[157] In 1928, Casey was faced with two men accused of forcing entry to a shop and several offices, from which they were alleged to have stolen more than £88 in cash, together with a telescope and sundry other items. Instead of referring them to the Full Court, as would certainly have happened in an earlier period, Casey decided that the case fell within his purview and tried the men himself. Allocating terms for each count, he sentenced them both to just six months.[158] This change in the categorisation of serious theft at least partly explains why property cases tried in the Full Court dropped from seventeen annually in the 1860s to just two per year in the 1920s.

---

[154] 28.4.1849, GG, *Crime*, vol. 32; *Star*, 28.4.1849.
[155] 23.11.1901, GG, *Crime*, vol. 52; *Gazette de Guernesey*, 30.11.1901.
[156] On the basis that offences which he personally felt merited more than two months' imprisonment or a fine exceeding £10 should go to the Full Court.
[157] See Article XI, *Loi ayant rapport à l'Institution d'un Magistrat en Police Correctionnelle*, O in C, 17.3.1925.
[158] 5.3.1928, GG, *Crime*, vol. 59.

Miscellaneous offences

The 'miscellaneous' category accounted for a growing proportion of both Police and Full Court business as our period progressed. By the final decade of our study, it comprised between a quarter and a third of the Court's entire criminal work. These offences fell into two classes: 'old' offences which the Court had been prosecuting for centuries, and 'new' offences which the Court had never prosecuted before. We shall look at a selection of offences in the former category first.

Worker combinations

There were six prosecutions for forming a workers' combination in our period, all of them relating to the same incident, and all tried summarily.[159] The accused were a group of English and Irish stone-crackers. In the winter of 1853, they had organised a strike aimed at raising the piece rate for broken stone from 2s 2d per ton to 2s 4d per ton. Leading a crowd of more than 200 men and carrying a board inscribed 'Bread for Life!', they had made their way from St Sampsons harbour to nearby quarries and stone-yards where they attempted to persuade stone-crackers to down tools. The six men were punished with prison sentences of between two and four days, and were all made to deposit £2 against their good behaviour for six months or leave the island. These prosecutions were Guernsey's last for forming workers' combinations. The organisers of a stone-crackers' strike in 1864 were not criminally prosecuted.[160] In the United Kingdom, trades unions and their activities were decriminalised by the 1871 Trade Union Act.[161] Guernsey had no corresponding legislation, but a local stone-workers' union is known to have been formed by at least the 1880s, and was allowed to conduct its activities without judicial interference.[162]

---

[159] 6.12.1853, GG, *Crime*, vol. 34; *Star*, 6.12.1853; *Comet*, 8.12.1853.

[160] *Comet*, 16.1.1864.

[161] J.V. Orth, 'The English combination laws reconsidered', in F. Snyder & D. Hay (eds), *Labour, Law and Crime: An Historical Perspective* (London, 1987), pp. 123–4.

[162] R.-M. Crossan, *Poverty and Welfare in Guernsey, 1560–2015* (Woodbridge, 2015), p. 102.

'Witchcraft' (as fraud on the credulous)

In the spring of 1857, the *Comet's* editor observed, 'at this very hour, when the blaze of civilisation dazzles every eye, Guernsey affords as lamentable an illustration of mental darkness – of superstition on the one hand, and imposture on the other – as ever existed in the dark ages.'[163] He was alluding to the case of Mary Ann Dawson which was at that point being investigated. The fifty-one-year-old spinster, who was also known as Mrs Pollard, had been charged with exercising the profession of *désorceleuse* for money. The previous year, 1856, had seen the passage of *la Loi relative à l'Application des Peines tant au Criminel qu'en Police Correctionnelle* which had made it a crime summarily punishable by up to eight days' imprisonment to purport to practise sorcery.[164] However (perhaps because Dawson's gains were deemed too considerable to try her in the Police Court) the new law was eschewed in favour of prosecution on indictment. In due course, the Full Court found the fifty-one-year-old guilty as charged and sentenced her to two months' imprisonment, half of which was to be in solitary confinement on bread and water.[165]

The next major case was that of twenty-six-year-old Amy Lake in 1914. Mrs Lake was accused of extracting cash and goods worth around £20 from two local people in return for lifting the 'spells' she herself claimed to have cast on them.[166] The twenty-six-year-old was not, however, tried on indictment. The Dawson precedent had by this time been forgotten, and Mrs Lake was sentenced to just eight days under the *Application des Peines* Law.[167] HM Comptroller Arthur Bell was reported to have told the Court he was sorry they could not inflict a heavier penalty but this was all that the law allowed.[168] Within a matter of months, the Law Officers remedied this perceived problem by drafting an amendment to the *Application des Peines* Law which raised the maximum term for this offence to two months if tried

---

[163] *Comet*, 5.3.1857.
[164] Appendix 7.
[165] 30.3.1857, GG, *Crime*, vol. 35; *Comet*, 2.4.1857.
[166] 16.1.1914, IA, AQ 0227/10.
[167] 29.1.1914, GG, *Crime*, vol. 55.
[168] *Star*, 29.1.1914.

summarily, whilst also making serious instances indictable, in which case the maximum penalty would rise to two years.[169] In submitting their draft for Home Office perusal, the Law Officers contended:

> We are of opinion that a prosecution in the Police Court is not sufficient to meet the appalling state of things existing in this Bailiwick with regard to the prevailing belief in witchcraft. We are unhappily well aware that a large number of persons of all classes – farmers, fruit growers and artisans besides the ignorant classes – are imbued with the idea that they can be, and are bewitched … and … that they can have recourse to certain well-known persons who have the reputed power of being able to remove spells from themselves, their families, or their cattle … These so-called sorcerers and sorceresses are well known … to extort relatively large sums of money, jewellery and other valuables from their victims.[170]

Notwithstanding the image conjured up by the Law Officers, the law was not used in any serious cases in what remained of the period covered by this study.

Libel

We saw in Chapter 6 that libels could be prosecuted in two ways: semi-civilly by means of *causes en adjonction* if the libel concerned private individuals, and purely criminally if the libel concerned public functionaries in the exercise of their duties. In the current period, there were only two cases where libels were prosecuted purely criminally. Both cases occurred in the early 1850s and both concerned Jurat Thomas Le Retilley. In the first case, John Le Noury was prosecuted for having a notice printed in a newspaper alleging that Jurat Le Retilley had committed forgery in relation to the succession of his (Le Noury's) late sister.[171] He was punished with a fine of 70 *livres tournois* (£5).[172] In the second case, John Sarchet was prosecuted for libelling Jurat Le Retilley in a letter to the Bailiff which was said to have 'undermined the respect due to the Court and to the administration of Justice in this Island'. He too was

---

[169] *Loi supplémentaire à la Loi relative à l'Application des Peines tant au Criminel qu'en Police Correctionnelle*, O in C, 23.3.1915. See also *Billet*, 23.7.1914 and *Star*, 23.7.1914.
[170] Law Officers to Home Office, 7.9.1914, NA, HO 45/14143.
[171] *Gazette de Guernesey*, 24.1.1852.
[172] 14.2.1852, GG, *Crime*, vol. 33; *Comet*, 16.2.1852.

fined 70 *livres tournois*.[173] After 1853, purely criminal prosecutions of libel completely ceased.

It was noted above that a law of 1861 created an option for dealing civilly with libels, while leaving open the option of *une cause en adjonction* for those who preferred it.[174] Between 1861 and the end of our period, there were a total of eleven libel prosecutions *en adjonction*. The first and most interesting occurred in 1876. The plaintiff was Rachel Clucas and the defendant Scipion Filippi de Faby. Mrs Clucas was the widow of Thomas Clucas, who had resigned as a Guernsey Jurat in 1857 to become Judge of Alderney. De Faby was a thirty-one-year-old French army officer who had fought in the Franco-Prussian War and moved to Alderney after the French defeat. While in Alderney, he had become personally and financially embroiled with Clucas, leading to resentments on both sides. After Clucas's death in April 1876, de Faby had published a vituperative article about the former Judge in his newspaper, *La Gazette des Iles de la Manche*, in which he alleged *inter alia* that Clucas knew nothing about law, left all his duties to his deputy, and spent his time indulging his two 'passions', *l'eau de vie* and *la paillardise*.[175] Mrs Clucas was successful in obtaining the *adjonction* of HM Procureur, and de Faby was in due course found guilty of libel. He was fined £200 and ordered to pay Mrs Clucas a further £200 in damages.[176]

All of the ten remaining libels prosecuted *en adjonction* after 1876 concerned living persons. Moreover, all concerned individuals with a public role, as the convention had become entrenched with de Faby that libels were only to be prosecuted semi-civilly 'when the public were themselves interested in the case'.[177] By this time, *causes en adjonction* were clearly filling the void left by the cessation of public libel prosecutions.

In the last *cause en adjonction* of our period, which took place in 1916, the plaintiff was HM Receiver Victor Carey. Carey obtained the *adjonction* of HM Procureur in an action against English grower Arthur J.F. Gibbons for

---

[173] 30.6.1853, GG, *Crime*, vol. 34.
[174] O in C, 5.8.1861.
[175] *Gazette des Iles de la Manche*, 6.5.1876.
[176] 10.6.1876, 15.7.1876, GG, *Crime*, vol. 42. It is not entirely clear to me from the trial record whether de Faby was convicted because he had smeared the deceased Judge's reputation or, less directly, that of his wife. In any event, there were many Guernsey precedents of *causes* for the defamation of the dead (see Chapter 3, p. 98).
[177] Thomas Godfrey Carey, cited in *Star*, 23.5.1882.

libelling Carey in a letter to the Guernsey Banking Company. The Court found Gibbons guilty as charged and fined him £75, in addition to which he was ordered to pay Carey damages of £75.[178] No further libels were prosecuted *en adjonction* in what remained of our period, and this may have been the last case of its kind. The possibility of prosecuting an action *en adjonction* was formally removed in 1950 by The Royal Court (Miscellaneous Provisions) Law. [179]

Bigamy

There were nine prosecutions of bigamy in the period covered by this chapter. The first three occurred between the 1840s and 1860s; there was then a fifty-year gap, and the remaining six took place between 1919 and 1929. The nineteenth-century cases were treated fairly uniformly. All three involved the union of someone who was already married to a person who was single. The married partners – two women and one man – were convicted of bigamy and given sentences of two months' imprisonment. The two single men who had married the bigamous women were each given one month for knowingly making false declarations when applying for a marriage licence. The single woman who had unknowingly married someone else's husband was not prosecuted.[180]

The twentieth-century cases followed the disruptions of World War I. In the first, which occurred in 1919, a Private in the Royal Guernsey Light Infantry was sentenced to the unprecedented sentence of four months for marrying a war widow while his first wife was not only still living but had recently given birth to their sixth child.[181] In the second, the following year, the Court reverted to the lighter sentence of two months because the man

---

[178] 15.7.1916, GG, *Crime*, vol. 56. For *causes* between 1877 and 1916, see 16.6.1877, GG, *Crime*, vol. 42; 27.5.1882, GG, *Crime*, vol. 44; 25.10.1884, GG, *Crime*, vol. 45; 7.2.1891, GG, *Crime*, vol. 47.

[179] Barclay, 'Defamation action in Guernsey', p. 255.

[180] 19.2.1848, GG, *Crime*, vol. 32; 4.6.1859, GG, *Crime*, vol. 36; 26.4.1866, GG, *Crime*, vol. 39.

[181] 8.2.1919, GG, *Crime*, vol. 56; *Guernsey Weekly Press*, 15.2.1919.

was judicially separated from his first wife and had not heard from her for twelve years.[182] In neither case was the bride prosecuted.

The third case, which occurred in 1922, resulted in two prosecutions because both parties were already married. The Court sentenced the groom, an ex-serviceman from Yorkshire, to three months' imprisonment and his Alderney-born bride to one month's imprisonment.[183] This was not however done without misgiving. The man's defence Advocate, Ambrose Sherwill, had asked the Court for an acquittal on the basis that bigamy was not a statutory crime in Guernsey and 'the ground on which the Court vested its jurisdiction … was most insecure.'[184] In an era when Guernsey's legal authorities were becoming sensitive to such lacunae, it was not long before this defect was remedied. *La Loi relative à la Bigamie* was ratified within a year of the trial.[185] The law formally constituted bigamy a felony and made it punishable by up to seven years' penal servitude. There were two prosecutions under the new Bigamy Law in what remained of our period, and both resulted in a two-month sentence for the bigamous parties.[186] The 1923 *Loi relative à la Bigamie* remains the law under which bigamy is prosecuted at the time of writing.[187]

Novel offences

Many other offences began to be prosecuted in our period without any legislation at all – some on a one-off basis, others on multiple occasions. In the latter category were 'white collar' offences such as embezzlement and false accounting. One of the first prosecutions of embezzlement occurred in 1845, when Hellier Dorey, Castel Procureur des Pauvres, was charged with

[182] 8.1.1920, GG, *Crime*, vol. 57; *Star*, 9.1.1920.

[183] 3.3.1922, GG, *Crime*, vol. 57.

[184] *Star*, 3.3.1922, 4.3.1922.

[185] O in C, 29.1.1923.

[186] 10.3.1925, GG, *Crime*, vol. 58; *Star*, 11.3.1925; 8.10.1929, GG, *Crime*, vol. 60; *Star*, 8.10.1929.

[187] Save that The Magistrate's Court (Guernsey) Law 1954 transferred jurisdiction over bigamies alleged to have been committed within the island from the Full Court to the Magistrate's Court.

embezzling c.£100 from his parish.[188] In a trial lasting two days, Law Officers Charles De Jersey and John Utermarck argued with defence counsel Thomas Falla as to how Dorey's crime might be defined and whether the Court had any right to try it.[189] Eventually, the Court deemed itself competent and sentenced Dorey to three months' imprisonment.[190] Every subsequent decade then had its share of embezzlement and/or false accounting prosecutions. In the 1850s and 1860s, many cases concerned sub-contractors working on the harbour construction projects.[191] In later decades, most prosecutions involved book-keepers employed by private companies, sports clubs and other community associations.[192]

The novel offences prosecuted on a one-off basis are too numerous to detail individually, but include blackmail; conspiring to damage a business rival; deserting the helm of a commercial vessel while at sea; criminal sabotage; and chequebook fraud.[193] Newspaper accounts of all of these cases have one feature in common. In each of them, the defence Advocate would argue that the Court had no jurisdiction because the alleged offences were not defined in any local statute. The Law Officers would then counter, as Arthur Bell did in the sabotage case, that 'the Report of the Commissioners, show[ed] that the Court had powers to deal with any … offences against Society, awarding punishments at their discretion where there was no specific statute.'[194] Notwithstanding that the Commissioners had condemned this practice,[195] the Law Officers' argument invariably prevailed, and in time

---

[188] Procureurs des Pauvres were responsible for the custody and management of parochial poor funds. Dorey had systematically entered larger sums in his ledger than he had actually dispensed to the poor, keeping the difference for himself.

[189] This dispute is recapitulated in *Second Report*, pp. 262–3.

[190] 10.11.1845, GG, *Crime*, vol. 32; *Star*, 10.11.1845, 13.11.1845.

[191] In 1856, for instance, four sub-contractors were sentenced to prison terms of between three and six weeks for submitting accounts to St Peter Port harbour contractors Le Gros and De La Mare for work they had not done (11.10. 1856, GG, *Crime*, vol. 35).

[192] One of the most serious cases concerned a book-keeper sentenced to sixteen months' imprisonment for embezzling more than £200 from shipowners Onesimus Dorey & Sons in 1923 (16.10.1923, GG, *Crime*, vol. 58).

[193] References, in sequence, are 7.12.1859, GG, *Crime*, vol. 36; 15.5.1869, GG, *Crime*, vol. 40; 23.11.1895, GG, *Crime*, vol. 49; 23.3.1921, GG, *Crime*, vol. 57; 11.9.1920, GG, *Crime*, vol. 57.

[194] *Star*, 22.3.1921, 23.3.1921.

[195] *Second Report*, p. xvii.

became enshrined as part of local orthodoxy. As HM Comptroller told a British government inquiry in 1946, 'one can establish that a man has committed a crime, that is, one that is not a statutory offence, provided he has committed an act which is "malum in se".'[196]

Drugs offences

We will finish our exploration of offences brought within the Court's jurisdiction during our period with a look at a branch of offending which was in due course to occupy a significant proportion of Court time. In this case, however, legislation was central to the process.

Prior to the mid-nineteenth century, drugs of all kinds could be freely bought and sold throughout Europe. In 1868, the United Kingdom became one of the first countries to place restrictions on this trade, when The Pharmacy Act limited the sale of certain drugs, including opium and its derivatives, to qualified persons only.[197] In 1882, this Act was replicated locally by *l'Ordonnance relative au Débit des Poisons*, which restricted the sale of thirty named substances to doctors and pharmacists authorised to practise in Guernsey.[198]

During World War I, the sale of opium and cocaine to British servicemen was banned under the Defence of the Realm Regulations, which were extended to Guernsey. When these Regulations expired after the War, Westminster tightened controls on civilians as well as the military by the passage in 1920 of the Dangerous Drugs Act, which comprehensively criminalised the importation, sale, and possession of a list of substances which included opium, morphine, heroin, cocaine, and barbiturates.[199] In 1924, Guernsey again followed suit with a law based on the Dangerous Drugs Act.[200]

---

[196] 'Evidence given before the Privy Council Committee on Proposed Reforms in the Channel Islands, Guernsey, September 1946', p. 212 (Royal Court Library, IA).

[197] P. Haber, *Drugs of Dependence: The Role of Medical Professionals* (London, 2013), p. 87.

[198] Ord, 16.1.1882.

[199] Haber, *Drugs of Dependence*, pp. 88–9.

[200] *Loi ayant rapport à l'Importation, l'Exportation, la Manufacture, la Vente et à l'Emploi d'Opium et autres Drogues Dangereuses*, O in C, 16.4.1924.

The first prosecution under Guernsey's new law took place in September 1924. It concerned a forty-two-year-old Englishman who was sentenced to three months' imprisonment after being found in possession of cocaine he had ordered from Holland.[201] The 1924 law was repealed and re-enacted in 1931 by another of the same name which replicated a recent change in the United Kingdom by extending restrictions to cannabis.[202] This remained the principal law under which drugs offences were prosecuted in Guernsey until its replacement by more up-to-date legislation in the 1960s and 1970s.

Punishments

A break-down of sentencing data from our sample quinquennia shows the following ranking of punishments: the commonest form was imprisonment, which was used in 51 per cent of the period's criminal cases; fines were next at 23 per cent; in third place at 9 per cent were bind overs to keep the peace or be of good conduct; banishment, transportation and other forms of ejection came fourth at 5 per cent; and last of all, at 2 per cent, came corporal punishment.[203] In addition to the above, there was also one case of capital punishment, and a number of novel penal options such as 'first offender' disposals, probation orders and blacklisting, which were introduced too late in our period to make a statistical impact. Sentences usually combined more than one form of punishment. The following paragraphs will discuss each mode of punishment in turn, beginning with the least used.

---

[201] 13.9.1924, GG, *Crime*, vol. 58. The man was a middle-class drug addict who was maintained by remittances from his father (*Star*, 11.9.1924).

[202] O in C, 12.2.1931. Cannabis had been added to the United Kingdom's restricted list in 1928.

[203] These figures are exclusive of semi-civil actions and prosecutions under Ordinances, which could only be punished by a fine.

Capital punishment

There had been six hangings in Guernsey in the period 1680–1764, and nineteen in 1765–1844. In the current period, there was just one. The execution of John Tapner in 1854 differed from previous executions in that it was not carried out in public but in a walled enclosure behind the prison. Credit for the change of venue was claimed by French writer Victor Hugo, who attributed it to the distaste he had aroused in an open letter to a local newspaper a fortnight before the execution.[204]

In December 1855, Victor Hugo was shown the apparatus used to execute Tapner.[205] It had been newly made for the occasion, and featured a platform with a trap-door about three feet square.[206] Tapner's execution was botched, and the small size of the trap-door undoubtedly played a part. Tapner was merely stunned by his fall through the trap, and managing to unfasten his hands, had attempted to pull himself back up by grabbing on to the sides. Seeing this, the Prévôt had ordered the hangman to pull the prisoner down by his legs, and keep him pulled down while pressure from the noose asphyxiated him. The incident found its way into the British press,[207] and the Home Secretary, Lord Palmerston, called on the Prévôt to submit an account of what had happened. The Prévôt described the events as they had unfolded, and added 'the sufferings of the culprit did not last more than four minutes'.[208]

Tapner's ordeal was due as much to the hangman's failure to secure his hands as to the under-sized trap. Now aged sixty-four and ensconced as

---

[204] H. Juin (ed.), *Victor Hugo, Choses Vues: Souvenaux, Journaux, Cahiers, 1849–1869* (Paris, 1972), p. 310.

[205] By this time, Hugo had moved from Jersey to Guernsey, where he was to reside until 1870.

[206] Juin (ed.), *Victor Hugo, Choses Vues*, pp. 310–11.

[207] *The Times*, 15.2.1854.

[208] Prévôt to Lieutenant Governor, 2.3.1854, NA, HO 45/5194. Botched executions were not uncommon in other parts of the British Isles at this time. The situation was somewhat palliated by the adoption in the 1880s of the 'long drop', based on the ratio between body weight and drop, which was designed to ensure a speedier end by rupturing the spinal cord (V.A.C. Gatrell, *The Hanging Tree: Execution and the English People, 1770–1868* (Oxford, 1994), pp. 46, 49–51, 54).

Exécuteur des Hautes Oeuvres since 1830, John Rooks had performed only one other execution. Jersey had abolished the office of public executioner in 1837, and was now procuring an experienced hangman from England as and when required.[209] The month after Tapner's execution, John Rooks went into retirement on a Crown pension of 12s weekly.[210] He died early in 1855. No one was appointed to replace Rooks as hangman, and in 1857 the office of public executioner was abolished.[211]

John Tapner was the last person to suffer the death penalty for a crime committed in Guernsey. Following the commutation of death sentences passed on Nugent Loughnan and Timothy Kelly in 1856, the Royal Court issued no further such sentences until 1935. Between that date and 1947, the Court passed a further four capital sentences (all for murder), but all were commuted by the British authorities to life imprisonment.[212] In the United Kingdom, the death penalty for murder was abolished by The Murder (Abolition of Death Penalty) Act 1965.[213] In Guernsey, the death penalty for murder was abolished by The Homicide (Guernsey) Law 1965, and execution as a judicial punishment for any crime was ruled out by the 2000 Human Rights (Bailiwick of Guernsey) Law.

Corporal punishment

Although the Royal Court stopped sentencing women to whipping in 1819, it continued to inflict this punishment on men and boys. Peter Stafford Carey,

---

[209] L. Sinel, *Jersey through the Centuries: A Chronology of Events and Matters of Interest* (Jersey, 1984), p. 50.

[210] Lieutenant Governor to Home Office, 3.3.1853, NA, HO 45/5194; Lieutenant Governor to Bailiff, 27.4.1854, GG, Royal Court General Letter Book (first series), vol. 8.

[211] O in C, 27.8.1857.

[212] For these sentences, see 14.4.1935, GG, *Crime*, vol. 63; 13.7.1937, GG, *Crime*, vol. 65; 10.6.1947, 28.7.1947, GG, *Crime*, vol. 72.

[213] This measure was provisional to begin with but confirmed after a quinquennial review in 1969. Thereafter, capital punishment was still technically available for arson in Royal Dockyards, treason, and piracy with violence. The death penalty was abolished for the first of these in 1971, and for the last two in 1998.

who became Bailiff in 1845, was a supporter of corporal punishment, but, in emulation of the policy now current in England and Wales, ordered on assuming office that it should be administered out of public view.[214] Such punishments were henceforth carried out within the prison enclosure.

The hangman, John Rooks, was responsible for the infliction of whippings until his retirement in 1854. In 1856, HM Receiver was formally charged with hiring a private person to administer whippings, and a piece-work rate was authorised from Crown revenues.[215] When the prison acquired warders in later years, the person paid to administer floggings was generally one of the warders.

Prior to the mid-1800s, adolescents as well as adults could be flogged with the cat o'nine tails. In 1848, however, it was laid down that only over-eighteens should be flogged with the cat, and that younger boys should be flogged with the birch.[216] Adult floggings were generally a complement to local imprisonment for native islanders who had committed serious crimes but where transportation or penal servitude were felt disproportionate. The flagellatory excesses of the late 1700s were no longer in evidence, but adult floggings could still be severe. On two occasions in the 1840s, a man was sentenced to 100 lashes for aggravated theft.[217] As late as 1892, six men were given fifty-lash sentences for their part in a violent attack on two other men.[218] The last adult whipping in our period occurred in 1914, when a man was sentenced to twenty-four lashes and a prison term for a serious assault.[219]

---

[214] *Second Report,* p. 181. In England and Wales, the public whipping of men had ceased in the 1830s.

[215] Treasury to Home Office, 10.3.1856, NA, HO 45/6269; Lieutenant Governor to Bailiff, 15.3.1856, GG, Royal Court General Letter Book (first series), vol. 8.

[216] This was the result of an instruction from the Privy Council after the mother of a fifteen-year-old had petitioned against her son's sentence to forty lashes of the cat for theft (28.11.1848, GG, *Ordres du Conseil et Actes du Parlement,* vol. 6).

[217] 21.10.1848, 12.5.1849, GG, *Crime,* vol. 32.

[218] 10.12.1892, GG, *Crime,* vol. 48. The men were additionally sentenced to six months' imprisonment.

[219] 31.1.1914, GG, *Crime,* vol. 55.

Birching was a commoner punishment than whipping. In each year of our sample quinquennia some four or five boys were sentenced to the birch. The 1856 *Application des Peines* Law set the maximum number of strokes a boy could receive at twenty-four.[220] Just under half of boys in our sample received the full quota. This seems broadly to have been reserved for teenagers, while under-thirteens might receive half that number or fewer. There was no lower age limit for birching in our period, and the youngest age at which a boy was birched was seven.[221]

In England, Wales and Scotland the judicial corporal punishment of both men and boys was abolished by the 1948 Criminal Justice Act. In Guernsey, the flogging of juveniles and adults was explicitly retained in the Corporal Punishment (Guernsey) Law of 1957.[222] Although there were no adult whippings after the 1940s,[223] birching, for which a lower age limit of twelve and a maximum of twelve strokes was set in 1957, remained common until the end of the 1960s.[224] Both whipping and birching were abolished when the 1957 Corporal Punishment Law was repealed in 2006.[225]

---

[220] O in C, 24.6.1856. The original *projet de loi* had set the maximum at forty, but this was deemed excessive by the Home Office (13.7.1855, Bailiff to Colonel Bainbrigge (deputising for Lieutenant Governor); Bailiff to Lieutenant Governor, 8.4.1856, GG, Royal Court General Letter Book (first series), vol. 8).

[221] See 18.3.1920, GG, *Crime*, vol. 57.

[222] O in C, 27.11.1957.

[223] The last took place in 1944, when a man received twelve lashes as part of his sentence for burglary and rape (F. Gahan, 'The law of the Channel Islands, IV: criminal law in Guernsey', *Solicitor Quarterly*, 2 (1963), p. 158).

[224] For birching in the 1960s, see www.corpun.com/archto75.htm#guernsey.

[225] By the Criminal Justice (Miscellaneous Provisions) (Bailiwick of Guernsey) Law.

Plate 43. Birching rack, Guernsey prison, 1915
Courtesy of Guernsey Museums & Galleries (States of Guernsey)

Transportation and penal servitude

We noted in Chapter 6 that Guernsey's Court began sentencing criminals
to transportation in 1835. In the first ten years, only five people were
sentenced to transportation. However, numbers increased after Peter
Stafford Carey became Bailiff, and between 1845 and the end of
transportation in the late 1860s, the sentence was handed down a further
fifty-seven times (exclusively to males). Transportation was used only for
the most serious crimes, which had to have been charged *félonieusement*.
Some 69 per cent of sentences were for burglary or robbery. A further 7
per cent were for manslaughter, 3 per cent were for rape, and the
remainder for sundry offences such as counterfeiting and forgery. The
terms for which people were transported varied between seven years and
life, and all such sentences entailed forfeiture of property.

The transportation of convicts from Britain to Australia was at its peak in the early 1830s. From 1840, the Australian colonies began to refuse convicts, so that by 1852, the only colony still open to transportees was Western Australia, which continued accepting convicts until 1868.[226] With capacity for transportation declining, the British authorities were forced to find an alternative way of dealing with serious criminals. This came in the form of a series of Penal Servitude Acts of which the first was passed in 1853. The 1853 Act allowed prisoners sentenced to transportation to serve their terms in British convict prisons rather than Australia.[227] It also introduced the ticket-of-leave system, whereby remission was granted on licence half-way through a sentence to any convict not guilty of idleness or misconduct. The National Archives at Kew hold records of convicts released on licence from 1853 onwards.[228] The earliest licence issued to a Guernsey convict dates from 1854 and was in respect of William Croucher, a burglar sentenced to seven years' transportation in 1850.[229] A search of these records showed that 36 per cent of those sentenced to transportation in Guernsey were released early by the authorities in England. These tended to be men on seven-year sentences, typically released after serving three or four years in an English prison.

In 1857, Westminster's second Penal Servitude Act officially abolished transportation as a judicial sentence and replaced it with sentences to penal servitude. Nevertheless, since penal servitude could also be served overseas, a small number of British convicts continued to be sent each year to Western Australia until this option was finally closed down in 1868. Perhaps with this in mind, the Guernsey Court continued to issue sentences to transportation until that date – in the full knowledge,

[226] H. Johnston, *Crime in England, 1815–1880: Experiencing the Criminal Justice System* (Abingdon, 2015), pp. 80, 84.

[227] Convict prisons were national institutions built by the British government from 1816 onwards. At the height of transportation, they were used as staging-posts for transportees. These prisons included Millbank, Pentonville, Portland, Portsmouth, Dartmoor, Brixton, and Parkhurst.

[228] These are preserved in the series PCOM 3.

[229] NA, PCOM 3/7/682.

presumably, that those so sentenced were unlikely ever to reach Australia.[230]

In 1869, the Home Office informed the Guernsey authorities that transportation had officially ceased and invited them to adopt Westminster's Penal Servitude Acts.[231] Loath to subject themselves to United Kingdom legislation, the States chose instead to enact their own law.[232] They did so in 1870 in the form of *la Loi relative à la Servitude Pénale*.[233] In order to obviate the need for an Order in Council to give effect to each sentence (as had been the case with transportation), the new law simply permitted the Royal Court to add a sentence of penal servitude to a sentence of banishment using the wording '*adjugé à être banni hors de ce Bailliage pour subir la servitude pénale pendant* xxx *ans sous la discipline prescrite par la législation du Royaume Uni*'.[234] Laying down a minimum sentence of five years, *la Loi relative à la Servitude Pénale* also partly replicated Westminster's 1870 Abolition of Forfeiture Act by abolishing forfeiture in all cases of banishment.[235] The first people formally to be sentenced to penal servitude in Guernsey were fifty-year-old Samuel Toms and twenty-four-year-old Alfred Rosser, who in August 1870 received terms of seven and five years respectively for burglary.[236]

Between 1870 and the end of our period, the Royal Court handed down two or three penal servitude sentences each year. All except one were given to men.[237] They were given for serious offences similar to those for

---

[230] The website convictrecords.com.au lists arrivals of individual transportees in Australia. Arrival in Australia can only be confirmed for two Guernsey convicts after 1857: Thomas Geake, sentenced to life for the manslaughter of his wife in 1861 and Nicholas Melhuish, sentenced to ten years for arson in 1863 (2.12.1861, 6.2.1863, GG, *Crime*, vol. 37).

[231] *Billet*, 25.5.1870.

[232] *Billet*, 15.6.1870.

[233] O in C, 19.7.1870.

[234] 'Sentenced to be banished from this Bailiwick to undergo penal servitude for xxx years under the discipline prescribed by United Kingdom legislation'.

[235] Note, however, that the Royal Court continued to treat themselves to dinners at Crown expense each time a person was sentenced to penal servitude until 1881, notwithstanding that these dinners supposedly marked the issue of sentences entailing forfeiture (GG, *Mémoires de la Cour Royale*).

[236] 13.8.1870, GG, *Crime*, vol. 41.

[237] For the exception, see n. 67, above.

which criminals had earlier been sentenced to transportation. The maximum penal servitude sentence handed down by Guernsey's Court in this period was twenty years, which was given in some manslaughter cases. The next step down was ten years, then seven, then five. In 1891, Westminster's fifth Penal Servitude Act reduced the minimum term to three years, and Guernsey replicated this in its 1892 *Loi portant modification à la Loi relative à la Servitude Pénale*.[238] From this point onwards, terms of five and three years preponderated.

As had previously been the case with transportees, the costs of all Guernsey prisoners undergoing penal servitude were paid by the Westminster government from the moment they entered a British prison. This remained the position until 1929. In this year, HM Treasury resolved that Guernsey should henceforth bear the costs of insular convicts undergoing penal servitude in England on the precedent that the States had agreed in 1928 to pay the costs of youths sentenced to English Borstals. After a period of negotiation between Treasury, Home Office, States and HM Receiver General, it was agreed in September 1929 that the maintenance costs of local convicts sent to English gaols should in future be borne by Guernsey's Crown revenues. The arrangement was backdated to 1 April 1929.[239]

---

[238] O in C, 26.11.1892. The 1891 Penal Servitude Act also formally authorised (for the first time) the imprisonment under penal servitude in England, under the same terms as persons so sentenced in England, of convicts sentenced to penal servitude in the Channel Islands.
[239] Home Office to HM Receiver General, 2.8.1929; Receiver General to Home Office, 28.8.1929; Treasury to Home Office, 9.9.1929, NA, T 161/694/7.

Plates 44–55. Guernsey convicts sentenced to penal servitude in England
NG-PR/1/D/5/2, Dorset History Centre, Dorchester[240]

[240] Local prisons in the south of England were used as staging-posts for Guernsey prisoners bound for convict prisons elsewhere in the country. Many of them transited through Dorchester Prison, which kept photographs of all inmates admitted to the prison from 1887.

Banishment and other forms of ejection

Banishment ranked high in the scale of penal severity and was only used with prisoners tried on indictment. In the period covered by this chapter, it was used on about forty occasions, mainly with men, usually in cases of aggravated thefts or serious assaults, and always as a complement to a period of local imprisonment. Banishment could be for life, but the most common sentence between 1845 and 1929 was six years.[241]

Until the mid-nineteenth century, banishment was used with both natives and non-natives. After Peter Stafford Carey's installation as Bailiff in 1845, its use against natives declined and in time petered out altogether. The last banishment of a native occurred in 1851, when St Peter Port-born Joseph Berger was sentenced to three months' imprisonment and six years' banishment for burglary.[242] As in the previous period, premature return from banishment was treated as a crime. Berger himself returned twice. On each return, he was imprisoned (for eight days and one month respectively) and then re-ejected to serve the rest of his term.[243]

The final use of banishment in our period occurred in 1915, when a Jerseyman was sentenced to five months' hard labour and three years' banishment as a punishment for burglary.[244] After this time, banishment seems to have been abandoned as a penal sanction, although there was never any statutory repeal of the Court's power to banish.

More common than sentences of banishment were orders given to offenders to deposit bail against their future good conduct or leave the island. As noted in Chapter 6, this practice had originated without statutory foundation in the mid-1700s and was used as a sanction for summary offences. During the eighty-five years covered by this chapter, a total of 1,329

[241] There were just two instances of perpetual banishment in this period: of an Englishman for burglary in 1870, and a Frenchman for theft and forgery in 1913 (29.1.1870, GG, *Crime*, vol. 40; 8.11.1913, GG, *Crime*, vol. 55).
[242] 17.5.1851, GG, *Crime*, vol. 33.
[243] 21.5.1853, 15.10.1853, GG, *Crime*, vol. 34.
[244] 16.10.1915, GG, *Crime*, vol. 56.

orders to find bail or leave were issued by the Court, invariably as an adjunct to a fine or prison sentence.

In the previous period, orders to find bail or leave had sometimes been used with natives and issued merely on the suspicion or anticipation of wrongdoing. After the arrival of Peter Stafford Carey, the Court only issued such orders to non-natives, and in respect of offences duly proven. In 1856, *la Loi relative à l'Application des Peines* limited the sum which could be exacted by way of bail to a maximum of one-half of the maximum fine for the offence committed, and restricted the term of exile offenders could be obliged to serve to a maximum of one year.[245] The law also formally made returning before the end of a prescribed term a crime punishable by up to one month's imprisonment.

The use of orders to find bail or leave was particularly popular with the Court in the early decades of our period. Thereafter, their use gradually diminished. In the quinquennium 1920–4, there were a total of just five orders to find bail or leave. The very last I have found dates from March 1925. It concerned a Frenchman convicted of stealing a suit who was sentenced to one month's imprisonment and ordered to find bail in the sum of £20 or leave the island for a year.[246] Henry Casey, sworn in as Police Court Magistrate in September 1925, issued no further such orders.[247] The Royal Court's power to issue orders to find bail or leave, like its power to banish, was never statutorily repealed.

Bind overs

The issue of orders to find bail or leave should not be confused with bind overs proper. These were modelled on the power exercised by English JPs and

---

[245] The limitation on sums exacted by way of bail did not apply to offences such as theft and assault which were not subject to any maximum fine.

[246] 24.3.1925, GG, *Crime*, vol. 58.

[247] Casey did occasionally recommend the deportation of foreign nationals (see, for instance, 16.12.1925, GG, *Crime*, vol. 58), but this was done under the 1922 *Loi portant Réglementation sur l'Admission et l'Enregistrement des Etrangers* which allowed the Court to recommend that the Lieutenant Governor use his powers under the law to deport foreign nationals convicted of a criminal offence.

Judges to require a person to enter into recognisances, with or without sureties, to keep the peace or be of good behaviour for a set term. They were adopted in the late eighteenth century to replace the action for *trêves* but were not commonly used until Peter Stafford Carey's appointment as Bailiff in 1845. Over the course of our four sample quinquennia, bind overs were used in about one-tenth of Police Court cases. In 37 per cent of cases, they were added to a fine or prison sentence, and in the remaining 63 per cent they were used on their own. Some two-thirds of bind overs were secured by a promissory oath, and one-third by a pecuniary surety. The duration of orders and sums to be deposited were governed by the 1856 *Loi relative à l'Application des Peines* in the same way as orders to find bail or leave. After the 1870s, it became standard practice to make a pecuniary bind over formally exchangeable for a prison term (or an extra prison term if the bind over were already an adjunct to a gaol sentence). Thus in 1883 Mark Smith's four-week gaol sentence for assaulting his wife was complemented by an order to deposit £5 against his good behaviour for three months or serve an extra two weeks in prison.[248] After Henry Casey's installation as Police Court Magistrate in 1925, the use of bind overs increased, though Casey followed standard English practice in deploying them.

Imprisonment

The period dealt with by this chapter saw imprisonment at its height as a punishment for crime. As noted above, over half of criminal cases across our four quinquennia incurred a carceral sentence.[249] Local imprisonment as a sanction for crime was at its all-time peak between the 1850s and 1880s, when around two-thirds of those convicted by the Royal Court were sentenced to terms in the town gaol. Thereafter, it gradually declined, and, by 1920–4, the proportion of offenders given gaol terms had fallen to 39 per

---

[248] 21.7.1883, GG, *Crime*, vol. 44.

[249] About 4 per cent of these sentences provided for detention in an English convict prison or reformatory and a further 2 per cent in one of Guernsey's Hospitals.

cent. This paralleled a decline in the use of imprisonment over broadly the same period in England and Wales.[250]

Local prison sentences remained short throughout our period. Just under two-thirds were for terms of three weeks or less, with the remaining third mainly for one to two months, and only 5 per cent for more than two months. Until the early 1900s, most sentences recorded in crime registers specified a portion to be spent at hard labour and/or a portion in solitary confinement. After 1900, references to solitary confinement were dropped, and it became usual to categorise the entire sentence as being at 'hard labour' (whatever the reality behind prison walls).

Fines

In 23 per cent of cases determined by the Court in our quinquennia (other than prosecutions under Ordinances or *causes en adjonction*), the guilty party was punished by a fine.[251] The majority of fines were levied in the Police Court, where the offences most likely to incur such a punishment were minor assaults and disorderly conduct. The majority of Police Court fines were small. In the 1860s, the commonest fine was 2s 6d. This rose to 7s 6d in the early 1900s, and 10s by the 1920s. In 86 per cent of cases, offenders were punished by fining alone, and in a further 13 per cent of cases, offenders were additionally issued with a bind over or an order to find bail or leave.

Novel sentencing options

The end of our period saw three major sentencing innovations. These were 'first offender' disposals, blacklisting and probation. The first came into being with the passage in 1896 of *la Loi relative aux Personnes accusées de Crime pour la Première Fois*.[252] Based on Westminster's 1887 First Offenders Act, this gave

---

[250] V. Bailey, 'English prisons, penal culture, and the abatement of imprisonment, 1895–1922', *Journal of British Studies*, 36 (1997), pp. 287, 319.

[251] Excluding semi-civil and Ordinance-related prosecutions.

[252] O in C, 1.8.1896.

both the Police Court and Full Court discretion to release without convicting any first-time offender guilty of any offence punishable by imprisonment, providing the offender agreed to keep the peace and come up for judgment whenever called upon. The law listed as criteria for the exercise of such discretion 'the accused's age, his character, his antecedents, extenuating circumstances, and the slightness of the offence'. Some 5 per cent of offenders who came before the Court in 1900–4 and 1920–4 were released under the terms of the First Offenders Law for offences including petty theft, minor assault, child cruelty, indecent exposure, and even the carnal knowledge of minors.[253]

Blacklisting was introduced in 1920, following an increase in alcohol-related offending after the First World War.[254] This enabled the Court to ban from procuring alcohol for a specified period any person who had been twice convicted under certain sections of the 1856 *Loi relative à l'Application des Peines*, or twice convicted of an offence committed under the influence of alcohol.[255] The maximum penalty for procuring alcohol while blacklisted (or supplying a blacklisted person with alcohol) was a £20 fine or six-month prison sentence. Blacklisting was first used in November 1920, when a thirty-two-year-old war veteran convicted of assault was sentenced to six weeks' imprisonment and blacklisted for a year.[256] The Court issued a further eighty blacklisting orders between 1920 and 1929.[257]

In 1929, probation was introduced to Guernsey by *la Loi relative à la Probation des Délinquants*.[258] Based on Westminster's 1907 Probation Act, this law applied only to offences triable in the Police Court. It repealed the 1896 First Offenders Law and replaced it with similar provisions regarding the release of offenders without convicting, while also allowing the Court to

---

[253] For examples of the last three (in sequence), see 3.1.1901, GG, *Crime*, vol. 52; 25.5.1922, GG, *Crime*, vol. 57; 28.8.1928, GG, *Crime*, vol. 59.

[254] *Loi ayant rapport à la Constitution d'une Liste d'Interdits* (O in C, 11.6.1920). Alderney had had a blacklist since 1913.

[255] The Court was also empowered to blacklist at its discretion any person whose parents, friends, local Douzaines or other official body applied for the individual to be blacklisted.

[256] 25.11.1920, GG, *Crime*, vol. 57; *Star*, 26.11.1920.

[257] Blacklists were kept at the Greffe. Each entry included a copy of the listed person's photograph and details as to name, age and duration of listing. These details were circulated to licensed outlets. In 1960, the 1920 law was repealed and replaced by The Intoxicating Liquor (Prohibition Orders) (Guernsey) Law.

[258] O in C, 5.11.1929.

place such offenders under probation for up to three years, during which they were obliged to observe certain conditions set by the Court (usually relating to residence and alcohol consumption).[259] Probation entailed supervision by a Probation Officer whose job it was to monitor adherence to the conditions and, more generally, to 'advise, assist, and befriend' those undergoing probation. If an offender was subsequently proven to have broken any of the conditions under which he had been released, the Court could, without further proof of guilt, convict and sentence him for the original offence. In December 1929, Captain George Steele and Mrs Blanche Mahy were sworn in as Guernsey's first Probation Officers.[260]

Conclusion

This conclusion will be limited to a brief assessment of developments in Guernsey's criminal justice system between 1845 and 1929, since a more substantial evaluation will follow in the next pages. It is sufficient to observe that, in assessing improvements to the system, we must distinguish the law as set down on paper and the law as it was experienced by offenders and victims. In terms of the former, progress must be acknowledged as considerable. Criminal procedure was modernised, the rules of evidence were updated, and a number of important substantive laws were passed. In terms of lived experience, a more equivocal conclusion is in order. There were undoubtedly improvements, not least the more sympathetic treatment of neonaticide and the tempering of disproportionately harsh attitudes to theft. Nevertheless, the personal values of those who operated the system conditioned their exercise of justice, and, in Guernsey, these values remained fundamentally conservative and patriarchal. For offenders, this translated into the prolonged use of archaic punishments such as whipping and banishment and the toleration of pre-Dickensian prison conditions. For victims – in particular female victims – it translated into the persistent downplaying of crimes such

[259] Criteria for the exercise of discretion were the same as those listed in the First Offenders Law, save that they now pertained to all offenders rather than just first-timers.

[260] 3.12.1929, GG, *Ordonnances*, vol. 23; *Star*, 4.12.1929. In force for nearly ninety years, the 1929 Probation Law was finally repealed and replaced by The Probation (Bailiwick of Guernsey) Law 2018.

as child-molestation and wife-beating, as well as victim-blaming in cases of rape. Change in these respects required a wholesale cultural shift, not only in the judiciary but in society at large, and this shift would be another fifty years in coming.

Conclusion

Analysis of the fifty-five crime registers spanning the period between 1680 and 1929 enables us to identify two overarching trends. The first of these is the transition from an essentially 'private' criminal justice system catering for the needs of the individual, to a 'public' system dedicated to enforcing order on behalf of the community. The second is the progressive anglicisation of Guernsey's criminal law. The former might be said to embody the social history aspect of this study, and the latter the legal history aspect. This Conclusion will concentrate on an analysis of these two trends, and begin with a brief discussion of the statistics.

Figure 7. Criminal cases per decade, 1680–1929

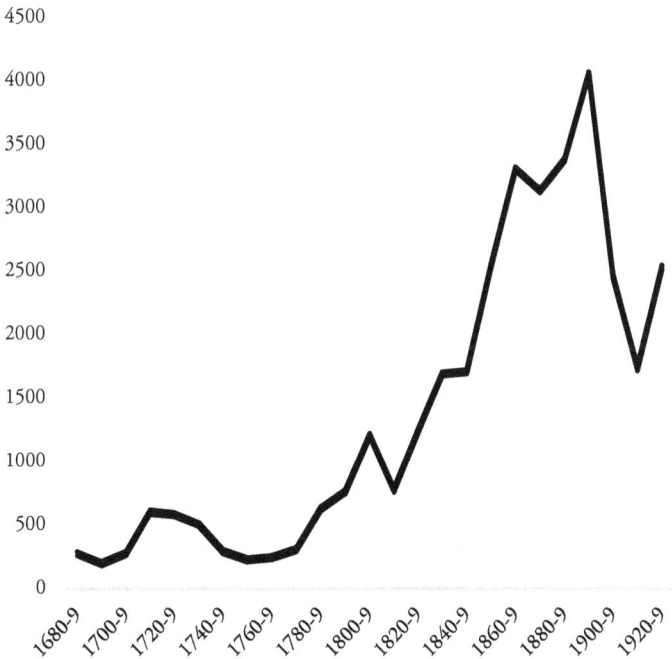

Figure 7 depicts in graphic form changes in the numbers of criminal cases determined by Guernsey's Royal Court in each of the twenty-five decades covered by this study. In the opening period, 1680–1764, the average number of cases was fairly stable at thirty-seven annually, with the graph showing random fluctuations but no definite trend.[1] A sustained upward movement is only discernible from the late 1770s, but by the 1790s, the Court was dealing with an average of seventy-eight cases per year, and in the following decade with 122 cases a year. After a short-lived fall coinciding with economic depression and emigration in the post-Napoleonic period, the trajectory continued upwards, reaching more than 250 cases per year by the 1850s and peaking at more than 400 in the decade 1890–9. A decline then set in with the turn of the century, which was deepened by the departure of young men in World War I, causing numbers to fall to an annual average of 175 in the decade 1910–19. With the return of demobilised servicemen in 1918/19, crime figures rebounded, and by the final decade of our period, the average annual number of cases had risen to 255.

Royal Court records from the late 1600s and early 1700s show that, after the prolonged turbulence of the Reformation and Civil War period, society had settled into a relatively relaxed state. The day-to-day maintenance of order was largely left to parochial Constables, who disciplined their co-parishioners in a face-to-face manner, defusing situations before they got out of hand, separating belligerents, issuing warnings, sometimes also using the parish stocks. This translated into low numbers of summary prosecutions, which in the period 1680–1764 accounted for barely one-tenth of the Royal Court's criminal business. Aside from a tiny number of serious crimes, the rest of the Court's criminal work was equally divided between prosecutions under regulatory Ordinances and actions *en adjonction*.

The low number of summary prosecutions had an effect on the form of Court proceedings. Writing about the late-sixteenth-century Royal Court, Arthur Eagleston drew attention to what he called 'the extraordinary fluidity of the island system of law and legal procedure', contrasting Guernsey's laxity with the 'strict rules of procedure' in English courts.[2] Whether this was an entirely accurate portrayal of Guernsey's Court (or even of English courts) in the late 1500s is a moot point, but my own study has shown that, far from being 'fluid', criminal procedure in the late 1600s and early 1700s was highly formalistic, with 90 per cent of cases requiring multiple sittings.

---

[1] Minor upswings in the first 100 years generally arose from bursts of higher than usual Ordinance-related prosecutions.

[2] A.J. Eagleston, *The Channel Islands under Tudor Government, 1485–1642* (Cambridge, 1949), pp. 156, 157.

This situation began subtly to change in the last third of the eighteenth century, as the number of summary prosecutions rose at the expense of other types of action. The reasons for this increase were complex. At a purely local level, the increase was influenced by mounting immigration, rising urbanisation and growing social inequality. However, change was also more generally in the air. Vic Gatrell has described a 'transformation in perceptions of criminality' all over the British Isles in the years after 1780. A multiplicity of factors – industrialisation, the Revolution in France, unrest at home – combined to engender what Gatrell termed 'a mounting disciplinary assault' on the lower ranks, who were felt to threaten 'dominant and newly articulated definitions of order.'[3] Something of this change in attitudes was undoubtedly transmitted to Guernsey.

From the 1780s onwards, the formalism of earlier decades was progressively less in evidence. Idiosyncratic innovations such as orders to find bail or leave were introduced and ancient practices such as abjuration resurrected to help manage the increasing volume of prosecutions. In the 1820s and 1830s, the Police Court came into existence to expedite summary business. In the 1850s, a town police force was established to clamp down on popular misbehaviour. By this point, summary prosecutions accounted for four-fifths of criminal business, and actions *en adjonction* were all but extinct. In functional terms, the criminal justice system had turned from a dispute-resolution service for the few into a tool for the control of the many. The drive to manage all forms of misbehaviour continued unabated for the next fifty years. Ultimately, with an average of more than 400 prosecutions annually in the 1890s, the pursuit of petty deviance reached a peak – only to fall away sharply after 1900.

Why, we may ask, did prosecutions drop when Guernsey's population went on rising? Gatrell and other historians have highlighted a similar decline in England and Wales, for which many reasons have been identified. On the side of the police and judiciary, there was a distinct decline in the propensity to prosecute very trivial offences. This was matched on the side of the populace by a downturn in the propensity to offend, which, some speculate, may partly have been caused by the deterrent effect of the police, whose intervention people learned to pre-empt by not engaging (at least publicly) in

[3] V.A.C. Gatrell, 'Crime, authority and the policeman-state', in F.M.L. Thompson (ed.), *The Cambridge Social History of Britain, 1750–1950*, 3 vols (Cambridge, 1990), 3, p. 244.

problem behaviours. A major role is also thought to have been played by schools, churches, temperance associations and youth organisations like the Boys' Brigade, which collectively inculcated notions of Victorian 'respectability' into the lower ranks.[4] Rising standards of living also came into play, and in Guernsey's case, these owed much to the flourishing early-twentieth-century horticultural industry. With an increasing proportion of the island's population now aspiring to respectability and possessed of the means to achieve it, the pattern which set in at the turn of the century was to endure until at least the 1950s.[5]

The second major trend identified in our opening paragraph concerned anglicisation. In 1680, *L'Approbation des Lois*, validated by Order in Council of 1583, was held to be the basis of insular law. Comprising just twenty-seven pages in printed form, it consisted of a brief survey of Guillaume Terrien's 1574 commentary on Norman law, specifying what did or did not accord with local law and usage.[6] Terrien's commentary was divided into sixteen sections, only one of which was devoted to criminal law. This section, based largely on French royal legislation and decisions of the Norman *Parlement*, focused primarily on procedure. Guernsey's response to it occupied just four pages of *L'Approbation*, and central to this response was the blanket endorsement of Terrien's account of procedure.

At the start of our period, this translated into a fairly scrupulous observance of French criminal procedure, but a necessarily looser approach to substantive law. Here, however, Guernsey did not greatly differ from neighbouring Normandy, where, as far as substantive criminal law was concerned, courts practised what Professor Zoë Schneider has called a 'bricolage of justice' comprising elements of custom and royal legislation, together with case precedents and equity, and – the ubiquitous gap-filler –

---

[4] For discussions of all these factors, see V.A.C. Gatrell, 'The decline of theft and violence in Victorian and Edwardian England', in V.A.C. Gatrell, B. Lenman & G. Parker, *Crime and the Law: The Social History of Crime in Western Europe since 1500* (London, 1980), p. 300; M. Eisner, 'Modernity strikes back? A historical perspective on the latest increase in interpersonal violence (1960–1990)', *International Journal of Conflict and Violence*, 2 (2008), pp. 290, 303–4.

[5] With the exception of the years 1940–5, which, for obvious reasons, were aberrant.

[6] T. Tramailler (ed.), *L'Approbation des Lois, Coutumes, et Usages de l'Île de Guernesey ratifiée au Conseil Privé le 27 Octobre 1583* (Guernsey, 1822); G. Terrien, *Commentaires du Droict Civil tant Public que Privé Observé au Pays & Duché de Normandie* (Rouen, 1574).

Roman law.[7] It was in this last point that Guernsey's Court parted company from its Norman counterparts, because, in Guernsey, the major gaps in criminal law were filled not by Roman law but by English law.

The Court's recourse to English law appears to have been entirely voluntary. The sole external intervention in our period came in the form of the 1690s Orders in Council which effectively aligned Guernsey's treatment of murder and manslaughter with English practice. This alignment, however, required no coercion. Without any explicit instruction to do so, the Royal Court adopted English sentencing practices for manslaughter and even went so far as to use the English term 'manslaughter' in crime registers. The same willingness characterised the Court's early replication of English policy on infanticide and concealment, its adoption of the English concept of felony in the 1720s, and its application of English standards of proof from the 1730s.

The Court's increasing recourse to English law over ensuing decades led to a growing reliance on English legal authorities and English case precedents. By the mid-nineteenth century, this had effectively reversed the judiciary's orientation from France to England. So thorough-going was the shift that, in 1847, Court members freely admitted to the Royal Commissioners that, while pre-Revolutionary French jurists might still occasionally be consulted on procedural matters, 'Russell and Archbold' were now their principal guides as to 'criminality and the nature of offences'.[8]

By this stage, Guernsey's criminal practice was essentially in a transitional stage. It comprised an amalgam of survivals from the French and Norman past, idiosyncratic insular innovations, and, to an increasing extent, the application of English case law without the accompanying statutory underpinnings. This disturbed the Commissioners, and as the obvious remedy, they proposed the adoption of a criminal code based on English law, and the assimilation of criminal procedure to English norms.

It did not take long for the Commissioners' proposals regarding procedure to be adopted. Peter Stafford Carey, an English barrister appointed Bailiff in

---

[7] Z.A. Schneider, *The King's Bench: Bailiwick Magistrates and Local Governance in Normandy, 1670–1740* (Woodbridge, 2008), pp. 96, 103, 105, 160.

[8] *Second Report of the Commissioners Appointed to Inquire into the State of the Criminal Law in the Channel Islands: Guernsey* (London, 1848), p. 10. The works referred to were W.O. Russell, *A Treatise on Crimes and Indictable Misdemeanours*, 2 vols (London, 1819) and J.F. Archbold, *Summary of the Law relating to Pleading and Evidence in Criminal Cases* (London, 1822).

1845 with a brief to reform the system, had already identified the anomalies he wished to tackle, and soon after his installation he set about adjusting criminal procedure to the English norms with which he was familiar. In a series of laws between the late 1840s and mid-1860s, Carey removed most vestiges of ancient French procedure, such that by the end of his tenure, just a shadow of these remained.

Carey, however, eschewed the Commissioners' suggestion of a criminal code based on English law. This was not because Carey was opposed to English law, but because, for reasons of his own, he was wary of substantive enactments. In this respect, it is significant that his one major venture into substantive criminal law, the 1856 *Loi relative à l'Application des Peines*, was based on Westminster's 1824 Vagrancy Act and various 1840s English Summary Jurisdiction and Police Acts. Carey moreover made heavy use of English authorities in his Court work and encouraged other Court members to do likewise.

Guernsey's enactment of its own substantive criminal laws only tentatively began in late Victorian times, under the stewardship of Law Officers and Bailiffs such as Edward Chepmell Ozanne and Arthur Bell, who were troubled by legislative lacunae in respect of sexual offences. Unsurprisingly, these lawyers sought English models for the criminal laws they drafted, which were all directly based on English statutes.

Two further major steps towards anglicisation occurred in 1915 and 1925. In 1915, ex-Metropolitan policeman Edwin Green was appointed Inspector of the States' Police. Green took over the duty of bringing cases to Court, and – as Magistrate Henry Casey later pointed out – Inspector Green 'had a knowledge of English criminal law, and so he would frame a charge after the English fashion.'[9] In 1925, Casey (an English barrister fresh from London) assumed sole responsibility for the Police Court, without so much as a Law Officer to guide him. With charges already framed in English terms, Casey based his judgments not on local custom and precedent, of which he

---

[9] 'Evidence given before the Privy Council Committee on Proposed Reforms in the Channel Islands, Guernsey, September 1946', p. 217 (Royal Court Library, IA). Green had experience of prosecuting in England, where, although private prosecutions of criminal offences still remained possible, some 80 per cent of criminal prosecutions were now initiated and carried forward by the police (B.S. Godfrey, *Crime in England, 1880–1945: The Rough and the Criminal, the Policed and the Incarcerated* (Abingdon, 2014), p. 37).

knew little, but on English law, which he knew well. His approach encompassed not only assault and theft, which had never been the subject of local statutory enactments, but also many of the offences under the 1856 *Application des Peines* Law whose penalties were now out of date and inadequate. In his evidence to the 1946 Privy Council Committee on Proposed Reforms in the Channel Islands, Casey stated unequivocally, 'the Police Court deals with charges that are drawn up on English lines always ... I only convict ... on a charge that is based on English law ... I really deal in English criminal law and nothing else, except insofar as I am administering the Guernsey law laid down in Ordinances or Orders in Council.'[10] Elsewhere in his evidence, however, Henry Casey observed that there were only 'very few instances where a special Order in Council has been passed to deal with a particular crime,' which left almost all of the major offences undefined.[11] The full extent of the local legislative deficit was spelled out in an exchange between a Committee member and HM Comptroller W.P. Doyle:

> Q. You could not say what is larceny? – A. No
> Q. What is housebreaking? – A. No
> Q. What is murder? – A. No
> Q. Are none of these things defined? – A. No.[12]

Pressed on whether these local lacunae meant that English law did after all govern Guernsey's justice system, Henry Casey answered 'that is the difficulty, Sir; it does and it does not.' Although, technically, English law did not run in the island, 'if you have a murder trial here, you will find that all the English authorities have been quoted as if English law did run here, and you will find that the English Common Law does run in criminal trials for the simple reason that English decisions are enforced here.'[13] This was clearly unsatisfactory, and one matter on which both Doyle and Casey were agreed

---

[10] 'Evidence given before the Privy Council Committee on Proposed Reforms', p. 218.
[11] *Ibid.*, p. 217.
[12] *Ibid.*, p. 212.
[13] *Ibid.*, p. 218.

was that Guernsey's criminal law would soon have to be made the subject of statutory enactments.[14]

Work on this task began soon after the visit of the Privy Council Committee. In 1949, a Blackmail Law was passed, and in 1950 a Currency Offences Law. At first, enactments were well-spaced, proceeding slowly through the 1958 Larceny Law, the 1965 Homicide Law and the 1979 Criminal Justice Law. The 1980s then saw an acceleration in tempo, with the 1982 Summary Offences Law, the 1983 Theft Law, the 1983 Sexual Offences Law, and the 1983 Domestic Violence Law all ratified within the space of a few months. Further criminal legislation followed in ensuing decades.

What all these laws had in common was that, like the Edwardian ones, they were based on English statutes. Indeed, this was made increasingly inevitable by the fact that post-war Advocates, Law Officers and legal draftsmen were primarily English-qualified, and the English system was the one with which they were all most familiar.[15] The Royal Commissioners of 1847 would not have been displeased. It might have taken 150 years for Guernsey to embrace English criminal law, but by the early twenty-first century, the Commissioners' chief recommendation had been all but accomplished.

Compared with the situation fifty, one hundred or two hundred years earlier, this development has undoubtedly been to the benefit of those experiencing Guernsey's criminal justice system. However, as the Scottish historian aptly observed, 'the law draws physical boundaries in geographical space, shaping and giving identity to that space'.[16] Any role Guernsey's criminal law might have played in sustaining a distinctive insular identity has now disappeared. Guernsey's civil law, more deeply rooted in its Norman substrate, must now bear that burden alone.

---

[14] *Ibid.*, pp. 210, 217.

[15] At the time of writing, however, candidates for the Guernsey Bar must still complement their British qualifications with Caen University's *Certificat d'Etudes Juridiques Françaises et Normandes*. This essentially covers civil law.

[16] Introduction, n. 3.

Appendix 1

Bailiffs, 1680–1929

A name in **bold** indicates that the Bailiff was previously a Jurat
A name in *italics* indicates that the Bailiff was previously HM Procureur
Ages are rounded up to the nearest year (this applies also to Appendices 2 and 3)

Name	Year of appointment	Age at appointment	Length of tenure
Edmund Andros (Lieutenant Governor 1704-6)	1674	37	39 years
Jean De Sausmarez	1714	unknown	14 years
Josué Le Marchant	1728	42	24 years
Eléazar Le Marchant (brother of the above)	1752	63	6 years
Samuel Bonamy	1758	50	13 years
William Le Marchant	1771	50	29 years
Robert Le Marchant (son of the above)	1800	45	10 years
Peter De Havilland (previously an Advocate)	1810	63	11 years
Daniel De Lisle Brock	1821	58	21 years
John Guille	1842	54	2 years
Peter Stafford Carey (English barrister)	1845	42	38 years
John Utermarck	1883	65	9 months
Edgar MacCulloch	1884	76	11 years
Thomas Godfrey Carey	1895	63	7 years
Henry Giffard	1902	64	6 years
William Carey (previously an Advocate)	1908	55	7 years
Edward Chepmell Ozanne	1915	63	7 years
Havilland De Sausmarez (English barrister)	1922	61	7 years
Arthur Bell	1929	61	6 years

Appendix 2

Law Officers, 1680–1929

1. Procureurs

A name in **bold** indicates that the Procureur was previously Comptroller
A name in *italics* indicate that the Procureur became Bailiff

Name	Sworn in	Age at appointment
Josué Tramalier (Tramailler) (previously served as Greffier)	14 Sep 1667	unknown
Elizée Roland (previously served as Greffier)	14 Jun 1701	c.46
William Le Marchant (also Receiver while serving as Procureur; subsequently elected Jurat)	4 Feb 1708	27
Jean De Sausmarez (also Receiver while serving as Procureur)	8 Dec 1744	38
Hirzel Le Marchant (son of Bailiff William Le Marchant, and brother of Bailiff Robert Le Marchant)	17 May 1774	22
Thomas De Sausmarez (nephew of Bailiff William Le Marchant, and son of Procureur Jean De Sausmarez)	2 Nov 1793	37
Charles De Jersey	21 Aug 1830	47
John De Havilland Utermarck	12 Jul 1851	33
Thomas Godfrey Carey	18 Aug 1883	51
Edward Chepmell Ozanne	14 Dec 1895	43
Arthur William Bell	5 Feb 1916	48
Herbert Le Patourel	3 Oct 1929	54

2. Comptrollers

A name in *italics* indicates that the Comptroller became Procureur
A name in **bold** indicates that the Comptroller became a Jurat

Name	Sworn in	Age at appointment
Daniel Carey	14 Sep 1667	unknown
Daniel Painsec	26 Sep 1682	unknown
Elizée Roland (previously served as Greffier)	27 May 1699	c.44
William De Beauvoir	14 Jun 1701	32
Henry Mauger	19 Feb 1724	28
Josué Le Marchant	19 Jan 1745	22
Eléazar Le Marchant (nephew of Comptroller Josué Le Marchant, step-son of Bailiff William Le Marchant)	6 Jul 1765	22
Thomas De Sausmarez (son of HM Procureur Jean De Sausmarez, nephew of Bailiff William Le Marchant)	12 Jul 1777	21
Jean Carey Métivier (previously served as Prévôt)	2 Nov 1793	35
Pierre Coutart	26 Nov 1796	75
John Condamine	5 Aug 1797	34
Peter Le Cocq	16 Jun 1821	47
Charles De Jersey	16 Nov 1822	39
John Thomas De Sausmarez (son of HM Procureur Thomas De Sausmarez)	21 Aug 1830	39
John De Havilland Utermarck	11 Sep 1845	27
Peter Jeremie	9 Nov 1861	54
James Gallienne	14 Oct 1871	53
Edward Chepmell Ozanne	8 Dec 1877	25
Arthur William Bell	14 Dec 1895	27
William Henry Foote	15 Feb 1916	31
Herbert Le Patourel	23 Oct 1920	45
Ambrose Sherwill	3 Oct 1929	39

Appendix 3

Advocates, 1680–1929

Name	Sworn in	Education	Other offices
Etienne Agenor	unknown		
Pierre Gosselin	unknown		
Josué Tramalier (Tramailler)	unknown		Greffier, Comptroller, Procureur
Elizée Roland	22 Jan 1677		Greffier, Comptroller, Procureur
Daniel Painsec	28 Apr 1679		Comptroller
Pierre Henry	28 Oct 1679		
Henry De Jersey	28 Oct 1679		
Jean Bonamy	27 Oct 1690		Greffier
Josué Priaulx	1694		
Nicolas De Jersey (*fils* Henry)	31 Oct 1702		
Aaron Guillaume	28 Oct 1710		
Jean Pallot	28 Oct 1710		
Jean Hubert	28 Mar 1714		
Thos Tramalier (Tramailler)	25 Apr 1716		
Pierre Coutart	5 Jul 1718		
Richard Bailleul	27 May 1721		
Jean De Sausmarez	23 Jul 1726		Receiver, Procureur
Jean Bonamy	27 Oct 1726		
Jean Andros	14 May 1740		Jurat
Pierre Coutart (*fils* Pierre)	5 Apr 1756		Sergeant
John Cornelius	9 Jul 1764		Sergeant
Eléazar Le Marchant	9 Jul 1764		
Matthew De Sausmarez	9 Jul 1764	Oxford	
Peter De Havilland	17 Apr 1767		Jurat, Bailiff
Peter Hubert	1 Jan 1774		

Thomas Andros	26 Aug 1775		
John Bonamy	15 Apr 1776		Greffier
Thomas De Sausmarez	12 Jul 1777		Comptroller, Procureur
John Carey Métivier	9 Jun 1780		Prévôt, Comptroller
John Jeremie	6 Oct 1794		
Peter Le Cocq	6 Oct 1794		Comptroller, Jurat
John Condamine	15 Oct 1796		Comptroller
Charles De Jersey	30 Mar 1805		Comptroller, Procureur
John Métivier	6 Oct 1808		
John Thomas De Sausmarez	24 Jun 1815		Comptroller, Jurat
John Jeremie	4 Aug 1815	Dijon	Gov., Sierra Leone
Richard Hicks Champion	9 Apr 1820		
Robert MacCulloch	3 Jan 1824	Caen	
Hilary Ollivier Carré	6 Jul 1824	Caen	Jurat, Greffier
Thomas Falla	6 Jul 1824		
Peter Bredthafft	16 Sep 1826	Caen	
George Radford	30 Oct 1827	Caen	
Peter Jeremie	8 Aug 1829		Comptroller
Henry Tupper	5 Jun 1830	Rennes	Jurat
James Gallienne	12 May 1838	Caen	Comptroller, Greffier
Charles Guille	28 Jul 1838		
John Utermarck	27 Apr 1839	Caen	Comptroller, Procureur, Bailiff
Thomas Godfrey Carey	17 Jun 1854	Caen	Procureur, Bailiff
Peter Le Ber	27 Apr 1861	Caen	
Edward Chepmell Ozanne	13 Apr 1874	Caen	Comptroller, Procureur, Bailiff

Amelius Corbin	13 Apr 1874	Caen	
William Moullin	13 Apr 1874	Oxford, barrister	
William Carey	8 Jul 1875	Caen	Bailiff
William Lainé	8 Jul 1875	Rennes	
Theophilus De Mouilpied	24 Feb 1876	Caen	
Cecil Carey	5 Oct 1885	Caen	
Arthur Bell	10 Jul 1890	Caen	Comptroller, Procureur, Bailiff
Wyndham Peel	8 Feb 1896	Cambridge, barrister	
Harold Randell	5 Feb 1898	Rennes	
Victor Gosselin Carey	5 Feb 1898	Caen	Receiver, Bailiff
Julius Bishop	9 Jan 1901	Caen	Deputy Greffier, Jurat
Arthur De Sausmarez	26 Oct 1901	Caen	
Hedley Ninnim	7 Nov 1903	Caen	
Herbert Le Patourel	1 Jul 1905	Caen	Comptroller, Procureur
William Foote	20 Jan 1908	Caen	Comptroller
Eugene Carey	14 Mar 1910	Caen	
George Ridgway	1 Apr 1911	Caen, barrister	Comptroller
John Martel	25 Aug 1919	Caen	
Ambrose Sherwill	1 May 1920	Caen, barrister	Comptroller, Procureur, Bailiff
Alan De Jersey Carey	7 Jun 1924	Caen, barrister	
Walter Langlois	18 Jan 1926	Caen	
William Arnold	2 Jul 1927	Caen, barrister	Comptroller, Procureur, Bailiff
Victor M.G. Carey	26 Nov 1927	Caen	

Appendix 4

Hangmen sworn in after 1680

Name	Sworn in	Origin
Etienne Robert	27 Feb 1697	St Andrews, Guernsey
Pierre Marie, alias Le Noury	2 Mar 1717	France
Guillaume Fritau	21 May 1737	France
Jacques Le Large	1740 or 1741	France
John Whitehead	16 Jul 1763	England
Jean Marie Chapelle	7 Jun 1781	Dinan, France
John Christie	12 Nov 1781	Ireland
Pierre Suzanne	18 Oct 1783	Havre de Grâce, France
Pierre Froment	13 Dec 1788	France
Jean Marche	2 May 1789	Clermont, France
Joseph Godefroi Le Cognac	2 May 1791	Ile de Bréhat, France
Louis Daudeville	13 Feb 1792	Bayeux, France
Louis Hochet	13 Oct 1821	France
Louis Le Sauxnier	4 May 1822	Saint-Cyr, France
Louis Hochet (same as 1821)	10 May 1823	France
Jean Baptiste Mendon	28 Sep 1827	France
John Rooks	16 Oct 1830	St Peter Port, Guernsey

Appendix 5

Principal Bar Ordinances, 1906–48

In addition to the French and British academic qualifications specified in these Ordinances, candidates for the Guernsey Bar were required to pass an examination in Guernsey law and procedure and to be British subjects who had lived in Guernsey for at least five years since the age of ten.

Ord, 3.2.1906 – either
(a) a BA degree from a British university, or
(b) a *Baccalauréat-ès-Lettres* from a French university
plus either
(a) a *Licence en Droit* from any French university, or
(b) a *Diplôme de Docteur-ès-Lois* from Caen University

Ord, 29.10.1938 – either
(a) a certificate of admission as an Utter Barrister of an English Inn of Court
plus *un Diplôme de Bachelier en Droit* from a French university, or
(b) a certificate of admission as a Solicitor of the Supreme Court of England
plus *un Diplôme de Bachelier en Droit* from a French university

Ord, 3.8.1946 – either
(a) a certificate of admission as an Utter Barrister of an English Inn of Court
plus a certificate from a French university showing that the candidate had successfully passed the first year of a *Licence en Droit* or held *un Diplôme de Bachelier en Droit*, or
(b) a certificate of admission as a Solicitor of the Supreme Court of England
plus a certificate from a French university showing that the candidate had successfully passed the first year of a *Licence en Droit* or held *un Diplôme de Bachelier en Droit*

Ord, 3.7.1948 – either
(a) a certificate of admission as an Utter Barrister of an English Inn of Court
plus the *Certificat d'Etudes Juridiques Françaises et Normandes* from Caen University or a *Diplôme de Bachelier en Droit* from any French university, or
(b) a certificate of admission as a Solicitor of the Supreme Court of England
plus the *Certificat d'Etudes Juridiques Françaises et Normandes* from Caen University or a *Diplôme de Bachelier en Droit* from any French university

Appendix 6

Principal recommendations of the 1846 Royal Commission into the State of the Criminal Law in the Channel Islands, with dates of fulfilment

Summarised from *Second Report of the Commissioners Appointed to Inquire into the State of the Criminal Law in the Channel Islands: Guernsey* (London, 1848), pp. xxxix–xlii.

1. Grant Alderney court jurisdiction over minor criminal offences – **1848**
2. Remove the limit on the number of witnesses in criminal trials, and reduce the list of recusable witnesses – **1849**
3. Record in writing the statements of witnesses produced by the police at committal hearings – **1850**
4. Abolish proceedings *au grand criminel* and substitute a *viva voce* trial – **1850**
5. Introduce paid police – partly **1853**; fully **1915**
6. Abolish forfeiture in criminal cases – **1870** (abolition technically only applied to cases of banishment or penal servitude, and not to cases of capital punishment; however, after 1854, there were no cases of capital punishment)
7. De-restrict the number of Advocates and institute regulations for their admission – **1896**
8. Require Jurats to pronounce on guilt or innocence before prescribing a punishment – **c.1900**
9. Abolish the *interrogatoire* – **1923**
10. Appoint a paid magistrate to preside over the Police Court – **1925**
11. Ensure that a prisoner is not tried by the same persons who committed him for trial – **1925** (this was achieved when the new paid Magistrate assumed responsibility for committal proceedings)
12. Allow Full Court trials to be conducted partially in English – **c.1850**
13. Abolish the legislative power of the Royal Court and transfer it to the States – **1948**
14. Remove the Jurats from the States – **1948**
15. Abolish *causes en adjonction* – **1950**
16. Institute a criminal appeal court – **1964**
17. Make the Bailiff sole judge of law – **1964**
18. Align Guernsey's substantive criminal law with English criminal law – **in progress**
19. Introduce jury trial – **never**
20. Make the Bailiff and Jurats Justices of the Peace in order to give them jurisdiction under English Acts of Parliament – **never**

Appendix 7

Offences defined by
Loi relative à l'Application des Peines tant au Criminel qu'en Police Correctionnelle
(O in C, 24.6.1856)

A. Offences liable to a sentence of imprisonment (with or without hard labour and/or solitary confinement on bread and water):

i. *déréglement* (disorderly conduct)
ii. *vagabondage* (a range of 'vagrancy' offences as understood under English law)
iii. cruelty to animals.

i. *déréglement*

This is punishable by up to eight days' imprisonment, in part or in whole with hard labour and/or solitary confinement on bread and water.

The following will be liable to conviction for *déréglement*:

1. beggars found loitering in a public place
2. persons who have employed or encouraged children to beg
3. persons who have behaved in a disorderly or indecent fashion in a public place while drunk
4. persons who have appeared before the Court in a drunken state
5. persons found lying drunk in the open air or on someone else's premises
6. beggars or others without means of subsistence found lying in the open air or on someone else's premises and who have been unable to give a good account of themselves
7. prostitutes who have behaved in a disorderly or indecent fashion in a public place
8. persons purporting to tell fortunes, interpret dreams, or practise witchcraft
9. persons who have disturbed the public peace, especially at night, by making undue noise
10. persons who, or whose families, have fallen chargeable to their parishes while having the means to support themselves and their dependants by working or otherwise

ii. *vagabondage*

This is punishable by up to one month's imprisonment, in part or in whole with hard labour and/or solitary confinement on bread and water.

The following will be deemed guilty of *vagabondage*:

11. persons twice convicted of *déréglement* within a year and a day
12. persons guilty of *déréglement* who violently resisted a constable or other officer during their arrest
13. persons who have entered a building, yard or other enclosed space for an illegal object
14. persons found in possession of files, hooks, picklocks, false keys and other tools for breaking into houses and committing thefts
15. persons found carrying weapons with the intention of committing a criminal offence
16. persons setting up lotteries and other gambling games in streets and other public places
17. persons exposing or distributing images, engravings or printed matter contrary to public morals or religion
18. persons soliciting charitable alms under false pretences
19. persons who neglect or abandon their families and leave them without the means of subsistence
20. persons sent back to their place of legal settlement who return and fall chargeable
21. persons sent away for a certain period because they have been unable to find bail for their good conduct who return before the expiry of the term
22. beggars who use threatening behaviour, enter inhabited dwellings without permission, solicit alms under false pretences, feign injuries or infirmities, or wilfully alter their appearance
23. persons who break public lamps, or the windows of an inhabited dwelling or public building

iii. cruelty to animals (this is left undefined).

B. Offences liable to a fine

The following will be liable to a fine:

24. persons disrupting religious services (fine of up to 40s)
25. persons riding horses or driving vehicles dangerously or with excessive speed (up to 40s)

26. persons offering for sale food which is spoilt or dangerous (up to 40s)
27. persons publicly insulting others (up to 20s)
28. persons allowing mischievous or ferocious animals to wander (up to 20s)
29. persons exciting or not restraining their dogs when attacking or chasing passers-by (up to 20s)
30. persons firing guns in public places (up to 20s)
31. persons letting off fireworks in public places without the permission of the Constables (up to 20s)
32. persons selling spirituous liquors for consumption on the premises to minors under 14 (up to 20s)
33. persons exciting or not restraining their dogs when attacking or chasing other people's animals (up to 10s)
34. persons throwing ordure, stones or other missiles at people's dwellings and buildings, or into their gardens, yards and other enclosures (up to 10s)
35. persons throwing missiles or ordure at other people (up to 10s)
36. persons found drunk in a public place or on private property (up to 5s) (such persons will be deemed guilty of *déréglement* if the offence is repeated within a year and a day)
37. prostitutes who have molested passers-by or others in a public place (up to 5s) (such persons will be deemed guilty of *déréglement* if the offence is repeated within a year and a day).

The law lays down that persons unable to pay fines to which they are sentenced will instead serve prison sentences to be determined, up to certain maxima, by the Court.

The law does not define petty theft or minor physical or sexual assault but explicitly recognises the right of the Police Court to punish them in accordance with *la Loi et Coutume du pays*.

This law was amended in 1878 to add food adulteration and malicious damage to trees or enclosures to the list of offences for which it provided (O in C, 26.3.1878). It was further amended in 1896 to enable the Police Court to order persons convicted of maliciously damaging lamps, windows, fences, hedges, walls, gates, bushes or trees, to pay compensation to the owners of the damaged property in addition to sentencing them to a fine or prison term (O in C, 26.10.1896).

Appendix 8

Homicide cases, 1845–1929

Date	Accused	Victim	Type	Verdict	Sentence
3.1.1854	John Tapner	acquaintance, f	wilful killing	murder	hanging
19.12.1856	Nugent Loughnan	stranger, m	fight	murder	hanging
19.12.1856	Timothy Kelly	stranger, m	fight	murder	hanging
18.11.1856	Daniel Statt	wife	domestic	acquittal	
30.5.1857	Andrew Brehaut	wife	domestic	acquittal	
26.4.1858	Joseph Brouard	acquaintance, f	domestic	acquittal	
16.7.1880	William Kaines	wife	domestic	acquittal	
6.6.1853	William Curran	wife	domestic	manslaughter	life transportation
26.4.1858	Nicolas Brouard	cohabitee	domestic	manslaughter	life transportation
2.12.1861	Thomas Geake	wife	domestic	manslaughter	life transportation
18.3.1890	Edward Hooper	wife	domestic	manslaughter	20 years
18.3.1899	René Trouvé	cohabitee	domestic	manslaughter	20 years
1.8.1854	Luke Lawrence	stranger, m	fight	acquittal	
18.11.1876	Joseph Hammoniaux	acquaintance, m	fight	acquittal	
18.10.1886	Patrick Quin	acquaintance, m	unplanned violence	acquittal	
27.10.1894	David Kaill	acquaintance, m	unplanned violence	acquittal	
7.2.1898	Charles Wilson	acquaintance, m	fight	acquittal	
16.1.1871	Thomas Stevens	stranger, f	unplanned violence	manslaughter	3 months & 6 yrs banishment
11.7.1906	Frenchman	acquaintance, m	fight	manslaughter	20 years
13.7.1914	Guernseyman	acquaintance, m	fight	manslaughter	6 months
6.4.1916	Englishman	acquaintance, m	fight	manslaughter	10 years
13.5.1921	Englishman	acquaintance, m	fight	manslaughter	3 months
25.2.1871	Clarence Macpherson	stranger, m	unplanned violence	unfit to plead	
22.6.1889	Edward Bourke	acquaintance, m	poisoning	acquittal	
27.8.1858	John Woods	acquaintance, m	planned violence	attempted murder	7 yrs transp.
1.11.1920	Guernseyman	wife, son	domestic	attempted wounding	18 months
2.11.1921	Guernseyman	stranger, m	unplanned violence	attempted murder	7 years
30.6.1926	Guernseyman	wife	domestic	attempted murder	7 years
4.4.1894	David Le Lievre	son	neglect	manslaughter	6 months
8.5.1897	Francis Clarke	son	neglect	acquittal	
30.6.1860	Richard Dorey	stranger, f	dangerous driving	manslaughter	2 months
14.11.1928	Guernseyman	stranger, m	dangerous driving	acquittal	
23.11.1928	Guernseyman	stranger, m	dangerous driving	acquittal	

Date	Accused	Victim	Type	Verdict	Sentence
28.9.1850	Elizabeth Jeffrey	baby	infanticide	acquittal	
24.2.1852	Charlotte Simmonds	baby	infanticide	acquittal	
2.2.1866	Susan Harris	baby	infanticide	manslaughter	3 months & 6 yrs banishment
19.10.1901	Violet Gallichan	baby	infanticide	concealment	2 months
31.8.1857	Adeline Godechal	acquaintance, f	fight	acquittal	
25.8.1894	Phoebe Woodland	father	poisoning	attempted murder	2 years
4.4.1894	Theresa Le Lievre	son	neglect	manslaughter	6 months
8.5.1897	Lydia Clarke	son	neglect	manslaughter	6 months
16.6.1900	Maria MacPherson	patient, f	negligence	manslaughter	3 years

Extracted from GG, *Crime*, vols 34–60

The names of offenders after 1900 have been withheld or changed

Appendix 9

Inquests

This short survey is based on the 920 inquests recorded in crime registers over the quinquennia analysed in detail for this book.[1] The first part consists of an examination of the legal and procedural aspect of inquests, the second of a discussion of everyday Court practice.

Legal and procedural

The holding of inquests, known in Guernsey as *levées de corps*, originated in Norman customary law, which stipulated that people who had been killed could not be buried until seen by the judicial authorities.[2] According to Jersey commentator Philippe Le Geyt, this provision was later extended by French jurists to include anyone unexpectedly found dead anywhere.[3] The comprehensive French approach was in due course adopted in the Channel Islands, and by the 1680s, Guernsey's Court was convening two or three inquests each year.

Inquests were essentially an inquiry into possible crime, and it was for this reason that they were recorded in crime registers. If no crime was found to have occurred, the Court would simply give permission for the deceased person to be buried in the normal way. If the verdict was foul play, permission for burial would be accompanied with an order to launch a criminal investigation. If the verdict was suicide (also a crime), the procedure to be followed varied as the period progressed.[4]

---

[1] For the dates of these thirteen quinquennia, see opening paragraphs of Chapters 3, 6 and 9. Unless otherwise stated, statistics cited here are derived from this source.

[2] J.A. Everard (tr), *Le Grand Coutumier de Normandie* (Jersey, 2009), pp. 274–8.

[3] P. Le Geyt, *Les Manuscrits de Philippe Le Geyt, Ecuyer, Lieutenant-Bailli de l'Ile de Jersey, sur la Constitution, les Lois et les Usages de cette Ile*, 4 vols (Jersey, 1846–7), 2, pp. 554–5.

[4] See Chapter 3, pp. 105–6 and Chapter 6, pp. 195–6.

Inquests were conducted by the Ordinary Court, which comprised the Bailiff or Lieutenant Bailiff and a minimum of two Jurats.[5] At least one Law Officer also took part. In the early part of our period, Jurats and Law Officers usually went to view the body *in situ*, where they also took the testimony of witnesses. The final stage of proceedings then took place in the courtroom, where the Law Officer delivered his *conclusions* and the Jurats voted on a verdict, as in a criminal trial. Inquest proceedings were not open to the public, and the deceased's family or friends were expected to pay the costs, which in 1734 stood at 10 *livres tournois* (14s 4d).[6]

From the beginning of our period until the late eighteenth century, the number of witnesses at an inquest was limited to twelve, all of whom gave their testimony on oath. They were usually joined by at least one doctor, who also gave sworn evidence. It was suggested in Chapter 2 that these twelve-man panels might represent a throwback to the Norman *harèle*, or parochial jury of presentment, which had disappeared from Guernsey by the mid-sixteenth century.[7] Early crime registers usually described the witnesses in inquests as *douze hommes* (or *témoins*) *dignes de foi*. Sometimes these *douze hommes* were the local Douzaine, particularly in cases where there were no eye-witnesses, as in 1771, when St Saviours Douzenier Pierre Tourgis was called to give evidence at an inquest on someone found dead in a snowdrift.[8] On other occasions, the twelve men were actual eye-witnesses to the event, such as the twelve soldiers called to testify at the inquest of a murdered fellow soldier in 1738.[9]

---

[5] Just over one-third of all inquests were conducted in the presence of only two Jurats in the period between 1680 and 1929. On most other occasions, three or four Jurats would typically sit with the Bailiff or his Lieutenant. Only a small proportion of inquests were attended by more than seven Jurats: 7 per cent in 1680–1764; 19 per cent in 1765–1844; 1 per cent in 1845–1929. Such well-attended inquests generally involved deaths strongly suspected to have been caused by foul play.

[6] 4.5.1734, GG, *Crime*, vol. 11.

[7] In Jersey, inquests were organised by a court officer known as the Vicomte, who would select a twelve-man jury to accompany him and a Law Officer to view the body, hear witnesses, and then deliver a verdict in court (*First Report of the Commissioners appointed to Inquire into the State of the Criminal Law in the Channel Islands: Jersey* (London, 1847), p. xxxvi).

[8] 5.2.1771, Notebook of Pierre Tourgis, IA, AQ 0712/34.

[9] 23.3.1738, GG, *Crime*, vol. 11.

Procedures in relation to inquests began to change from the late eighteenth century, concurrent with the general deformalisation of process. Change happened slowly and gradually, but by the time the Royal Commissioners visited in 1847, the twelve-witness limit had been lifted, and any person who presented him- or herself with evidence was considered a competent witness. Furthermore, inquests were now funded from Crown revenues, and the Court only viewed corpses *in situ* where a crime was suspected.[10]

Further procedural modifications were introduced in subsequent years. A law of 1850 opened inquests to the public.[11] A law of 1919 transferred the organising function to the Island Police,[12] and the Police Court Magistrate's Law of 1925 delegated the holding of inquests to the new stipendiary, who henceforth examined witnesses and delivered verdicts alone.[13]

Inquests in practice

The three periods into which this book is divided – 1680–1764, 1765–1844 and 1845–1929 – saw increasing numbers of inquests. In the first, there were an average of two inquests a year; in the second, eleven per year; and in the third, thirty-three per year.[14] Three-quarters of these inquests concerned males, and more than four-fifths concerned adults.

In the minority of inquests which concerned children, two-thirds of deaths were attributed to an accident. The two commonest forms of accident to which children succumbed in our period were drowning and burning/scalding. Eighteenth- and nineteenth-century children were left unsupervised to a greater degree than today, and their elders showed little

---

[10] *Second Report of the Commissioners Appointed to Inquire into the State of the Criminal Law in the Channel Islands: Guernsey* (London, 1848), pp. xxii, 84, 155–6, 215–17.

[11] *Loi relative à la Procédure en cas de Félonie et de Levées de Corps*, O in C, 12.12.1850. Some inquests relating to deaths in particularly sensitive circumstances nevertheless continued to be held *in camera*.

[12] *Loi ayant rapport à la Police Salariée pour l'Île Entière*, O in C, 20.12.1919.

[13] *Loi ayant rapport à l'Institution d'un Magistrat en Police Correctionnelle*, O in C, 17.3.1925.

[14] Compared with the present day, this was a high number. The three years 2017–19, saw an average of only twenty inquests per year in a population half as large again as in the 1920s (Royal Court Annual Report, 2019, accessed 14.1.2021 at http://www.guernseyroyalcourt.gg).

awareness of basic precautions which might keep them safe. Wells, pits, ponds, *douits* and other bodies of water were left unfenced, and many children, like two-year-old Mathieu Tostevin in 1822, met their ends by falling into them.[15] Similarly, most dwellings contained unguarded fireplaces, and a significant number of children, like two-year-old Arthur Lowe in 1881, either fell into them or had their clothing catch fire.[16] Other common causes of accidental child deaths were falls from a height (particularly when bird-nesting), kicks from animals, and collisions with carts and carriages.

Just under one-third of child deaths were ascribed to natural causes. The majority of these were doubtless due to childhood infections, but this level of detail was hardly ever given. On the rare occasions when a specific cause was identified, this was usually 'convulsions', which, in most cases, would have been caused by an underlying condition.

Foul play was identified as the cause of death in just 2 per cent of child inquests. Such cases almost always involved infants whose bodies were found in wells, under bushes, on the sea shore, etc. The provenance of these corpses was seldom established, and those who caused their deaths were rarely identified. In one particularly sad case from 1880, investigations into the death of a mother followed the inquest of an infant found buried in a garden in St Peter Port. The mother lived in the house to which the garden belonged, and her identity came to light when she died from complications of childbirth without ever having revealed to anyone that she was pregnant.[17]

Among adults, 38 per cent of unexpected deaths were attributed to accidents, 34 per cent to natural causes, 26 per cent to suicide, and fewer than 1 per cent to foul play. Most adult deaths ascribed to foul play related to the cases of murder and manslaughter detailed in the chapters of this book. Of the 26 per cent of deaths attributed to suicide (a verdict returned exclusively in respect of adults), four-fifths were of males. Suicides were particularly common during the stressful Napoleonic years. Sixteen individuals took their own lives in the quinquennium 1800–4 alone, of whom nine were soldiers.[18] Suicide however affected people from all walks of life. Among members of

---

[15] 21.9.1822, GG, *Crime*, vol. 25. *Douit* was (and is) the Guernsey name for a drainage channel.

[16] 18.10.1881, GG, *Crime*, vol. 43. Arthur and his four-year-old sister had been left alone at their home in St Sampsons. This, again, was not uncommon.

[17] 3.10.1880, 4.10.1880, GG, *Crime*, vol. 43.

[18] 11.1.1800, 14.5.1800, 13.12.1800, 18.5.1801, 20.3.1802, 6.9.1802, 10.3.1803, 29.4.1803, 16.5.1803, 14.6.1803, 17.1.1804, 29.4.1804, 3.7.1804, 1.8.1804, 20.11.1804, 22.12.1804, GG, *Crime*, vol. 21.

the elite who died by their own hand were the clergymen cousins Peter and Henry Dobrée, and siblings De Vic Tupper (a Jurat) and Amelia Brock Tupper, children of Advocate Henry Tupper.[19] In 41 per cent of suicides, hanging was the chosen method; a further 18 per cent were by drowning; 16 per cent were by gunshot, and in 12 per cent, victims cut their own throats or wrists.

Of the 38 per cent of adult deaths attributed to accidents, a majority, like those of children, were due to drowning. Shipwreck victims washed up on Guernsey's beaches accounted for a fairly substantial proportion of these. Multiple inquests were held in the aftermath of the wrecks of the privateer *Success* in 1810, the barque *L'Europe* in 1849, the steamers *Channel Queen* in 1898 and *Saint Malo* in 1915.[20] Other adult victims of drowning were shore-gatherers or inshore fishermen overwhelmed by rip tides or high seas. Yet others were drowned after falling into St Peter Port or St Sampsons harbours. The quays of these harbours were poorly lit, without barriers, and adjacent to well-frequented public houses. Many of those who drowned in the harbours fell into them while intoxicated late at night.[21]

In an era when almost no precautions were taken to ensure workplace safety, many other adult deaths were ascribed to industrial accidents, most frequently on building sites, in timber or flour mills, on the harbour quays, and – particularly – in quarries. In 1861 alone, no fewer than three men died in quarry accidents, all struck by flying debris or crushed in landslides as a result of explosions to loosen stone.[22] No compensation was payable nor States support available to families who lost breadwinners in such accidents at this time.

The remaining third of adult deaths were attributed to natural causes. Female deaths accounted for a greater proportion of these than they did of deaths from accidents or suicide. As was the case with children, detail as to causative illnesses was rarely supplied.

One interesting feature of deaths ascribed to natural causes is that, after the mid-1860s, some 28 per cent of them occurred in one or other of the

---

[19] 18.4.1879, 13.9.1879, GG, *Crime*, vol. 43; 12.1.1892, GG, *Crime*, vol. 47; 31.1.1895, GG, *Crime*, vol. 49.

[20] 24.10.1810, GG, *Crime*, vol. 22; 20.11.1849, GG, *Crime*, vol. 33; 2.2.1898 (and following days), GG, *Crime*, vol. 50; 23.11.1915, GG, *Crime*, vol. 56.

[21] In 1908, the Court specifically drew attention to the lack of barriers around St Sampsons harbour after a forty-year-old was found drowned in it the morning after a Saturday night drinking session at the Mariner's Inn (27.2.1908, GG, *Crime*, vol. 54).

[22] 2.1.1861, GG, *Crime*, vol. 36; 2.5.1861, 3.10.1861, GG, *Crime*, vol. 37.

island's two lunatic asylums. Both asylums were departments of the island's parochial workhouses (the Town Hospital's asylum opened in 1851, and the Country Hospital's in 1882). Crime registers recorded a total of 345 asylum inquests between 1864 (when it became policy to subject all asylum deaths to inquests) and 1929. In the period between the 1880s and 1920s, when both asylums were operating, there were about five or six asylum deaths each year. Against a combined asylum population generally around fifty or sixty, this represented a mortality rate of about ten per cent. The average age of a person dying in the asylums in this period was fifty-five, with 20 per cent of asylum inquests relating to people in their twenties and thirties.

All asylum deaths, save one at the end of our period, were attributed to natural causes without further elaboration, on evidence supplied by the asylums' own medical officers.[23] This evidence was accepted without question by the Court, even though conditions in the asylums were notoriously poor.[24] In at least one instance, the Hospitals' own records belie the evidence supplied to the Court. Minutes of a Town Hospital Committee meeting in 1891 show that a fifty-four-year-old man whose inquest ascribed his death to natural causes had in fact hanged himself from the window bars of his cell.[25]

One historian of coroners' courts in England has suggested that deaths at the bottom of the social order – those of vagrants, prostitutes, drunkards and asylum inmates – were often not considered worth serious probing.[26] This was undoubtedly also true of Guernsey, not only in respect of asylum deaths, but of other deaths attributed to both illness and accidents.

---

[23] The only death not ascribed to natural causes was a suicide which occurred at the Country Hospital's asylum in 1929 (16.10.1929, Crime, vol. 60; *Star*, 16.10.1929).

[24] Buildings were vermin-ridden and staff untrained. Physical restraint was liberally used, including chaining, strapping, straitjacketing, and confinement in unheated, bedless, stone-flagged cells (R.-M. Crossan, *Poverty and Welfare in Guernsey, 1560–2015* (Woodbridge, 2015), pp. 164, 169, pp. 166–76).

[25] 1.9.1891, GG, *Crime*, vol. 47; 1.9.1891, 7.12.1891, IA, DC/HX 136–03.

[26] J.E. Archer, 'Mysterious and suspicious deaths: missing homicides in north-west England (1850–1900)', *Crime, History & Societies*, 12 (2008), p. 56.

Appendix 10

Language and the Court

At the opening of our study in 1680, the everyday language of most of Guernsey's country parishioners was *guernésiais*, a variant of Norman French which had established itself in the island after it became part of Normandy in the tenth century. Nearly all of them, however, would also have had some knowledge of 'standard' French, based on the Parisian dialect, which was used for writing and in which literacy was taught in local schools. The same would also broadly have been true of most lower- and middle-ranking town parishioners. Urban patricians, however, were educated to a higher level and sometimes spent time in France, so that while able to converse in *guernésiais* with servants and tradesmen, they may have preferred to speak as well as write in standard French among themselves.

Guernsey's Court records, which survive in continuous form from the 1520s, were not in *guernésiais*. Neither were they in what was known in England as 'law French'.[1] They were in a form of standard French, which seems to have been adopted as the language of law and administration in Guernsey in parallel with its adoption in such contexts in Normandy.[2]

Standard French was also the language in which the Court's oral proceedings were conducted: Advocates made their speeches in standard French; Jurats rendered their verdicts and sentences in standard French; and Bailiffs pronounced judgments in standard French. During the period covered by this book, both the language of record and the language of proceedings underwent protracted processes of change. These processes, though linked, were to some extent separate, so they will be discussed separately. We will begin with an account of the language of record.

Although the French used in Guernsey's crime registers aimed at French norms, it was not entirely that of mainland France. One difference was that

---

[1] This was a compound of Anglo-French, Old French and Old Norman which was adopted for use in English judicial proceedings and documents in the thirteenth century, and persisted, though to a declining extent, until English was officially made the monopoly language of the courts in 1730 (C. Laske, 'Losing touch with the common tongues – the story of law French', *International Journal of Legal Discourse*, 1 (2016), pp. 169–92).

[2] The gradual displacement of Latin in these contexts in provincial France had begun around 1300 (R.A. Lodge, *French: From Dialect to Standard* (London, 1993), pp. 98, 122–3).

it contained technical terms and expressions which had evolved for local use and were applicable only in a local context. Examples of such expressions would be *mis à la folle adjonction* (to be non-suited in a semi-civil action) or *être ajugé à donner caution ou vuider hors de l'île* (to be sentenced to deposit bail or quit the island).[3]

The French of the crime registers also exhibited many lexical, syntactic and orthographic eccentricities. Archaisms peppered the registers until as late as the 1790s. These might be lexical archaisms such as *ce jour d'huy* for *aujourd'hui* and *yceluy* for *celui*, or orthographical archaisms such as *deub* for *dû*, *soubessons* for *soupçons* (suspicions); *larrecin* for *larcin* (theft). Many other words were simply spelt idiosyncratically: *à fin de* (in order to) sometimes appeared as *afain de*; *tous* (all) as *touts*.

Guernésiais words were also intermittently used, without any apparent awareness that they were not standard French terms. Some which appeared with particular frequency in the seventeenth and eighteenth centuries were *banatre* (crabpot); *hechet* (gate); *barrat* (drain); *fossé* (hedgebank); *palaire* (tinker); *chivière* (wheelbarrow); *palotte* (basin); *doublier* (tablecloth). In addition to this, the syntax and grammar of register entries also exhibited features characteristic of *guernésiais* but not seen in standard French: the use of the base-ten numeral *nonante*; the use of *ès* instead of *aux* for *à + les*; and the use of *avoir* instead of *être* as auxiliary in the perfect tense of verbs of motion (*il a sorti de sa maison* instead of *il est sorti de sa maison*).

By the early nineteenth century, many of the lexical peculiarities had disappeared; however their place was increasingly taken by anglicisms, whose use seems to have been just as unconscious as the earlier use of *guernésiais* terms. In 1831, a signboard to be hung over a woman sentenced to the cage was recorded as bearing the words '*convaincue de vol*'.[4] This seems to have been a simple calque on the English word 'convicted', since *convaincue* in French means 'convinced', and the normal French term would have been '*jugée coupable*'. Similarly, in 1842, the register recorded the Court's criticism of a quarry-owner for not taking precautions '*lorsqu'on souffle des pierres*'.[5] This again seems to have been a calque on the English verb 'to blow up'.

---

[3] Note that, although I have here used modern French accents (and will continue to use them in what follows), such accents were not generally or consistently used in Court registers until the mid-nineteenth century.

[4] 3.12.1831, GG, *Crime*, vol. 28.

[5] 30.5.1842, GG, *Crime*, vol. 31.

A more usual French expression would have been '*lorsqu'on fait sauter des pierres*'.

Such practices continued until the end of our period, with a growing tendency to drop expressions and terms translated directly from English into the framework of stock phrases which formed the foundation of register entries – '*dans un état d'aberration mentale temporaire*'; '*enlever une fille pour un objet immoral*'; '*commettre un acte d'indécence grossier*'. None of these expressions were particularly incorrect in French, but they would not normally have been used in France, because they represented English concepts, based on English laws and/or translated from English legal parlance.

All this suggests that the practice of recording criminal proceedings in French had by the late nineteenth century essentially become artificial. This was not only because it no longer reflected the spoken reality of island life, but also because it no longer reflected the spoken reality of the courtroom. At this point we shall turn to the evolution of oral proceedings.

The sound of English voices in judicial proceedings probably predated the beginning of our study. The first of the registers examined for this project (volume 6, covering 1660–1704) already contained evidence of the use of English in Court. This came in the form of witness depositions, where the testimony of English-speakers was recorded, as spoken, in English.[6] Monoglot anglophone settlers and sojourners, already present in number, could not be expected to give their evidence any other way. Nevertheless, for the next hundred years, the use of English in Court remained firmly restricted to witness depositions, since French, or a variant of it, remained the mother tongue of most Guernseymen and its use came naturally to them.

Towards the end of the eighteenth century, this situation began to be seriously disrupted. The Anglo-French wars which raged for twenty-two years between 1792 and 1815 inhibited travel to France and encouraged a more complete re-orientation towards Britain. Elite families increasingly sent their sons to be educated in England (or at English-speaking 'academies' in St Peter Port), and these developed greater fluency in English at the expense of their fluency in French. At the same time, the English language was making inroads at other levels, as immigration from England rose, and British service personnel filled the streets. William Berry, an Englishman who lived in Guernsey at the end of the Napoleonic period, commented as early as 1814

---

[6] Some fifty pages at the back of volume 6 contain witness depositions.

that 'the whole Court, Jurats as well as Advocates, understand and in fact speak better English than French.'[7] He might also have observed that this was increasingly true of the Court's clientele.

Despite this state of affairs, the Court (at least in its more formal iteration as the Full Court) appears well into mid-century to have stuck to tradition and retained French as the language of proceedings.[8] In 1847, Court members told the visiting Royal Commissioners that witness evidence (together with citations from English legal authorities) remained the only English generally permitted in Court.[9] On hearing this, the Commissioners, concerned that such a practice could disadvantage monolingual English-speakers, suggested that it might be advisable, in cases where the accused did not understand French, 'to authorize the Court … on the application of [his] counsel … to direct that the proceedings should be in English'.[10] The hint was taken, and thereafter, though French remained the 'official' language of proceedings, the use of English was frequently permitted in Full Court trials, albeit on a concessionary basis only.[11]

In the Police Court, where proceedings were less formal and a majority of offenders were from St Peter Port, the process of anglicisation had started earlier and went further and faster. As early as 1860, a correspondent to the *Comet* newspaper wrote that a large proportion of summary trials were disposed of completely in English.[12]

In the Full Court, an informal transition from concession to discretion was made around the turn of the twentieth century. This seems to have coincided with the States' vote in 1898 to allow members of the assembly the option of making their speeches in English.[13] There is no indication in official

---

[7] Berry to Privy Council, 23.3.1814, NA, PC 1/4051.

[8] Notwithstanding the permission exceptionally given to Jurat Thomas Andros, a monoglot anglophone ex-London lawyer elected in 1843, to address the Court in English (R. Hocart, 'Elections to the Royal Court of Guernsey, 1821–1844, *TSG*, 19 (1979), pp. 507–8.).

[9] *Second Report of the Commissioners Appointed to Inquire into the State of the Criminal Law in the Channel Islands: Guernsey* (London, 1848), pp. 55, 167, 258.

[10] *Ibid.*, p. xli.

[11] A case in point is John Tapner's murder trial in 1853/4, of which large portions were conducted in English (see Anon., *Procès de Jean Charles Tapner, Condamné à la Peine de Mort par Arrêt de la Cour Royale de Guernesey à la Date du 3 Janvier 1854 pour Crime d'Assassinat suivi de Vol et de Tentative d'Incendie* (Guernsey, 1854), pp. 6–19).

[12] Letter from 'J.B.', *Comet*, 1.5.1860.

[13] For a detailed account of this episode, see R.-M. Crossan, *Guernsey, 1814–1914: Migration and Modernisation* (Woodbridge, 2007), pp. 271–4.

records of how and when the decision was taken to grant Court members a similar option, but a letter dated April 1906 from Jersey's Attorney General to Guernsey's Bailiff shows that the transition had already been made. 'Has the optional use of English in the Guernsey Court created any confusion?' the Jerseyman enquired.[14] 'No', answered the Bailiff; 'the option of using English in our Courts instead of French, so far from causing any confusion, has worked perfectly smoothly and brought great relief to both the Jurats and the members of the Bar, who are now free to express their thoughts in the language which they habitually use in private life, instead of translating them into a comparatively unfamiliar tongue.'[15]

This essentially left only the most formal elements of Full Court trials in what had by now become rather stiff and formulaic French. As Bailiff Ambrose Sherwill told the Privy Council Committee on Proposed Reforms in the Channel Islands in 1946, he had never known the substance of trials to be in anything but English since his own admission to the Bar in 1920.[16] In the interim, moreover, a complete shift to the exclusive use of English in the Police Court had followed the appointment of an English barrister as Magistrate in 1925.

By coincidence (or perhaps by design), the States had voted to implement a full change-over from French to English in the Royal Court just a few days before the Privy Council Committee arrived in the island.[17] The measure was subject to the provision that parties could still opt to use French if they wished and that certain documents (such as conveyances) should continue to be drafted in French. This full change-over was eventually implemented in 1948. The last remaining vestiges of oral French in criminal trials were dispensed with, and on Wednesday 26 May 1948 crime registers switched to English as the language of record.[18]

---

[14] A.H. Turner to Sir Henry Giffard, 28.4.1906, GG, Royal Court General Letter Book (second series), vol. 18.

[15] Giffard to Turner, 1.5.1906, GG, Royal Court General Letter Book (second series), vol. 18.

[16] 'Evidence given before the Privy Council Committee on Proposed Reforms in the Channel Islands, Guernsey, September 1946', pp. 190–1 (Royal Court Library, IA).

[17] The decision was made on 17 September 1946, and the Committee began taking evidence on 21 September (R. Hocart, *An Island Assembly: The Development of the States of Guernsey, 1700–1949* (Guernsey, 1988), p. 128).

[18] 26.5.1948, GG, *Crime*, vol. 72.

Bibliography

Primary Sources

Greffe, St Peter Port, Guernsey

Dépositions des Témoins de Nicolas Rougier, 1775 (Miscellaneous Books, no. 38)
Jugements, Ordonnances et Ordres du Conseil
Livres en Crime
Mémoires de la Cour Royale
Ordonnances
Ordres du Conseil et Actes du Parlement
Préjugés en Crime
Requêtes
Royal Court Letter Books

Guernsey Museum, St Peter Port, Guernsey

GUELI:GMAG 2004.50.23 – Correspondence concerning HM Prison, 1854–62

Priaulx Library, St Peter Port, Guernsey

Billets d'Etat
Census of Great Britain, 1851: Population Tables, Scotland and Islands in the British Seas (London, 1852)
Census of England and Wales, 1861: Population and Houses, England and Wales and Islands in the British Seas (London, 1862)
Census of England and Wales, 1871: Population and Houses, England and Wales and Islands in the British Seas (London, 1871)
Census 1881: Islands in the British Seas (London, 1883)
Census 1891: Islands in the British Seas (London, 1893)
Census 1901: Islands in the British Seas (London, 1903)
Census 1911: Islands in the British Seas (London, 1913)
Census 1921: Jersey, Guernsey and Adjacent Islands (London, 1924)

Census 1931: Jersey, Guernsey and Adjacent Islands (London, 1933)
Edith Carey's Lists of Jurats and Court Officers
Edith Carey's Scrapbooks
F.C. Lukis, 'Reminiscences of Former Days in Connection with Guernsey'
Guernsey Assize Roll, 1299 (tr J.H. Le Patourel)
Journals and Correspondence of Charles Mollet
Orders in Council (published volumes)
Ordinances (published volumes)
Watkins Manuscripts

Island Archives, St Peter Port, Guernsey

AM 001-13 – Ogier, D.M., 'Notes on Guernsey's Georgian prison and its
    antecedents' (unpub. typescript, 1999)
AQ 0001/22 – Notebook of Daniel De Putron, 1848–9
AQ 008/01 – Acts of the Ecclesiastical Court, 1664–1704
AQ 0227/10 – St Martins Police Occurrence Book, 1911–15
AQ 0712/34 – Notebook of Pierre Tourgis, c.1771–84
AQ 0966/01 – St Peter Port Douzaine Deliberations, 1848–73
AQ 0967/01 – St Peter Port Douzaine Deliberations, 1873–1910
AQ 0988/01 – St Peter Port *Ordonnances*, 1581–1766
AQ 40/04 – Guernsey Chamber of Commerce Minutes, 1849–89
AQ 44/05 – Guernsey Chamber of Commerce Minutes, 1889–1902
AQ 1003/01 – St Peter Port Tax Book, 1740–62
AQ 1004/01 – St Peter Port Tax Book, 1803–10
DC/HX 130-01 – Town Hospital Committee Minutes, 1842–9
DC/HX 136-03 – Town Hospital House Committee Minutes, 1890–3
PC 181-01 – Island Police Occurrence Book, January 1915–April 1917
PC 181-03 – Island Police Occurrence Book, May 1919–September 1920

Royal Court Library (Island Archives)

'Channel Islands Finance' (HM Treasury, 1909)
'Evidence given before the Privy Council Committee on Proposed Reforms in the
    Channel Islands, Guernsey, September 1946'
Examen d'une Question en Petit-Criminel, 1798
'Judicial Proceedings', vol. 13
'Privy Council', vols 2 & 3
'Statistical Papers, 1847–52'

National Archives, Kew

HO 17/26/132 – case of Marie Joseph François Béasse, 1830
HO 17/87/141 – case of Joseph Chapman, 1826–31
HO 45/090 – papers relating to Royal Commission, 1846
HO 45/213 – papers relating to the office of Bailiff, 1845–6
HO 45/399 – William Napier's observations on Guernsey, 1842
HO 45/930 – papers relating to Royal Commission, 1845
HO 45/931 – case of Wilhelm Fleckner, 1844–5
HO 45/938 – Comptroller's resignation, 1845
HO 45/4889 – despatch of a London detective to Guernsey, 1853
HO 45/5188 – Bailiff's request for a salary increase, 1854
HO 45/5194 – correspondence concerning hangman, 1854
HO 45/6268 – Bailiff's salary, 1856
HO 45/6269 – correspondence concerning flogging, 1855
HO 45/6390 – Comptroller's office, 1857–8
HO 45/6393 – Guernsey reformatory, 1857
HO 45/9293/7221 – Comptroller's office, 1861–77
HO 45/7969 – correspondence on extradition between Guernsey and the United Kingdom, 1867–9
HO 45/9314/14702 – extension of 1870 Extradition Act to Guernsey
HO 45/9320/16929 – Guernsey prison and penal servitude, 1871–6
HO 45/9492/5006 – report on Channel Island militias, 1869
HO 45/9578/83489 – correspondence on certified reformatories, 1879–86
HO 45/9595/94762 – Channel Island prisons, 1880–90
HO 45/9811/B6950 – correspondence on certified reformatories, 1889–95
HO 45/10072/B5960A – reorganisation of Guernsey militia, 1889–1904
HO 45/10143/B18108 – Bailiff's salary, 1895–1901
HO 45/10978/B15797 – Crown Officers' salaries, 1919–21
HO 45/14143 – corresponding concerning sorcery law, 1914–15
HO 45/17337 – correspondence concerning Borstals, 1910–38
HO 45/233135 – correspondence concerning Sodomy Law, 1929–48
HO 45/24658 – Stipendiary Magistrate, 1914–25
HO 45/24671 – Guernsey Police, 1914–52
HO 98/88 – Statistical Return, 1847
HO 284/336 – correspondence concerning Sexual Offences Law, 1983
MEPO 2/1821 – Guernsey Police, 1914–30
PC 1/2247 – correspondence relating to Royal Commission, 1845
PC 1/3190 – murder and manslaughter in the Channel Islands, 1699
PC 1/3463 – Orders in Council issued for seizing Persons in the Plantations and Guernsey and Jersey

PC 1/4022 – Bailiff's salary, 1813
PC 1/4051 – correspondence concerning Royal Commission of 1815
PC 1/4296 – appointment of St Peter Port assistant constables, 1825–6
PCOM 3 – tickets-of-leave issued to male convicts, 1853–87
SP 36/23/89 – correspondence concerning Françoise Litton, 1731
SP 78/273/37 – correspondence concerning the despatch of quarrymen to
    Guernsey, 1767
T 64/153 – Customs Commissioner's Report on Guernsey, 1800
T 1/16938 – correspondence concerning certified reformatories, 1879
T 161/694/7 – correspondence concerning Guernsey prisoners in English prisons,
    1924–9

British Library

Add Ch 76094 – Thomas White sedition case, 1707
Add MS 6253 – *A Short Account of the Island of Guernsey A.D. MDCCXLIX*
    (Samuel Bonamy)
Add MS 6253 – *The State of Guernzey writen by Christopher Lord Hatton* (copied
    from the original by Samuel Bonamy)

Dorset History Centre

NG-PR/1/D/5/2 – Dorchester prisoner photograph album

Archives départementales du Calvados, Caen

D/708–794 – Caen University law faculty matriculations, 1680–1785

Parliamentary Papers

1833 XXXVII (1831 census analysis)
1844 XXVII (1841 census analysis)
1852–3 LXXXVIII (1851 census analysis)
1883 LXXX (1881 census analysis)
1893–4 CVII (1891 census analysis)
1903 LXXXIV (1901 census analysis)

Guernsey newspapers and magazines

Comet
Gazette de Guernesey
Gazette des Iles de la Manche
Guernsey Advertiser and Weekly Chronicle
Guernsey Evening Press
Guernsey Weekly Press
Indépendance
Mercure de Guernesey
Miroir Politique
Monthly Illustrated Journal
Star
The Chit Chat
The Guernsey and Jersey Magazine
The Guernsey Times

Non-Guernsey newspapers and magazines

Bath Chronicle & Weekly Gazette
The Eclectic Review
The Times

Secondary Sources

Pre-1920 publications

Allen, E., *A Summer Stroll through the Islands of Jersey and Guernsey* (Jersey, 1809)

Anon., *Almanach Journalier à l'Usage de l'Ile de Guernesey* (Guernsey, 1797)

Anon. (ed.), *Documens relatifs à l'Ile de Guernesey, Revus et Corrigés d'après les Pièces Originales, No. 1* (Guernsey, 1814)

Anon., *A Guide to the Island of Guernsey* (Guernsey, 1826)

Anon. (ed.), *A Treatise on the History, Laws and Customs of the Island of Guernsey by Mr Warburton, a Herald and Celebrated Antiquary in Charles II's Reign* (Guernsey, 1822)

Anon., *The Stranger's Guide to the Islands of Guernsey and Jersey* (Guernsey, 1833)

Anon., *Barbet's Guide for the Island of Guernsey* (Guernsey, 1844)

Anon., *Bichard's Guide to the Islands of Guernsey, Alderney, Sark & Herm* (Guernsey, 1863)

Anon., *Procès de Jean Charles Tapner, Condamné à la Peine de Mort par Arrêt de la Cour Royale de Guernesey à la Date du 3 Janvier 1854 pour Crime d'Assassinat suivi de Vol et de Tentative d'Incendie* (Guernsey, 1854)

Ansted, D.T. & Latham, R.G., *The Channel Islands* (London, 1862)

Bear, W.E., 'Garden farming', *Quarterly Review*, 166 (1888), pp. 407–38

Bear, W.E., 'Glimpses of farming in the Channel Islands', *Journal of the Royal Agricultural Society of England*, 24 (1888), pp. 365–97

Berry, W., *The History of the Island of Guernsey* (London, 1815)

Blackstone, W., *Commentaries on the Laws of England*, 4 vols (Oxford, 1765–9), 1

Boland, H., *Les Iles de la Manche* (Paris, 1904)

Bouverie, F.W.B., *The Eleventh Hour* (Guernsey, 1854)

Bruce, H.A., *Life of Sir William Napier, K.C.B.*, 2 vols (London, 1864)

Bruneau, A., *Observations et Maximes sur les Matières Criminelles* (Paris, 1715)

Carey, L., *Essai sur les Institutions, Lois et Coutumes de l'Ile de Guernesey* (c.1750; Guernsey, 1889)

Clarke, L.L., *Redstone's Guernsey Guide; or the Stranger's Companion for the Island of Guernsey* (Guernsey, 1841)

Cauvet, J., 'Le droit criminel de la Normandie au treizième siècle', *Revue de Législation et de Jurisprudence*, 3 (1851), pp. 265–301

Dally, F.F., *A Guide to Jersey, Guernsey, Sark, Herm, Jethou, Alderney, etc.* (London, 1858)

Dally, F.F., *A Guide to Guernsey* (London, 1860)

Dally, F.F., *The Channel Islands: A Guide* (London, 1860)

Dally, F.F., *Agriculture of the Channel Islands* (Guernsey, 1860)

De Guérin, T.W.M., 'The English garrison of Guernsey from early times', *Transactions of the Guernsey Society of Natural Science and Local Research*, 5 (1905), pp. 66–81

De Guérin, W.C.L., *Our Kin: Genealogical Sketches, Pedigrees, and Arms of Sundry Families* (Guernsey, 1890)

Dicey, T., *An Historical Account of Guernsey* (London, 1751)

Dodd, C.R., *The Annual Biography* (London, 1843)

Duncan, J., *The History of Guernsey* (London, 1841)

Esmein, A. (tr J. Simpson), *A History of Continental Criminal Procedure with Special Reference to France* (Boston, 1913)

First Report of the Commissioners appointed to Inquire into the State of the Criminal Law in the Channel Islands: Jersey (London, 1847)

Fry, K. & Cresswell, R.E. (eds), *Memoir of the Life of Elizabeth Fry*, 2 vols (London, 1847), 2

Hale, M., *History of the Pleas of the Crown*, 2 vols (London, 1736), 1

Hannay, D., 'Sir William Napier', *Macmillan's Magazine*, 86 (1902), pp. 209–26

Havet, J., *Les Cours Royales des Iles Normandes* (Paris, 1878)

Hemery, J. & Dumaresq, J., *A Statement of the Mode of Proceeding & of Going to Trial in the Royal Court of Jersey* (Jersey, 1789)

Heylyn, P., *A Full Relation of Two Journeys: The One into the Main-Land of France, the Other into some of the Adjacent Ilands* (London, 1656)

Hugo, A., *Victor Hugo: A Life by One who has Witnessed It*, 2 vols (London, 1863), 2

Inglis, H.D., *The Channel Islands*, 2 vols (London, 1834), 2

Jacob, J., *Annals of Some of the British Norman Isles Constituting the Bailiwick of Guernsey* (Paris, 1830)

Jeremie, J., *Historical Account of the Island of Guernsey* (Guernsey, 1821)

Lee, G.E. (ed.), *Actes des Etats de l'Ile de Guernesey, 1651–1780* (Guernsey, 1907)

Lee, G.E. (ed.), *Actes des Etats de l'Ile de Guernesey, 1780–1815* (Guernsey, 1910)

Le Geyt, P., *Les Manuscrits de Philippe Le Geyt, Ecuyer, Lieutenant-Bailli de l'Ile de Jersey, sur la Constitution, les Lois et les Usages de cette Ile*, 4 vols (Jersey, 1846–7)

Le Gros, G. & Toulmin Nicolle, E. (eds), *Rolls of the Assizes held in the Channel Islands in the Second year of the Reign of King Edward II, A.D. 1309* (Jersey, 1903)

Lelièvre, M., *Histoire du Méthodisme dans les Iles de la Manche, 1784–1884* (Paris, 1885)

Le Marchant, T., *Remarques et Animadversions sur l'Approbation des Lois et Coustumier de Normandie usitées ès Jurisdictions de Guernezé*, 2 vols (c.1660; Guernsey, 1826)

Long, C. (ed.), *Sequel to the Annals of Guernsey by John Jacob, Esq.* (Guernsey, 1872)

Montgomery Martin, R., *History of the British Colonies*, 5 vols (London, 1835), 5

Quayle, T., *A General View of the Agriculture and Present State of the Islands on the Coast of Normandy* (London, 1815)

Rider Haggard, H., *Rural England*, 2 vols (London, 1902), 1

Robinet de Cléry, G.A., 'Etude sur l'organisation politique, administrative et judiciaire des îles anglo-normandes', *Bulletin de la Société de Législation Comparée*, 2 (1890), pp. 164–95

Robinet de Cléry, G.A., *Les Iles Normandes, Pays de Home Rule* (Paris, 1898)

Second Report of the Commissioners Appointed to Inquire into the State of the Criminal Law of the Channel Islands (London, 1848)

Smith, M., 'Letters from Colonel William Napier to Sir John Colborne', *English Historical Review*, 18 (1903), pp. 725–53

Stephen, L. (ed.), *Dictionary of National Biography* (London, 1885)

Taylor, A.S., *Elements of Medical Jurisprudence* (1836; London, 1849 edn)

Terrien, G., *Commentaires du Droict Civil tant Public que Privé Observé au Pays & Duché de Normandie* (1574; Rouen, 1654 edn)

Third Report of the Committee of the Society for the Improvement of Prison Discipline (London, 1821)

Tramailler, T. (ed.), *Approbation des Lois, Coutumes, et Usages de l'Ile de Guernesey* (1715; Guernsey, 1822 edn)

Tupper, F.B., *The History of Guernsey and its Bailiwick* (Guernsey, 1854 and 1876)

Tupper, H., *Observations of Advocate Tupper of Guernsey Explaining Recent Events and Grievances* (Guernsey, 1844)

Vallaux, C., *L'Archipel de la Manche* (Paris, 1913)

Post-1920 publications

Ahier, P., 'The house of correction in Jersey', *Annual Bulletin of la Société Jersiaise*, 20 (1971), pp. 284–8

Andrew, D.T., 'The code of honour and its critics: the opposition to duelling in England, 1700–1850', *Social History*, 5 (1980), pp. 409–34

Anon., 'Guernsey executions, from the papers of the Rev. H. Le M. Chepmell', *Quarterly Review of the Guernsey Society* (Autumn 1949), pp. 6–10

Anon., 'St Julian's Avenue – a centenary', *The Review of the Guernsey Society*, 28 (1972), p. 3

Appleby, J.C., 'Neutrality, trade and privateering, 1500–1689', in Jamieson, A.G. (ed.), *A People of the Sea: The Maritime History of the Channel Islands* (London, 1986)

Archer, J.E., 'Mysterious and suspicious deaths: missing homicides in north-west England (1850–1900)', *Crime, History & Societies*, 12 (2008), pp. 45–63

Arnot, M.L., 'Understanding women committing newborn child murder in Victorian England', in S. D'Cruze (ed.), *Everyday Violence in Britain, 1850–1950: Gender and Class* (Harlow, 2000)

Bailey, V., 'English prisons, penal culture, and the abatement of imprisonment, 1895–1922', *Journal of British Studies*, 36 (1997), pp. 285–324

Bailhache, P. (ed.), *A Celebration of Autonomy, 1204–2004: 800 Years of Channel Islands' Law* (Jersey, 2005)

Baker, J.H., 'Criminal courts and procedure at common law, 1550–1800', in Cockburn, J.S. (ed.), *Crime in England, 1550–1800* (London, 1977)

Baldry, W.Y., 'Disbanded regiments', *Journal of the Society for Army Historical Research*, 56 (1935), pp. 233–5

Barclay, J., 'The defamation action in Guernsey: past, present and future', in Dawes, G. (ed.), *Paris 1259: Studies in the History and Law of Continental and Insular Normandy* (Guernsey, 2016)

Barrie, D.G. & Broomhall, S., *Police Courts in Nineteenth-Century Scotland*, 2 vols (Farnham, 2014), 1

Beattie, J.M., 'Crime and the courts in Surrey, 1736–1753', in Cockburn, J.S. (ed.), *Crime in England, 1550–1800* (London, 1977)

Beattie, J.M., *Crime and the Courts in England, 1660-1800* (Oxford, 1986)

Bebbington, D.W., *Evangelicals in Modern Britain: A History from the 1730s to the 1980s* (London, 1989)

Behlmer, G., 'Summary justice and working-class marriage in England, 1870-1940', *Law and History Review*, 2 (1994), pp. 229-75

Bennett, A.R., *History of the States of Guernsey Telephone System* (London, 1926)

Berridge, V., 'Drugs and social policy: the establishment of drug control in Britain, 1900-1930', *Addiction*, 79 (1984), pp. 17-29

Bourke, J., *Rape: A History from 1860 to the Present* (2007; London, 2008 edn)

Brett, C.E.B., *Buildings in the Town and Parish of St Peter Port* (Guernsey, 1975)

Brewer, J. & Styles, J. (eds), *An Ungovernable People: the English and their Law in the Seventeenth and Eighteenth Centuries* (London, 1980)

Bridrey, M.E., 'Les études de droit normand au collège des droits de l'ancienne université de Caen', in *Travaux de la Semaine d'Histoire du Droit Normand tenue à Guernesey du 26 au 30 Mai 1927* (Caen, 1928)

Bromley, J.S., 'A new vocation: privateering in the wars of 1689-97 and 1702-13', in Jamieson, A.G. (ed.), *A People of the Sea: The Maritime History of the Channel Islands* (London, 1986)

Brookes, B., *Abortion in England, 1900-1967* (1988; Abingdon, 2013 edn)

Brown, B.J., 'The demise of chance medley and the recognition of provocation as a defence to murder in English law', *The American Journal of Legal History*, 7 (1963)

Brown, M. & Donlan, S.P. (eds), *The Laws and other Legalities of Ireland, 1689-1850* (Farnham, 2011)

Brown, M. & Donlan, S.P., 'The laws in Ireland, 1689-1850: a brief introduction', in Brown, M. & Donlan, S.P. (eds), *The Laws and other Legalities of Ireland, 1689-1850* (Farnham, 2011)

Burnett, J., *Plenty and Want: A Social History of Food in England from 1815 to the Present Day* (1966; London, 1989 edn)

Carbasse, J.-M., *Histoire du Droit Pénal et de la Justice Criminelle* (2000; Paris, 2014 edn)

Carey, E.F., 'La Plaiderie', *TSG*, 10 (1929), pp. 399–406

Carey, J.A., *Judicial Reform in France before the Revolution of 1789* (London, 1981)

Carman, W.J., *Channel Island Transport* (Guernsey, 1987)

Chalklin, C.W., *The Provincial Towns of Georgian England* (London, 1974)

Champin, M.-M., 'Un cas typique de justice bailliagère: la criminalité dans le bailliage d'Alençon de 1715 à 1745', *Annales de Normandie*, 22 (1972), pp. 47–84

Chapman, W.R., *His Praise in the Islands* (1984; Guernsey, 1995 edn)

Chauvel, C., 'The contribution made to the Christian life of the island', *The Review of the Guernsey Society* (winter 2006–7), pp. 88–95

Clark, A., 'Domesticity and the problem of wifebeating in nineteenth-century Britain: working-class culture, law and politics', in D'Cruze, S. (ed.), *Everyday Violence in Britain, 1850–1950: Gender and Class* (Harlow, 2000)

Clarke, R., 'Growth of the Village de Putron', *TSG*, 22 (1990), pp. 798–805

Cockburn, J.S. (ed.), *Crime in England, 1550–1800* (London, 1977)

Conley, C.A., 'Rape and justice in Victorian England', *Victorian Studies*, 29 (1986), pp. 519–36

Conley, C.A., *Certain other Countries: Homicide, Gender, and National Identity in Late Nineteenth-Century England, Ireland, Scotland, and Wales* (Columbus, Ohio, 2007)

Connolly, S.J. (ed.), *Kingdoms United? Great Britain and Ireland since 1500: Integration and Diversity* (Dublin, 1999)

Conway, S.R., 'The recruitment of criminals into the British army, 1775–81', *Bulletin of the Institute of Historical Research*, 137 (1985), pp. 46–58

Conway Davies, J., 'The records of the Royal Court', *TSG*, 16 (1959), pp. 404–14

Coysh, V., *Royal Guernsey: A History of the Royal Guernsey Militia* (Guernsey, 1977)

Crossan, R.-M., 'The retreat of French from Guernsey's public primary schools, 1800–1939', *TSG*, 25 (2005), pp. 851–88

Crossan, R.-M., *Guernsey, 1814–1914: Migration and Modernisation* (Woodbridge, 2007)

Crossan, R.-M., *Poverty and Welfare in Guernsey, 1560–2015* (Woodbridge, 2015)

Crossan, R.-M., *The States and Secondary Education, 1560–1970* (Guernsey, 2016)

Crossan, R.-M., *A Women's History of Guernsey, 1850s–1950s* (Benderloch, 2018)

Croucher, A.E., *A Short History of St Stephen's Church, Guernsey* (Guernsey, 1983)

Crowther, M.A., 'Crime, prosecution and mercy: English influence and Scottish practice in the early nineteenth century', in Connolly, S.J. (ed.), *Kingdoms United? Great Britain and Ireland since 1500: Integration and Diversity* (Dublin, 1999)

Crozier, J. (ed.), *Catholicism in the Channel Islands* (Guernsey, 1951)

Davies, O., *Witchcraft, Magic and Culture, 1736–1951* (Manchester, 1999)

Davies, S.J., 'The courts and the Scottish legal system, 1600–1747: the case of Stirlingshire', in Gatrell, V.A.C., Lenman, B. & Parker, G. (eds), *Crime and the Law: The Social History of Crime in Western Europe since 1500* (London, 1980)

Davis, J., 'A poor man's system of justice: the London police courts in the second half of the nineteenth century', *The Historical Journal*, 27 (1984), pp. 309–35

Dawes, G., *Laws of Guernsey* (Oxford, 2003)

Dawes, G. (ed.), *Commise 1204: Studies in the History and Law of Continental and Insular Normandy* (Guernsey, 2005)

Dawes, G., 'The Guernsey Advocate – a short history', *The Jersey Law Review* (February 2005)

Dawes, G., 'A brief history of Guernsey law', *The Jersey Law Review*, February 2006

Dawes, G. (ed.), *Paris 1259: Studies in the History and Law of Continental and Insular Normandy* (Guernsey, 2016)

Day, A., 'A Russian army on Guernsey and Jersey', *The Review of the Guernsey Society* (Summer 1997), pp. 40–5

D'Cruze, S. (ed.), *Everyday Violence in Britain, 1850–1950: Gender and Class* (Harlow, 2000)

D'Cruze, S. & Jackson, L.A., *Women, Crime and Justice in England since 1660* (Basingstoke, 2009)

Dean, T., *Crime in Medieval Europe, 1200–1550* (Harlow, 2001)

De Garis, M., *Dictiounnaire Angllais–Guernesiais* (Chichester, 1982)

De Guerin, B.C., *History of Agriculture on the Island of Guernsey* (Guernsey, 1947)

Delorme, M.-L., 'Criminels et justiciables: l'exemple du bailliage d'Argentan (1720–1750)', *Annales de Normandie*, 61, 2012, pp. 55–79

De Sausmarez, C.H., 'The story of William Le Marchant, 1770'–1800: a lost page of Guernsey history, *TSG*, 17 (1965), pp. 717–46

De Sausmarez, H., *The Extentes of Guernsey 1248 and 1331* (Guernsey, 1934)

De Sausmarez, H., 'Guernsey's Précepte d'Assise of 1441: translation and notes', *Jersey & Guernsey Law Review* (June 2008) (reprinted from *TSG*, 1934)

Désert, G., 'Aspects de la criminalité en France et en Normandie', *Cahier des Annales de Normandie*, 13 (1981), pp. 221–316

Dickinson, J.R. & Sharpe, J.A., 'Courts, crime and litigation in the Isle of Man, 1580–1700', *Historical Research*, 72 (1999), pp. 140–59

Dickinson, J.R., 'Criminal violence and judicial punishment in the Isle of Man, 1580–1700', *Proceedings of the Isle of Man Natural History and Antiquarian Society*, 11 (2000), pp. 127–42

Doggett, M.E., *Marriage, Wife-Beating and the Law in Victorian England* (Columbia, 1993)

Donnachie, I., 'Scottish criminals and transportation to Australia, 1786–1852', *Scottish Economic and Social History*, 4 (1984), pp. 21–38

Donovan, J.M., *Juries and the Transformation of Criminal Justice in France in the Nineteenth and Twentieth Centuries* (Chapel Hill, 2010)

Du Feu, C.A.R., 'Elizabeth Fry and the Jersey prison', *Annual Bulletin of la Société Jersiaise*, 20 (1970), pp. 180–91

Eagleston, A.J., *The Channel Islands under Tudor Government, 1485–1642* (Cambridge, 1949)

Edge, P.W., *Manx Public Law* (Douglas, 1997)

Edge, P., 'A criminal code – lessons from the Isle of Man?', *Jersey & Guernsey Law Review*, 1 (2017), pp. 101–9

Eisner, M., 'Modernity strikes back? A historical perspective on the latest increase in interpersonal violence (1960–1990)', *International Journal of Conflict and Violence*, 2 (2008), pp. 289–316

Ekirch, A.R., 'The transportation of Scottish criminals to America during the eighteenth century', *Journal of British Studies*, 24 (1985), pp. 366–74

Emsley, C., *Crime and Society in England, 1750–1900* (1987; Harlow, 1996 edn)

Emsley, C., '"Mother, what *did* policemen do when there weren't any motors?": the law, the police and the regulation of motor traffic in England, 1900–1939', *The Historical Journal*, 36 (1993), pp. 357–81

Emsley, C., *Crime, Police, and Penal Policy: European Experiences, 1750–1940* (Oxford, 2007)

Emsley, C., *Crime and Society in Twentieth-Century England* (Harlow, 2011)

Everard, J.A. & Holt, J.C., *Jersey 1204: The Forging of an Island Community* (London, 2004)

Everard, J.A. (tr), *Le Grand Coutumier de Normandie: The Laws and Customs by which the Duchy of Normandy is Ruled* (Jersey, 2009)

Everard, J.A., 'L'ancienne [sic] Coutumier de Normandie: the laws and customs by which the duchy is ruled', in Dawes, G. (ed.), *Paris 1259: Studies in the History and Law of Continental and Insular Normandy* (Guernsey, 2016)

Farmer, L., *Criminal Law, Tradition and Legal Order: Crime and the Genius of Scots Law, 1747 to the Present* (Cambridge, 1997)

Feeley, M.M. & Little, D.L., 'The decline of women in the criminal process, 1687–1912', *Law & Society Review*, 25 (1991), pp. 719–58

Fortescue, J.W., 'The Napiers', *Blackwood's Magazine*, 236 (1934), pp. 115–39

Gahan, F., 'The law of the Channel Islands, IV: criminal law in Guernsey', *The Solicitor Quarterly*, 2 (1963), pp. 148–160

Garnham, N., 'The criminal law, 1692–1760: England and Ireland compared', in Connolly, S.J. (ed.), *Kingdoms United? Great Britain and Ireland since 1500: Integration and Diversity* (Dublin, 1999)

Garnham, N., 'The limits of English influence on the Irish criminal law and the boundaries of discretion in the eighteenth-century Irish criminal justice system', in Brown, M. & Donlan, S.P. (eds), *The Laws and other Legalities of Ireland, 1689–1850* (Farnham, 2011)

Garnot, B., *Crime et Justice aux XVII*[e] *et XVIII*[e] *Siècles* (Paris, 2000)

Gatrell, V.A.C. & Hadden, T.B., 'Criminal statistics and their interpretation', in Wrigley, E.A., *Nineteenth-Century Society: Essays in the Use of Quantitative Methods for the Study of Social Data* (Cambridge, 1972)

Gatrell, V.A.C., Lenman, B. & Parker, G. (eds), *Crime and the Law: The Social History of Crime in Western Europe since 1500* (London, 1980)

Gatrell, V.A.C., 'The decline of theft and violence in Victorian and Edwardian England', in Gatrell, V.A.C., Lenman, B. & Parker, G. (eds), *Crime and the Law: The Social History of Crime in Western Europe since 1500* (London, 1980)

Gatrell, V.A.C., 'Crime, authority and the policeman-state', in Thompson, F.M.L. (ed.), *The Cambridge Social History of Britain, 1750–1950*, 3 vols (Cambridge, 1990), 3

Gatrell, V.A.C., *The Hanging Tree: Execution and the English People, 1770-1868* (Oxford, 1994)

Gégot, J-C., 'Etude par sondage de la criminalité dans le bailliage de Falaise (XVIIᵉ-XVIIIᵉ siècles): criminalité diffuse ou société criminelle?', *Annales de Normandie*, 13 (1966), pp. 103-64

Girard, P.J., 'Development of the bulb and flower industry in Guernsey', *TSG*, 13 (1939), pp. 284-98

Girard, P.J., 'The Guernsey grape industry', *TSG*, 15 (1951), pp. 126-44

Girard, P.J., 'Country life and some insular enterprises of the late 19ᵗʰ century', *TSG*, 19 (1972), pp. 88-105

Girard, P.J., 'Adolphus Bichard's reminiscences of the stone industry', *TSG*, 21 (1982), pp. 202-8

Godfrey, B.S., *Crime in England, 1880-1945: The Rough and the Criminal, the Policed and the Incarcerated* (Abingdon, 2014)

Gonthier, N., *Le Châtiment du Crime au Moyen Age, XIIᵉ-XVIᵉ Siècles* (Rennes, 1998)

Grass, T., *Two Centuries of Baptists in Guernsey: The Story of an Island Community* (Isle of Man, 2013)

Gray, D.D., *Crime, Policing and Punishment in England, 1660-1914* (London, 2016)

Gregory, J., *Victorians against the Gallows: Capital Punishment and the Abolitionist Movement in Nineteenth-Century Britain* (London, 2012)

Haber, P., *Drugs of Dependence: The Role of Medical Professionals* (London, 2013)

Hanson, T., 'The language of the law: the importance of French', *The Jersey Law Review* (June, 2005)

Hay, D., Linebaugh, P., Rule, J.G., Thompson, E.P. & Winslow, C., *Albion's Fatal Tree: Crime and Society in Eighteenth-Century England* (London, 1975)

Hay, D., 'Poaching and the Game Laws on Cannock Chase', in Hay, D., Linebaugh, P., Rule, J.G., Thompson, E.P. & Winslow, C., *Albion's Fatal Tree: Crime and Society in Eighteenth-Century England* (London, 1975)

Hay, D., 'Property, authority and the criminal law', in Hay, D., Linebaugh, P., Rule, J.G., Thompson, E.P. & Winslow, C., *Albion's Fatal Tree: Crime and Society in Eighteenth-Century England* (London, 1975)

Hendrick, H., *Child Welfare: England, 1872-1989* (London, 1994)

Hocart, R., 'Elections to the Royal Court of Guernsey, 1821'-1844, *TSG*, 19 (1979), pp. 494-514

Hocart, R., 'Sir Edgar MacCulloch', *TSG*, 21 (1983), pp. 274-7

Hocart, R. (ed.), 'The Journal of Charles Trumbull', *TSG*, 21 (1984), pp. 566-85

Hocart, R., *An Island Assembly: The Development of the States of Guernsey, 1700-1949* (Guernsey, 1988)

Hocart, R., *Peter de Havilland: Bailiff of Guernsey: A History of his Life, 1747–1821* (Guernsey, 1997)

Hocart, R., *The Country People of Guernsey and their Agriculture, 1640–1840* (Guernsey, 2016)

Hocart, R., *Guernsey in the Reign of Charles II* (Guernsey 2020)

Holt, J.C., 'Jersey 1204: the origins of unity: a note on the Constitutions of King John', in Bailhache, P. (ed.), *A Celebration of Autonomy, 1204–2004: 800 Years of Channel Islands' Law* (Jersey, 2005)

Hovasse, J.-M., *Victor Hugo*, 2 vols (Paris, 2001–8), 2

Innes, J., 'Prisons for the poor: English bridewells, 1555–1800', in Snyder, F. & Hay, D. (eds), *Labour, Law and Crime: An Historical Perspective* (London, 1987)

Jackson, L.A., *Child Sexual Abuse in Victorian England* (London, 2000)

Jamieson, A.G. (ed.), *A People of the Sea: The Maritime History of the Channel Islands* (London, 1986)

Jamieson, A.G., 'Channel Island shipowners and seamen, 1700–1900', in Jamieson, A.G. (ed.), *A People of the Sea: The Maritime History of the Channel Islands* (London, 1986)

Jamieson, A.G., 'The Channel Islands and smuggling, 1680–1850', in Jamieson, A.G. (ed.), *A People of the Sea: The Maritime History of the Channel Islands* (London, 1986)

Jamieson, A.G., 'Voyage patterns and trades of Channel Island vessels, 1700–1900', in A.G. Jamieson (ed.), *A People of the Sea: The Maritime History of the Channel Islands* (London, 1986)

Johnston, P.K., 'Duelling in Guernsey: T. Andros v. K. Beauvoir [sic]', *The Review of the Guernsey Society* (Summer 1976), pp. 44–6

Johnston, P.K., 'Four Guernsey duels', *The Review of the Guernsey Society* (Summer 1998), pp. 57–8

Johnston, H., *Crime in England, 1815–1880: Experiencing the Criminal Justice System* (Abingdon, 2015)

Juin, H. (ed.), *Victor Hugo, Choses Vues: Souvenirs, Journaux, Cahiers, 1849–1869* (Paris, 1972)

Kagan, R.L., 'Law students and legal careers in eighteenth-century France', *Past & Present*, 68 (1975), pp. 38–72

Kelleher, J., *The Triumph of the Country: The Rural Community in Nineteenth-Century Jersey* (1994; Jersey, 2017 edn)

Kelleher, J., 'The mysterious case of the ship abandoned off Sark in 1608: the customary law relating to *choses gaives*', in Dawes, G. (ed.), *Commise 1204: Studies in the History and Law of Continental and Insular Normandy* (Guernsey, 2005)

Kellett-Smith, S.K., 'Quarrying and mining on Herm and Jethou', *TSG*, 17 (1961), pp. 246–63

Kent, J., 'The English village constable, 1580–1642: the nature and dilemmas of the office', *Journal of British Studies*, 20 (1981), pp. 26–49

Kilday, A.-M., *A History of Infanticide in Britain, c.1600 to the Present* (Basingstoke, 2013)

King, P., 'Decision-makers and decision-making in the English criminal law, 1750–1800', *The Historical Journal*, 27 (1984), pp. 25–58

King, P., 'Punishing assault: the transformation of attitudes in the English courts', *Journal of Interdisciplinary History*, 27 (1996), pp. 43–74

King, P., 'The rise of juvenile delinquency in England, 1780–1840: changing patterns of perception and prosecution', *Past & Present*, 160 (1998), pp. 116–166

King, P., 'The summary courts and social relations in eighteenth-century England', *Past & Present*, 183 (2004), pp. 125–72

King, P., 'Newspaper reporting and attitudes to crime and justice in late-eighteenth- and early-nineteenth-century London', *Continuity and Change*, 22 (2007), pp. 73–112

King, P. & Ward, R., 'Rethinking the Bloody Code in eighteenth-century Britain: capital punishment at the centre and on the periphery', *Past & Present*, 228 (2015), pp. 159–205

Langbein, J.H., *Prosecuting Crime in the Renaissance: England, Germany, France* (Cambridge, Massachusetts, 1974)

Langbein, J.H., 'Albion's fatal flaws', *Past & Present*, 98 (1983), pp. 96–120

Laragy, G., '"A peculiar species of felony": suicide, medicine, and the law in Victorian Britain and Ireland', *Journal of Social History*, 46 (2013), pp. 732–43

Laske, C., 'Losing touch with the common tongues – the story of law French', *International Journal of Legal Discourse*, 1 (2016), pp. 169–92

Le Foyer, J., *Exposé du Droit Pénal Normand au XIIIᵉ Siècle* (Paris, 1931)

Le Herissier, R.G., *The Development of the Government of Jersey, 1771–1972* (Jersey, 1973)

Lenfestey, G., 'The development of public sewers in Guernsey, 1826–1966', *TSG*, 25 (2002), pp. 374–80

Lenfestey, J.H. (ed.), *List of Records in the Greffe, Guernsey, Volume 2* (London, 1978)

Lenfestey, J.H. (ed.), *List of Records in the Greffe, Guernsey, Volume 3* (Guernsey, 1983)

Le Patourel, J.H., *The Medieval Administration of the Channel Islands, 1199–1399* (London, 1937)

Le Patourel, J.H., 'The law of the Channel Islands, I: the origins of the Channel Islands legal system', *Solicitor Quarterly*, 1 (1962), pp. 198–210

Le Patourel, J.H. *et al* (eds), *List of Records in the Greffe, Guernsey, Volume 1* (London, 1969)

Le Quesne, G., 'An abortive penal code', *The Jersey Law Review* (October 2002)

Le Quesne, J.G., 'The development of constitutional autonomy during the nineteenth century', in Bailhache, P. (ed.), *A Celebration of Autonomy, 1204–2004: 800 Years of Channel Islands' Law* (Jersey, 2005)

Lenman, B. & Parker, G., 'The state, the community and the criminal law in early modern Europe', in Gatrell, V.A.C., Lenman, B. & Parker, G. (eds), *Crime and the Law: The Social History of Crime in Western Europe since 1500* (London, 1980)

Lewer, D. (ed.), *John Mowlem's Swanage Diary, 1845–1851* (Wincanton, 1990)

Locker, J.P., '"Quiet Thieves, quiet punishment": private responses to the "respectable" offender, c.1850–1930', *Crime, History & Societies*, 9 (2009), pp. 9–31

Lodge, R.A., *French: From Dialect to Standard* (London, 1993)

Loveridge, J., *The Constitution and Law of Guernsey* (1975; Guernsey, 1997 edn)

MacDonald, M., 'The secularization of suicide in England, 1660–1800', *Past & Present*, 111 (1986), pp. 50–100

MacKay, L., 'Why they stole: women in the Old Bailey, 1779–1789', *Journal of Social History*, 32 (1999), pp. 623–639

Malcolmson, R.W., 'Infanticide in the eighteenth century', in Cockburn, J.S. (ed.), *Crime in England, 1550–1800* (London, 1977)

Margot, A., 'La criminalité dans le bailliage de Mamers (1695–1750)', *Annales de Normandie*, 22 (1972), pp. 185–224

Marr, J., *The History of Guernsey: The Bailiwick's Story* (1982; Guernsey, 2001 edn)

Marr, J., *Guernsey People* (Chichester, 1984)

Marshall, M., *Criminal Law of the Bailiwick of Guernsey* (Guernsey, 1975)

Marshall-Fraser, W., 'A history of the press and of publications in the Channel Islands', *TSG*, 15 (1954)

Martel, E., 'Philological report', *TSG*, 17 (1965), pp. 708–10

McDonald, W.F., *Criminal Prosecution and the Rationalization of Criminal Justice* (Washington, 1991)

McGowen, R., 'History, culture and the death penalty: the British debates, 1840–70', *Historical Reflections*, 2 (2003), pp. 229–49

McKerrell, G., 'Prosecuting in Guernsey', *Jersey & Guernsey Law Review*, February 2012

McLaren, A., 'Abortion in France: women and the regulation of family size, 1800–1914', *French Historical Studies*, 3 (1978), pp. 461–85

McShane, A. & Walker, G. (eds), *The Extraordinary and the Everyday in Early Modern England* (Basingstoke, 2010)

Mer, L.-B., 'La procédure criminelle au XVIIᵉ siècle: l'enseignement des archives bretonnes', *Revue Historique*, 274 (1985), pp. 9–42

Mitchison, R. & Roebuck, P., *Economy and Society in Scotland and Ireland, 1500–1939* (Edinburgh, 1988)

Mogensen, N.W., 'Crimes and punishments in eighteenth-century France: the example of the pays d'Auge', *Social History*, 10 (1977), pp. 337–53

Moir, E., *The Justice of the Peace* (Harmondsworth, 1969)

Moore, R.D., *Methodism in the Channel Islands* (London, 1952)

Napier, P., *Revolution and the Napier Brothers, 1820–1840* (London, 1973)

Neveux, F., 'The French conquest of Normandy (1204)', in Dawes, G. (ed.), *Commise 1204: Studies in the History and Law of Continental and Insular Normandy* (Guernsey, 2005)

Nézard, M.H., 'Allocution, Séance d'Ouverture', in *Travaux de la Semaine d'Histoire du Droit Normand tenue à Guernesey du 8 au 13 Juin 1938* (Caen, 1939)

Nicolle, S.C., *The Origin and Development of Jersey Law* (1998; Jersey, 2009 edn)

Ní Mhunghaile, L., 'The legal system in Ireland and the Irish language, 1700–c.1843', in Brown, M. & Donlan, S.P. (eds), *The Laws and other Legalities of Ireland, 1689–1850* (Farnham, 2011)

Ogier, D.M., 'The authorship of Warburton's treatise', *TSG*, 22 (1990), pp. 871–7

Ogier, D.M., *Reformation and Society in Guernsey* (Woodbridge, 1996)

Ogier, D.M., 'Chief Pleas dinners', *Guernsey Law Journal*, 28 (2000), pp. 79–82

Ogier, D.M., *History of the Buildings of Guernsey's Royal Court* (Guernsey, 2004)

Ogier, D.M., 'New-born child murder in Reformation Guernsey', in Dawes, G. (ed.), *Commise 1204: Studies in the History and Law of Continental and Insular Normandy* (Guernsey, 2005)

Ogier, D.M., *The Government and Law of Guernsey* (2005; Guernsey, 2012 edn)

Ogier, D.M., 'Glimpses of the obscure: the witch trials of the Channel Islands', in McShane, A. & Walker, G. (eds), *The Extraordinary and the Everyday in Early Modern England* (Basingstoke, 2010)

Orth, J.V., 'The English combination laws reconsidered', in Snyder, F. & Hay, D. (eds), *Labour, Law and Crime: An Historical Perspective* (London, 1987)

Osborough, W.N., 'Eighteenth-century Ireland's legislative deficit', in Brown, M. & Donlan, S.P. (eds), *The Laws and other Legalities of Ireland, 1689–1850* (Farnham, 2011)

Ozanne, N.M., 'La Cour Ecclésiastique', *The Review of the Guernsey Society*, 48 (1993), pp. 104–9

Parks, E., *The Royal Guernsey Militia: A Short History and List of Officers* (Guernsey, 1992)

Philips, D., '"A new engine of authority": the institutionalization of law enforcement in England, 1780–1830', in Gatrell, V.A.C., Lenman, B. & Parker, G. (eds), *Crime and the Law: The Social History of Crime in Western Europe since 1500* (London, 1980)

Plucknett, T.F.T., *A Concise History of the Common Law* (1929; Boston, 1956 edn)

Poirey, S., '*L'esprit* of Norman customary law', in Bailhache, P. (ed.), *A Celebration of Autonomy, 1204–2004: 800 Years of Channel Islands' Law* (Jersey, 2005)

Priaulx, T.F., 'Le Corps des Ecrivains', *Quarterly Review of the Guernsey Society*, 37 (1981), pp. 34–6

Reader, W.J., *Macadam* (London, 1980)

Robin, A.C., 'The population of the Bailiwick of Guernsey', *TSG*, 16 (1955), pp. 51–69

Rowbotham, J., '"Only when drunk": the stereotyping of violence in England, c.1850–1900', in D'Cruze, S. (ed.), *Everyday Violence in Britain, 1850–1950: Gender and Class* (Harlow, 2000)

Rowland, G., 'Sir Edgar MacCulloch', *TSG*, 26 (2007), pp. 224–9

Rowland, G., 'Sir Havilland De Sausmarez, Bt', *TSG*, 26 (2007), pp. 229–37

Rule, J.G., 'Wrecking and coastal plunder', in Hay, D., Linebaugh, P., Rule, J.G., Thompson, E.P. & Winslow, C., *Albion's Fatal Tree: Crime and Society in Eighteenth-Century England* (London, 1975)

Schmitt, J.-C., 'Le suicide au Moyen Age', *Annales. Economies, Sociétés, Civilisations*, 31 (1976), pp. 3–28

Schneider, Z.A., *The King's Bench: Bailiwick Magistrates and Local Governance in Normandy, 1670–1740* (Woodbridge, 2008)

Sharp, E.W., 'The evolution of St Peter Port harbour,' *TSG*, 18 (1967), pp. 226–66

Sharp, E.W., 'The evolution of St Sampson's harbour,' *TSG*, 18 (1968), pp. 301–14

Sharp, E.W., 'The shipbuilders of Guernsey', *TSG*, 27 (1970), pp. 478–502

Sharpe, J.A., *Crime in Early Modern England, 1550–1750* (1984; London, 1999 edn)

Sherwill, A.J., 'Some notes as to the origin and history of la Clameur de Haro and on its use in Guernsey in the twentieth century', *TSG*, 14 (1947), pp. 129–32

Shoemaker, R.B., 'The taming of the duel: masculinity, honour and ritual violence in London, 1660–1800', *The Historical Journal*, 45 (2002), pp. 525–45

Sinel, L., *Jersey through the Centuries: A Chronology of Events and Matters of Interest* (Jersey, 1984)

Snyder, F. & Hay, D. (eds), *Labour, Law and Crime: An Historical Perspective* (London, 1987)

States of Guernsey, *Guernsey Facts and Figures, 2016* (Guernsey, 2017)

Stevens Cox, G., *St Peter Port, 1680–1830: The History of an International Entrepôt* (Woodbridge, 1999)

Stevens Cox, G., 'Crime and punishment in medieval Guernsey', in Dawes, G. (ed.), *Commise 1204: Studies in the History and Law of Continental and Insular Normandy* (Guernsey, 2005)

Stevens Cox, G., *The Guernsey Merchants and their World* (Guernsey, 2009)

Stevenson, K., '"Ingenuities of the female mind": legal and public perceptions of sexual violence in Victorian England, 1850–1890', in D'Cruze, S. (ed.), *Everyday Violence in Britain, 1850–1950: Gender and Class* (Harlow, 2000)

Stevenson, W., 'The Middle Ages, 1000–1500', in Jamieson, A.G. (ed.), *A People of the Sea: The Maritime History of the Channel Islands* (London, 1986)

Storch, J.D., 'The policeman as domestic missionary: urban discipline and popular culture in northern England, 1850–1880', *Journal of Social History*, 9 (1976), pp. 481–509

Swift, R., 'Heroes or villains? The Irish, crime, and disorder in Victorian England', *Albion: A Quarterly Journal concerned with British Studies*, 29 (1997), pp. 399–421

Syvret, M. & Stevens, J. (eds), *Balleine's History of Jersey* (1950; Andover, 1998 edn)

Thompson, E.P., *Whigs and Hunters: The Origin of the Black Act* (London, 1975)

Thornton, T., *The Charters of Guernsey* (Bognor Regis, 2004)

Thornton, T., *The Channel Islands, 1370–1640: Between England and Normandy* (Woodbridge, 2012)

Travaux de la Semaine d'Histoire du Droit Normand tenue à Guernesey du 26 au 30 Mai 1927 (Caen, 1928)

Travaux de la Semaine d'Histoire du Droit Normand tenue à Guernesey du 8 au 13 Juin 1938 (Caen, 1939)

Trotter, J.M.Y, 'The cost of an execution', *Quarterly Review of the Guernsey Society*, 15 (1959), pp. 73–5

Turner, J., 'Summary justice for women: Stafford Borough, 1880–1905', *Crime, History & Societies*, 16 (2012), pp. 55–77

Turner, J., Taylor, P., Morley, S. & Corteen, K. (eds), *A Companion to the History of Crime and Criminal Justice* (Bristol, 2017)

Van Leuven, N., 'Constitutional relationships within the Bailiwick of Guernsey – Alderney', *The Jersey Law Review* (June 2004)

Warren, J.P. (ed.), *Extracts from the diary of Elisha Dobrée* (Guernsey, 1929)

Wheadon, E.A., 'The history of the tomato in Guernsey', *TSG*, 12 (1935), pp. 338–50

Whelan, C., 'Grave and criminal assault – the landscape past and present', *The Jersey Law Review* (October 2006)

Wright, G., *Between the Guillotine and Liberty: Two Centuries of the Crime Problem in France* (Oxford, 1983)

Wrightson, K., 'Two concepts of order: justices, constables and jurymen in seventeenth-century England', in Brewer, J. & Styles, J. (eds), *An Ungovernable People: the English and their Law in the Seventeenth and Eighteenth Centuries* (London, 1980)

Zedner, L., 'Women, crime, and penal responses: a historical account', *Crime and Justice*, 14 (1991), pp. 307–62

Zell, M., 'Suicide in pre-industrial England', *Social History*, 11 (1986), pp. 303–17

Unpublished Theses and Dissertations

Bennett, A., 'A history of the French newspapers and nineteenth-century English newspapers of Guernsey' (unpub. MA dissertation, Loughborough University, 1995)

Davies, S.J., 'Law and order in Stirlingshire, 1637–1747' (unpub. PhD thesis, St Andrews University, 1984)

Kirkegaard, K.M.S., 'Clameur de haro – the Norman connection' (unpub. Master's thesis, Copenhagen Business School, 2008)

Moore, S., 'The decriminalisation of suicide' (unpub. PhD thesis, London University, 2000)

Websites

www.ancestry.co.uk
www.convictrecords.com.au
www.corpun.com
www.gov.gg/data
www.gov.gg/population
www.guernseylegalresources.gg
www.guernseyroyalcourt.gg
www.histpop.org
www.jerseyeveningpost.com
www.sueyounghistories.com
www.visionofbritain.org.uk

Index

www.ingramcontent.com/pod-product-compliance
Lightning Source LLC
Chambersburg PA
CBHW060448030426
42337CB00015B/1520